Britannia, Europa and Christendom

Britannia, Europa and Christendom

British Christians and European Integration

Philip M. Coupland

D
2025.5
.G7
C68
2006

First published 2006 by
PALGRAVE MACMILLAN
Houndmills, Basingstoke, Hampshire RG21 6XS and
175 Fifth Avenue, New York, N.Y. 10010
Companies and representatives throughout the world

PALGRAVE MACMILLAN is the global academic imprint of the Palgrave Macmillan division of St. Martin's Press, LLC and of Palgrave Macmillan Ltd. Macmillan® is a registered trademark in the United States, United Kingdom and other countries. Palgrave is a registered trademark in the European Union and other countries.

ISBN-13: 978-1-4039-3912-8 hardback

This book is printed on paper suitable for recycling and made from fully managed and sustained forest sources.

A catalogue record for this book is available from the British Library.

Library of Congress Cataloging-in-Publication Data

Coupland, Philip M., 1966–
    Britannia, Europa and Christendom : British Christians and European integration / Philip M. Coupland
        p. cm.
    Includes bibliographical references and index.
    ISBN 1–4039–3912–8 (cloth)
    1. Europe–Relations–Great Britain. 2. Great Britain–Relations–Europe.
3. European cooperation. 4. European Union. 5. Christianity–Europe.
6. Christianity–Great Britain. 7. National characteristics, British. 8. National characteristics, European. I. Title.

D2025.5.G7C68 2007
341.242'2088270941–dc22   2006043624

10   9   8   7   6   5   4   3   2   1
15   14   13   12   11   10   09   08   07   06

Transferred to Digital Printing in 2009

For Jane,
who made this possible

Contents

Acknowledgements

Although purely a personal project, this book originates from the research I conducted while at the University of Glasgow as a member of the Churches and European Integration (CEI) project (2001–2004), which was funded by the European Commission. I am thankful to all participants in the CEI project from the universities of Helsinki, Lund, Münster and Tartu and especially to Nicholas Hope, project co-ordinator at the University of Glasgow, and Pauliina Arola, project secretary, for their friendship and support. Without the inspiration and encouragement of my colleague and friend Katharina Kunter this book might not have appeared. My grateful appreciation is also due to all individuals and institutions that co-operated with my research. Derek Ford kindly provided a copy of his highly informative but otherwise obtainable MA thesis. Without access to the papers of the late Noël Salter the final chapter would have been very much the poorer. In that regard, I am grateful to Elizabeth Salter and Uwe Kitzinger, who were both most hospitable and generous with their time, opening their homes to me and answering my questions and emails. Elizabeth sadly died in May 2006 - I treasure her warm approval for my treatment of Noël's story. Michael Walsh, John Pinder and Dianne Kirby also read and commented on individual chapters and I am especially indebted to Keith Robbins for reading and commenting on the original proposal and the complete draft. Ken Medhurst, Grace Davie and other members of Faith in Europe (formerly Christians and the Future of Europe) invited me to their meetings and responded readily to my questions and requests. In addition to the various British national and university archives and libraries which were opened to me, thanks are also due to the Keston Institute, the European Movement, Chatham House, the archives of the Atholl family at Blair Castle, Lambeth Palace Library, the Church of England Records Centre, the library of the World Council of Churches in Geneva and Georgetown University Library, Washington, DC. Finally, I would like to thank Michael Strang and his colleagues at Palgrave for their patience and understanding.

Introduction

Christendom and the idea of Europe

Despite the hard facts of geography and thirty years' membership of the European Union (EU), the 'question of Europe' continues to loom large in Britain. Whatever is specifically at issue – political, socio-economic or cultural; major or trivial – the question of Britain's whole relationship to continental Europe, and, therefore, its wider geo-political alliances and its position in the world generally is never far from the surface. Irrespective of what is on the table the whole baggage of 'Britishness' is invariably there beneath. In this way, current debate and decision making draws continually on the historical and cultural roots of national identity. Inevitably at the same time is being asked what it means to be 'European', what Britain and the other countries of the western peninsula of Asia might have in common, what unites them. While the cultural heritage of the Renaissance, Enlightenment and Industrial Revolution might be suggested, transcending these is the jagged but unbroken line of tradition leading back through Medieval Europe as 'Christendom' to the Roman Empire of Constantine; of a continent sharing the same faith and unified by the authority of a universal Church.

Underlining the present and continuing significance of the 'spiritual' in the constitution of a common European identity, during their tenures as president of the European Commission, both Jacques Delors and Romani Prodi have spoken of the need for Europe to have a 'soul'.[1] This is a theme which the current incumbent, José Manuel Barroso, returned to in 2004. Speaking in Berlin at a conference on 'Europe and Culture', which took as its motto 'a soul for Europe', Barroso noted that the preamble of the highly contentious Constitutional Treaty which the

1

Commission was then struggling to have accepted across the Union, stressed that Europe was 'united in its diversity', words which were, he admitted, 'reassuring and ambitious'. The continent's cultural identity was 'made of its different heritages, of its multiplicity of histories and of languages, of its diverse literary, artistic and popular traditions'. Among the treasures of this heritage was 'medieval Christianity, which was by its nature European, united around the same faith, with its network of universities and European cultural elites'. The EU, its president believed, had 'reached a stage of its history where the cultural dimension can no longer be ignored'. There was a necessity to create a 'sense of belonging to Europe' and for citizens to 'have the opportunity to experience their European identity in their everyday lives'.[2]

'Identity' is no mere decoration for politics and economics, it is the cultural cement which builds individuals into communities and makes the structures of the State and civil society viable. At the beginning of a new century the future of the EU is under greater doubt than ever before. Amid the pressures entailed in the incorporation of Eastern Europe into the EU, of resurgent nationalism even among its founder members, and Turkey's application for membership, the cement of community is in greater demand than ever. In 1992, Delors stated that '[i]f in the next ten years we haven't managed to give a Soul to Europe, to give it spirituality and meaning the game will be up'. That this deadline has already passed unrealised is not of special significance – a decade is a brief moment in the growth and decay of such a cultural formation. However, this sense of urgency was not misplaced; early in his Berlin speech, Barosso spoke also of 'a new sense of urgency'.[3] In fact a 'soul' may be more needful at this point in the history of Europe and the EU than ever before. However, in an increasingly culturally and religiously diverse continent, the explicit and implicit tensions entailed in even speaking of such a goal not only remain but may increase at what is perhaps the beginning of a new epoch of conflict between the West and East.

*

In Britain today, church leaders also speak on this question. In 1999, George Carey, then Archbishop of Canterbury, took Delors's statement as the starting point for a public speech on 'The Millennium and the Soul of Europe'.[4] More recently, his successor, Rowan Williams, spoke on the relationship of Christianity and European identity as part of a debate entitled 'Is Europe at its End'.[5] Although vocal on the topic, it is more questionable whether such utterances from Christians, even of the eminence of the Archbishop of Canterbury, have been at all influential.

Their pronouncements tend to share the obscurity of the Advanced Dental Institute in Baden-Württemberg – the venue at which Carey was speaking. In Britain, Christianity, in neither its formal institutional, nor its wider cultural forms, has so far played a large part in recent debates about Britain's future vis-à-vis continental Europe. However, within living memory, both the Churches and religious identity have been centrally implicated in the politics determining the nation's relationship to continental Europe.

During the 1940s William Temple and George Bell, as respectively, Archbishop of York (and then of Canterbury) and Bishop of Chichester, were committed to European unity and successively chaired the British Churches' Peace Aims Group (PAG). This group was the most influential of a number of such bodies established in wartime to influence post-war reconstruction, and it contributed a Christian perspective to one of the most creative and radical periods of British social and political thought. During the 1940s the Churches' were also an important channel through which the British government sought to influence American opinion and build the 'English-speaking alliance'. Then, as now, this 'alliance' was at the heart of British foreign policy, and conflicted with full participation in European integration. For the Labour governments of 1945–51, Europe remained a vitally important issue as they struggled to protect the national interest in the face of economic crisis and decline, the beginnings of the Cold War and the end of empire. To draw Europe and the West together in an alliance against the perceived Russian threat, the then foreign secretary, Ernest Bevin proposed a 'Western Union'. This was not to be a federation but a 'spiritual union' and Bevin drew on the support of those whose business was the spiritual: the Churches. At the same time, in the face of the division of Europe by what, in 1946, Winston Churchill called the 'iron curtain', the Churches became opponents of the division of Europe and, ironically, the willing or unwitting participants in a rupture which would distort European and world politics up to the fall of the Berlin Wall in 1989 and the collapse of the Soviet Union in 1991. More recently, the Churches and Christian elites played a significant role in the long and highly successful campaign for Britain to join what was then called the 'Common Market'. In 1975 this culminated in a referendum in which the Churches did not hesitate to throw their support behind British membership and a people not normally known for their Europhilism gave their approval by a substantial margin.

In these and other episodes, the Churches entered into the theologically problematic zone where the spheres of God and Cesar overlapped, where it was unclear who was influencing whom. Given that the Churches at the time were closely linked to the establishment, and were unmatched in the size and heterogeneity of their membership, over which they had the potential to exert an influence backed by a rare authority, their neglect by historians is puzzling. In the context of the continued controversy of Britain's relationship to the rest of Europe this omission is all the more surprising.

British Christians, Europe and Christendom

Although the interest of British Christians in the 'question of Europe' might be traced back to the Quaker William Penn's essay 'Toward the Present and Future Peace of Europe' of 1693,[6] it was the pressures of modernity – in particular the political crises and wars of the twentieth century which caused the Churches to take a serious interest in foreign affairs. This was apparent in the enthusiastic support they gave to the League of Nations after the Great War[7] and in the inclusion of the topic of international relations in the Conference on Christian Politics, Economics and Citizenship (COPEC). When COPEC first sat in 1924 it declared '[t]he Christian doctrine of International Relationships' as 'the dark continent of Christian ethics'.[8] The inroads made into that territory reflected the particular preoccupation of Christians with the moral implications and human consequences of war, but also a belief that the Churches could make a special contribution to solving the problem of a world divided into squabbling nation-states.

Christian universalism and the Nation

Whereas the contemporary world was divided by 'race', ideology and nationality, Christians posited humanity as a single, equal community. For example, drawing on the scriptures and on 'natural law', the Papal encyclical *Summi Pontificatus* (1939) spoke of 'men as brothers in one great family', who should be 'united by the very force of their nature and by internal destiny, into an organic, harmonious mutual relationship'.[9] Although reference to natural law was central to Catholic thinking, many Anglicans also employed it. For example, the Anglo-Catholic authority V.A. Demant stressed that 'solidarity' was 'elemental in the created order'.[10] Part of the importance of natural law was its claim to inclusivity. As the Catholic and academic A.C.F. Beales explained, natural law existed 'before the coming of Christ' and followed from 'the facts of man's natural existence'. Hence Christianity, despite its religious exclusivity, could claim that its social teaching could provide a 'world order to suit all creeds, all colours and all men'.[11]

Although superficially Christian universalism was similar to cosmopolitan thinking, such as that of H.G. Wells, who looked forward to a world state, Christians permitted the nation a definite place in their plans. Beales stated that even in the 'world-cosmopolis – there will still be nations'.[12] Archbishop Temple similarly dismissed socialist internationalism. A class was united by economic interest, but a nation was 'a fellowship of many diverse types in a common heritage of tradition, sentiment, and purpose covering every phase of human existence'.[13] The nation, his ecumenical colleague Joseph Oldham agreed, with its 'long heritage ... and its encompassing web of tradition and custom' was a 'great moulding force'.[14] The Christian attitude to the nation was not merely pragmatic but warmly affirmative – national differences enriched human life. As Demant explained, 'difference and separateness' were not the cause of 'conflict and disunion', but an 'aspect of creation'.[15] Pius XII saw no tension between Christian universalism and patriotism, even Christ had showed a 'preference for His Own country and fatherland, as He wept for the coming destruction of the Holy City'.[16] The nation was an expression of love. Bishop Bell wrote of how, in fulfilment of the 'fundamental human law ... love', 'men and women are grouped in families, and families again in nations'. The nation, like the family, was 'God given'. A 'passionate patriotism' was natural and proper.[17] This stress on the nation as an extension of the family was strong in Catholic thinking. John Eppstein defined patriotism as 'the love of the family and of that human setting from which it is not normally possible to separate a man's conception of his family, a place, friends, neighbours, language, traditions – his native land'. Patriotism had a necessary place in the international order as the basis for that '"moral responsibility" essential to "tranquillity of order". Without patriotism, no peace', he wrote.[18] Likewise, Oldham concluded that a 'true internationalism' was 'not the antithesis between, but the fulfilment of a true nationalism'.[19]

In this way, Christians posited the ideal of a universal community, enriched by national difference. Between every community is a nexus of power relations, an arena of struggle and negotiation which, ideally, should be disciplined by moral order. Within a society, Church and State were divinely appointed to specific and different *functions*, but both of them were to be subordinate to divine moral authority: 'God is Himself the source of justice of which the State is not lord but servant'.[20] The Church, should be able 'to recall the State continually to the Divine law ... 'to protest and criticize' when it 'transgresses the law of God'.[21]

In Christian thinking, the road to international harmony between the national particular and the human universal was through a similar submission of 'secular' power to moral authority.

In this regard the Church itself would possess a crucial role. Since the late nineteenth century, the non-Catholic denominations of the fractured Christendom had, through the ecumenical movement, themselves begun to slowly close the historical fissures which divided them, in a process which led in 1937 to their decision to found a World Council of Churches (WCC). As a 'universal community' in itself, the Church was to be the source of the 'ethos' underpinning international political order. While there were many churches, in a theological sense they were also 'the Church' – 'that fellowship which … overleaps all barriers of social status, race, or nationality', to 'call the nations to order their lives as members of the one family of God'.[22] The political implications of this became clear in their application to the individual. The superior relationship in Christian thought was between a person and God, and this was to be the determinant of their actions in all other spheres. The claims of religious identity were 'such as to transcend all other loyalties', and, hence, all claims of states or nations. While a patriot, it was the believer's higher duty to 'test rigorously all claims of national interest by His Gospel'.[23]

The Churches as a supra-national world community, and the transcendence of religious identity over nation and ideology, became important resources and symbols in Christian contributions to the debate about the reconstruction of world order. Although the universality of the Church was often fractured, the *ideal* remained a key symbol. William Paton, the inspiration behind the wartime Churches' Peace Aims Group, saw it as the 'great thing' that Christians brought to the statesmen creating 'the new world order'.[24] And, unlike the cosmopolitan dream, his colleague Oldham held that it was 'not an ideal but a fact'.[25] These different assumptions about the inter-relationship of religious and national identities would critically inform the Churches' role in response to European integration.

The golden age of Christendom and its decay

Although Europe in the twentieth century was the antithesis of the ideal ordering of brotherhood, nation and Church, history provided a moment when it had conformed more closely to it. Asking the question '[w]here … may we expect to find the Christian vision of the world foreshadowed?' the COPEC report of 1924 answered: 'Christendom'.[26]

The 'myth' – by which I mean an idealisation of actuality – of medieval 'Christendom' was not without its dark side. When Christians were being called on to support Ernest Bevin's 'Western Union', *The Christian News-Letter* commented that 'in Europe Christianity has not only been a culture-making but a culture-breaking force'.[27] Nonetheless, Temple saw within it that which was 'permanently precious',[28] and it has remained a powerful symbol to this day.[29]

Temple also described the adoption of Christianity as the state religion of the Roman Empire as the 'turning point of history'. With the coronation of Charlemagne as Holy Roman Emperor in 800, and the 'Hildebranine reformation' of Pope Gregory VII three centuries later, emerged the particular relationship between spiritual authority and secular power which defined Christendom. Gregory, Temple wrote, 'sought to prepare the way for the coming of the Kingdom of God on earth by securing the subordination of all temporal princes to the spiritual throne of St. Peter, if the apostolic see could control the potentates of the earth, the supremacy of the divine law in all things would be established'.[30] The spiritual then governed the secular – The Catholic and historian Christopher Dawson wrote of how the Church was not 'a state within a state, but a super-political society of which the state was a subordinate, local and limited organ'.[31] In his contribution to the widely read series of Penguin 'specials' of the 1940s, Rev. James Parkes wrote of how, in Christendom, the Church was 'as much part of civilisation as the blood is of the body'.[32] Europe remained a community of distinct societies, but was also Christendom because they shared a cultural – a 'spiritual' – identity which was fundamental to their political relationships. Christendom was, Temple wrote, 'the fellowship of professedly Christian nations considered as a unity'.[33]

If Christendom stood as a golden age in Christian historical narrative, the story of its decay was at the heart of the Churches' diagnosis of the causes of international anarchy. From an Anglican point of view one reason for the dissolution of Christendom lay in the circumstances of its realisation. Papal authority had triumphed by becoming a strong *political* power, thereby becoming 'worldly' with all the temptations that entailed. The Church lost moral authority, and so cultural influence. With the loosening of its authority over secular power, the unity of Christendom broke down and Europe took on a new political form, becoming a 'chaos of national sovereignties'. Underlining this fundamental break, Temple wrote of how '[p]olitics had openly thrown off the yoke. National sovereignty was recognized as absolute. The national state acknowledged no earthly superior and (in practice) no divine superior'.[34]

The disintegration of Christendom brought with it the nationalisation, and concomitant fragmentation of Christianity. With the Reformation, national churches emerged, and 'religious cleavage was added to national animosity'.[35] Religion became a 'national' business, conducted beneath the authority of the State. The circumstances of the early stirrings of the aberrant force of nationalism was not without its irony. Each great power claimed to be 'the heir and guardian of the universal ideal of Christendom', to be 'chosen' to have a 'special mission to the world', so laying down grounds for conflict.[36] The dissolution of the unity of the Church in the West, both paralleling and implicated in the political disunity of Europe, left 'nothing which actually held together the nations in any fellowship', Temple believed.[37] Dawson agreed: while the peoples of Europe still shared a common 'cultural patrimony', Christianity was no longer 'the rallying point of Western unity' because the Church itself was divided.[38]

Accompanying the disintegration of Christendom and the Church was a long cultural revolution. 'The Renaissance and the Reformation', Temple stated, 'together undermined the structure of Christendom'.[39] The emergence of the notion of national sovereignty and, eventually, nationalism, was in many ways the symptom of what Pius XII described as a 'deep spiritual crisis'. This was attributable to the interlinked fragmentation of the Church and the rise of secular belief systems which displaced Christianity. In Catholic thinking, it was the trinity of 'Protestantism, then Humanism, then Materialism' which was the culprit.[40] Excepting the inclusion of Protestantism, Bell pointed to a similar list.[41] Moral and religious agnosticism brought a forgetfulness of the charity and solidarity of Christian universalism which made the 'peaceful intercourse of peoples' almost impossible.[42]

Christian historical narrative, therefore, attributed international anarchy to an ever-wider misalignment of political power and moral authority. In the twentieth century this process culminated in the 'totalitarian' state, which was interpreted as not merely another stage in the decay of Christendom, but as an apocalyptic threat to civilisation itself. For Christians, the crisis of European society was fundamentally spiritual. Bell wrote of how, with the appearance of totalitarianism, the long-term conflict between 'the forces of the spirit and the forces of materialism' became 'one manifestly between Christianity and anti-Christ'.[43] In both its atheistic Stalinist and pagan fascist forms, the totalitarian state effectively proclaimed itself God. Each inculcated its own all-encompassing cosmology, worldview, and scale of values. Each made exclusive claims on the human subject and cut the fundamental bond between them and their 'Creator'. Dawson, who saw the roots of totalitarianism in the Russian Orthodox and Lutheran deviations, saw it as signalling a 'psychological breach with the old European Christian tradition'.[44] This was a threat unseen since the barbarian invasion fifteen centuries earlier, 'the dark forces ... chained by a thousand years of Christian civilization' had been 'set free to conquer the world'.[45]

Totalitarian states were not only diseased internally but injured the relations between peoples. As with all good things which became corrupt, patriotism thus took on a 'demonic' form as nationalism. The report of the 1937 Oxford conference stated that '[t]he deification of nation, race, or class ... is idolatry, and can only lead to increasing division and disaster'.[46] This development was most extreme in the fascist states but was also injurious to world order among the democracies too. Nation-states had repudiated moral authority, held themselves to be sovereign and, therefore, to be bound only by their own self-interest. The consequence was an anarchic power-politics which wrecked the League of Nations. Beales declared the 'specious' notion of 'absolute sovereignty' as 'perhaps the greatest snare', it was 'utterly anarchic and destructive of all hopes of world organisation'.[47]

The Second World War was interpreted as the cataclysmic climax of these historical processes. 'The Europe now in danger of falling to pieces was built on foundations which have been steadily crumbling', the Bishop of Chichester wrote in 1940, in an article pressing for the earliest declaration of the principles on which the new Europe would be built.[48] The editor of *Theology*, Alec Vidler, proclaimed the war as 'God's judgement on Europe', for the 'apostasy of Christendom'.[49]

The reborn Christendom

The Christian diagnosis of the international crisis posited a 'spiritual' deficit. '[B]ehind ... political struggles and ... economic confusion lies something much deeper', Paton believed. To build a new structure for a community without a new 'spirit' was futile: 'No plan of political federation or economic reorganization will work by itself'.[50] The League had failed because it created 'a juridical skeleton of international order, but not the living body of a spiritual community'.[51] There was no 'organic connection' between the nations, no 'common ethos', by which the Oxford conference meant 'a common foundation of moral convictions'. Without such an ethos international relations would continue to be governed by 'power-politics' alone.[52] This was not a belief peculiar to clergy, Alfred Zimmern, an authority on international relations, who made the same point.[53] In one sense, therefore, the Christian cure for international disorder was summed up by Beales' words: 'the road back is the only road out'.[54]

If medieval Christendom was the lost golden age of Christian reconstruction discourse, Christendom reborn was its utopia. A new order required the renewal of the relationship between political power and moral authority symbolised by Christendom. For George Bell the historical precedent was clear and its lesson decisive:

> The real trouble is a spiritual trouble; and the real rebuilding must be spiritual. Who would have thought that a few years after the convulsions of the times of Virgil, a new world order would have arisen, through the death and resurrection of Christ? It was the inspiration of the same Christian faith 500 years later, when Europe was again in darkness, that ushered in the dawn, with St. Augustine, St. Benedict, St. Gregory and St. Boniface, as the lantern bearers. And if there is such darkness and suffering to-day, a new awakening of men's spirits can only come to Europe, through a reillumination of the Christian faith, a new and deep spiritual reformation.[55]

While wary of specifics, Christian thinkers did indicate the fundamentals of the new order they sought. In the first instance, the reborn Christendom would still be composed of nations. The difference would be, as Temple's concept of the 'Christian nation' indicated, that 'the Christian standard for judgement' would have its rightful place within and between them.[56] Pius XII found such a standard in 'international natural law', which would restore 'that unity of religious teaching and of moral code which of old gave consistency to pacific international relations'. He laid out the basis of such an order in his 'Five Peace Points', which secured the support of British Protestant leaders too.[57] Just as the exercise of the God-given authority of the State internally was only legitimate inasmuch as it conformed with the good of its citizens, so, Beales suggested, any exercise of sovereignty 'must not conflict with the rights of the *whole* society of peoples'.[58] Temple concurred, if unity and fellowship were good within a nation then they were between nations too: 'to seek the interest of one at the cost of the others' was 'an intellectual blunder and a moral fault'.[59] Whereas it had been impossible to appeal to the League of Nations on the basis of their Christian identity, in a new Christendom states would work collectively and sacrificially towards a 'Christian policy' on the basis of justice rather than self-interest.[60]

Just as the disintegration of the Church was part of the breakdown of Christendom, its reunification – or at least a will to that end – was essential to make it 'a vital and vitalizing force in the world' once again.[61] Hence, the growth of the church into a 'world community'[62] and the ecumenical movement were crucial symbols and resources. Bell described the latter as 'a living expression of a supra-national fellowship, transcending race and nation, class and culture'.[63] Even in wartime, it remained 'a main ground of hope for the Rebirth of Christendom in the future'. The 'ecumenical sense' was the 'nucleus of the spirit of true fellowship' which would be of 'priceless value in binding the nations together'.[64] Linking religious identity to international order, Paton saw that 'friendship in Christ' would 'minister to the need for an international ethos that shall underpin the structure of law'.[65]

Much of the discussion of Temple and others dealt with concepts not unfamiliar to secular thinkers. However, Christian discourse necessarily transcended the point to which the sceptic might follow. Temple, having delved deeply into the 'worldly' aspects of the question, wrote that '[t]his world can be saved from political chaos and collapse by one thing only, and that is worship'.[66] Likewise, Beales wrote that 'the best machinery in the world' would fail without 'the Sacraments, and, above all, ... Grace'.[67] As we will see below, Paton's grasp of international affairs was ruthlessly shorn of sentimentality, nonetheless, he pointed to a higher source of 'power' that made redemption and forgiveness conceivable. Only there was the means 'to remake broken man', to 'provide the possibility on which the constructive work of statesmen may be built'.[68] To those 'searching for world order', Bell's reply was that the answer was in 'the person of Jesus Christ ... Order is not found or created by man. It is given by God'.[69]

Christendom and the new Europe

What then was the relationship of the utopia of a reborn Christendom to hopes for a new Europe? From one perspective, it was impossible to speak 'for Europe' except as a Christian.[70] 'Europe' was not defined by shared 'race', ethnicity or language. It was not made by its geography, being a north-west extension of the Asiatic landmass, rather than a discrete space. Europe, Dawson contended, was 'a man-made continent, an historical creation',[71] it was 'the result of the European culture rather than vice versa'.[72] And Christendom had made Europe, not Europe Christendom.[73] At the beginning of the Cold War Bernard Griffin, Archbishop of Westminster, justified his interest in European unity by stating that it was 'by God's providence' that the continent had been 'chosen' as the centre of the Church.[74] The Church was the 'primary factor in the culture of Europe', it was 'the Mother of European civilisation'.[75] The 'Christian community in the past', Dawson wrote, 'underlay the social organization of Western culture'.[76] While admitting that 'the idea of Europe' could be traced back to even older roots – Temple attributed it to the fusion of influences not only from Palestine, but Greece and Rome too – nonetheless, the Church as 'the spiritual bridge', had transmuted classical culture.[77] In December 1945, George Bell linked the golden age to the future, stating that just as 'Christendom and Europe' were once 'interchangeable terms' so 'one of the principle goals of our thinking and action should be the recovery of Christendom. We want to see Europe as Christendom'.[78]

*

The presence of the Christendom narrative in the discourse of the British Churches endowed them with an elegant affinity towards the political cause of European unity. Furthermore, the years of the 1940s and 1950s, when the Churches were speaking of Europe and Christendom in the same breath, coincided with a series of moments of great potential for the British state to play a leading, actually a *pivotal* role in the creation of new Europe. Whenever British political will engaged in this project, the Churches played an active and sometimes significantly influential part too.

A commonplace judgment is that this was a moment when political will failed and a historic opportunity was rejected. Stated so baldly that is a gross over-simplification, but it does communicate the consequence of British decision-making, if not the complex of circumstances, contingencies and calculations which led to it. The political history for this has already received some of the dissection and analysis which it demands. However, the reasons that the British Churches – despite their frequent references to the cultural tradition of European Christendom, and the claims of ecumenism and human 'brotherhood' – followed a similar line of retreat have not been previously examined. To explain this outcome, this book provides a narrative of the Churches' often intimate relations with the secular political forces which, for convenience, might be called 'the European movement'. In so doing, it brings to notice a little of the complex circuitry which runs beneath the surface of any functional democratic polity. The chapters below also analyse the specific 'ideological' reasons which either consciously or unconsciously premised actions taken, opportunities embraced or rejected. In so doing, it interests itself in the Churches' developing understanding of the relationship between power and ideals in international relations. It also unpicks the problematic relationship between, on the one hand, the potential integrating factors of the historical tradition of Europe as united 'Christendom', and Christianity as a supranational religious identity, and, on the other, particularistic factors of culture, and national identity. For institutions whose relationship to the State and Nations in the United Kingdom was intimate, and who were at the heart of imperial history, patriotism was a powerful force.

Inasmuch that this study concentrates on the period from the outbreak of the Second World War in Europe in 1939 to the popular confirmation of British membership of the European Community (EC) in 1975 it might be seen to be remote from the questions facing Britain and the rest of Europe at the beginning of the twenty-first century. The reality is that the problems of the present are rooted in the decisions and actions of the past and that the debates and discussions of the past anticipate those of the present. At the outset of this introduction Barroso was quoted as saying of the search for a 'soul for Europe', that in 2004 the EU had 'reached a stage of its history where the cultural dimension can no longer be ignored'.[79] The pages that follow show that in actuality, while easy answers have been as elusive as they are now, discussion of the cultural identity of Europe has never done more than paused for breath.

1
Christian Peace Aims and Federal Europe

Whereas the Church of England has often been described as the 'Conservative Party at prayer', for a brief moment in wartime Britain some commentators believed that it was veering radically to the Left. Although the notion that the occupants of pew and pulpit had anything in common with Harry Pollitt's communists could figure only in the most paranoid reactionary minds, during the war years the Churches in Britain did call for radical social and political changes at home and abroad. This radicalism was embodied and symbolised nowhere more than in the person of Dr. William Temple, Archbishop of York, who in 1942 became head of the Church of England and, therefore, the leading figure in Britain's Christian community as a whole. Intellectually acute, eloquent, and well-connected, Temple was also a sincere Christian socialist, determined not only to work out the theological implications of Christianity for British social life and international relations, but to actively work for radical change.

The wartime activism of Temple and like-minded colleagues was part of the general tendency whereby, since the nineteenth century, Christians had looked beyond the narrowly spiritual or ecclesiastical, to work out the implications of their beliefs in response to the socio-economic, cultural, political and ideological challenges of modernity. More specifically, at the beginning of the war, it was also part of a general political development which might be called the 'peace aims movement'.

The Churches in wartime politics

Already during the 1920s and 1930s there had been little reason to sustain optimistic liberal assumptions about the inevitability of 'progress'. These had been dealt a heavy blow by the mass, industrialised slaughter

of 1914–18, followed by chronic economic malaise and political insta-
bility. Hence when, after 20 years of crisis, Europe collapsed into general
war once again, the fundamental institutions of Western societies had
already been subjected to a sustained and searching critique. Whereas
the Great War had begun in a spirit of national fervour and enthusiasm
and only later gave birth to the cry of 'Never again', the outbreak of
another European war in 1939, followed in Britain by the crisis of defeat
and near extinction in 1940, provoked an altogether different mood
of grim determination and critical reflection. For this reason, from
its beginning, thinking people – great and small, and of all political
complexions – concluded that the war should be fought not only to
defeat the Axis powers but also to achieve the positive 'peace' aim of a
new social and political order at home and abroad. Their collective aim
was to transform the system which produced slump, fascism and war
and thus create a new and better world.

Initially, peace aims were the concern of the political and intellectual
elites who composed independent 'think tanks', like Political and
Economic Planning (PEP) and the Royal Institute of International
Affairs (RIIA); pressure groups such as Federal Union (FU) and the
League of Nations Union (LNU); and the peace aims committees of both
the major and minor political parties. However, at the end of 1942,
when Allied victories in North Africa and at Stalingrad turned minds
towards the possibility of peace and when the public imagination was
captured by the Beveridge Report on social security, the peace aims
agenda came to dominate the political mainstream in the years leading
up to the 1945 election.

Through their own groups, conferences – such as at Malvern in 1941 –
and publications, and via their individual participation in the archipel-
ago of secular groups and parties, Christians played a full part in the
peace aims debate. However, the contribution of the Churches is particularly deserving of detailed study inasmuch that they occupied a unique
and potentially highly influential position in the discursive and political structures of the time. Whereas even in the radicalised atmosphere
of the home front, peace aims activists found it relatively difficult to
obtain a hearing beyond the already converted, the Churches enjoyed
an access to the mass media which was matched only by the parties of
the wartime coalition government. For example, Christian thinking
about peace aims or 'reconstruction' featured in a series of contributions
to the hugely successful topical series of 'Specials' published by Penguin
books and, perhaps most importantly, in a succession of broadcasts on
the most significant demotic medium of the day, the BBC.

However, it was not only the political salience of the peace aims movement which opened space for the Churches at the heart of public discourse. From the outset of the conflict, the British State had recognised the importance of propaganda as a war weapon. Inevitably in a total war the condition of public morale, in terms of mass support for the prosecution of the war, was as crucial as the supply of munitions. One way towards this end was to represent the war effort as serving a higher purpose than narrow national interest. This was an approach advocated by the peace aims movement, which suggested that a statement of aims would encourage popular support for the war, especially among the working classes. British propaganda did make some use of peace aims rhetoric. However, although the cabinet had established its own dedicated committee under Arthur Greenwood, public reference to peace aims was politically problematic inasmuch that it aroused the hostility of many elements of the Conservative side of the coalition drawn together for the duration of the war, including Winston Churchill.[1]

A less controversial answer to the question 'What are we fighting for?' was to represent the war as a defence of a so-called British way of life, based on a historical narrative of progressive but peaceful, gradual change, the institutions of parliamentary democracy and the rule of law, a culture of public 'tolerance' and individual freedoms of association, confession and speech. However, the 'British way' was not something static but an exemplar to the wider world, something to be positively advanced. Indicating this function, the first pamphlet in the series provided for forces' education on the topic was clear: 'By turning this war into a struggle to make a decent life genuinely possible for all, we shall equip ourselves with a faith which is as fine as the Nazi faith is evil, without being one whit less dynamic'.[2]

The easy presence of the language of 'evil' and 'faith' here was typical of much wartime rhetoric. The representation of the war against Nazi Germany as not merely a conflict over national interest but as a cultural clash, between ways of life, between opposed moralities, allowed the Churches to speak to, and for, the nation in a way permitted to few other institutions in wartime Britain. Whereas religious affiliations were conventionally considered to be a private and personal matter and so excluded from the public and political sphere, the Christian heritage in the language and thus the culture of the nation was still considerable at this point in the twentieth century. The assumptions, practices and personnel of the Churches were still very much part of the fabric of everyday existence and subtly influential because of their unexamined ubiquity. As one of a number of studies pondering, evoking or dissecting the nature of the nation in wartime noted, the Churches were '... like cricket, part of the English background'.[3] For this reason, for example, when Prime Minister Churchill at the time of the Battle of Britain bracketed together faith and nation, stating that 'Upon this battle depends the survival of Christian civilization. Upon it depends our own British life, and the long continuity of our institutions and our Empire',[4] he intersected with the general, unscrutinised assumptions of Britons, irrespective of whether they were active churchgoers or not. Similarly, in one of his influential 'postscripts' on the BBC, J.B. Priestley referred to the same binary opposition when speaking of the silhouette of the dome and cross of St. Paul's cathedral against the flames of the Blitz as 'an enduring symbol of reason and Christian ethics seen against the crimson glare of unreason and savagery'.[5]

This patterning of public discourse would have opened a space for a prominent contribution from the Churches in the public sphere in any case, but the recruitment of Christians to support this function was a deliberate government policy, as evinced by the establishment of a Religions Division at the Ministry of Information (MOI). Similarly, the innovation of national days of prayer at key moments in the war served to tie the Churches tightly into national identity and destiny. The sharply sarcastic 'Cassandra' (William Connor) of the *Daily Mirror* included a chapter entitled 'The Church' in *The English at War* and noted that '[w]ith impressive speed the rulers of England signed up the Almighty for the duration of the war. It was a contract made possible firstly by the widespread and very real national conviction that we were in the right, and secondly, by the enormous array of spiritual and political talent which we could muster to prove the point'. By his identification of Nazism with evil, Cosmo Gordon Lang gave Germany 'a proper theological habitation and a name'.[6]

In assessing the relative influence of the Churches, we should also note that although Temple might have been suspected of turning the Church of England into the Communist Party at prayer, there was a very important difference between those two bodies. Whereas the Communist Party of Great Britain (CPGB) – even at what would turn out to be the zenith of it fortunes – was politically marginal, the Church of England was intimately tied into Britain's establishment and thus had ready access to the corridors of power. Nowhere was this more apparent than in the membership and activities of the Church's Peace Aims Group, which was chaired by Temple and is discussed in detail below.

While other parts of the Churches' general contribution to the peace aims discourse are also drawn out of obscurity here, it was through Peace Aims Group that Church and State came together most influentially.

Christians in the peace aims movement

In 1940 John Strachey – a leading British Marxist who would later be a minister in the Attlee government – described 'making plans for the world' as 'the new national industry'.[7] The Churches formed an important sector in this 'industry' from the outset; in fact even before the actual declaration of war Church leaders issued a joint statement, 'Religion and the Organisation of Peace', in July 1939. After the declaration of war the Church of Scotland's Committee for Church and Nation turned their attention to post-war reconstruction as did the unofficial Anglican Wartime Council (AWC), established in autumn 1939.[8] The Anglo-Catholic Christendom Group, which published an eponymous journal of Christian sociology, edited by the Maurice Reckitt, and Joseph Oldham's discussion group 'The Moot' did likewise. Oldham had a long involvement in overseas mission and a pioneering role in the ecumenical movement, in particular its Life and Work wing.[9] He was not only eminently well connected to church leaders but also to many others in public life. His group, like the Peace Aims Group, well illustrated the informal dimension of the relationship of the Churches to the establishment. For example, among those gathered with Oldham and other leading British churchmen in September 1939 were T.S. Eliot, the leading academic Walter Moberly and the influential social theorists Karl Mannheim and R.H. Tawney.[10] Also invited to the meeting were Charles G. Vickers and Oliver S. Franks. During the war Vickers served on the Joint Intelligence Committee of Chiefs of Staff and was a director in the government's Department of Economic Warfare; Franks would be British ambassador to Washington at the beginning of the Cold War. Oldham was also the initiator and secretary of the Council on the Christian Faith and the Common Life which, in autumn 1939, started *The Christian-News Letter*, which became an important forum for discussion of peace aims. Three years later, Oldham would be the initiator of the Christian Frontier Council, so-called because its aim was to work on the frontier where Christian values and concerns met and overlapped with those of the secular world.

As Martin Ceadel's research indicates, the 'pacifist' wing of what he calls the British 'peace movement' was also a force behind 'idealist' conceptions for international relations. Christians – often Quakers – played an important part in peace groups, of which the Peace Pledge Union and the Fellowship of Reconciliation were the most significant religiously inspired bodies.[11] In 1939 the Quaker Maurice Rowntree sketched out the blueprint for a pacifist world utopia, which seems to have evoked little notice.[12] In wartime, support for the total rejection of force was negligible, even among Christians, who were more likely to accept defensive war as a necessary evil. Even for the Rev. Albert Belden 'personal pacifism' in the immediate present was inadequate and he called for a rank-and-file movement to overcome the conservatism of ecclesiastical hierarchies to create an 'Ultimate-Pacifist World-Church', which, when the day came, would with 'one vast official collective step' honour its pledge to 'refuse the Act of War', and usher in a new age of 'Pax Christi'.[13]

While Christian unity had not yet achieved the strides that Belden hoped for, since the turn of the century the ecumenical movement had grown in size and importance. Inaugurated in 1925, its Life and Work section concerned itself with the application of Christian faith and values to social and political questions. In 1937, following the Life and Work conference at Oxford, a provisional committee was set up to oversee the merger of Life and Work with the ecumenical movement's Faith and Order wing (which dealt with specifically ecclesiastical concerns) to create the World Council of Churches (WCC). This was not finally achieved until the Amsterdam conference of 1948, but despite its provisional status during the war years, the WCC 'in formation' acted as a crucial central forum and nerve centre for the Churches of Britain, continental Europe and America.[14]

Much of the work of the ecumenical movement was through its national committees. The British committee of Life and Work, which was called the Commission of the Churches for International Friendship and Social Responsibility (CCIFSR) and was also chaired by Temple, contributed to the peace aims debate in 1942 with its statement 'The Christian Church and World Order'.[15] In the same year the Commission came together with the British section of the World Conference on Faith and Order and the Council on the Christian Faith and the Common Life to create the more sparely titled British Council of Churches (BCC).[16] The BCC continued the work of the CCIFSR through its International Affairs Department, which produced the memorandum 'Christian Influence on Peace Settlement' in April 1944. This offered support for a series of general principles for international reconstruction drawn from the Atlantic Charter (1941) and other wartime agreements.[17] It was also under the aegis of the WCC that the

Peace Aims Group was inspired and convened by William Paton, who was associate general secretary of the Council, and chaired by Temple.[18]

The groups mentioned so far represented the membership of the various Protestant Churches in Britain. While the Catholic Church represented only a relatively small proportion of British Christianity, it was not only significant on account of its ability to mobilise its disciplined membership, but also as the British outpost of a world church which was also a major power in continental European and world politics. Forbidden to participate in bodies created by the other churches, Catholics had their own exclusive organisations to propagate their church's teaching on political and social questions. However, the most significant Catholic contribution to the peace aims movement came through the body Sword of the Spirit, founded in August 1940. Sword brought together influential members of the English Catholic intelligentsia with the blessing of Arthur Hinsley, Cardinal Archbishop of Westminster. The group had a ready-made programme in the form of the principles of Pius XII's encyclical *Summi Pontificatus* (On the Unity of Human Society), promulgated on 20 October 1939, and in the aims articulated in his allocution to the College of Cardinals of 24 December in the same year, which was commonly known as the 'Pope's Five Peace Points'.[19] These offered principles predicated on 'natural law' for the reform of the domestic and external relations of states.

However, besides its contents, it was of great significance that the Papal allocation, by addressing 'all Christians ... all men of good will on earth',[20] indicated a softening in the Vatican's formerly inflexible attitude towards co-operation with other Christians. Given the symbolic importance of the lost unity of Christendom in the Christian discourse on international relations in Europe and the stress that it placed on the ecumenical community and religious identities as supra-national forces, any sign that the deepest cleavage among the Churches might have started to narrow was important. Reflecting this potential, in December 1940, the Pope's five points together with five additional 'points' drawn up by the British Protestant Churches appeared in what was often referred to as the 'ten peace points' letter to *The Times*. Given that the Catholic Church at this time denied the legitimacy of other churches, the appearance of the Archbishop of Westminster's signature alongside those of Canterbury and York – Lang and Temple – and the name of W.H. Armstrong, the Moderator of the Free Church Council, was a historical and, it seemed, portentous moment. Another of the key figures in this history, George Bell, Bishop of Chichester, welcomed the Five Peace Points and became the major Anglican participant in the co-operative activities which followed the ten-point letter and the inauguration of Sword of the Spirit.[21] Chichester, after Temple, was probably the most publicly visible Anglican in wartime Britain, and certainly the most outspoken; he was also foremost among British Christians in terms of the depth and consistency of his support for European unity. Although, as Michael Walsh has shown, the ecumenical promise of Sword of the Spirit was to be ultimately stifled following the death of Hinsley in 1943 and because of the attitude of the Catholic hierarchy generally, wartime nonetheless saw considerable co-operation between Protestants and Catholics.[22]

Christians, Europe and Federal Union

The scope of Christian peace aims was ultimately comprehensive, requiring a moral and spiritual revolution touching all aspects of social and political life. Applied to international relations this necessarily implied a global focus. However, in many ways, both implicitly and explicitly, the problem of international relations in the 1940s was European in its causes and, therefore, in its solution too. Nationalism and the totalitarian systems of fascism and communism were all of European origin; the breakdown of peace for the second time in 20 years was the political consequence of ideological and socio-economic conflicts which made the outbreak of the second world war an episode in an on-going European 'civil war'. Furthermore, while Christianity was itself becoming a truly global religion, Europe continued to have a special place in Christian thinking as the historical home and base of the faith.

As has already been suggested above, Christians had their own historical argument supporting European unity, built around the key symbolic myth of 'Christendom'.[23] The essential claim of this 'myth' – that is an idealization, a distillation of an idea – was that medieval Europe had been united by Christianity. At that time, society took Christian values as its point of reference and Church, State and society were one, and all Europe was united under the moral authority of the Church. Through schism, apostasy, secularization and the rise of nationalism and other secular creeds, the authority of the Church had been denied in social life and in international relations. The consequence: international anarchy, a problem that could only be remedied by the rebirth of Christendom, by Europe's residual Christian cultural heritage becoming once more the primary influence in its affairs. Although for some Protestants the ideal of Christendom may have sat uneasily with their belief that it was at the Reformation that the 'true' Church was born, even for Presbyterians like William Paton and Joseph Oldham Christendom represented what the former described as the 'first and greatest bond of what we call Europe'.[24]

The Federal Union boom

At the beginning of the war, therefore, the peace aims debate in Britain was mainly orientated towards solving the problem of European nationalism, a preoccupation reflected in a considerable interest in federalist schemes aimed to break the dangerous coupling of nationalism and the modern state. *Union Now* (1939) by the American Clarence Streit became a bestseller, as did W.B. Curry's Penguin 'Special' *The Case for Federal Union* (1939). These were only the most prominent of many books and pamphlets published on the topic, including contributions by men of the eminence of Sir William Beveridge.[25] Even George VI suggested that Britain sponsor a European federation, a suggestion which the foreign secretary, Lord Halifax, politely declined.[26] Both the prime minister, Neville Chamberlain and the leader of the opposition, Clement Attlee, spoke positively about federalism – the latter's declaration 'Europe must federate or perish' pithily encapsulated the thinking and attitude of the moment and became a rallying cry for federalists. Although driven more by expediency and desperation than federalist fervour, the Churchill government's move of 16 July 1940 to offer the collapsing French state incorporation in 'one Franco-British Union' nonetheless could be – and was – seen as a significant precedent.

British enthusiasm for federalism took an organised form in Federal Union, which, begun by a handful of enthusiasts at the time of the Munich crisis in 1938, grew so rapidly that by the beginning of 1940 it had 170 local groups and was signing up 500 new members a week.[27] In its official statement of policy FU pledged itself:

(1) To obtain support for a federation of free peoples under a common government, directly or indirectly elected by and responsible to the peoples for their common affairs, with national self-government for national affairs.
(2) To ensure that any federation so formed shall be regarded as the first step towards ultimate world federation.
(3) Through such a federation to secure peace, based on economic security and civil rights for all.

To this end the present policy of FU is

(1)To work for an Allied statement of Peace Aims challenging the idea of race superiority with a declaration of the rights of man, and the method of aggression with a declaration of readiness to federate with any people whose government is prepared to recognise these rights.

(2)To welcome any steps towards a federation of the Allies or any other groups of peoples, provided that at the time of its formation the federation is declared open to accession by other nations, including Germany.[28]

This formulation gave sufficient space for FU to be ideologically heterogeneous. The first major area of difference was over which combination of the United Kingdom, the continental European democracies, the British Commonwealth and the United States would be theoretically ideal and/or practically possible. While there were many different opinions on this question, the major fault line was between those for whom Britain and the other European democracies would be the core of the union and those who stressed an 'Atlantic' union. The second major divide was between those federalists who were otherwise L/liberal or C/conservative in their allegiances and those who held that a viable federation required not just a 'pooling' of national sovereignty but socialism as well.

It was agreement over the abrogation of national sovereignty which both held this otherwise diverse group together and identified them as a species of E.H. Carr's 'utopians' rather than the practitioners of *realpolitik* and jealous guardians of national sovereignty who traditionally inhabited the Foreign Office.[29] As to the specific powers which would be ceded from the national state, it was stated that: 'The Federation would control foreign policy, Armed Forces and armaments. It would have substantial powers over tariffs, currency, migration, communications and similar matters. It would also have power to ensure that colonies and dependencies were administered in the interests of the inhabitant and not for the benefit of any particular country'.[30]

Clerical thinking on the future of international relations also took on a distinctively federalist flavour at this time. While Christians saw the nation as a providential community, they also understood nations as primarily *cultural* rather than *political* entities. Consequently, there was no automatic right for a nation to constitute itself as a state and neither was absolute sovereignty a necessary basis for international organisation. Although Arthur Headlam, Bishop of Gloucester and chairman of the Church of England's Council on Foreign Relations, deprecated the idea of a federal union as 'impracticable', 'harmful' and 'impossible',[31] public expressions by Christians were generally much more positive. Just as with the LNU, many Anglican and Free Church clergy and lay people were actively involved in FU, and it established a Churches' Committee.[32] One insider believed that it was the donations of Christians – 'this not often articulate body of opinion' – which kept FU afloat financially.[33] The secretary of the organisation was Gerald Bailey, a member of the Society of Friends, and among its most significant thinkers and propagandists was another Quaker, John Hoyland.[34] George Catlin sat on the Union's board of directors and – apart from being the husband of Vera Brittain and father of Shirley Williams, a Labour Party supporter and academic expert on international relations – was a Catholic. Other significant Christian participants included the founder of the CommonWealth party, Sir Richard Acland MP, Monica Wingate and Phillip Edwards, who joined FU as an Anglican curate and later became its chairman.[35]

Interest in FU and federalist ideas generally was spread across the denominations. The AWC began to investigate the topic in late 1939, and in April the following year hosted discussions with Charles Kimber, general secretary of FU.[36] While stressing that it was '*not* opposed to Federation', the AWC vehemently stressed that FU was putting the supra-national political cart before the national economic horse, and outlined proposals that showed the Anglo-Catholic, social credit and ruralist qualities which were the hallmark of the Christendom Group.[37] Kimber criticised the memorandum as 'Fascist or Nazi in the sense that it advocated the kind of "national renewal" that Hitler was originally after'.[38] The AWC agreed to publish a joint pamphlet with Church Social Action on the subject but in all likelihood the radical change in the war situation in 1940 stifled this initiative.[39] The same year the Church of Scotland's Committee on Church and Nation stressed the need for peace aims to include 'a New Europe', and while preferring not to venture beyond what it believed to be its sphere of competence to detail the *method* for achieving this end, offered two different federal plans as possible solutions.[40] Indicating the prominence of this topic at the time, the Catholic journal *The Month* commented that 'Occasionally one single key-word is put forward as the passport to the brave new world. In 1919 this was "self-determination", to-day it is "Federal Union"'.[41]

The three most significant ecclesiastical figures in what would become the Peace Aims Group, Temple, Bell and Paton, also took a close interest in FU. Even before war had broken out or the Peace Aims Group founded, Paton was in contact with Arnold Toynbee, director of studies at the RIIA, asking his opinion of FU. Following on from a suggestion 'from America', he sought to get Gerald Bailey or another leading federalist to represent that line of thinking at the conference on the international crisis that the WCC convened at the hotel Beau Séjour, near Geneva, in July 1939. As he explained in an earlier letter inviting Toynbee to attend, the conference was to be 'composed partly of experts like yourself and partly of people who carry guns in the churches' and it aimed to see if there was anything that the Churches could do to 'stem the drift towards war'.[42] Apropos the sought-for-federalist, Paton added a rider stipulating that they should be able to 'take a sufficiently Christian line to be helpful in a gathering which is ... concerned with what the Churches can and ought to do'.[43] Although the reason is unclear, ultimately the British delegation consisted of 'gun carrying' Christians such as the Methodist Henry Carter, J. Hutchinson Cockburn of the Church of Scotland, and the Anglican W.R. Matthews, backed-up by the expertise of Toynbee's fellow academic and RIIA member, Sir Alfred Zimmern. At this seminal event, which Paton chaired, theologians, economists, experts in international law and other specialists gathered to discuss what the Churches could do in the face of the international crisis.[44] As to Paton's own position on federalism, he remained sceptical but interested; later he declined an offer to join the FU council but remained in contact with it.

Temple had an established interest in the reform of international relations. Before the war he was among the many influential supporters of The New Commonwealth, which had emerged out of the LNU, with the aim of making the League effective by establishing an international tribunal, whose judgements would be enforced by a 'world police force'.[45] The archbishop was also among the signatories of the statement 'Religion and the Organisation of the Peace' published in the summer of 1939, whose prescription was for universal federalism, including a 'Pan-Europa'.[46] Similarly, in August the same year, he urged that Britain 'repudiate the claim to be judge in its own case as the first step towards the federal goal' and, at the beginning of the war, stated on the BBC that a 'Federal Union of Europe', was the 'only hope of a permanent settlement'.[47] International justice could not be achieved by voluntarism – 'by mere *laisser-faire*' – and he declared that 'one form or other of federalism must be our goal'.[48] Peace would require the integration of Germany in a united Europe where economic and political sovereignty would be 'pooled' and individual states would function only in an 'administrative and cultural' capacity.[49] Federalism was compatible with Christian thinking as a form of 'mutual interdependence' and 'brotherhood'.[50] The

archbishop also noted a 'close coherence ... between the federal principle and the spirit of Christianity'.[51] At one stage, Temple looked to
the emergence of a mass-movement of Christians and others of like
mind. He imagined this revolutionary movement – 'a great multitude
of folk ... growing on the principle of a snowball ... ready as true disci-
ples of Christ ... to turn the world upside down' – coming together on
the basis of a common statement of beliefs and aims, and knowing each
other 'by the wearing of some kind of badge or symbol'.[52] Temple
became a FU supporter in the summer of 1939 and gave the organisation
the widest possible exposure, naming it on the BBC and in published letters to the *Daily Telegraph* and *Morning Post* later that year. He also
penned a Christmas message for the group and offered detailed comments on its policy.[53] When he became primate of the Church of
England in 1942 FU sent a telegram welcoming the 'appointment of a
fellow-Federalist to Canterbury'.[54]

George Bell was also enthusiastic about federalism and referred to
Streit's *Union Now* favourably before an audience at Oxford in 1939 and
also in his best-selling Penguin 'Special' of 1940, where he described the
'full dress plan of Federal Union' as being among a number of events
having 'great potentialities'.[55] He became a FU supporter in 1939,
accepting an invitation to join its Brighton and Hove branch.[56]

The Bishop of Chichester had close connections with the Confessing
Church in Germany and throughout the war was a devoted ally and
vital contact of Christians in the anti-Nazi resistance there. By extension, he was also a brave advocate of the 'other' Germany, the 'non-
Nazi' Germany. In consequence, he used every opportunity to speak of
the necessity for stating a positive aim beyond simply defeating
Germany. If Germany was simply to be fought to 'unconditional surrender', annihilated and perhaps thereby handed over to Bolshevism,
every patriotic German, Christian as well as Nazi, would be forced to
rally behind Adolf Hitler. Instead, Bell argued for peace aims offering a
positive future for a democratic Germany, along with guarantees to its
European neighbours. Having spoken in favour of peace negotiations in
the House of Lords in December 1939, he then sketched the positive
measures needed when proposing a resolution to the Convocation of
Canterbury in January 1940.[57] The second paragraph of the resolution
called for convocation to:

'... associate themselves with the declaration often made by His
Majesty's Government, that it is no part of the war aims of this country to bring about the destruction of Germany; and that they

earnestly desire that life and independence be secured for the German nation, on the sole condition that the German nation itself respects the right of all other nations, both great and small, strong and weak to a similar life and independence'.[58]

In his speech supporting the resolution he repeatedly called for Allied governments to make public their conception of the 'new order in Europe' for which the war was being fought. As to his own thinking about such a new Europe, in *Christianity and World Order* he balanced his belief that while Streit's and other federal proposals had 'great potentialities', they were also 'vain things' inasmuch that the 'supreme need' was not for 'schemes or constitutions or blue prints, but a new spirit, a conversion of human persons' 'more than constitution making was required'.[59] As is discussed below, proposals for the post-war settlement from the anti-Nazi resistance envisaged a future for Germany as part of a European federation. In the years that followed Bell's support for this solution to the 'problem of Germany' was stalwart and he increasingly ignored any scruples about speaking on the political and economic details of such a settlement.

In October 1939 *Federal Union News* spoke of the '[a]dded keenness' which had come to the group following Temple's mention of it on the BBC and dwelled on 'the image of a vast number of his listeners wondering what this Federal Union is'.[60] Undoubtedly this public advocacy for federalism on the chief popular mass medium of the day – subverting the BBC's usual proscription of radical political topics – was influential. The public opinion research group Mass-Observation found that FU was one of the few peace aims proposals which the ordinary man and woman 'in the street' had heard of.[61]

The Peace Aims Group

Hence the approach of Temple, Paton and Bell during the period from the Beau Séjour conference to the first meetings of the Peace Aims Group in 1940 had a strong federalist flavour and definite European emphasis. The foundational meeting of the group was on 3 January 1940 at Edinburgh House, headquarters of the International Missionary Council.[62]

Those assembled on this occasion discussed and accepted the paper written in late 1939 by W.A. Visser t' Hooft, in consultation with Hans Schönfeld, the director of the Life and Work Study Department of the WCC in Geneva. T' Hooft, with Paton, was joint secretary of the Council. Entitled 'The Responsibility of the Church for the International

Order', this document laid down the basis for the investigation and analysis of the international crisis and the formulation of peace aims by a network of study groups.[63] As a worldwide body whose links were not broken by the war, it was envisaged that this work by the ecumenical movement would be especially significant. This document noted that while the political and economic origins of the crisis were being discussed, experts in those areas were also saying that 'spiritual and religious factors must especially be studied' and it was this sphere which the Churches claimed as their area of special competence.

In the first instance, the study groups were directed to critically examine the extent to which the crisis was a consequence of the 'breakdown of "Christendom"'. Subsidiary to this, the groups were directed to focus on the key ideological conflicts of the age between fascism, communism and democracy.[64] The major task of the groups was to be the 'preparation of a just peace'. International stability required the creation of 'an international ethos': '[n]ational sovereignty must find its counterbalance and limitation in international solidarity'.[65] In respect of the Churches' role here, the paper asked: 'Dare we share the expectation, which finds expression in many quarters, "that out of this chaos there will shall be a rebirth of Christendom"'. As a preface to this constructive side of the Churches' mission, the paper noted 'we will have to be especially on our guard against the kind of idealism which refuses to face historical realities and which is thus inclined to repeat the mistake of the 1918–1939 period, that is to, to construct an impressive system without laying solid foundations for such a system'.[66] The Geneva document reiterated the same point when it came to discuss the Churches' role in examining the various proposals then appearing in such profusion:

> The specific Christian contribution ... is to test the projects of federalism (whether on a world, a European, or a more restrictive sense) or proposals for a reorganized League of Nations, on the basis of the realistic Christian conception of history and men, of nation and state. The Christian task is to warn, on the one hand, against a utopianism which seeks to solve by mere organization what are ultimately spiritual issues, and on the other hand, against an amoralism which regards political relationships solely in the light of military and economic power.[67]

This emphasis on Christian idealism tempered by political realism would be a decisively influential aspect of British Christian work in this area.

While concerning itself ultimately with universals, the practical emphasis of the paper was on the problem of Europe. It was the war there, which would have 'a decisive bearing on the whole problem of the future world order'.[68] The principle underlying the 'future organisation of Europe' should concern the Churches in a 'special way': 'Is self determination the decisive consideration? Should the national principle be the guiding principle in a future settlement? Or is the cultural heritage (which more often means the confessional heritage) a more important principle to be kept in mind in forming political units, and by what common political ideal are these units to be held together?'[69]

These proposals were a development from the paper which emerged from the Beau Séjour conference earlier that year.[70] Paton had suggested 'a sharpening up of the July Geneva document in relation to the present situation'.[71] One telling change was the reference to federalism in the later document – a few months earlier the Churches had concluded that it was 'wiser to improve and develop existing institutions, where possible, than to establish new ones'.[72] Over the intervening months, not only had existing institutions failed and collapsed but the stock and public visibility of federalism had correspondingly shot up. It may also be significant that the anti-Nazi resistance in Germany had already produced a memorandum including the suggestion for what would have been an a 'United States of Europe'.[73] Paton was handed this document at an International Missionary Council (IMC) meeting in Copenhagen in October where the decision was taken to found national study groups to continue the work begun at Beau Séjour.[74]

Hence, the January meeting was really only an intermediate step in a process which Paton had been deeply involved in since the summer before. He had already been in contact with most of the prominent members of what would become Peace Aims Group. In November he had met to discuss the proposed group with Sir John Hope Simpson, Arnold Toynbee, H.J. Paton and Alfred Zimmern, all prominent members of the RIIA.[75] Paton had also shown Toynbee and other 'experts' drafts of the Geneva paper and received their comments and passed on details of the German peace proposals to them.[76] Although it would not be as influential as the Peace Aims Group link to Chatham House, a similar co-operative relationship was established with PEP.[77]

Chatham House, the State and the Peace Aims Group

Thinking on the function of religion in international order was not restricted to clergy or the members of specifically Christian lay organisations, but also took in two men who, among British writers, came closest to German historicism in their use of history. For Arnold Toynbee, author of the twelve volume *A Study of History* (1934–61) and the director of studies at Chatham House, religion was at the heart of the historical development of world order. In his comments on 'The Responsibility of the Church for the International Order' he was unequivocal in his stress on the necessity of a shared religious ethos as a basis for political order and that the 'disappearance of the sense of common Christendom' was behind the failure to create a viable international order after the Great War.[78] Similarly, Lionel Curtis, the initiator of the Round Table groups and a founder and honorary secretary of the RIIA, was also author of the massive and much discussed tome *Civitas Dei: The Commonwealth of God* (1934; 1937; 1938). Both men were also early supporters of FU, Curtis being the honorary secretary of its Oxford branch.[79] A number of leading members of the RIIA – including Curtis, who became a strong supporter of European federation[80] – were to be influential upon, or in contact with the Peace Aims Group. However, Toynbee was to be especially significant at the interface between Church and State.

Founded in 1920, the RIIA emerged from the informal gatherings of officials – including Curtis – attending the Paris Peace Conference of 1919. The Institute functioned not only as a permanent forum for elite discourse on international relations – if necessary, 'off the record' – and to research foreign affairs, but also influenced the thinking of the ruling classes at home and abroad. As Christopher Brewin writes, it operated 'to answer questions of interest to the Government, and especially to monitor and influence elite opinion abroad'.[81] Generously funded by the leading sections of finance and manufacturing capital, the editors and proprietors among its membership gave it ready access to the broadsheet press, including the leading organ of the British establishment, *The Times*. Among its membership were to be found leading politicians from all mainstream parties, a considerable cohort of serving and retired officers from the armed forces and a similarly significant portion of the professorial section of the Oxbridge mafia.[82] Inasmuch that the British state cannot be meaningfully examined in abstraction from the social origins of its chief agents and the assumptions and mores of the wider elite culture from which they emerged, neither can Chatham House and the formal state be neatly separated. This overlap was never more apparent than during the war years. From 1939 to 1943 Chatham House was funded by a Foreign Office grant to operate the Foreign Research and Press Service (FRPS), whose large staff of academics operated at Balliol College, Oxford under the direction of Toynbee. In 1943 the marriage between Chatham House and State was formalised when the FRPS moved to London and became the Foreign Office Research Department.[83]

The remit of the FRPS required it to perform three official functions. It was to produce a digest providing an analysis and interpretation of the foreign and commonwealth press. Originally circulated only among government departments, this material later became available to Fleet Street and to the RIIA. The second function, 'Standing Orders and Enquiries from Government Departments', entailed the FRPS answering enquiries on international affairs. These two functions relied on its third objective, the continuous research into the background of current international questions, including peace aims. In both its research and current work, the FRPS not only trawled the press but utilised 'official and unofficial information from British and foreign sources' and maintained 'personal contact ... with several Government Departments and with individuals who are able to communicate valuable information', including 'secret intelligence'.[84] The FRPS not only had unrivalled access to intelligence but the digests, analyses and interpretations which it prepared inevitably endowed it with potential to influence executive decision making. While much of the work of FRPS was secret and in the background, that did not mean that it was without scope for wider influence. While the service operated under the RIIA charter that forbade propaganda activities, a 'special arrangement' existed whereby FRPS staffs were permitted to write for the press or broadcast on the BBC. Furthermore, inasmuch that the leading figures of the FRPS continued to participate in the wider intellectual and political world, including that of the Peace Aims Group, a definite and unbroken conduit for influence existed.

Peace Aims Group was similarly close to the State and Chatham House. Paton described the group's method as being 'to establish friendly confidential relations between those who know something of the Christian consensus and the experts who are advising the government with respect to post-war arrangements'.[85] Following his discussion of the proposed group and its ecumenical partners with Toynbee and his RIIA colleagues in late 1939, Paton was in no doubt about its potential for influence:

> The group were extremely keen that this should be done and again and again expressed their sense of its importance. Toynbee, I think, felt this most of all, judging by what he said to me. You know of course, that all these men are working under the aegis of the Chatham

House, but in quite close contact with the Foreign Office. ... I am quite clear that there is open to us a method of work whereby the results of informed Christian thinking would be taken into serious account at least by our own Government.[86]

Time was found in the exceptionally busy wartime diaries of Toynbee and his colleagues and not only did the Foreign Office provide the means for the group to remain in close contact with its opposite numbers in Switzerland and America, but the doors of senior civil servants, cabinet ministers and ambassadors opened readily to the churchmen.

To an extent this reflected a common culture. While impossible to quantify, the Christian values underpinning the ethic of public service integral to the 'gentlemanly' ideals of a public school education were undoubtedly significant: they provided a vocabulary connecting secular and spiritual elites and the possibility of a shared world-view. Furthermore, the culture of the upper and upper-middle classes in general – its familial links, shared schools and universities, common accents and manners – allowed a ready interchange whenever different sections of Britain's relatively small and cosy ruling class came together. When Paton was asked by his American opposite numbers to describe Peace Aims Group's relationship to 'significant government leaders' he pointed out that he came from 'a small country with an established church' and that '[d]irect contact with the Foreign Office is continuous. There are pretty general contacts with other divisions and departments of the government. Many of those who hold leading posts share the point of view of Christian leaders and are themselves genuinely Christian men'.[87] However, this shared culture, while important, does not fully explain the relationship between institutions of vastly differing power. Like all those active in the peace aims movement the Church stood at the door of the State hoping to influence the shape of the future, but in this case the door was opened because the State itself saw just such a potential in the Church.

It was perhaps telling that when Paton agreed to speak at the FU conference 'The War Weapon of Propaganda', *Federal Union News* remarked: 'If you believe the Church as a political power is played out, you will change your mind when you have heard Dr. Paton'.[88] Hugh Martin's words showed his colleague to bring together faith and considerable political facility: 'He could push and scheme and wrangle and at times be brusque and overriding – but always for the Kingdom of God and never for himself'.[89] The doors of Whitehall opened to the highest levels for him. In preparing his statements on peace aims, Paton consulted not only Toynbee and others from Chatham House and received 'copious letters and cables to and from America' but also was in contact with the foreign secretary, Lord Halifax.[90] However, the key influence was the Chatham House Circle and most specifically Arnold Toynbee. Since before the Beau Séjour conference Paton had been an assiduous consumer of Chatham House reports and in wartime pressed Toynbee for insights on 'the lines along which your policy is shaping itself'.[91] He also submitted the drafts of his own writing, including his major peace aims statement *The Church and the New Order*, to detailed critique by Toynbee and others of the RIIA circle.

In a letter to a colleague Toynbee described Paton as 'an extremely able, discreet and sensible student of international affairs' and was sufficiently confident in his abilities to suggest that the churchman be asked to join Chatham House's own reconstruction committee – Toynbee also suggested confidentially that his 'connections' would make him a 'valuable recruit'.[92] Correspondingly, Paton clearly saw Toynbee as his mentor, writing on one occasion 'I am greatly encouraged by your approval, for I know myself to be very much an amateur in this field'.[93] On another occasion he again spoke of himself as 'an amateur' who had 'the opportunity for consultation with the men who do know the inside problems of this present situation and who have great responsibility in government circles'.[94] This student–mentor relationship also reflected a more general principle of Christian thinking on the correct relationship between Church and State. This tended to stress that while the former was to be the ultimate judge of the morality of the actions of the State and the ends it pursued, the latter was responsible for the formulation of policy and its execution or, as Paton put it, '[i]t is the Church's task to say we believe that this and this must be done. Experts tell us how'.[95] Given that, in reality, means can rarely, if ever, be considered separately to ends, this artificial distinction was inevitably frequently breached; nonetheless it did seem to encourage the belief that the 'men from the ministry' – or as Paton called them, 'experts on concrete questions' – really did 'know best'.[96] Given that the workaholic Paton not only formally controlled the Peace Aims Group as its secretary, but was very much its motivating spirit and driving force, his student–mentor relationship with Toynbee gave the latter considerable influence.

Peace Aims Group and European federalism

The Peace Aims Group's collaboration with PEP linked it to an influential 'think-tank' which maintained a federalist position on the future of

Europe throughout the war.[97] As to Chatham House's thinking during the final weeks of peace and the period of the so-called 'Phoney War', his has already been indicated by Curtis and Toynbee's involvement with FU. Curtis had been a longtime advocate for the transformation of the relationship between Great Britain and the Dominions by welding them into an 'organic' – that is a federal – union, and in July 1939 he set up a study group to examine the problem of 'world order and European settlement'. By this stage Curtis had come to see the European democracies unified with Britain and the Commonwealth as the possible core of what would eventually become a world federal union. Toynbee's thinking moved on similar lines.

In his paper 'First Thoughts on a Peace Settlement' Toynbee argued that if Britain and France each jealously hoarded their sovereignty then their destiny was to lose it. Not only that, but to see the liberal and democratic way of life and civilisation itself lost to German fascist world domination. The only way out was for the two countries to match German power by pooling their sovereignties to become 'a single Anglo-French state'. This 'political union', a 'full and permanent' federation, would then become the nucleus for 'predominantly democratic and Christian-minded superstate'. It was envisaged that it would be possible to incorporate the 'more highly civilised parts' of Germany and Italy and thus provide links to connect the smaller states of Europe to the Anglo-French Axis. Around this European core would be added the European colonial empires, the Americas and other states on the 'southern and eastern fringes of Europe'.[98] Underlining the two men's shared conviction, Toynbee wrote to Curtis, concerning the series of 'world order papers' that the Chatham House committee was working on, that 'our whole purpose in publishing is to win the widest attention and support for the federal union idea'.[99]

The fall of France and the Church and the New Order

Then, as one contemporary saw it, 'the whole outlook of the war was suddenly changed by the German break-through in France'.[100] Among the consequences of the sudden collapse of the western front in May 1940 was a severe reality check to federalist visionaries, as any new order in Europe was more likely to be a fascist one, as indeed was the promise of Nazi propaganda. Despite this, and war news which for the next couple of years would be a gloomy tale of one Axis triumph after another, a necessary faith in an ultimate Allied victory, combined with the belief that these events made a new post-war system in Europe even more urgently needful, ensured that reconstruction remained an important topic.

As early as 26 June 1940,[101] Paton began a process of exploring a possible declaration of peace aims with members of Peace Aims Group and others and it was agreed that once the threat of invasion was passed, that lobbying for war aims would begin.[102] Initially he spoke of the need for a 'fresh statement of the central convictions with which our own Government and people are imbued' and enclosed a series of 'notes on peace aims' which he had received from Walter Oakeshott, headmaster of St. Paul's School and a member of the Council of the Christian Faith and the Common Life.[103] This process would lead in early 1941 to Paton's article 'War and Peace Aims and the Church's Task' published in the *Christian News-Letter* and, finally, to a book, *The Church and the New Order* (1941), in which the same argument appeared at length.[104] However, while written by Paton and a genuine reflection of his thinking, *The Church and the New Order* was also very much a collective enterprise, the product of the discussions of the group, of contacts with Christian leaders in the United States and British civil servants and politicians, and most particularly with Toynbee and his circle. Apart from the readership it received at home, *The Church and the New Order* was influential in America and among resistance groups in Germany. The argument of Paton's book was also made to a very much wider audience via the BBC.[105] The Rev. Eric Fenn, assistant director of religious broadcasting at the Corporation, worked closely with Paton and the group and believed that the talks 'had a good deal of public effect'.[106]

As Paton outlined at their outset, the purpose of the discussions he initiated was to either draft an appeal to the Government to issue its own peace aims or for the Churches to issue their own statement. Given that it was only peace aims adopted by a state which could hope to be realised, the latter course of action was only an indirect way to the same end, by influencing public opinion. In the case of a statement by the Churches, Paton reported that Oakeshott had suggested that 'it would be desirable to get the unofficial support of Lord Halifax, and also the support of some prominent newspapers'.[107] Paton allowed that while the government's peace aims, should they be issued, were likely to be conservative, others were 'free to scout ahead ... testing and criticising ideas and informing the public mind'.[108]

In 1941 Prime Minister Churchill continued to resist the declaration of peace aims. An official declaration of aims – it would be 'momentous' when it came, Paton believed – was vital for two reasons: 'the first is the blockade and its effect upon Continental countries; the second is the importance of the American attitude'.[109] This first issue had been on Paton's mind right from the outset of the new phase of the war begun by the French armistice with Germany in 22 June 1940.[110] He had gone so far as to speak to the Ministry of Economic Warfare on the subject.[111] He pointed out that the peoples of Britain's erstwhile allies, bombarded with Nazi propaganda and ground down by the deprivations conse-quent on the British naval blockade, might become resigned to the 'much advertised "new order in Europe"' of the Nazis.[112] It was, he argued, 'widely recognized that a mere return to national sovereignties' would not 'solve Europe's problems' and that the peoples of continen-tal Europe, weakened and demoralised, might come to accept the Nazi 'new order' as the only form of European order available.[113] Paton stressed that there were 'strong reasons for indicating, at least in broad outline, what is the nature of the European (or even of the world) order that we should wish to see set up'.[114]

As to a possible Christian blueprint for a new Europe, the broad prin-ciples on which it could be based might be found in the statement agreed at Beau Séjour, and among the British Churches, where agree-ment was truly ecumenical to the extent of including Catholic approval in the ten-point letter of December 1940.[115] At its base reconstruction, as with all political, social and economic questions, was a moral and hence religious question. In this way the Churches could provide a moral datum for the praxis of the State. However, Paton did not leave things there but then went on – speaking in his 'personal' capacity – to speculate as to how these broad principles could be made concrete. Oakeshott had contended : 'The new order will not be a Europe of sover-eign nation states'. He noted 'the fusion of France and Britain' proposed by Jean Monnet – later to be the founding father of united Europe – which so nearly took place between Britain and France in 1940, that '[i]f such a fusion was right for France and Britain it might be right for oth-ers too'. He hoped for a 'Europe of the future' where nations might be 'merged economically and politically' but at the same time be able to each 'live their own life, to speak their own language, to preserve their own civilization'.[116] Except in name, this was a fully federal Europe. Paton agreed that '[i]n some way or another a European unity has to be found'. In this regard, even Germany's 'new order', while being merely a gloss on the subordination of Europe to a conqueror's interests,[117] was not without significance:

> … it is an organization of Europe. There will be no going back to the multitudinous divisions, barriers and national autarchies which have

prevented Europe from achieving the life of the community which in reality Europe is. ... We shall be compelled (but surely not against our will) to move towards a genuine new order worthy of civilized men, and we should recognize in that compulsion and in the inevitable destruction of so much that was old and familiar, a challenge to find new and better ways of human living.[118]

Paton also saw the proposal of 'a complete political union' between France and Britain as '[p]olitically, far the most important event of the war ... Events annulled it, but the offer was made. It might be made again, and not only to France'.[119] Toynbee, who read and commented on the manuscript of *The Churches and New Order*, had also drafted for the Foreign Office the Act of Perpetual Association intended to join the two states.[120]

Paton was familiar with federalist blueprints such as RWG Mackay's *Peace Aims and the New Order*.[121] However, the problem posed by a 'full-dress plan for federalism' was not *what* it was but *how* it could be achieved: the problem of 'the transition from one order of things to another'.[122] While seeing the utility of the pooling sovereignty, Paton's strictly 'realist' approach led him to consider federalism as impractical in the 'immediate future': 'Because I do not think that the immediate future is to be opened up by advancing political federation I do not discuss here the rights and wrongs of Federal Union'.[123] Both the theoretical criticism that such blueprints took for granted a moral, economic and political context which could not be assumed to exist after the war and the powerful memory of how national interest wrecked the League prompted his scepticism.[124] He then went on to outline 'a line of thought which seems to be gaining increasing support among those most competent to form a judgement', by which he could only have meant his mentor Toynbee and his other Chatham House contacts.

The core to this approach was the notion that the immediate essential practical measures necessary 'for policing, for feeding, for the rationing of raw materials and for the many tasks of reconstruction' in the devastated continent would themselves begin to create the 'nucleus of a permanent organization of government'; 'the foundation of a permanent order'. Both the scale of the devastation of the continent and the interdependence of the European states meant that 'the rebuilding of Europe's life ... should be followed irrespective of national frontiers'. Here was the notion of the creation of a single economic life for Europe, admission to which process Paton imagined would be contingent 'upon acceptance of a fundamental charter of human rights'.[125] Similarly, the co-operation between Britain and the various free forces of occupied Europe appeared to offer 'hints of the future' in the 'realms of defence and political organization'.[126] All this was not incompatible with the federalism. However, despite endorsing the aborted Anglo-French union, Paton did seem to break with the federalists in the political sphere, preferring the more informal defensive arrangements and political relationship of Britain and the Dominions based on a 'community of ideals and understanding of life'.[127] This preference for the ad hoc, pragmatic and evolutionary over the innovation specific formal structures would be characteristic of the dominant approach within the Peace Aims Group, as it has been in the wider history of Britain's relationship to European institutions.

Although Temple at this time was a genuine federalist in a way in which Paton never was, he did share much of his colleague's thinking in *The Church and the New Order*, also uniting idealism with political realism. The archbishop commented during one of his wireless talks in autumn 1940 that 'the actual Federation of Europe is a colossal task. We must keep it before us as our goal; but if we attempt to rush it, any measure of temporary success will be wiped out in the ensuing set-back'.[128] Hence, in May 1940, believing that a single unified Europe would be impossible in the aftermath of the war, he offered a blueprint in the *Fortnightly Review* for a Europe divided into five smaller federations, one of which would see Britain, France and possibly also the 'Benelux' countries pooling sovereignty.[129]

For Temple, as with many other thinkers, including those of PEP whose broadsheet he quoted in his article 'The Future of Germany'[130] the solution of the 'problem of Germany' was integral to answering the 'problem of Europe' as a whole. Temple anticipated that the negative qualities in the German 'character' identified and publicised by Robert Vansittart[131] would demand a considerable process of re-education under Allied occupation, but linked this to the positive measure of the promise of 'as good a life as for any people on earth'. A peaceful and prosperous Germany in a peaceful and prosperous Europe would be achieved by a gradual process, by which economic and political power would be detached from its national bases so that, in time, the state would function at national level only in an 'administrative and cultural' capacity. In the first instance, planned economic reconstruction after the war would not be conducted on a national basis, and the consequent changes in economic life would have a psycho-cultural effect encouraging the 'exclusive aspects of nationalism to fade out'. After five years of peace a 'Congress of European nations' would be appointed to deal with the outstanding political problems of the continent, which, Temple hoped, would 'become in effect, at last (perhaps fifty years later) by full right the federal Council of a united Europe'. This united Europe would play its part in the League of Nations which would be 'a forum for international discussion; ... the focus of the moral judgement of the civilized world'. 'But', the archbishop stressed, 'Europe is a separate and special problem, for which a separate and special solution must be found'. In this way a united federal Europe would grow organically, rather than being imposed by treaty before the cultural and political conditions for its existence pertained. One recurrent problem of interpreting peace aims proposals for the future of Europe is whether they are intended for *us* or *them*, however, by his stress on the necessity for Britain to fight the temptation 'once more to withdraw from Europe and leave the small nations to their fate'[132] Temple left no doubt that he saw Britain as integral to the future of the continent.

*

During the 12 months before the fall of France the supporters of European unity among the Churches, as elsewhere, could be accused of a degree of political naivety born out of hope, earnestness and the desperation of crisis. They also shared with the Allied leaderships and populations generally what would turn out to be a misplaced general confidence in the strength and efficacy of the democratic societies. Within a few weeks in 1940, the situation was transformed. As has been indicated, British Christian belief in European unity and even an ultimate federal union survived even this brutal reality-check, qualified but intact. However, the tremendous dynamism unleashed by the war was by no means spent, but rather was of a growing power and historical consequence.

2
Britain, America and Europe

In 1940, A.C.F. Beales, who made a special study of peace aims, captured the 'realist' and 'idealist' poles of current thinking: 'the idealist is canvassing the already famous FU while on the other side the cynic is murmuring that war aims are being left vague deliberately, so that no predatory victory in the future may be have been forsworn in advance'.[1] With the benefit of hindsight, British enthusiasm for federalism in 1940 stands out as an aberration in the long-term emphasis of policymakers on jealously safeguarding national sovereignty. Up to 1940, proposed solutions for the problems behind the war looked to a radical rearrangement of the international politics of Europe, and frequently stressed a federal future. Likewise, British strategic planning in the war against Germany was based around an Anglo-French alliance. In a sense, the Churchill government's proposed 'indissoluble union' between Britain and France of June 1940 was the logical culmination and, as it turned out, conclusion, of both these discourses.[2] The rapid, unanticipated and catastrophic defeat of the Allies revolutionised this situation. After the fall of France, the only power which could contemplate transforming European political relations was Germany, which did indeed announce its intention to create a 'new European order'. France and the smaller continental democracies were no longer authors of their own destiny, let alone of the future of Europe as a whole, and – even if Germany was eventually defeated – could scarcely be expected to be so for some long time.

For Britain at this moment, and for many months to come, the issue was not reconstruction, but survival. Defeat in 1940 weighted the balance of power mightily against a nation standing alone with straitened and diminishing resources to pursue a war, whose scope and demands would continue to expand. What for the British in 1939 had begun as a

40

European war became after 1941 a *world* war in every sense. Already deep into its relative economic decline, the conflict bankrupted the country and made it dependent on American aid to both pursue the war and rebuild afterwards. While economically drained, Britain was simultaneously militarily over-committed, its forces fighting against the Axis across the globe. At the same time, the political and strategic assets, which made a small northern European island a world power, were also under pressure. The Dominions of the so-called white Commonwealth increasingly drifted into the American sphere of influence while Britain's hold on the colonial empire was increasingly criticised where it was not – as in India – visibly slipping away.

Britain alone could not defeat Germany. At one stage an alliance with Russia to check German power might have been possible, but in 1939 that state had forged a desperate pact with its ideological *bête noir*. By 1941 this situation was reversed and Hitler's invasion of the Soviet Union pushed that state into the Allied camp. When Germany's last *blitzkrieg* gamble narrowly failed in 1941, the balance began to slide slowly away from fascism. However, with every day that the German drive for hegemony in Europe was driven closer to defeat, the potential threat of Russia increased. Unlike in the 1930s, when British policy hoped to maintain some kind of balance of power by means of an alliance with France to curb Germany in the west and by an appeased Germany holding the pass against Russia in the east, in the 1940s 'peace' offered the prospect of an ideologically unfriendly totalitarian military superpower covering most of eastern and central Europe and with little standing between it and the straits of Dover. There was only one possible source of strength to preserve Britain and its empire against the Axis in war and the Soviet Union in the post-war period: the United States of America. In the 'official mind' the economic and political support obtainable through the so-called English-Speaking alliance was vital, firstly to defeat the Axis and, secondly, to maintain Britain's interests in the rebuilding of world order in peacetime.[3]

Likewise, the RIIA had a long-established emphasis on Anglo-American co-operation, which strengthened as hostilities progressed.[4] Toynbee's position changed dramatically. He had stated that in the case of military defeat his proposals for a Franco-British union would become 'waste paper'.[5] As the quotation from Beales indicates above, federalist approaches were at the time and afterwards identified with the so-called idealist approach to international relations, a classification drawn from the distinction between 'realist' and 'idealist' or 'utopian' approaches within E.H. Carr's highly influential book *The Twenty Years*

Crisis, 1919–1939 (1939).[6] However, in order to properly understand Toynbee's stance we need to note that although, as a federalist, he was one of Carr's 'utopians', the historian's thinking was also based on a model of power politics as blunt as that of any 'realist'. He recognised that ideals had to be backed by power. An alliance of Britain and France had been essential to match German power, so with France defeated, Toynbee necessarily looked across the Atlantic to the only other major democratic nation. At a meeting at Chatham House – also attended by the Bishop of Chichester – the historian spoke of how, in a world moving towards unification 'we have a choice of Germany becoming the crystallisation point … or the English speaking peoples becoming the crystallisation point'. Compromise, a 'middle path', was not possible.[7]

The 'theology of power'

Whereas Carr's use of the catagories 'idealist' and 'realist' and their subsequent employment by others tends to oversimplify, these terms are not without value.[8] They distinguish optimistic, progressive modes of thinking, which assume human actors to be reasoning subjects able to improve their world, from pessimistic approaches stressing that ultimately all values, laws and philosophies are merely the feints and counters in a game of *power* driven by the greedy pursuit of sectional interests. This terminology also points to a rhetorical structure which was particularly strong in a proudly empiricist British political culture, in which 'realism' connoted 'commonsense' and suggested political viability whereas 'idealism' indicated head-in-the-clouds theorising and promised marginality. For a number of reasons it might be assumed that Christians would appear towards the more fanciful end of the idealist side of the spectrum. Had they not been at the head of the pacifist response to the crises of the interbellum period, which often took naïve optimism to extremes? Had they not supported the failed policies of disarmament and the League? Alfred Zimmern, while himself holding that 'spiritual values' were at the very core of world order, was unequivocal in his criticism of this school of thought. He wrote of '… the havoc that these irresponsible and vociferous camp-followers of the Society of Friends have wrought … on well-meaning but unthinking minds … they … have brought shame upon our country and let loose a flood of suffering and evil upon the world'.[9]

However, many Christian thinkers at this time also held a dual position in which 'idealist' and 'realist' tendencies co-existed and Paton and many of his colleagues accepted Toynbee's evaluation. The churchman asked: 'British thinkers have mainly based their ideas upon the permanence of the Anglo-French accord: Now that France is for the moment laid low where in the world can we look for friends who share our own broad outlook upon human freedom and can unite to those ideas the needful power?'[10] There was only one possible answer, in Paton's words, 'Anglo-American co-operation' was 'an absolute prerequisite' in all foreign policy calculations.[11]

At the same time that Christian thinking might stress the power of the 'spirit' to act on material facts, it could with justification also claim to be more 'realistic' in its estimates of the potential for change within human nature than many secular thinkers. On the one hand, Christians posited moral values as the necessary foundation on which any social and political order was raised. On the other, they also stressed that, by accepting the notion of the 'fallen' nature of humanity, they were *more* realistic in their approach than many secular thinkers. On this basis the role of the state and the use of force were accepted as lesser evils in a sinful world. In Christian thinking the State represented a 'union between law and force'.[12] A social order, and the collective moral ethos which it expressed, could only be preserved from individual egotism by the state's power. But at the same time, moral authority was to regulate power. Sketching out the ideal relationship between power and principle, Christopher Dawson specified that '[p]ower must be the servant and not the master. Civilization is essentially the process by which power is progressively subdued, subordinated and directed to human and spiritual ends'.[13] The international arena presented the problem of the egotism of individual nations, but without a corresponding political answer. There, as the Oxford conference noted, law and force had not yet been brought into an 'effective partnership'.[14] There was no superior authority to constrain the evil of individual states. Therefore, international order required not only a Christian ethos, but also *power*.

This was a theological lesson which had been reinforced by the failure of the League of Nations and the inter-war disarmament conferences which the Churches had so enthusiastically supported. Apparently chastened by what many came to see as the 'utopianism' of their previous position, many Christian thinkers became preoccupied with answering what was then called the 'problem of power'. Writing of the 'frank realisation' of the power element in politics, Oldham stressed that there was 'no Christian virtue in clinging to the values and shibboleths of a world that has gone'.[15] The CCIFSR's statement of 1942, which represented the common mind of the Protestant Churches as much as anything did, commented that '[t]he problem of power is a principal problem of the modern world'.[16]

As the theologian Alec Vidler argued, the notions of 'original sin' and the 'fallen' nature of humanity denied that society was governed by reason and the inevitability of progress and hence required that Christians reject the various secular utopianisms of the age. This did not mean that spiritual values could not change the world for the better but it did imply that creating moral order was a challenge of Sisyphean proportions. If there *was* any way out of the crisis, and Vidler was sceptical that there was, one prerequisite was that the 're-christianization of Europe' be begun in England. But, alongside such a cultural revolution, had to come a 'victory of power', whereby pagan totalitarianism would be defeated at its own game so that power could instead be used for 'moral purposes … for the establishment of an international order in which power is used, not merely for the unbridled pursuit of national interests but for enforcing international relations according to a standard of justice for all'. Referring to the lesson that Carr dealt out to those who believed 'politics could become an affair of pure morality' – Vidler wrote of how 'power politicians' had to be defeated 'on their own ground and by their own methods'.[17] Given his role here, it was profoundly significant that Paton was so firmly convinced on this point too. He concurred with Carr's criticism of the 'utopianism which results from … ignoring … the necessity of power to any effective political structure'.[18] He captured the dualism of the 'theology of power', declaring that: 'To plan as if men were good but stupid, as if the world were not sinful but only needing organization, is condemned by Christian realism. To accept the evolution of history as the last word, and to eliminate the moral appeal and the ideal aspiration from the life of societies is condemned by Christian utopianism'.[19] As he wrote elsewhere, '[p]ower must be checked by something outside the sphere of material forces'.[20]

Paton also wrote of how Carr, 'in theory … does insist on a balance between realism and utopia, but in practice, it seems to be he leaves little room to the sphere of moral ideal'.[21] Inevitably, to keep these two positions in proper proportion, to avoid idealism being driven out by 'realism' presented a severe challenge. A drift towards the extremities of idealism promised political impotence; but travel in the opposite direction risked denying any possibility of positive change. Furthermore, realism and utopianism where not equal partners: the flower of hope turned its face towards the status quo of power politics, thickly armoured and deeply entrenched. At the beginning of 1940, while seeking to hold both of these two forces in tension, Paton was already inclined towards realism. He wrote that Carr's book 'ought to be made compulsory reading for all members of the LNU, of FU and of the equivalents in the United States'. He asked speculatively, and perhaps sceptically: 'How much identity of fundamental idea and principle is necessary to a federal union of sovereign states?'[22]

Christendom, the Empire and the Anglo-American alliance

For Paton and his colleagues the Anglo-American alliance was the answer to the problem of power, not only because of the economic, military and political capacities of these nations but because they also united power with ideals. As Linda Colley and others have discussed, post-Reformation religious conflicts and the wars against France had not only made Protestantism and 'Britishness' synonymous, but had created that identification in opposition to the 'Catholic' Continent.[23] By the 1940s, even if this negative linkage of religion and nationality was of diminishing effect, the 'positive' aspects of Britishness continued to be influential. As an 'imagined community'[24] a nation is composed by its distinctive symbols, landscape, literature and so on, but of particularly importance in this context was the way in which its collective 'character' was imagined. George Bell, for example, held that Britain was fighting for 'ideals of liberty and justice',[25] and many saw 'British' political culture to be a repository of the Christian tradition.

Not only this, but the Empire, or 'Commonwealth' as it was increasingly called at this time, was often represented as an example to the world of a 'spiritual' unity of otherwise distinct nations. Ties of language, kinship and history seemed to stretch naturally to the wider 'British' community of the Commonwealth to which the Churches, through mission, had a particularly close relationship.[26] Even Beales, who, as a Catholic, was much more inclined to think 'European', wrote of the Commonwealth as demonstrating 'a cohesion and common loyalty' which were the 'envy of the world', and being the consequence not of formal instruments but of 'history and tradition, and of inherited standards of freedom'.[27] Given the stress on Christendom as being in the first instance a cultural or 'spiritual' form of unity, the widespread notion of British institutions as organic formations which had grown up to reflect the pacific, ordered and 'democratic' spirit of the British 'way of life' fostered a belief in an affinity between British institutions and the reborn Christendom to come. As Ortega y Gasset suggests, nations might exist in their history but they are also 'a doing': 'the national past projects its attractions – real or imaginary – into the future'.[28] Christian notions of 'Britishness' imagined a world community and a global political power, which was itself anointed by Providence to be a historical force. Temple preached that '[i]f we believe at all in the Divine Providence we cannot doubt that so great and distinctive a fact as the British Empire has its place in the providential scheme'.[29] Archbishop Cyril Garbett underlined the depth and security of such beliefs: 'I find it hard to exaggerate the complete and absolute confidence we had in the greatness and security of the British Empire; we believed it had been chosen by God to bring justice and good order to all the earth, and that for centuries to come it would stand as a rock against all storms'.[30]

On their own, such assumptions did not *necessitate* a disengagement from the European movement. For example, in 1942, Oldham saw the 'Anglo-Saxon peoples' as a community uniting power, moral authority and grace as a resource for leadership in Europe.[31] Reckitt and Casserley believed in the 'unique role in international life allotted by Providence to a nation which is at the same time a member of the European family of nations and the keystone of a world empire'. Britain had been appointed to be the 'indispensable link' between the old world and new, and to carry out 'her world-wide cultural mission' to create a 'sane world order'.[32] In these examples, service to God, Empire and Europe were apparently one. However, Oldham's reference above to the 'Anglo-Saxon peoples' is of significance for referring to a putative community of interest, culture, and 'race' between the United States and British Commonwealth. Despite existing predominantly in the British imagination, such a construction was congruent with foreign policy at the time in which the nation's future as a world power was inextricably linked to an Anglo-American alliance.[33] William Paton, believed that the United States and the Commonwealth stood among the greater powers of 'the West, with its twin tradition going back to Palestine and Hellas'. He saw in an Anglo-American alliance power and moral authority combined: 'they combine the fact of power with an ingrained distaste for the absolute state'.[34] Likewise, Temple saw the 'United States and the British Commonwealth of Nations' as 'the culmination of human history' in this regard,[35] and Oldham believed that the 'Anglo-Saxon peoples' possessed a 'political tradition' combining the 'vital moral element' with power. They were 'heirs to a great tradition ... not by merit but by grace'.[36]

The demand for ideals to be backed with the power which the League had lacked, alongside with the British preference for the organic evolution of political institutions over the imposition of model constitutions, and the various ruling myths of British national identity, together damned European federalism. While continuing to play homage to the heritage of Christendom in European history, many British Christians also came to assume that the continent would be too weak and divided to be a viable political unit and, therefore, they looked to a world order built around an Anglo-American Axis. Paton was unequivocal on this point: 'I believe with intense conviction that upon collaboration between the United States and the British Commonwealth nearly everything in a secular sense depends, but I believe chiefly because it seems to me the hopeful beginning of world order and the plainly indicated path to it'.[37]

Whitehall, the British Churches and American opinion

Paton and the Peace Aims Group did not merely accept the Anglo-American alliance theoretically but actively worked to cement and sustain it throughout the war. In 1940 this was a considerable challenge. The American public, while having no especial affection for Nazi Germany, was also overwhelmingly against American intervention in another European war. President Roosevelt was friendly to the British cause, but neither Congress nor popular isolationism could be overridden, and certainly not in election year. For this reason, influencing policymakers, public figures and the general climate of opinion in America was a crucial front in the war of words between Britain and Germany.

As to the significance of religion in this campaign, if the United States represented the most important target of British propaganda, the Churches were among the most influential institutions within American society. An early MOI document noted that the Protestant community there was the 'largest ... in the world', numbering some seventy five millions and that '[s]ome of the Churches exercise a powerful influence on public opinion'.[38] An important constituency of opinion in any case, the Churches were especially significant because of their contribution to the pacifist wing of isolationism. As sources of anti-British feeling, the German origins of the significant Lutheran denomination in America had to be considered, as did the strong Irish strand within US Catholicism. As a secret briefing paper for the minister stated, it was 'difficult to exaggerate the influences of the churches in the life of America', and that 'American public opinion cannot be moved to a whole-hearted support of the allied cause unless the churches are moved'.[39]

In the war of words the Peace Aims Group served an important role in Britain's struggle to overcome isolationism and entered into close collaboration with the Foreign Office and the MOI. In intention, all British propaganda was covert, or at least aimed to be so. Beyond the general assumption that anything that could be identified as 'propaganda' was ineffective, it became the formal rule that for the British state to appear to seek to influence its onetime colony in such a way would be counterproductive, provoking anti-British and pro-isolationist opinion. One British report likened the American response to propaganda as being akin to a 'phobia', arising from a fear that they were 'about to become the victim of European, particularly British, propaganda "like the last time"'.[40] Hence another early memorandum advised that, because Americans would 'resent' such publicity, that it was 'understood that none will be directed from this side'. 'Open' or 'ostensible' propaganda was not to be used.[41] However, it was simultaneously understood that all opportunities which could be used to influence opinion covertly and *obliquely*, should be employed.

The key to successful propaganda was for its intentions and origins to be disguised and so informal personal networks were a crucial conduit for state influence. The Churches offered considerable potential here. Not only were the Anglican and Free Church denominations strongly represented in America, but British Christians could draw on links built up though co-operation in the ecumenical movement and International Missionary Council which went back to the end of the nineteenth century. Paton believed that the 'closest link which joins the British Commonwealth and the United States is the friendship and understanding provided by the Churches and the myriad of enterprises in which across the ocean they are joined'.[42] In essence, the aim of British propagandists was to use these networks as a way of influencing American opinion free of the taint of official propaganda. The director of the Religions Division of the MOI, Hugh Martin, a Baptist and previously editor of the Student Christian Movement Press, was well-equipped to his role. He explained: '[t]he work of the Religions Division is built upon personal contact with leaders of the Churches here and abroad. The officers of the Division are in most cases either on terms of personal friendship or are known by reputation to the correspondent. ... He is not likely to respond so cordially or so confidentially if he is instructed to write to an anonymous official instead of someone he knows and trust'.[43] It was 'vital in approaching the churches to avoid the impression that they were being used for merely political ends'.[44] This approach was also essential inasmuch that the Ministry found that written propaganda was ineffective, if it was 'much more fruitful ... to encourage Church leaders themselves to expound the issues at stake to their own people'.[45] As will be shown here, the success of the Division in achieving subtlety was patent in its results. As a retrospective study commented: '[t]here is no doubt that the value of the Religions Division was genuinely recognised in Church circles. It was not, as some had feared, looked on as a department for exploiting the Church'.[46]

Two principal 'oblique' methods of influence were available. The first was through direct contacts with members of the American Churches. The MOI pursued a number of such contacts at a personal level and through the circulation of its publications. Of particular importance was the relationship Martin forged with Henry Pitney van Dusen (1897–1975). Van Dusen was professor of Systematic Theology at the Union Theological Seminary, New York and the Secretary of the Federal Council of Churches in America, the body which represented all the main non-Catholic Christian denominations. He had been awarded his Ph.D. by Edinburgh University in 1932, was married to a Scot, and has been described as 'a great admirer of the British'; someone who 'never tried to conceal a feeling of almost special kinship with them [the British], and probably felt himself something of an Anglophile'.[47] Also a convinced interventionist, van Dusen crowned all his other virtues by a network of contacts which not only took in the churches' leadership but also penetrated into the highest echelons of American social and political life.

In a discussion of 4 July 1940, between representatives of the American and Religions Divisions of MOI, it was agreed that the 'main idea' was to 'get the Van Dusen Group to assume interest and responsibility for making known the point of view of British Christianity in church circles in America'.[48] Van Dusen had agreed, Martin wrote, to place 'articles in American papers without divulging the fact that they come ultimately through this Ministry'.[49] He described the American as 'the liaison officer between myself and the group of pro-British American churchmen who have been working with my division since the outbreak of war'.[50] Concerning the value of this link Martin wrote in a secret memorandum: 'We are fortunate in having a large number of influential friends in the leadership of the Protestant Church'. Van Dusen's group had been 'particularly generous in their expenditure of time and energy and money and have guided the American policy of the Religions Division of the MOI. They could not do more to help ...'[51] Their co-operation had been 'magnificent'.[52]

A second technique was the inter-visitation of church leaders, which was stressed as being of the 'utmost importance'.[53] Martin personally oversaw visits to the United States.[54] In so doing, he liaised with van Dusen, the American Section of MOI and with the British Library of Information and Aubrey Morgan of the British Information Service (BIS) in New York to organise and, if necessary, fund such visits. Certain individual clergy, including Temple, were deemed to be 'persona grata in the

USA' and their visits to the States provided opportunities for 'useful informal publicity'.[55] Visits by Christian leaders and theologians with 'sound' – that is, non-pacifist – thinking on the war, as unofficial 'ambassadors' in the British interest, to conduct 'vigorous propaganda' would, it was hoped, encourage the 'most cordial possible relationships' between the two countries. Martin styled such visitations as being a 'national service' and of being of 'considerable national importance'.[56] On one visit, John Baillie, Professor of Divinity at Edinburgh University, spoke no less than 78 times in 42 days, invariably to audiences of a thousand or more, on such topic as 'The Moral issues of the War'. He hoped that he had 'succeeded in winning some affection and empathy for Britain'.[57] Even after Pearl Harbor the Ministry continued to promote such visits, there were, Martin wrote '[f]ew things are more important than the promotion of friendly understanding between Britain and America'.[58]

In wartime, travel to the United States was impossible without the permission and active support of the British government and even then scarcely straightforward. It was indicative of the importance of Paton's visits that he was accorded priority status for the highly prized seats on the transatlantic Pan-American Airways service, which were reserved for VIPs. 'It would be ridiculous', Martin wrote with regard to Paton's second visit in 1942, to ask 'a man of his standing to waste three weeks on a cargo boat'.[59] In order to assess the importance of these visits, we should note that the travel of British dignitaries to the United States to conduct propaganda was not necessarily welcomed. In 1940, the British ambassador, Lord Lothian, wrote that 'flooding' America with such visitors would do 'more harm than good' and he commented that he had yet to find a single American or Briton who thought that Duff Cooper's recent visit had been at all beneficial.[60] What was needed, Lothian stressed, was for information and arguments germane to the British case to be fed to sympathetic natives so that America could 'make its own mind up'.

The value of Paton's work here, we might surmise, was that his behind-the-scenes meetings allowed the British argument to be made to sympathetic public leaders, who then propagated among the general public the same message, laundered clean of the taint of propaganda. Writing to Dr. Granville-Barker, of the British Library of Information in New York, Martin wrote that Paton, possessing 'many strong links in the United States of America' was 'of the utmost service to us here in all our work. Visits of him would always be of great value … For contacts with leaders of the American Churches and for lectures and addresses to selected groups nobody could be better'.[61] Similarly, according to (Rev.) Ronald R. Williams, who followed Martin as director of the Religions Division, Paton, by 'moving independently in America, but undermining isolationism with almost every word he spoke', 'was very useful precisely because of this fine balance of independence from and support for the British Government'.[62]

Paton, Van Dusen and the destroyers-for-bases deal

Paton made the first of his two wartime visits to the United States in 1940, leaving in February during the so-called phoney war and returning as the Allies were rapidly defeated in the West. The German attack began on 7 May and by the end of the month the British Expeditionary Force had retreated to the beaches of Dunkirk. Not long after Paton's return the German army entered Paris (14 June) and by the 22nd the French government capitulated. Paton wrote later that the temper of US public opinion which he found at that time was 'broadly speaking, ... opposed utterly to the Nazi way of life; almost as unanimously it desired, and was resolved, to keep out of "Europe's War"'.[63]

A detailed account of how Paton spent his time in America is difficult to reconstruct – possibly his letters at this time may have been lost in the turmoil of war. Alternatively, the long lag entailed in trans-Atlantic correspondence may have meant that he did not choose to report back in this way. During his visit he was in regular contact with Lord Lothian – a leading Chatham House man, then British ambassador to Washington – and with the British Library of Information in New York, which was also responsible for British propaganda.[64] Paton addressed a series of public meetings but also made contact with influential individuals. Before leaving he sought the advice of Lionel Curtis at Chatham House on who the 'right people' in the field of international relations were to see,[65] and he also drew up a list of 'people to see' after a meeting with PEP.[66] Following from these suggestions,[67] he reported having had 'a long and valuable talk' with the foreign affairs and military expert Professor Edward Mead Earle. Among Earle's many distinctions was work with the Office of Strategic Services, the wartime forerunner of the Central Intelligence Agency.[68] Paton was unable to see to the economist and Democrat Everett Coil,[69] who was ill, but met his 'second in command' and also spoke with Bruce Bliven, editor of the prominent liberal journal *The New Republic* and New York correspondent of *The Manchester Guardian*.[70]

Paton also made contact with some of the church leaders with whom he would collaborate closely over the next few years, including van

Dusen and the leading theologian Reinhold Niebuhr.[71] As already noted, van Dusen was a very active collaborator with the MOI and was central to the WCC debates over peace aims throughout the war. He was also acquainted with Paton from ecumenical meetings before the war and was even related to him by marriage to the Scotsman's cousin. A convinced interventionist from the outset of the war, in 1940 van Dusen was in the vanguard of those in America who sought to come to Britain's aid in the face of calamitous defeat and the looming possibility of invasion. In retrospect, he spoke of his bid 'to conspire to bring the United States into the war'.[72]

Not long after Paton's departure, van Dusen was instrumental in calling together what became the 'Century Group', which included many of the leaders of political, business, cultural, religious and scholarly life on the East coast, many of whom also had British links.[73] It was indicative of the sway that this group wielded that van Dusen was among those Americans who initiated and then lobbied for the adoption of what became the idea of 'lend-lease', which was so vital to Britain's survival during the war.[74] On 4 July, a month after Paton's return, as the representative of the Century Group, van Dusen met with Lord Lothian. At the heart of their discussion was America's foreboding at the strategic consequences should Britain be defeated. If this should happen, and – most importantly of all – if the ships of the Royal Navy be destroyed or surrendered to the *Kriegsmarine*, then the balance of naval power would be shifted overwhelmingly against America. The detailed account which van Dusen sent to Paton stated that the 'destruction or surrender of the British Fleet would place the United States in a position, exceedingly precarious from the point of view of national defence ...'[75] The fleet was, the Century Group held, Britain's 'one and only one great asset, which ... might be proven to be of sufficient importance to enlist active American participation in the war'.[76] The *quid pro quo* proposed was that the British government should pledge that, in the case of invasion, it would not surrender but carry on the struggle at sea from bases in the Empire. In exchange for this, the group suggested that the American government should agree to enter the war against Germany. In essence, the discussions between the two governments at the time also centred on the fleet. The Americans were concerned to save it in the case of a German invasion, whereas the British were desperate to secure vital war materials and, ideally, an American declaration of war, to *prevent* such an eventuality occurring. Unwilling to concede either the viability or desirability of an agreement whereby the United States might, in the prime minister's words, 'pick up the debris of the British fleet', London painted the unpleasant possibility of a quisling successor of a defeated Churchill delivering Britain's navy to the enemy.[77]

When Lothian met with van Dusen, the ambassador mentioned the urgent need for a transfer of US destroyers to the Royal Navy, to help protect Britain's essential Atlantic lifeline, which the German navy's U-boats were then working very successfully to sever. Defeat in the Atlantic would not only have cut off the flow of material essential for Britain's war effort but ended the imports necessary to feed its population. Churchill had first proposed such a 'loan' of ships in a personal message to the president on 15 May, but despite continued contacts stressing the urgency of the request, there had been no progress, with Roosevelt citing the difficultly of securing the approval of Congress for such a deal.[78] Following his meeting with van Dusen, Lothian, who had previously doubted the possibility of such a deal, wrote to the prime minister in more positive tones.[79] Finally, on the 22 August and after much more manoeuvring, the Americans agreed to exchange destroyers for concessions giving them the right to build bases on British territory in Newfoundland and in the Caribbean, a deal which Lothian had first mooted towards the end of May.

During these negotiations the British faced not only the challenge of the continuing force of isolationism but also the common, and at different points, dominant belief that the British position was hopeless. Even for those otherwise favourable to supporting London, this second point raised the problem of delivering valuable war weapons which might shortly be in enemy hands, thereby further weakening America on the seas. It is undoubtedly the case that van Dusen was a significant agent in influencing the climate of opinion by countering isolationist arguments, articulating arguments for intervention and for showing that Britain was by no means out of the war. However, in addition to this more or less public stance he was also deeply involved in the covert web of intrigue surrounding these events. He was fully cognisant with a whole range of contacts made by Century Group members with the US administration and leading Republicans to enable the bases for destroyers deal. For example, Henry Sloane Coffin (president of Union Theological Seminary) and the media mogul Henry Luce saw Secretary of State Cordell Hull, while Lewis Douglas sounded out the Republican presidential candidate, Wendell Wilkie. Vitally, Wilkie intimated that he would not try to make political capital if the bases for destroyers deal went ahead, and, in the event, foreign policy was not central to his campaign.

It is also highly likely that van Dusen was a player in the so-called secret diplomacy presided over by William Stephenson, of the Secret Intelligence Service (MI6), and head of British Security Coordination (BSC) in the United States. Whether the theologian was conscious or unconscious of his role here is not yet known. The Century Group certainly had access to secret British Intelligence. Writing to Paton, van Dusen mentioned that his knowledge of the desperate British destroyer situation had come from 'a confidential authoritative memorandum from the British Admiralty in London'.[80] The most convincing evidence for van Dusen's involvement is that it was he who claimed to have originated the idea of asking General Pershing – an American national hero – to speak in favour of the destroyers deal, in a speech written by Century Group member Herbert Agar.[81] This speech was vital in gathering wider public support behind the destroyers deal, an achievement which BSC claimed in its unpublished history to have achieved through the persuasion of Pershing by 'an intermediary'.[82] The same text claimed that its liaison with William Donovan of the Office of Strategic Services – the American equivalent of SIS – was vital in Donovan convincing the president to act in the destroyers deal.[83] Of the same period in August, van Dusen wrote 'for the last four days every pressure has been concentrated upon the President in the matter of the destroyers'.[84] Circumstantially, we might also note that the British Library of Information, with which van Dusen was in close contact, shared an address with British Security Coordination at the Rockefeller Centre on Fifth Avenue, New York.

Following his contacts in the United States, Paton – Margaret Sinclair writes – could 'leave for home satisfied that firm foundations had been laid between British and American churchmen on [the] question of the Church and post-war reconstruction'.[85] Sources do not exist to support any precise statement about the extent of Paton's role in 1940 in preparing the ground for the militarily and symbolically important ships-for-bases deal and in van Dusen's work in breaking down isolationism, but it is likely to have been significant. Paton was clearly 'in the know' about the nature and extent of the American's secret work in the British interest, as van Dusen sent him detailed reports of what he was doing. Van Dusen also used Paton as an intermediary for sending his proposals for ways in which America could help the British government. Paton passed one of these on to the foreign secretary with his commendation as to the 'quality' of the group, as having 'weight with thoughtful America, and of whose disinterested spirit one need have no doubts'.[86] It was indicative of his concerns at this time, that not long after his return, Paton stressed to the Peace Aims Group the necessity of meeting German propaganda in America with a statement of Britain's moral purpose in the war. This would counter Republicans 'standing for isolationism' who might seize on similar themes to attack FDR for his friendly stance to Britain in the presidential election campaign.[87]

Paton's active approach to Anglo-American relations and the substantial resources he drew on to influence them was also very clearly in evidence in respect to Britain's economic blockade of occupied Europe. In America, humanitarian concern that the continent might be plunged into famine by British policy was growing and proposals made by former president Herbert Hoover to provide 'famine relief' had considerable potential to create public ill will against Britain. Paton's task here was to ensure that the British argument for its policy was convincingly made in the right quarters. He wrote of having 'been into this business rather deeply' by letter and cable with the American church leadership and, on the British side, 'some of the leading Church peoples and also the Government people concerned'.[88] The extent of Paton's influence was clear: 'The fact is that the American Church leaders have been unwilling to support Hoover, whatever they themselves thought about it, without being sure of our attitude and they have completely accepted the arguments which ... I presented to them'. Paton's close relationship with the British ambassador to Washington was clear too in his letter to Charles Raven: 'Very privately to you, I understand that Lothian has some plan of his own which he thinks would meet the desires of the best Americans and would not weaken the British war effort to defeat Germany. I am hoping to see Lothian before he goes back to America and will pump him on this ...'[89] Inasmuch that the voice of the American churches on such a delicately poised ethical question was likely to have great authority, Paton's influence can only have been beneficial to the British interest. Suggestively, Granville-Barker in New York later alluded to the success of Paton's first visit as 'spectacular'.[90]

An Anglo-American Christian declaration on peace aims

As we now know, FDR was successful in securing another term and America became increasingly supportive of the British war effort. Following the president's joint declaration with the British prime minister that summer ('The Atlantic Charter') and his uncompromising response to German attacks on US shipping, van Dusen could report to an Anglo-American meeting in October 1941 that American opinion was increasingly reconciled to war.[91] Nonetheless, even in late 1941, a

formal declaration of war was still unlikely and the interventionist faction faced 'an exceedingly difficult task' in changing Christian opinion,
which remained strongly pacifist and isolationist. For this reason, even
before the United States had entered the war, Paton and PAG sought a
peace aims statement, which would be an Anglo-American document;
having 'the assent of responsible people in both countries'.[92] This,
Paton believed, would be 'politically very far reaching'.[93]

He found ready agreement with this aim from van Dusen and the
Commission to Study the Bases of a Just and Durable Peace. In 1940,
van Dusen's circle had successfully lobbied the Federal Council of
Churches, the collective body of American Protestantism, to establish
this body, commonly referred to as the Commission on a Just and
Durable Peace. Chaired by John Foster Dulles, the Commission set out
not merely to study the question of world order, but to change the
American public mind towards taking an active role in reforming international politics. Indicating the scale of its intentions the first edition
of its handbook *A Just and Durable Peace* was of 450,000 copies.[94]
Intensive discussions would pursue between PAG and the Commission,
not only via extensive correspondence, but also through a series of joint
meetings on both sides of the Atlantic. At the first Anglo-American
gathering, held at Balliol College, Oxford, over two days at the beginning of October 1941, van Dusen represented the American side and sat
at the table with representatives of the British Churches, Chatham
House and PEP. He explained that there were two reasons why the 'formulation, discussion and declaration of what were called "peace aims"
was of quite incalculable importance as far as the United States was concerned'.[95] Firstly, he believed that it would be impossible for America to
fully commit itself to the war unless it knew what post-war world it was
fighting for. In this context peace aims preceded war aims.

Two months later, following the unanticipated Japanese attack on the
US naval base at Pearl Harbor in Hawaii and the unexpected German
declaration of war, any such reasons for hesitancy were speedily
despatched. The United States committed fully its huge resources to the
Allied cause and this, Paton believed, was 'the most important fact of
all'.[96] However, while America's belligerency made the defeat of
Germany possible, it did not alter the fundamental facts about Britain's
weakness as a world power and the spectre of peacetime isolationism
continued to haunt the British. Paton detected a 'deep American reluc-
tance to get into any permanent responsibility for Europe' and a corresponding preoccupation with its own hemisphere.[97] It was highly
important then, that even before his country was at war, van Dusen was

looking for ways to encourage America's full involvement in the post-war settlement, which was his second argument for peace aims in October 1941. He believed that, unless countered by a positive policy, the factors promoting isolationism would be stronger than after the 1914–18 war. Writing to van Dusen a year later, Paton referred to the community of interest between the two men: 'You ... want to strike a blow ... against the people who are getting ready for an isolationist policy after the war. I feel that this is so important for the whole world and we ought to do all we can to help you'.[98]

While ready to do almost anything to encourage the Anglo-American alliance, the British state was wary of any discussion of peace aims and would not commit itself to anything which went beyond the moderate principles of the Atlantic Charter. Nonetheless, it continued to support generously Paton and PAG in its contacts with its opposite number in the United States. To the British state the importance of the Commission was twofold – firstly, it was a channel through which to influence the not inconsiderable general body of American Protestant opinion. After Toynbee had mentioned the value of Paton's 'connections', J.V. Wilson, his assistant director of research at the FRPS, acknowledged 'the importance of the movement with which Paton is in close contact as a channel of possible influence, especially in America'.[99] Secondly, in addition to their potential to influence US opinion as a whole, these contacts were also a route to the east coast political elites. Besides van Dusen's personal network, Commission Chairman John Foster Dulles's (1888–1959) career in international affairs began as a personal secretary at the Hague Peace Conference in 1907 and ended as Eisenhower's Secretary of State for Foreign Affairs in 1958. Besides reaching the summit of political power, he had a parallel career in the ecumenical movement, participating in the key conferences at Oxford and Beau Séjour. Tellingly, when in Britain to attend a PAG meeting, he also managed to see 'most members of the British Government'. During that stay he was very positive about the Anglo-American alliance, speaking of the two nations as the 'corner stones' of the post-war world order.[100]

Indicating the importance of these Anglo-American talks, Harold Cockburn, who was the brother of Hutchison Cockburn of PAG and responsible for religious press activities at the BIS in New York, endorsed a joint statement as a way of countering US isolationism.[101] Paton commented that his letter 'greatly reinforces the importance of our going as far as we can to meet our American friends'. The group's work had also received the endorsement of Sir Archibald Clark Kerr, who was 'enthusiastic about the idea of a combined Anglo-American declaration of

Christians'.[102] Clark Kerr was perhaps the foremost British career diplomat of the time, holding posts key to forging the post-war order, as ambassador to Moscow in wartime and then Washington at the beginning of the Cold War.[103] Similarly, both Toynbee and Kenneth Grubb stressed the importance of agreement.[104]

Toynbee we have already met, Grubb was also a man of significant influence. Grubb was a leading lay figure in the Church of England, he had previously been a missionary in South America and would be involved in ecumenical organisations for the rest of his career. He was also a patrician figure very much at home in the world of Britain's ruling classes, who brought to Christian analysis of foreign affairs not only political subtlety but knowledge of intelligence and policy withheld from the public domain. In wartime, Grubb held the post of overseas controller at the MOI, so was closely in touch with the inside track of foreign policy. He enjoyed 'close and cordial' relations with Robin Cruikshank, head of the American section of MOI, and Aubrey Morgan, who was in charge of the BIS. He also worked closely with Rae Smith, the American director of the British arm of the J. Walter Thomson advertising agency, often meeting unofficially over dinner at Grubb's club. Smith was sympathetic to the British cause, and the two men worked to draw up the principles upon which national and regional plans for MOI propaganda were based. Grubb also collaborated with Elmer Davis of the US Office of War Information and the Office of Strategic Studies in Washington. He also alluded to his 'close and informal contacts' with the secret arms of the British state – 'entities of a more mysterious and wraith-like order' – whether these links were involved in his role here is not known.[105] Paton described Grubb as 'a man of great influence in government circles', to whom the group 'kept close ... in nearly everything we do'.[106]

In the end, the intention of creating a joint statement was not quite fulfilled – the Commission's 'Six Pillars of Peace' was issued independently on 19 March 1943 and the Peace Aims Group's declaration 'A Christian Basis for Reconstruction' appeared later in its support.[107] Nonetheless, taken together, the two statements showed that Paton's original aim of creating a symbolic community of opinion had succeeded. However, for those who had hoped for a positive British endorsement of the goal of a new Europe, the British statement was a disappointment. Whereas the American declaration allowed for the possibility of a federal Europe within an overall world plan, and met with approval among continental Christians for that reason,[108] the Peace Aims Group would decide to excise a similar declaration from its published statement.

As to the reason for this, at one meeting it was suggested that federal integration might deter American engagement in Europe.[109] This suggestion engaged with the longstanding fear that any positive British involvement with a united Europe would have a negative consequence for the nation's other global relationships. There was, of course, nothing intrinsic to an Anglo-American alliance which ruled out British participation in an European unity. Christian pro-European thinkers rarely, if ever, conceptualised a united Europe in exclusive terms. There was also a significant body of American opinion which favoured Britain taking a lead in Europe. At the very outset of the interchange between the two groups, van Dusen had suggested that a world order based around 'Hemispheric or regional federations', including 'a European federation with Great Britain as its leader, would be amenable to "realistic statesman"'.[110] Dulles, who drafted the Commission's statement, himself favoured a federal solution. He envisaged a federal Europe existing beneath the umbrella of an improved world association of nation-states. This association would, on occasion and by agreement, aggregate certain powers to a global 'Executive organ', as a first step towards true world government. Alongside a federal Europe, Dulles imagined a parallel 'evolution of the English speaking peoples towards greater political unity' which 'might avoid, for England, the apprehension she might otherwise feel in the face of a projected federation of Continental Europe'.[111]

At the first Anglo-American meeting at Balliol, van Dusen outlined the various schools of thought on post-war world order. Of these, three stand out as significant:

> (2) regionalism. There was tremendous sentiment in the US which said that they had no desire to mix in Europe's affairs, that this should be Britain's job, but they would strengthen Britain's hands. America had her job in the Western hemisphere, and, together with China, would see what could be done in the Far East. This idea would get the support of the less extreme isolationists and also of the support of a great many people who were in favour of entering the war but doubt whether America has the ability or the interest to take a leading part in world affairs. (3) British and American collaboration, the principle which Dr. Paton had expounded in his book. This view of course had the support of the pro-British part of American people. (4) return to collective security through an association of member states. This was the view held by most of what this group would consider their opposite numbers in the U.S.[112]

In this way, van Dusen summarised the dominant modes of opinion of the American political classes (2); the thinking of Paton – and, therefore, Toynbee, Chatham House and the British state (3); and the powerful idealist section among US Christian elites (4).

Paton, and through him the Chatham House circle and the British state, were influential here in ensuring that 'option 3' became a preferred one. Before the meeting Paton wrote to Toynbee that 'Van Dusen himself agrees with the general line that you and I have taken – that Anglo-American leadership is really essential. At the same time he feels that nearly all the best people in America have turned the same way and are thinking in terms of the all-in association of the nations of the League of Nations kind'.[113] Van Dusen also indicated his agreement a little later in an article based on the text of his speech at the Oxford meeting. He noted there that of all the options for the future only two were likely to 'engage the support of Christian leaders – British–American collaboration *or* return to an Association of Nations'. Van Dusen held that it was American leaders 'with a keen awareness of *Realpolitik* who are also most intimately sympathetic with dominant British opinion' – among whom he was undoubtedly numbered himself – who favoured a world rebuilt around the Anglo-American Axis.[114]

It was illustrative of Toynbee's sway that at the October meeting it was 'universally agreed' that he would draft the British group's statement, a decision which, given that the historian probably never properly shook off his agnosticism, was not without irony. Some weeks after the meeting Paton's enthusiasm was undiminished: 'I rejoice in the fact that you see so clearly the immense importance of the Anglo-American Christian link. I do not think that we are wrong in feeling that, if we can secure something like a common body of convinced opinion it might be politically very far reaching'. In the event, Toynbee could not draft a statement for PAG due to the pressure of other commitments, although he agreed to comment on the group's work. Despite this disappointment, Paton pressed Toynbee to accompany him on a return visit to meet van Dusen and his Commission colleagues.[115] Once again Paton was disappointed. Toynbee was unable to travel, having been ordered to rest for six weeks, but despite this, his opinion was ably represented at the closed meeting at the Princeton Inn. At the meeting, held over three days in March 1942, Paton spoke of his contacts with 'the men who know the inside problems of this present situation and who bear great responsibility in government circles'. He cited 'feeling on the part of finest Christian opinion' – by which almost certainly meant Toynbee – that: 'what the British Empire has been at its best should be reflected in some international system'. He could not say exactly what this would be, but did feel 'that this was the only possible thing now for the kind of world in which we live. If America and England cannot understand each other no other can or will'. Hence, Paton continued, 'great importance attaches to which view wins in the world – regionalism', or his preferred option, 'world organisation, with Anglo-American leadership at its heart'.[116]

This did not necessarily mean that Europe was completely ignored. Dr. J. Hutchison Cockburn, moderator of the Church of Scotland, who accompanied Paton, stressed the need for 'regional agreements' to prevent a return to the old power politics of Europe, but all the same, even for the Scotsman, whatever happened to continental Europe was subsidiary to a world order built around an Anglo-American Axis. On the American side, Dr. Raymond Leslie Buell, formerly research director and then president of the Foreign Policy Association saw 'the virtual elimination of France' as opening the possibility of 'virtually a league based on Washington and London as centres of power'. Europe, without American involvement, would be dominated by either Germany or Russia, hence 'an extra European solution' was needed, 'a mere European federation' being insufficient.[117] In Paton's presentation, as in the assumptions of his hosts, all other foreign affairs questions – of the future of Germany, of Russia's place in the new world order – were secondary to a vision of world power founded on some form of Anglo-American alliance.

Harley Granville-Barker, head of the MOI's outpost in New York, the British Library of Information, later described Paton's visit as being 'a tonic to the flabbiness of some of his and our acquaintances here – a tonic very much needed'. His was 'a highly successful journey'.[118]

At the first Oxford meeting, it had been agreed that if America was to be drawn into playing a full part in the post-war world order, it was necessary that the 'peace settlement must always be discussed from the British side in terms of a world settlement and not only of a European one'.[119] On the face of it, this was not inherently unfriendly towards European unity. Although a worldwide catastrophe required a global solution, the existence of regional unities beneath the umbrella of a world organisation was accepted as a valid and practical option and was treated as such by the American side in its final statement. However, in the context of ambitions to remain a nation whose power was global in its reach, influence, and ambitions, and built primarily on empire and the Atlantic alliance, this British stance placed a substantial barrier against full-hearted leadership in the building of the new Europe.

In July 1942, when PAG met at Balliol again, this time with J.F. Dulles, Dr. George Stewart and Dr. Walter van Kirk from the American side, the topic was again discussed under the heading of 'The Question of Germany'.[120] Initially, Routh spoke at some length, noting that while the war was now on a world scale, 'Europe had been the storm centre of world politics'. He also believed that 'people in Britain were in fact realising they were Europeans'. Furthermore, one 'positive' aspect of the German 'new order' was that it recognised that 'the units of power, political and social organisation, must be very much larger in than they had been in the past' The 'parcelation of continents into small national units was to some extent an obsolete conception'. This quality was the pattern for the future and must be taken into account in any peace aims. Routh was clear that a Europe united by German fascism could not last – ultimately it was internally unstable, and externally it was 'inconceivable that the German idea of Europe should be tolerated for very long by Britain, Russia or the United States'. If Routh himself had any idea of the future shape of Europe beyond the Nazi new order he did not detail it. However, an exchange between Toynbee and Bishop Bell made clear that a federal Europe was not an acceptable solution.

Bell, who had visited Sweden and met with elements of the German resistance not long beforehand, had been 'struck by the insistence on the European problem, and the fear in well-instructed quarters ... that Britain was so absorbed in her part ... of the war that she tended to overlook the very grave problem of Europe as a whole'. Bell urged a positive response to the German resistance, as it would make 'the establishment of future order in Europe and Germany less difficult'. While not going into detail, the bishop's suggestion of the future incorporation of German forces into a 'European Army' indicated the direction of his thinking. However, Toynbee replied that 'European federation ... was not enough; federation must be on a world scale'.[121] Whether the bishop and the historian discussed this point further is unclear, because Paton excised the rest of that page and the following one from the minutes. The reasoning behind Toybee's position was indicated later in the day and once more his primary focus was on power relations. The stability and longevity of the Roman Empire demonstrated that international order demanded a predominance of power. The Germans had made their bid in those terms and had created order, but only at the cost of 'awful conditions of life'. The ideal alternative would entail:

> order and security from world wars got at the least heavy price in loss of freedom and justice. Hitler's price is very heavy on both of these

things. The ideal would be to combine the maximum amount of effective world government with the maximum amount of liberty and justice, and this could be brought about by federal union. In this, however, relations between the USA and Russia were the keystone.[122]

However, while a world federation was the *ideal*, Toynbee ruled it out as an *'immediate* solution' (oe), presumably because of the 'difficult' relations between those two powers. Instead he proposed 'something like the League of Nations of the inter-war period' built around a continuation of the wartime 'inter-allied organisation' of the 'four big powers: USA, the British Commonwealth, Soviet Russia and China'.[123]

However, when he visited America, accompanied by Kenneth Grubb in October 1942, Toynbee was successful in steering the Americans towards his idealistic goal of world government. Van Dusen had arranged a series of meetings between the historians and various US luminaries. These included the 'Time-Life-Fortune' group, who Toynbee and Grubb met in a several intimate private gatherings which included, among others, Henry R. Luce, proprietor of *Time* and other influential magazines, the financier T.W. Lamont of J.P. Morgan, and Dulles. Van Dusen wrote of how during this meeting 'Grubb's abilities shone with increasing brightness' and how both men 'made an excellent impression on the TIME crowd'. Toynbee was 'utterly charming, the most delightful of Christian gentlemen', although van Dusen was surprised and somewhat disappointed by the Englishman's diffidence.[124] However, it seems that despite his reserve, Toynbee did influence the thinking of the Americans on the overall scope and structure necessary for the post-war world.

In his introductory statement at the Princeton Inn meeting,[125] Dulles expressed his regret that is was necessary to 'by-pass the solution which was his own desire but which he felt had little chance of realisation, e.g. world government'. It was at this point, van Dusen wrote, 'Toynbee followed, to both Dulles' and my surprise, by insisting that there were no adequate solutions of the main problems of the world order apart from world government. His specific proposal was a re-constitution of a World Association of Nations, to which all the United Nations would initially belong, and the Axis powers as soon as possible'. The meeting, having discussed 'every possible alternative to world government', came to accept that it was 'the only living option'. The 'one concrete proposal' to then emerge from the meeting was that a joint Anglo-American public statement be prepared and that in that document, van Dusen recorded: '[t]he conviction of our group was that the one point which most needs to be asserted is the necessity of world government'. It was the conclusion of the meeting, he believed that it was 'not only insincere but dangerous to lend countenance to half-way measures'.[126] Immediately after the meeting Dulles set to work to draw up a draft statement outlining a world government with 'real though strictly limited power – military, economic and political'. Among the responsibilities of this world body would be the 'reorganisation of Europe'.[127] This last point was a definite change from Dulles's support for a federal Europe earlier the same year.[128] As Bell wrote in criticism, this later proposal suggested 'a body of powers outside or on the fringe of Europe, ruling Europe for its own good'. This was a 'perfectly impossible proposal' and 'certain to arouse widespread resentment within Europe itself'.[129]

The drive behind Toynbee's enthusiasm for world government was almost certainly personal rather than official. Such an objective was incompatible with Whitehall's assumptions about national sovereignty, and did not even accord with the thinking of the Peace Aims Group. Dennis Routh subjected the Dulles's statement to what he saw as 'destructive criticism', suggesting that world government would be neither possible nor popular. Any government was not an end in itself, but the means to pursue the common purposes of the constituency in whose name it governed. The affairs of the nations of the world were insufficiently 'mixed-up' because the 'necessary basis of "like-mindedness"' did not yet exist.[130] When shown Dulles's draft, Temple was unconvinced and even alarmed at the prospect of such a statement being published under the imprimatur of the Churches.[131] Hutchinson Cockburn was critical that the proposals did not take into account the 'intense nationalism' extant in the world.[132] A.D. Lindsay believed there to be no popular support for world government and Grubb held that 'the prompt and irrevocable' achievement of such an objective was 'a mere chimera'.[133] Neither did Toynbee's RIIA colleagues support such a policy. Zimmern wrote that its 'naïveté' took his breath away.[134] Even Paton expressed circumspect doubt at his mentor's role: 'We had … a good talk about the whole thing and he is inclined to think that the difference between the line taken by Routh and the line taken in your memorandum is mainly one of presentation. I do not myself feel quite convinced about this but he may be right'.[135]

The problem this presented was that, on one hand, Anglo-American amity needed to be fostered at almost any cost while, on the other, the US draft statement went far beyond what PAG felt it could be seen to endorse. Routh wrote of 'the importance of responding as forthcomingly as we can to any American approach and the difficulty of proposing an entirely different approach to this end'.[136] This was in Paton's mind when he wrote to the group, proposing they meet to discuss issuing a joint statement: 'these men are conscious continually of the danger of post-war isolationism winning ground in America and they feel that to get a united Anglo-American Christian statement along such lines ... would help in regard to that vital matter'.[137] Consequently, the PAG statement, 'A Christian Basis for Reconstruction', while strongly endorsing the US group's statement in general, also politely distanced itself from the Americans' supranational tendencies.[138]

As already noted, the final US statement, while discussing 'permanent political collaboration' on a global scale, also allowed space for European unity. It stated that 'Europe particularly illustrates the need for regional collaboration. To continue there the unco-ordinated independence of some twenty five sovereign states will assure for the future that, as in the past, war will be a frequently recurrent event'.[139] As such, it moved back to Dulles's previous position of European unity and away from Toynbee's all-or-nothing stance on world government. At the meeting when PAG was first able to discuss the Dulles draft statement and Routh's detailed critique of it, Temple showed that he was thinking on similar lines. He endorsed the Catholic writer Christopher Dawson's thinking in his *Judgement of the Nations*:

> Dawson was very much disposed to accept regionalism with the object of combining some world unification with a good deal of local freedom and effectiveness. He was very keen on the unity of Europe. The four regions might be those led by Great Britain, America, Russia, and broadly speaking, Asia. There would have to be some federal council uniting the regions together.[140]

The American side had suggested that Temple draft a statement which he duly did and this carried the suggestion that:

> To attempt a settlement of many vast problems affecting the whole world through a single international organization for world government seems to be impractical. It is wise to break the problem up into both regional and functional departments. Thus there might be – for purposes of security – a European Council and a Pacific Council. Similarly there should be an international Council for Economic Reconstruction with regional committees; but there would also have to be a supreme world council as the ultimate court of reference.[141]

However, at the final meeting before the publication of the PAG statement, in June 1943, it was decided to omit any reference to a European
Council.[142] Thus, in the final version even this relatively modest nod
towards European unity and federalism was replaced with a more vague
conception: 'It will not be possible to deal with the many and vast problems affecting the world through a single international organisation for
world government; it may be best, as has been suggested in several quarters, to have both functional and regional departments beneath a
supreme World Council'.[143]

Paton's memorandum before the meeting had emphasised the necessity for careful consideration 'of *the type of structure to which we would
wish our own nation to be committed*'. It also emphasised that 'the way to
advance is not to start with the formal political structure but to grow
into it'.[144] This emphasis on 'gradualism' was, as van Dusen saw at the
time, typical of the British approach and in contrast to the American
confidence in federalism.[145] However, the minutes of the meeting do
not specify any reason for the excision of Temple's reference to Europe.

At first glance, this change is particularly puzzling because the group's
deliberations over the statement coincided with the moment at which
the British wartime government was taking a definite interest in the
future of Europe. As we have already noted, from 1940 onwards the government had avoided any comment on peace aims, but then in late
1942 and during the first half of 1943, discussions in the war cabinet
included proposals for regional federations and for the eventual creation of a 'Council of Europe'. The paper entitled 'The United Nations
Plan', which Foreign Secretary Anthony Eden laid before to the cabinet
in January 1943, proposed the creation of a 'World Council of the Four
Powers', possibly also to include France. The primary aim of the Council
would be the pacification and economic reconstruction of Europe, and,
in time, the Reconstruction Commission might develop into a Council
of Europe. This would include all the continental European nations, the
UK, the Soviet Union and, if possible, the United States. In March 1943
the prime minister made the idea of a European Council public in a
radio broadcast and even spoke privately of the possibility of a 'United
States of Europe'.[146]

Although these were – at least until Churchill's broadcast – discussions
held behind closed doors, at least some members of the group knew the
direction that policy seemed to be heading. In fact Grubb had been himself
involved in the preparation of the paper that Eden presented to cabinet
in January 1943, and – in a letter marked 'secret' – he had communicated
the general '"bent" of government thinking' to Dennis Routh.[147] Paton

had also asked Routh to prepare a draft statement, to be discussed along-side Temple's, and this document would contribute significantly to the substance of the final draft.[148] Grubb and Routh, as two of the group's 'experts' would have been especially – perhaps decisively – influential in the discussions. In his letter Grubb indicated the policy being proposed:

> The paper opts for a four power Council (China, according to the FO is to be included *pro forma*), primarily responsible for 'policing' and disarming' the Enemy in Europe. ... The political policy behind the long-term aspect will be to prevent Germany acquiring power (eco-nomic and, naturally, military) by our again seeking some kind of "balance" in Europe, to promote regional agreements, to build up the economies of the small 'etats limitrophes', and subject to what we see when Europe opens up, to build up France.
>
> The 'United Nations' in the longer sense, will find their main expression in a general UN Reconstruction Commission, to which certain [illegible] may be invited.
>
> The Four-Power Council is intended to be, so to speak, the provi-sional Executive of a World-Council-in-the-further-future.
>
> Working towards the ultimate formation of a coordinated range of councils under a world council, it is proposed to promote the forma-tion of two groups of bodies: Political; and economic-and-general. By the former, I mean regional bodies with a prominent "power" taking (in most cases) the lead. E.g. Czecho-slov. and Poland; Balkan (part) with Greece; Pan American (USA leads), Far-East (part) – with China; Middle East (GB). We are working on the problems these councils might discuss.
>
> By "economics" – I mean the ILO and similar bodies with a limited scope, but world range. To this a machine will be added to "marry" these two groups.
>
> No one knows yet just how these far these ideas will appeal in the USA. ...[149]

Part of the clue for why the endorsement of a Council of Europe was dropped by the group may lie in the stress that Grubb laid on the renewed search for a 'balance' in Europe. This was intended to be a means of controlling Germany in the future, by not only restricting its economic strength and disarming it, but also by creating regional con-federations out of the smaller European nations to thereby balance the substantial power that even an emasculated Germany would possess. In this respect, the aim was not European unity at such, as integration was incidental to a purpose which was essentially and literally divisive. Furthermore, the membership of the UK, USA and USSR on any future Council of Europe would continue the one-sided political relationship begun by their domination of the planning and execution of the continent's reconstruction. However, probably the decisive reason that the group came to change its mind was that the Foreign Office was itself doubtful of whether there was any likelihood that a European Council would be viable. It is possible that Grubb shared this attitude, as his letter made no mention of a Council of Europe. Eden certainly did, and he was also able to produce an ace by reporting to Churchill that Harry Hopkins, Roosevelt's confident, was against a European Council as it would encourage isolationists to press for the United States to leave Europe to the Europeans.[150]

This last point was actually made independently by Lindsay at one PAG meeting.[151] There was also an array of other reasons why members of the group preferred to avoid commitments to European integration. In general, the course of events since 1940 had driven the question of Europe's future further down the agenda, as the war and the problem of the post-war settlement expanded to become global. Even when the future of the continent was discussed, the circumstances had been revolutionised in the intervening years. Although not a PAG member at this stage, Joseph Oldham was in close touch with its members and wrote of how he believed that the 'spate of discussion about the political shape of Europe and of the world after the war' and 'interest in blueprints of the future' had 'died away under the stresses of the actual struggle', but that in 1942 the question had now been opened again, albeit 'with perhaps a more sober sense of reality'.[152] 'Realism' had various implications in this context. Toynbee's point of view has already been indicated. Possibly Zimmern – another Chatham House man in government service – may also have been influential. He had suggested in the morning meeting that '... Europe was not a political concept if one thought of it from the point of view of security, for there were two or three separate problems. If one took in Russia, the problem became more vast'.[153] This was a position which he had held from the beginning.[154] Eric Fenn's fear was that after the defeat of Germany, a 'Communist Europe' was more likely than anything else. He anticipated the United States shifting its attention and resources to a long war against Japan and that Britain would be compelled by its weakness to follow suit. The rest of Europe would be powerless to influence the situation. Fenn wrote: 'Isn't there in our minds a pretty deep-seated doubt whether any of the governments in exile ... will be of much importance in the post-war world'. Paton agreed.[155] By this stage of the war even Temple had lost much of his once fervent faith in federalism becoming, as he put it, 'lukewarm'. Replying to Cyril Joad of FU, the archbishop explained that he believed that federalism could only come after a 'long educational campaign' and it was 'a complete delusion' that a federal constitution could be included in any peace treaty.[156]

The British statement was welcomed in the American press.[157] Dulles telegraphed the Commission's 'deep appreciation' and his belief that it marked a 'significant forward step in achieving essential goal of unity of British and American Christians on common program for world order'.[158] However, while advancing Anglo-American relations this was also moment when an opportunity for the British churches to publicise and endorse the idea of European unity was lost. In his first public comment on peace aims, Paton had written of being 'free to scout ahead' of government thinking.[159] However, for all its wholesome sentiments, the British statement was careful to watch the government's line and so stayed largely within the principles articulated in the 'Atlantic Charter' signed by Churchill and Roosevelt in 1941, while also politely distancing itself from the federalist tendencies in the American statement.[160] As van Dusen noted at the time, 'each nation desires radical change where it has no present interests at stake, or where its own interests counsel such change; each nation favours gradualism where its own interests appear imperilled'.[161]

From the perspective of European integration, Toynbee and Paton's thinking was destructive because it was so radically split between utopian idealism and pragmatic realism that it closed the space for intermediate solutions. Besides his perspective on the relationship between power and ideals, a second influential characteristic of the split between 'idealist' and 'realist' approaches in Toynbee's thinking was that, as an idealist, he advocated a world federal government as an *ultimate* aim. But as a realist, working to provide the intellectual basis for the day-to-day development of British policy, he argued that the only practicable *immediate* possibility was another 'League' of sovereign nation-states. Paton also came to argue for the initial creation of a new League of Nations, expressing his agreement with 'my friend Toynbee' to Margaret Richards of FU. In his letter declining an invitation to join the FU National Council, he envisaged a 'world scaffolding' based around Britain, the USA, the USSR and China with a 'closer democratic federation within it' but stressed that any federal arrangement should be allowed 'to grow at its own pace' rather than be included in any peace treaty.[162] He had earlier on indicated his belief that an international system in which power remained concentrated in the hands of separate states did not preclude the eventual creation of a supra-national federal system, it was just a question of 'stages and pace'.[163] As we know now, the 'pace' between such 'stages' has, so far, been very leisurely. The effect of this was to accept the status quo.

3
The Future of Europe, 1944–45

At the same time as being drawn towards building-up the British alliance with the United States, the Churches' Peace Aims Group correspondingly shifted its attention away from the rest of Europe. A powerful array of factors relating to national identity, confessional background, ecumenical and personal relationships and the ruling conventions of Church–State relations contributed to a predisposition to look beyond Europe in imagining the future. This potential was catalysed by a determination to avoid 'utopianism' at almost any cost which was prompted by the failure of the League of Nations, and the often uncritical support which the Churches had accorded it. However, without William Paton, these general propensities might have remained unexpressed or, even if articulated, have drifted impotently heavenward. Paton gave these ideas their legs: Through his energy, tenacity and facility; through the network of relationships spanning the Atlantic and linking Church and State which he fostered and tirelessly maintained.

Bishop Bell

In contrast, Paton's colleague George Bell remained a strong voice for European unity to the end of the war and afterwards. As we have seen, he criticised Dulles's proposals for the rule of 'Europe for its own good' by 'powers outside or on the fringe of Europe' as being 'impossible' and liable to arouse 'resentment within Europe itself'.[1] As to his own support for European unity he expressed himself not only privately but publicly in an address to the House of Lords around the same time.[2] Having discoursed in detail on the necessity of encouraging the anti-Nazi resistance in Germany by distinguishing between the war aim of destroying the 'Hitlerite state' and the future of Germany as a nation, Bell had then explained how the problem of Germany needed to be linked to a peace aim solving 'the problem of Europe': 'The key to the solution of the problem of Europe, which is fundamentally spiritual and moral, and then social and industrial and concerned with the character of industrial society, is to be found in a nobler faith and freedom for all nations living together ...' The incorporation of Germany into a united Europe was, Bell argued, the only solution to the problem of Germany; the imposition of Carthaginian peace, as advocated by Lord Vansittart,[3] would promise a 'further catastrophe twenty years hence'. Outlining his vision of the future, the bishop pointed towards a federal future: '... look at Europe as a whole, plan your transport system, your civil aviation system, your education system, your wireless and communications system, not least your system of armaments, for Europe as a whole, tell the German people that they and all other nations must have such and such restrictions imposed for the sake of Europe as a whole, then the whole situation, moral and psychological, will have changed'.[4]

During the process of drafting 'A Christian Basis for Reconstruction', Bell had pressed for 'much more about the problem of Europe, and the problem of Germany in relation to that' to be included in the statement.[5] In the event, as we have seen, any specific mention of Europe was excised from the group's published statement.[6]

European peace aims via Geneva

Just as Bell had failed to persuade PAG to properly include Europe in its vision of the future world order, there was also another voice struggling for a hearing on the margins of what had become an almost exclusively Anglo-American discussion. During the war years, Willem Visser t' Hooft, Paton's, fellow associate general secretary of the WCC, who was based in the Council's Geneva office, acted as a channel for the thinking of Christians in the resistance in occupied Europe and in organised anti-Nazi opinion in Germany. After the war, many of the new political class rebuilding Europe would come from such quarters.[7]

Through Geneva – in particular from the German resistance – came a consistent advocacy of a federal Europe with full British involvement. An unambiguous demonstration of the direction that 'continental' thinking was taking appeared in a paper sent from Geneva in early 1941 to the British and American groups. This held that the defeat of democracy and the rise of fascist totalitarianism had sundered nations from their historical traditions. There was a 'general understanding' that a return to the '"good old days" of national sovereignty and unrestricted capitalism' was 'impossible'. The European public were ready for 'radical solutions', and the need was for a 'new beginning in politics and economics'. The only viable future was 'some form of European federation', to insure against 'further wars and against economic ruin'. Such a federation would solve the 'the two eternal European problems: – the problem of the balance of power and the problem of minorities'.[8]

This paper of March 1941 spoke only about the future of 'continental' Europe, without commenting on its wider political relationships. In December notes sent by t' Hooft commenting on Dulles's statement 'Long Range Peace Objectives' added further important detail.[9] The paper, which was circulated among the members of PAG,[10] endorsed Dulles's criticism of the Atlantic Charter, which, it agreed, contained 'too much pre-war language and pre-war ideas'. It recognised and welcomed proposals for American aid towards immediate post-war reconstruction and recognised the urgency of the United States and British governments to plan for the 'transition period'. But at the same time as recognising this necessity, a distinctive tone of independence was also present: 'the ideal solution' was that 'the European nations should themselves be able to restore normal conditions on their territory'.

It was also anticipated that Dulles's statement on the long-term future of Europe would enjoy:

> ... wide acceptance among continental Christians. There are, of course, very many who do not yet understand the urgency of some form of federation, but there is among the spiritual and intellectual leadership of the European nations an increasing recognition that there must be limitation of the national sovereignties whose juxtaposition and opposition have proved fatal to European society. At the same time the economic argument for collaboration and common planning becomes stronger every day. Thus the number of those who are ready to think in terms of a European federated commonwealth is constantly growing, and that in *all* types of Countries.

However, the possibility of this new Europe emerging hinged on two questions not mentioned by Dulles: 'the underlying conception of international order, and ... of Germany's place in Europe'. The answer to these questions was 'spiritual', inasmuch that no federal structure could survive unless rooted in 'a common ethos, a common foundation of moral convictions'. This was no longer present – before a European federation could succeed 'Europeans ... must be re-educated, or better, re-Christianised'. Such a cultural transformation would do much to answer the 'problem of Germany' by creating the conditions whereby that state could be safely incorporated within a European federation on terms of political and economic equality. However, at the same time the author/s of the paper also recognised the 'question of power' and continued: 'At this point the relation of Great Britain to a European federation becomes an acute question. For a continental federation without Great Britain would in the long run be dominated by Germany. As seen from the Continent, the best solution would be that Great Britain would be part of two federations, namely the European one and of the British Commonwealth of Nations'. Continuing on this question generally, the paper stressed: 'We know now that the refusal to use power to repress international anarchy is itself a case of war. ... [T]he churches know 'what is in man', they dare not minimise the fact of evil and they should, therefore, be the first to recognise that in our world law cannot do without force'.

Until the end of the war the aim of a self-determined, federal future for a Europe in which Britain would play a leading role, continued to be articulated from continental Europe via Geneva to PAG. For example, commenting on the report of the conference held at Delaware by the Commission on the Bases of a Just and Durable Peace in 1942, the Geneva group noted the absence of suggestions of 'larger cultural or regional units as an intermediate type of community' and set itself discuss the question whether 'Christians living on the Continent of Europe have any special insights to share with those responsible for the Delaware Report, as regards the pros and cons of a European federation, or group of federations'.[11] Following the issue of the Commission's formal statement in 1943, the Geneva group welcomed what they saw as its acknowledgement of *'the necessity for federations* within the framework of the general international organisation'; but stressed that 'No European federation could possibly be lasting, that was created from without by means of direct or indirect force and coercion. The European federation must be created by the parties concerned'.[12] Resistance to the imposition of a solution from outside marked an obvious tension between continental Europeans and the Anglo-American party.

The continental side of the triangular WCC peace aims discussion also acted as a conduit by which the German resistance tried, unsuccessfully, to influence the British government. This faction expressed itself in comments on Paton's *The Church and the New Order*. As discussed above,[13] this work, representing the collective mind of the Peace Aims Group or at least the most dominant part of it, was criticised by Dietrich Bonhoeffer and Visser t' Hooft for throwing 'insufficient light' on British proposals for the future. Whereas it had become 'very clear on the continent' that 'in the political domain there must be effective limitation of national sovereignty' and that in the 'economic domain there must be limitation of economic individualism', Paton's book did not fully answer these questions. Linking peace aims to the resistance against Nazism, Bonhoeffer and Visser t' Hooft argued that without the prospect of a positive future there would be no means of rallying effective support among patriotic Germans, who, for the sake of an alternative, would be forced to remain loyal to the Nazi government. There were Germans who could be 'counted upon as loyal collaborators in a European community of nations', who should be 'given a chance for the sake not only of Germany, but for Europe as a whole'.[14]

This document was sent to Hugh Martin at the MOI with a covering letter stressing that it reflected '*actual developments and discussions with responsible persons*' in Germany, and the hope that it would be 'brought before responsible people in Britain'.[15] Similarly, a document from Adam von Trott , an official in the German Foreign Ministry and a leading anti-Nazi, had the same aim. This document made its way from Visser t' Hooft to Paton and from there to the prime minister, via Sir Stafford Cripps. A radical (Christian) socialist rebel in the 1930s, Cripps had attained office and influence in the wartime coalition. He was also among a number of prominent people who von Trott had made contact with while studying at Balliol college in the 1930s. Among von Trott's arguments was that '… federalism in Germany should be organically connected with federalism within Europe (including Britain) and close international co-operation with other continents'.[16] These proposals were followed up the next month by George Bell's intercession on the behalf of the resistance with the foreign secretary. However, after a meeting and an exchange of correspondence, Anthony Eden would not sanction any form of positive response in reply.[17]

Thus, the continental voice stayed on the margins of the Anglo-American discussion. Even before the Nazi occupation of most of Western Europe, Geneva's study of British peace aims literature commented on the apparent 'assumption … often implicitly made – namely that Great Britain would be in a position to carry through her own peace programme, irrespective of the wishes of her allies, for whose sentiments and interests some of the writers … showed scant consideration'.[18] The defeat and occupation of Britain's Allies in the West inevitably meant that this unconscious Anglo-Saxon arrogance gained a definite political reality. While conducted by Christians, the minutes of PAG meetings were marked strongly with the assumptions and manners of those accustomed to world power, and who anticipated that the continental nations would have only a very small role in their own future. Temple had proposed the 'Christian way' as a corrective to any tendency to seek an exploitative and self-interested settlement, a principle his colleagues would undoubtedly have endorsed. Nonetheless, the problem, which Reinhold Niebuhr's indicated at one Anglo-American meeting – 'to rise above our national selves' – remained unsolved.[19] Given that at a series of points in the Anglo-American discussions, Bell and the Geneva group had unsuccessfully pressed for the consideration that what Temple had called the 'separate and special problem' of Europe,[20] one possible inference is that the churchmen had come to share much of what passed for 'common sense' in the Foreign Office's world-view too.

The Future of Europe

While 'A Christian Basis for Reconstruction' was a disappointment to supporters of European unity, there was another opportunity for PAG to seize hold of the problem in its second, and final, public statement. Among the possible topics for discussion by Paton in August 1943 was 'treatment of enemy nations'. The continuing emphasis in his own thinking was obvious in his stipulation that whatever issue selected should also 'involve Anglo-American co-operation and, if possible, even wider international co-operation'.[21]

Nonetheless, this gave Bell the opportunity to press for the group to deal with the interlinked questions of Europe and Germany. He mentioned to Paton his concern about 'the weakness of the British and American position in not having a constructive statement as to its idea of the future of Europe and of Germany in Europe'.[22] In part, the bishop was prompted by the concerns he outlined in his memorandum sent to Foreign Secretary Eden in July 1943, as mentioned above. Britain's insistence on nothing less than 'unconditional surrender' might force Germany into the arms of the Soviets, given that Moscow was attempting to encourage anti-Nazi resistance through their front organisation the National Committee of Free Germany. Bell again stressed the need to offer a positive alternative in which the problem of Germany and the future of Europe would be interconnected. Otherwise, the consequences could be dire: 'Unless action of this kind is taken and taken with the utmost urgency, it is to be feared that Russia will have all Germany under its power, and will soon, with German aid, control the whole of Europe, while Britain will gradually decline into a small power with the function of a buffer state between Russia-cum-Germany and America'.[23]

Bell pressed for PAG to assemble and 'put out a statement *as early as possible* on what we think should be the policy for the defeated Germany', before then going on to 'consider the *satellite countries*, particularly the east of Europe'.[24] Bell was not alone in favouring a fuller consideration of the question of Germany and Europe. Routh was supportive;[25] Grubb saw it as a 'difficult' question on which the group might make a 'useful contribution'.[26] Although Zimmern and Toynbee wished to turn to Anglo-Soviet relations – also a concern for Grubb – these topics were not altogether unrelated to Bell's endeavour.[27]

What Paton's response to Bell's request was is unclear, but, suddenly and unexpectedly, he died towards the end of August, following an operation for a duodenal ulcer. This death – the first of the three that would strike the group – threw its activities into disorder. Temple wrote afterwards: 'There is hardly anyone who would have left a greater gap. He had so many things in hand and his judgement was implicitly trusted by all responsible people'.[28] In a similar vein, Joseph Oldham wrote:

By every calculation the whole Christian front has been seriously weakened by the removal of William Paton from a key position. It seems certain that important things that his imagination, initiative and executive ability would have made possible will in fact remain undone. He was equipped in a unique degree to take the lead in re-creating international friendships and international co-operation after the war. Nothing is gained in disguising from ourselves that the effects of his loss will be grave and far reaching.[29]

Paton's death partially severed the group from the network of intelligence and influence that he had naturally and tirelessly cultivated. As will be seen, much of the motivating energy behind the group dissipated as well. In the context of the deprivations, exigencies and the general pressure of life and work in wartime, such a group could only survive if it had passion behind it. However, Paton's death may also have changed the power-dynamics of the group and opened its agenda too. In any case, Bell continued to press Temple for PAG to reassemble, which it did in December 1943.[30] This meeting put in train a series of contacts which produced the public statement, 'The Future of Europe'.

In his memorandum to PAG members before its next meeting, Bell wrote of the need to begin to build practically on the principles laid down in its first public statement, especially because of ecclesiastical 'tendency to hug the general and avoid the particular'.[31] As to the topic to be discussed, he noted Paton's letter to him of 12 August concerning the group's need to discuss the 'problem of Russia'. With the failure of the German counter-offensive that summer and the war on the eastern front now unambiguously going in Russia's favour, it was urgent that their attitude towards the USSR be discussed. It was 'imperative' for the future of 'Europe (and the world)' that a joint policy be developed between the three major partners in the war in the West. At the same time, Bell indicated his Europhile tendency and his own agenda, adding that 'in order that the proper contributions of all partners may be given ... we should frankly consider Europe as a whole'.

Indicating the ambiguous British position to its essential, but politically and ideologically problematically, Bell chose his words with care even in an unpublished paper. He wrote that Russia 'could be a partner of immense value for the future history of Europe. But the best kind of partnership is not likely to be obtained if we fail to look at the danger points'. Returning to the dangers of a Russian take-over in Germany, he condemned the British approach as showing 'few signs of a sense of Europe as Europe, and too many indications of a giving way to the predominance of Russia in Germany and so in Europe'. He then outlined the possibility of the 'Red army's occupation of the whole of central Europe and some part of Germany' and possible future struggle between left and right over Western Europe. To face this threat the bishop called on the group to emphasise the principles of the Atlantic Charter endorsing national self-determination.

When the group met in December, its chief concerns were the grounds for establishing a *modus vivendi* with the Soviet Union and the future of the rest of Europe, most especially Germany. In their discussion there was an acceptance that, as Zimmern said, 'relations between Russia and the two English speaking powers are the primary thing'. Whereas there was an acceptance that the price of this for smaller nations would certainly be costly – specifically in the Baltic states and most probably elsewhere too, at the same time there was also a determination, most strongly represented by Bell, that while 'collaboration' with Russia was 'essential ... we must not give up too much for the sake of that'. It was Bell who orientated the discussion towards a general European solution. The British Government had shied away from any public consideration of this question and this gave the group a special responsibility: '... We have no new order at all. Here is the chance for a Christian group to recall people to the Atlantic charter in broad terms and say rather definitely what we think Europe ought to be. We must get back to the idea of Europe'. 'Plenty to say and ought to be said soon', the bishop concluded.[32] He received valuable support from Dennis

Routh of the MOI on this point, who regretted that the three-power European Advisory Commission had also been silent on the future shape of Europe. In this respect, the Archbishop of Canterbury believed that the group had a freedom of expression that the government lacked. In his summary of their discussions at the beginning of the afternoon session, Temple interpreted their deliberations as dealing with the 'contents of a public statement which the Group might make, on the subject of a Christian new order in Europe'.[33] Reconstruction would require the co-operation of all three of the major Allies and the group 'welcomed' Russia in this regard. The future organisation of the peace for the world would work through 'regional groupings', one of which would be a new Europe. Great stress was placed on the economic and social reconstruction of Europe – and of Russia too – and the ending of economic borders. Routh was asked to prepare a draft statement for circulation and amendment prior to a meeting in January.

Bell regarded what had taken place as being an 'excellent discussion on this question of Europe' and that the statement would point in a 'concrete way ... to the vital necessity of looking at Europe as a whole, and uniting the peoples of Europe into one great community on the basis of the European tradition'.[34] He hoped that the degree of agreement apparently existing within the group was such that a statement could be agreed by lunchtime the next time PAG met.

Routh's first draft dispensed with Bell's polite circumlocution concerning Russia, describing a Soviet victory as 'disastrous for the whole of Western Civilisation'. Emphasising the need for 'the renewal of a feeling of solidarity between Western nations', he argued that this was 'only possible on a Christian basis because a Christian standard alone can make a spiritual union and fruitful European co-operation possible'. Principles rooted in natural law would be acceptable as 'basis for practical action' more generally. Turning from the ethical basis of a new Europe to its economic and political form, Routh made the frequently heard point that the interconnectedness of modern societies made national boundaries obsolete, hence, he argued: 'boundaries of a state must no longer hinder ... developments. They should, on the contrary, be invisible, so to say, for passenger and goods traffic within the limits of the whole continent. Everything should be done that may help to create European citizenship or at least to pave the way to such citizenship'. A common 'European citizenship' would also come through education and the leadership of Christian elites but was also 'a matter of organization, of federative building-up'. Looking for an ideal balance between supranational organic collectivity and national particularity;

and alluding to the 'problem of Germany', Routh specified that '[a]lthough the rights of individual states must have their limits, no violence should be done to historically founded states, either by enforced coalition or by dividing them up. Arrangements must also be made in order to render the hegemony of larger states within the federation impossible'. Finally, on the key question of the relationship of this 'European federation' to wider international relations, it was specified that it 'must not cut off Europe from the rest of the world. It should, on the contrary, enable her to look after this continent's interests in other parts of the globe'.[35]

When circulated before the meeting these proposals prompted objections from Joseph Oldham, which he regretted were 'fundamental' and 'destructive'.[36] The influential voices of Zimmern and Toynbee indicated similar positions and that they believed that it was better not to proceed in such a direction.[37] Previously outside of the group, probably because of tensions in his relationship with Paton, after the Scotsman's death Oldham became involved. His credentials as a positive commentator on the question of Europe were well established. A couple of years earlier, when Political and Economic Planning had called for Britain to answer the problem of power in European politics by revolutionising its foreign policy to take a role of leadership in a united federal Europe, Oldham had supported the proposals.[38] British political leaders needed to 'learn to think in European terms' and 'be prepared, where necessary, to subordinate British interests to the larger good of Europe as a whole'. In 1942 Oldham advised his readers that this was a responsibility which 'must be accepted. To refuse would be to desert the peoples of Europe in their fundamental need ... to cast away the opportunity of playing a creative part in shaping the future of mankind'.[39]

In 1943 Oldham explained that Routh's draft was imprecise on the loaded question of the definition of the extent of 'Europe'. It envisaged a political unity for the continent which would make it the 'fourth political power' in the world – would Russia approve of this and, if not, would Britain be prepared to go to war on the issue? The Churches could not commit themselves to 'vague schemes without taking into account ... fundamental questions of power factors'. A few months earlier the South African prime minister, Jan Smuts, had presented his solution to the 'problem of power' by arguing that with Germany, Italy and France no longer great powers, the only way for Britain to hold its own against Russia and America was by strengthening its weak European position by an alliance between the British Commonwealth and the smaller democracies of Western Europe.[40] Oldham could see no

'*Christian* grounds' for preferring a united Europe over Smuts's proposals. The group took the Field Marshal's proposal as highly significant.
When later inviting the South African to Lambeth to discuss peace aims,
Temple commended the 'healthy political realism' of Smuts's treatment
of national autonomy versus the 'Victorian Liberalism' of the Atlantic
Charter.[41] At the previous meeting Zimmern had spoken of Smuts as
indicating a 'new perspective' on the 'balance of forces in Europe' and
indicated that it was based on information from inside the war
Cabinet.[42] Given the group's tendency to respect official policy, this last
point was important. This position also concurred with the model of
official thinking which Grubb had sketched earlier.[43]

At the beginning of the war Oldham had written about the past, present and possible future relationship between Christianity and the West
in *The Resurrection of Christendom*.[44] By 1944, however much a 'revival
of the European cultural and Christian tradition' might be desirable, he
had begun to doubt that this tradition was strong enough to 'provide
any kind of political unity'. In any case, the European Christian tradition was by no means uncontroversial, being bound up in the 'bour-
geoisie [sic] civilisation' then being 'sharply challenged' as a reactionary
force. As the war went on – death piled on death, atrocity on atrocity,
rubble on rubble – hopes invested in the potential of Europe as cultural
community waned. In comparison to the confident claims of the past,
Kenneth Grubb's comments were typical: 'Journalists speak of the "Soul
of Europe," "The European Tradition"; it is difficult to find them except
tortured and maimed beyond recognition'. 'The problem of Europe' was
no longer its 'former cultural unity. That has broken down as to make it
impossible to restore it'. Beyond the essential prerequisite of the restoration of an ordered and sufficient existence to the peoples of Europe it
was: '... even more requisite to restore hope in God as an essential prelude to all faith and will to do good. Without hope the dissolution of
European culture cannot be avoided To many men, if the agonies of the
past are to be repeated, the game of life is hardly worth the candle; it
would be better to roll up the map of experience and cast away the precious with the vile'.[45] Others were more positive, speaking in the House
of Lords, Bell still believed that Christianity as the 'original bond of
unity among the European peoples' might still 'prove one of the great
unifying forces of Europe' in its post-war reconstruction.[46]

Routh amended the statement to a limited extent before the planned
meeting, but decided not to comply with those criticisms from Oldham
and others which called 'the whole substance of the draft' into question. The group itself needed to decide 'how to proceed, or whether to

proceed at all'.[47] At the meeting, there was agreement to press forward, with a strong emphasis on the ideal of the unity of Europe and the argument that this would entail new social and economic institutions.[48] Point five of the published statement, when it eventually appeared, pressed for: 'The framing ... of far-reaching economic and social polices to secure for the peoples of Europe full employment and social security and the fullest use of available resources in achieving higher standards of life and well-being'.[49] Routh spoke of the need for changes in these areas which would be 'almost revolutionary'.[50] In reality, PAG was in step with the progressive sections of all parties in Britain then moving towards what became the post-war consensus supporting the Keynesian mixed economy and welfare state. Similarly, the attention to fundamental freedoms in the statement should be placed in the context of a wider wartime debate which would culminate in the United Nation's Declaration on Human Rights. To state ideals was integral to the function of the Churches' mission in society as the moral conscience of the state, but stated in the abstract rather than in relation to concrete proposals for the future of Europe they were unlikely to ruffle many political feathers.

The political future of Europe was rather more problematic for the group. At the meeting Oldham raised the question as to whether the statement should endorse 'some form of political union in Europe'. He noted that while Reinhard Niebuhr and the Americans were in favour, he preferred co-operation on concrete practical issues, a position which would characterise the official British approach to European integration in the years to come. This issue was seen to have particular implications to relations with Russia and to Britain's own position. With the aim of continued co-operation between the wartime Allies in mind, there was a concern that, as Temple stated, that the statement should not be 'interpreted as anti-Russian'.[51] Routh could not envisage 'Europe as a political entity apart from Russia and Britain' and believed that European unity was impossible without the co-operation of those two powers. Smuts's ideas would tend to divide Europe into two halves, risking an 'Anglo-Russian clash'. Bell spoke of the need for a form of 'common organisation of Europe', including a 'political framework' but also maintaining a proper respect for national autonomy. The assumptions expressed in Smuts's speech had made the smaller nations 'jumpy' on this point, the bishop noted. Faced with these complexities it seems that it was implicitly agreed to be favourable but not explicit about political structures in the published statement. This endorsed 'the creation and development of common institutions and agencies in the social and economic as well as the political sphere to give effect to these common purposes and to embody the growing sense of European unity'.[52] This stress on the creation of European institutions to replace or superintend national ones was a point at which the group moved closer – albeit circumspectly – towards the vanguard of progressive thought.

The vital question of Britain's position in relation to this united Europe was also complicated and somewhat unclear in these discussions. Routh's suggestions that European social and economic forms will be 'very much in advance of our own' and that '[t]hey will start with a clean slate' and that Britain might be 'left behind politically and we may be holding Europe back' suggested significant detachment. Similarly, Oldham saw the danger that Britain would 'miss the bus altogether by being politically behind'.[53] 'The Future of Europe', while mentioning that Britain was 'bound to Europe by ties of history, culture, geography and economic interdependence', and calling for material sacrifice to provide for the restoration of Europe, did not make clear what Britain's long-term position vis-à-vis the new Europe should be.[54] Oldham also deprecated anything which 'committed Christian people to some kind of European unity which was cut off from the British Empire'.[55] Some days afterwards he worked with Routh to rewrite parts of the statement over lunch,[56] and it may have been then decided to insert the comment that the 'thought and practice of the British commonwealth' offered an example to Europe.[57] In Oldham's own gloss on the statement all references to European unity were absent.[58]

With the text of the statement agreed, it then remained to decide when to release it and over whose names. The first question meant before or after the invasion of Europe, which the whole country was anxiously expecting to happen sometime in the next few months.[59] It was decided to issue it before D-day, in anticipation of the question of the future of Europe being thus reopened. Zimmern believed that in the 'lull with its accompanying malaise' before the invasion '[t]he public, both here and on the Continent is straining its ears to hear an authoritative voice'.[60] Eric Fenn at the BBC preferred that the statement, like the 1940 letter in *The Times* be signed by all major Church leaders.[61] The final statement appeared in April 1944 over the signatures of Temple, Dr. John Baillie and Prof. R.D. Whitehorn, the moderators of the Church of Scotland and Free Church Federal Council. Temple wrote to the Archbishop of Westminster, but Cardinal Griffin, although being in 'sympathy with practically all the suggestions contained' preferred not to sign.[62] Outside of the church press, 'The Future of Europe' was noted in *The Times*, appeared in the MOI's regular news sheet *Spiritual Issues of the War*, which was circulated mainly to clergy at home and abroad, and was also made available in a modest run of leaflets.[63]

'The Future of Europe' was stuffed with wholesome ideals but the decisiveness and single-mindedness of Oldham in 1942 or Bell at any-time was absent. Instead, like many such ecclesiastical documents, it tended, as Chichester had hoped to avoid, 'to hug the general and avoid the particular'.[64] The statement was significant inasmuch that it officially 'commended to the careful attention of Christian people' the project of European unity but at the same time, unlike earlier pronouncements, avoided intervening in the important debate about the specific political form for the new Europe. While calling for 'a system of European security which will allow the peoples of Europe to develop their national life free from the fear of recurring aggression and war' and for the 'reintegration of the German people into the European family of nations', unlike in the proposals from the Geneva group two years earlier, no specific way of achieving this was mentioned. Given the amount of attention paid to the 'problem of power' in the group's discourse, this suggested a failure, if not of nerve, of direction. Torn between the choice of controversy and safety, the Churches took the latter path. At this stage in the war, it would have required something particularly unequivocal to either catch the attention of the war-weary or distinguish itself among the plethora of statements, leaflets and pamphlets of the time. George Bell was disappointed by the final result. Writing to Joseph Oldham, he explained that he had hoped 'for something more direct and trenchant. ... The third draft ... for such a tense situation is too academic'. It seemed 'to address itself to the student' rather than the 'suffering populations in the warring countries or the statesmen'.[65]

The end of the war

After PAG had a final draft for 'The Future of Europe' it sought to focus its attention on Soviet Russia. As has already been discussed, this issue was already overshadowing all other work so, in February 1944, Grubb suggested to Temple the formation of a USSR sub-committee to survey Soviet domestic and foreign policy.[66] Chaired by Oldham and with the Rev. Herbert Waddams as its secretary, this small group was also intended to include Oldham, Zimmern, Canon P.E.T. Widdrington – honorary secretary of the Russian Clergy and Church Aid Fund and an expert on Orthodox Church, Jeffrey Wilson of Chatham House, John Macmurray, Professor of Philosophy at University of Edinburgh. Waddams had worked in the Religions Division of the MOI in wartime, and had accompanied Archbishop Garbett on his visit to the Soviet Union in 1943.[67] The committee met in April but despite the importance of the topic there is no evidence that it did so again. Grubb described attendance as 'disappointing', so possibly the pressure of other commitments killed it.[68] The Peace Aims Group proper did not meet again until November 1944. Grubb pressed for it to return to work and, after Temple and Bell had agreed, it was 'revived'.[69]

This time, proceedings were under the chairmanship of Bishop Bell as, some days before the group met, it, and the radical voice of the Churches in Britain generally, suffered a loss which Bell named as an 'irreparable'. Although it agreed to continue despite the death of Temple, in fact this was the last time the group would gather. The deaths of Paton and Temple took away much of its drive and influence and before the end of the war another of the most involved members, W.T. Elmslie, would be killed by a flying-bomb. Bell wrote later of the group being 'sadly broken by successive blows'.[70] Whether due to the pressure of circumstances; a judgement that, due to the loss of its most illustrious member, PAG was no longer the force it was; or a desire for distance from the politically 'unsound' Bishop of Chichester, for the first time no one from Chatham House, PEP or the MOI was present. In contrast to these absences, for the first time representatives of all three parties in the peace aims debate met face-to-face, with participants from Britain, the United States and, with the attendance of the French Protestant Dr. Marc Boegner and Visser t' Hooft, 'Europe'.[71]

Despite the end of the war being in sight, expectations were gloomy, especially among the continental participants. In contrast to the unfeigned assurance and unexamined superiority with which British and American PAG participants had discussed the re-ordering of the world over the previous years, Boegner and – in particular – t' Hooft's voices were those of embattled subordinates. Boegner was in close contact with de Gaulle and shared the General's determination that France should have a seat at the negotiating table too. The churchman stated his belief that 'no true peace in Europe can be established if France is not admitted to take part in the conversations on the new organization of Europe'. He also pointed to the vital necessity for an agreement between Germany and France if there was to be peace. Despite being native to a country only lately liberated from a brutal occupation, Boegner recognised that breaking-up Germany would only prompt a war of revenge in the future. A couple of years later the churchman would be prominent in the foundation of the European Movement (EM) in France. This was also the way of thinking of the representatives of the various European resistance groups with which t' Hooft was in contact.[72] He regretted the lack of 'political imagination' on the part of the British government in its failure to encourage the opposition in Germany and rejection of its advances. The anti-Nazi resistance envisioned a 'federal solution' for Germany and also made a 'strong and insistent demand for a European federation just at the moment when in other circles the dream is definitely given up and not considered a political possibility'. Geneva had been in contact with resistance groups across the occupied continent and these too placed their hopes for future peace in a 'federal solution', including Germany. However, the Dutchman continued, '[j]ust at the moment when some of the liveliest elements are getting ready for federation, I get the impression that the Anglo-Saxon nations have set their faces against it'.

When the meeting turned to the question of Russia in the afternoon session, the gloom darkened. T' Hooft spoke of the naïve and unrealistic attitudes to Russia which he found in Britain, and predicted that all of eastern and much of central Europe would find itself behind 'almost a "Chinese wall" … as far as contact with the West is concerned'. In the world generally he predicted that 'while Britain and America may … have something to do outside the Continent, The European scene at least is going to be dominated by Russia'. The hope of continental Europe was for 'a very firm attitude on the part of Britain and America to this wave of nationalistic and imperialistic forms which is sweeping over Russia and the extension of zones of influence …' In this situation it was 'nonsense to talk about a European federation now. Actually a process of federation is going on, but it will only be a partial federation. That too will make the unity of Europe harder to achieve rather than easier'.[73]

*

While it was true that many of the contributions to the great British federalist boom of 1939–40 were only weakly related to political reality, the pessimism of the new political 'realism' which became firmly entrenched from then on did not anticipate that – in continental Europe, at least – the first tentative steps in the federalist direction would soon be underway. The voice of the Churches as radical force was also stifled by tragedy. Joseph Oldham likened the impact of the death of William Paton to the consequences had Churchill been lost in 1940.[74] The next year, Temple too was dead. For many the Europhile George Bell was Temple's natural successor, but he was passed-over for the conservative Geoffrey Fisher, appointed to Canterbury by Churchill. Fisher was to be a prominent supporter of the United Europe Movement founded by the former prime minister a couple of years later. On the surface, this might be seen as a renewal of the Churches as a force for British leadership in European integration. The reality was more complex.

4
The Churches, the European Movement and Western Union

Any elation at the end of the war in Europe could only be momentary. The living looked out over a continent of rubble, the ossuary for the bones of the wasted millions. Material need was infinite but industry and agriculture in chaos. Even the possibility of peace and political stability following the defeat of fascism, which had always been a fragile hope, seemed increasingly unrealisable as tensions held in check by the expediencies of war were released. In this context, the idea of building a new Europe was fantastical. However, just as the necessity was great, so was the will. Between 1945 and the creation of the European Coal and Steel Community (ECSC) by the Treaty of Paris in 1951, the new Europe dreamed of by utopians like Aristide Briand and Count Richard Coudenhove-Kalergi between the wars became a mainstream political project.

This process of reconstruction and transformation sought to build a new Europe out of the ruins of wartime, a continent which was not only economically viable but also politically stable. There could not be another war between Germany and France. At the same time, the politics of the new Europe were not isolated from the rest of the world. While the nations of continental Europe possessed their own imagination and energy, they each exercised their will in the cockpit of the Cold War, in the interstices of the wider global power relations of Britain, America and the Soviet Union; or, perhaps more realistically, the two superpowers and Britain. In the foreign policy of each of the former wartime 'big three', European unity had its own particular significance. In the Cold War strategy of the United States, a united Europe would be better able to stand and survive on its own, both generally and against the ambitions of the Soviet Union. From the perspective of the Soviet Union it could equally appear to be a hostile Western bloc threatening its western flank. For post-war Britain, 'Europe' was one the three inter-locking circles on which, together with the Commonwealth and Atlantic alliance, its fragile and teetering survival as a world power rested.

Britain was simultaneously in, and outside of, Europe. These years were therefore also the opening chapter in Britain's turbulent post-war rela-tionship with European integration, when the government of Clement Attlee took up, and then later renounced, a leadership role in that process. Many commentators have spoken of this as a missed early opportunity to transform a global imperium into what it has now become: a regional power, a European nation. While it is a matter for careful debate whether the Labour government could, or should, have acted differently, this was undoubtedly a hinge point in Britain's history.

In the immediate post-war years there was a process of European inte-gration which the Superpowers, Britain and the governments of Western Europe all sought to influence. Inasmuch that the participants in this process sought to advance integration they were – whatever their other allegiances, motivations and intentions – part of a political phe-nomenon which might be called 'the European movement'. After 1947, there was also a formally constituted 'European Movement' created to realise this aim. The participants of these two 'movements', while over-lapping, did not necessarily share the same identities or intentions. The United States supported both the movement and the Movement while not being European. At different times and in different ways Britain was European and not-European, part of the Movement but not of the movement.

The same could be said of the British Churches too. The death of Archbishop Temple and the failure of the wartime Peace Aims Group to live up to its early potential as a force for European unity undoubtedly closed certain avenues. However, the Churches continued to play an active and important role in this history. The Churches in Europe gen-erally were in a relatively strong position in the 1940s. With notable exceptions, they had had a 'good war'. In Britain strong and co-operative links between Church and State had been sustained in wartime and continued afterwards. Elsewhere, the Churches were the only institu-tions to survive the rise and fall of fascism with their structure anyway intact. They were necessary to, and involved with, the process of recon-struction in Europe. Not only had national Churches survived, but the ecumenical movement had also emerged from the war as one of the only few international bodies still linking both sides of the conflict. The secular process of working towards greater unity in Europe was paral-leled by the ecumenists' analogous goal. Thus, it was fitting that in 1948 both the EM and the WCC had their respective inaugural meetings, in the year when the British government also started to engage with European unity with its proposals for Western Union.

The United Europe Movement

At the heart of the European movement were those elements of the continental political classes of the center-left and -right which had managed to survive the fascist era with their political legitimacy intact. Some of its leading figures emerged from prisons and concentration camps, many had been involved in resistance to fascism. In other circumstances the British contribution to this movement would have been modest, probably being composed mainly of the earnest but politically negligible activists of FU. It was particularly important then that the greatest living democratic politician of the age, Winston Churchill, threw his weight behind European unity. Churchill's stature and influence gave the movement in Britain and continental Europe a real political force and was also vital to securing essential political and financial support from America.

As mentioned above, as early as March 1943, Churchill had publicly advocated the creation of a 'Council of Europe', to exist alongside the 'great powers'.[1] In peacetime, he spoke in favour of the creation of a 'United States of Europe' in addresses to the Belgian Senate and House of Representatives in November 1945. He made a similar speech at The Hague the next May, and, even more influentially, the idea of European unity was integral to his 'Iron Curtain' speech made at Fulton, Missouri in May 1946. The culmination of this campaign was his address at the University of Zürich of September 1946. He called there for the building of 'some kind of United States of Europe', whose 'first step' would be a 'partnership between France and Germany'. Although he did not stress the point, it was to be significant that in all these speeches Churchill was careful not to include Britain in the proposed United States of Europe (USE).[2]

Churchill also anticipated a central role for non-governmental organisations in the campaign for European unity and his speeches generated considerable public interest. Following positive contacts with the leaders of the Dominions, a United Europe Committee was established in January 1947 which became, some months later, after its inaugural meeting, the United Europe Movement (UEM). Although holding mass meetings, first at the Albert Hall and then elsewhere in the UK, and being described as a 'movement', in reality, the UEM was not a popular body – It was not possible to become a 'member' of the Movement, only a 'supporter'. Its primary function was not to organise mass support but to influence and mobilise elite opinion in the UK and, most vitally, internationally. Although launched as a non-party body, the honorary committee of the UEM not only had no representative of Labour's political leadership but was overwhelmingly Conservative in its allegiance including, besides Churchill, most of the shadow cabinet. Whereas protocol made the combination of government office and membership of such a body problematic, it was political and ideological differences which made Labour keep its distance. Similarly, while having no trades' unionists on its executive, leading business interests were well represented and almost all of the UEM's considerable financial muscle came from that quarter initially.[3]

The European movement's relationship with the Churches began as early as January 1946 when Leo Amery wrote to the Archbishop of Canterbury, Geoffrey Fisher.[4] During Leo Amery's long and illustrious career in the Conservative party he had been an Empire patriot and supporter of imperial unity.[5] In wartime, he also became a supporter of European unity, writing a preface for the British edition of Count Richard Coudenhove-Kalergi's *Europe Must Unite!*[6] In his letter, Amery referred to the Archbishop's recent calls for 'a new European patriotism' and the harnessing of 'the instinctive force of patriotism to wider ideals' and emphasised his own belief in the importance of a 'spiritual, moral and instinctive foundation' over a 'facile optimism' in the 'machinery of peace'. Amery had recently spoken at the University of London on 'British Links with Europe' and enclosed his paper. The archbishop responded positively to the ideas of greater European cultural unity which the politician sketched out, replying that 'I wholly agree with you that mechanical schemes are going to get us nowhere. What you describe as the general instinctive outlook covers intellectual and spiritual affinities which are a really necessary basis of understanding'.[7] Later that year, Amery responded in a similarly positive way to Churchill's Zürich speech and urged his lifelong friend and colleague to press on with a campaign for European unity and pledged his own support and collaboration.[8] Amery would be one of the three vice-presidents of the UEM.

At the end of 1946, when the United Europe Committee from which the UEM would come was being formed, Amery personally delivered a letter from Churchill to Fisher.[9] Stressing the need for order and co-operation in Europe to prevent the 'catastrophe of a third World War' Churchill outlined the role of the Churches: 'To attain this we must arouse the fervour of a crusade', '[t]he sentiments to which we must appeal and the forces which we seek to stir are rooted in the spiritual depths of our fellow men and women. It is therefore essential that from the outset we should have the support of the Churches throughout Europe'.[10] Amery wrote personally to Fisher a few days later in a similar vein, once again stressing the Churchill group's approach, and emphasising the specific way in which it engaged with Christian ideas about Europe: '... by the term "Europe", we are thinking, not so much of any definite boundary at the moment, still less of the blue print of any constitution, but of the restoration of the spiritual unity that was once Western Civilisation and Christendom'.[11] Amery reported to Churchill that Fisher was 'most sympathetic to our general idea and is particularly anxious that we should keep it to the broad conception and not commit ourselves to any constitutional scheme'. However, the archbishop held back, not only unwilling to be 'a guinea pig' for the new movement but also cautious about lending the official support of the Church to a body 'which is in some quarters being criticised as anti-Russian'.[12]

Although not allowing his name to appear on the United Europe Committee's statement, Fisher suggested the Dean of St. Paul's, W.R. Matthews as an alternative.[13] Matthews, who Amery described as 'able' and having taken 'a good deal of interest in European questions', was prepared to play the role of guinea pig and became an active member of the executive committee of the new movement.[14] The Anglican bishops of London, Peterborough, Lichfield, Truro and Bath & Wells also added their names to the cause, as did the Deans of Chichester, Durham and Westminster.[15] Irrespective of his tactical caution, Fisher was fundamentally supportive, writing to Churchill: 'with the purpose which you have in mind I have the utmost sympathy, and I hope that the efforts of this group under your leadership will be effective in restoring a sense of cultural and spiritual unity among European states'. With relations with the Soviet Union worsening by the day, it was not long before the archbishop was prepared to show his full support by agreeing to chair what would be the inaugural meeting of the UEM at the Albert Hall in May 1947.[16] His presence, Churchill believed, would 'help to emphasize the moral character of the appeal we are making to the spirit of international brotherhood'.[17]

The official report of the meeting described it thus:

> The Royal Albert Hall was crowded to capacity ... In the centre there hung a large banner bearing the words "EUROPE ARISE!" The great platform was filled with some two hundred prominent supporters, including leaders in almost every sphere of British public life. The French federalist movements were represented by a delegation from

Paris, the Royal Box was occupied by ambassadors and other diplomatic representatives of European countries.

'The entry of the speakers was greeted with prolonged applause'.[18] Then the archbishop opened the meeting, stressing to those assembled that supporters of European unity, while holding 'every kind of opinion ... one belief, one credo they all hold. And your presence here filling this vast hall from floor to floor is evidence that you hold it too. We all believe in the unity of Europe and assert that belief as the remedy to the present chaos and despair'. The 'first and essential step' to unity was to 'recover the experience of spiritual, cultural, familiar unity out of which Europe, whose other name is Christendom, once was born'. Speaking of the contemporary moment, Fisher talked of how 'the accumulating poisons in Europe's system have brought its body politic near to death. We are again in a revolutionary age. This time it is catastrophic in its scope, appalling in its disruptive force and suicidal in its possibilities'. Concluding his introduction, the archbishop spoke of how: 'United Europe is a challenge to which all who will can rally. Mr. Churchill led Europe out of the jaws of death. He now leads a crusade for its coming life'.[19] In these clear, unambiguous and powerful words, heard not only inside the Albert Hall but also broadcast live on the BBC, Fisher signalled the Churches' support for European unity and Churchill's campaign. The statesman wrote to him afterwards: 'Your presence in the Chair and your opening speech made, I am sure, a deep impression not only upon the audience in the Hall, but also upon the millions who listened in on the wireless'.[20]

There was a repeated stress in the archbishop's contacts with the UEM on a preference for 'spiritual' and 'cultural' forms of unity over blueprints for political or economic structures. This engaged with the established Christian discourse on Europe which Fisher, as his words at another EM meeting in 1949 showed, he firmly embraced: 'All Europe was embraced in Christendom once, and drew from the Christian faith its teachings after the true freedom of man. ... It is because this spiritual basis of European unity is known and acknowledged, that I am proud to take the chair tonight'.[21] This stance also smoothed the way for the Churches to become involved because it avoided at least the appearance of overt involvement in secular political matters. Following on Fisher's agreement to chair the Albert Hall meeting Churchill made the same point: 'My whole idea is that, at this stage, we should confine ourselves mainly to the cultural and spiritual, and leave the more difficult questions of structure and constitution for the moment when our ideas are more dominant than they are to-day'.[22] Duncan Sandys, Churchill's son-in-law and honorary secretary of the UEM, reiterated this message preparatory to the Albert Hall meeting.[23] Just as Churchill had taken pains to describe Britain as a 'friend' or 'associate' of a united Europe, he would be equally careful to emphasise that the function of the UEM was to foster public support and governmental action promoting European unity in general rather than any specific structural 'blueprint' towards that end. In reality, this meant a preference for political unity built around the co-operation of autonomous nation-states rather than the creation of any supra-national federal system.[24]

Thus the characteristic emphasis on ad hoc measures, practical co-operation and close but informal relationships between national government over technocratic blueprints and impressive structures – which has characterised the dominant British approach to European unity for the last 60 years – was present in the Churches' support for European unity from the beginning. However, letters to Lambeth Palace from FU and from Lionel Curtis, sent in the hope of influencing Fisher before the Albert Hall meeting, show that other opinions were current too.[25] In reply to these letters, the archbishop took special care to make clear that, while endorsing the 'spiritual union' of European nations, he in no way supported federal integration.[26] At the Convocation of Canterbury in October 1947 when George Bell moved a resolution endorsing the 'progressive establishment of a United States of Europe with a common foreign, military and economic policy', the price for the resolution to be carried unanimously was that its federalist implications be neutralised. Fisher replaced Bell's formulation with: 'the progressive establishment of a United Europe in which the true spiritual values of its past culture will be preserved, developed and expressed in such common organs as may prove to be acceptable or desirable'. As the archbishop explained, the 'more general phrase' 'United Europe' was preferable to the 'United States of Europe' because it could encompass 'all those who wanted to see some recovery of the long tradition of European culture without requiring the support of any one political solution'.[27]

As long as it remained an active force, Fisher remained a dependable supporter of the UEM and the EM generally.[28] The Free Churches – including the Baptists, Methodists, Moravians, Congregationalists, and the English and Welsh Presbyterians – were also supportive. The leading non-conformist minister the Rev. Dr. Sidney Berry, who was, at the time, moderator of the Congregational International Council, was an early member of the UEM Executive Committee and the Free Church Federal Council (FCFC) also readily agreed to be represented on the

UEM Council.[29] In fact, J.M. Richardson, the moderator designate of the FCFC for 1947–48, wrote to Churchill inviting him to speak to their annual assembly in his capacity as chairman of the Committee for a United Europe. The prominent Liberal, former government minister, and Baptist lay-preacher, Ernest Brown, who was Churchill's go-between on this occasion and had impressed Richardson with his enthusiasm and his argument that the UEM could not 'get a better audience than this assembly which is representative of the best free church thought in the country'. The cause was, Richardson wrote, one 'to which we Free Church people are greatly attracted.[30] As secretary of the UEM, Duncan Sandys had been routinely refusing all invitations for Churchill to speak but pressed him to accept this one. It was 'a very exceptional opportunity which it would be a great pity to miss'.[31] In the event, as Churchill explained in a warm and personal note to Richardson, the pressure of other commitments meant that this was not possible.[32] Among the topics of the Free Church annual conference that year was 'reconstruction and regeneration in Europe' and Richardson became an active member of the Council of the UEM. It was also the moderator who gave the penultimate speech at the great Albert Hall meeting. Although plans to begin with a hymn were dropped because of 'contrary views' being expressed, Sandys hoped to wind-up the meeting 'on a religious note' with Richardson's speech.[33] The churchman was also to speak on behalf of the UEM on other occasions and joined the British delegation to the EM conference held in Paris that summer.[34] Another non-conformist minister, Gordon Lang also joined the committee and was – at least nominally – a joint secretary to the UEM, alongside Sandys. Lang was involved in a number of federalist groups and was Chairman of FU[35] but, in reality, his seat on the Committee was on account of his political credentials as a Labour MP. Even then he was only a choice of last resort after more eminent candidates made their excuses. Lang's appointment only superficially addressed the absence of support from Labour for this ostensibly 'non-party' organisation.

While it represented only some two and three-quarter million people, and has been described as having 'made little contribution to politics in Britain', the Catholic Church in England was a significant player on this question.[36] During the 1930s, English Catholicism made a disproportionate contribution to arts and letters and although the 'singular brilliance' of this cohort was waning in the 1940s,[37] it was still influential and often in the vanguard of the European movement. Douglas Woodruff and the influential periodical which he edited, *The Tablet*, supported any movements towards European integration from the beginning.[38] Both Barbara Ward – the academic and foreign editor of *The Economist* – and the historian Christopher Dawson also spoke for European unity to a wide audience.[39] In addition to the influence of an articulate elite of Catholics, the Church was the native representative of forces which, on the continent and in world generally, were highly significant in the projects of anti-Communism and European integration.[40] As discussed below, American financial support was vital to the EM. Considerable US aid also flowed to Luigi Gedda, the leader of the lay body, Catholic Action, which was very active in the successful campaign against the Italian left in the vital 1948 elections and who also became an important supporter of European unity.[41] However, unlike Fisher and the UEM, Catholic support for European unity was strongly orientated towards federalism. The same year of giving his approval for the UEM, Pius received a party of federalists. A British participant wrote of how they '[a]ll knew that the work they were doing had his approval and they were glad to earn his praise, which they knew was not empty praise'.[42]

When Amery met with Cardinal Bernard Griffin, the Archbishop of Westminster, to deliver Churchill's invitation to join the Council of the UEM, he found him to be 'a genuine sympathiser'. The cardinal wrote afterwards to Churchill: 'I am indeed very much in sympathy with your proposals, especially as I consider that the nations of Europe have a very important part to play in the shaping of world peace. I know that many of the nations in Europe are looking to this country for a lead and help and guidance'. However, like Fisher, he would not risk his credibility at the beginning of the campaign, instead suggesting that the Bishop of Nottingham, Edward Ellis, join the Council.[43] Nottingham wrote back giving his 'whole-hearted support' and, unbidden, offered to use his overseas influence to the benefit of the UEM. Churchill replied very warmly encouraging him to 'develop' such contacts and consequently Ellis wrote a supportive statement addressed to the powerful US Catholic community.[44] Writing of the UEM statement of policy, the bishop indicated one of the several points which drew Catholics to the movement: '[it] makes a special appeal to me as a Catholic Bishop. I see in it an endeavour to recapture a unity which existed when Europe was bound together by a common Faith when it was possible for England to have a Primate in the person of the Greek Archbishop Theodore; Germany an English Apostle in the person of Boniface; Italy to have Irish bishops, and the whole of Christendom to be ruled spiritually by an Englishman, Nicholas Breakspear'.[45]

As a foundational member of the UEM Committee, the bishop was joined by his colleague, the Bishop of Menavia on its Council. The Archbishop of Birmingham, Joseph Masterson, was also a Council member and an active supporter, speaking alongside Harold Macmillan and Victor Gollancz at a public meeting in his diocese.[46] At Griffin's request the leading Catholic lay-people John Eppstein, director of the British Society for International Understanding; Count Michael de la Bedoyère, editor of the *Catholic Herald*; the Conservative MPs Christopher Hollis and William Teeling, were also invited to join the Council.[47] It was hoped that Griffin would lend his support for UEM by speaking at the Albert Hall, but being in Rome the same day, he sent a short, but positive, message of support which was read out.[48]

The European Movement

The EM was formally constituted at a meeting organised by Duncan Sandys in July 1947. The EM, chaired by Sandys until 1950, was the pan-European umbrella organisation to which all the main pro-European groups were affiliated. Besides the British UEM, it included the French all-party group Le Council Francais pour l'Europe Unie, led by Edouard Herriot, whose creation had been fostered and inspired by the Churchill group.[49] The Economic League for European Co-operation (ELEC) brought together those of all parties interested in the economic dimensions of integration, and was founded by Paul van Zeeland, former prime minister of Belgium, in October 1946; the chairman of its British branch was the international civil servant Sir Harold Butler. Europe's Christian Democrats were represented through Les Nouvelles Equipes Internationales (NEI), founded in Liège in May 1947. The fifth and final part of the EM, the European Union of Federalists, founded in Paris in December 1946, was headed by Dr. Henri Brugmans.[50] It was the EM – then called the International Committee of Movements for European Unity[51] – which convened the foundational Congress of Europe at the Hague in May 1948. After that, it campaigned successfully for the creation of the Council of Europe, founded in 1949, and continued to lobby European governments in the cause of European unity from there on.

In 1948, just as leadership towards the creation of the EM came from the Churchill group, so did much of its finance. The primary initial source of funds were the British industrial and financial interests which had made donations into the coffers of the UEM. Then, after the summer of 1948, the bulk of EM funding came from America. Once again,

Churchill was the key figure in achieving this. In response to a visit by Sandys, Joseph Retinger – Secretary General of the EM – and Edward Beddington-Behrens – head of the EM finance sub-committee, the American Committee on United Europe (ACUE) was established. This body was directed by Allen Welsh Dulles, later to be the director of the CIA, and William J Donovan, former head of the wartime Office for Strategic Services. Beddington-Behrens and Retinger shared similar histories, having both served in the British wartime Special Operations Executive (SOE). In conformity with the established US foreign policy of encouraging European integration, the ACUE was to secretly fund the EM with CIA money from 1948 onwards.[52] As Richard Aldrich writes 'Churchill, at once the most prominent advocate of European unity and the best know transatlantic evangelist, was the vital link between ACUE and the European Movement'.[53] There was a rich irony in Churchill's role here, inasmuch that by this link, the ACUE lavishly bankrolled European federalism which soon came into collision with the anti-federalist British wing of the Movement.

The complexity of the EM at a continental level was compounded by the creation of subordinate national EM councils at the end of 1948. In the British case the UK Council of the European Movement (UKCEM) was the umbrella body for the national branches of the five groups already named, where they existed and, various other groups distinct to Britain. In this case the UEM, ELEC and the British Section of NEI were joined with the Socialist Movement for the United States of Europe, FU, and the Parliamentary All-Party Group for European Union. As discussed below, as time went on, other groups would become affiliates, including the British League for European Freedom (BLEF) and the Christian Movement for European Unity (CMEU).[54] The United Kingdom Council of the European Movement was inaugurated at a meeting at the House of Commons in February 1949. Its honorary patrons included Fisher, Griffin, the Moderators of the FCFC and the Church of Scotland and the Chief Rabbi.[55] However, in a sense, much of the apparent complexity of the different layers of the EM was only on paper. In practice the UKCEM was dominated by the interests and personalities behind the UEM and had little impact or existence beyond that.

Western Union as a spiritual union

It would not be unreasonable to imagine that the British Labour government would be a force for European integration. Socialism was born in Europe. Democratic socialism, even in its particular British form, was strongly internationalist in its ideology and rhetoric. The prime minister, Clement Attlee, was himself a convinced internationalist and, a few years earlier, had uttered the much repeated phrase 'Europe must federate or perish'. Among the parliamentary party there were advocates of a united socialist Europe. In particular RWG 'Kim' Mackay, MP, was a leading proponent of federalism and would become an influential figure in the early EM.

At the same time, there was a gamut of other negative influences which made the question of Europe deeply divisive for the party. For its first two years in office, Labour's foreign policy sought to forge some kind of *modus vivendi* with the Soviet Union. In deference to Moscow's opposition to anything which looked like the creation of a Western 'bloc', Labour eschewed support for European unity. There was also a significant cohort within Labour's ranks, who while not taking their orders from Moscow – although there were crypto communists too – were sympathetic to the Soviet Union and whose socialism had drawn significantly from the Marxist-Leninist school of thought. A great part of the heart of Labour, especially among the trades unions, was also decidedly 'British' in the imperial sense and firmly embraced the economic, political and emotional ties which drew the nation to the world beyond Europe. Finally, although – behind the surface of Commons' rhetoric – the business of politics drew Labour and Conservatives into considerable day-to-day co-operation, the EM was so dominated by Churchill and other leading Tories that it remained an object of suspicion.

Therefore, as already noted, the Attlee government deliberately distanced itself from the UEM. However, at the beginning of 1948, with Foreign Secretary Ernest Bevin's proposals for a 'Western Union', Labour began its own involvement with the European movement. Historians have been divided over whether this represents a genuine engagement with European integration or was merely an expedient device in the struggle to shore-up Britain as a world power.[56] Although the weight of evidence suggests the latter, alternative outcomes were possible, and hence Western Union should be analysed not only as a tactical move in a geopolitical game but also as an intervention in the opening stages of European integration. As Dianne Kirby has shown in relation to the Cold War,[57] integral to Western Union was the notion of it as a 'spiritual union' or 'spiritual federation'. Bevin also recruited as Cold War warriors those social forces whose business was the spiritual: the British Churches.

That 'spiritual union' was more than a rhetorical ornament is shown by the way in which Bevin – having mentioned the idea of 'a sort of spiritual federation of the west' with his American counterpart, George Marshall, after the collapse of the London Conference of Ministers in December 1947 – outlined his thinking in detail to the Commons on 22 January 1948.[58] After summarising the thwarted attempts to establish a *modus vivendi* with the Soviet Union, Bevin went on to state that since 1945 the government had 'striven for the closer consolidation and economic development, and eventually for the spiritual unity, of Europe as a whole'. The foreign secretary then juxtaposed this form of unity with the 'unification' of Eastern Europe by force. The Soviets' approach was:

> ... not in keeping with the spirit of Western civilisation, and if we are to have an organism in the West it must be a spiritual union. While, no doubt, there must be treaties or, at least understandings, the union must primarily be a fusion derived from the basic freedoms and ethical principles for which we all stand. It must be on terms of equality and it must contain all elements of freedom for which we all stand. That is the goal we are now trying to reach. It cannot be written down as a rigid thesis or in a directive. It is more a brotherhood and less of a rigid system.[59]

Bevin's pursuit of a 'spiritual' basis for Western Union was probably not related to any active personal faith and he used the term 'spiritual' to refer broadly to the great world religions, and to a general notion of 'western civilisation', rather than narrowly to Christianity. Nonetheless, he was working in sympathy with a significant tendency in public discourse.

The practice of constructing Europe or 'the West' as a cultural community opposed to a morally and normatively deviant Other was nothing new and had been essential to the rhetorical struggle against Nazi Germany.[60] Furthermore, the basis of this unifying culture was frequently traced to a religious root, as evinced by, for example, Winston Churchill's references to the defense of 'Christian civilisation' in his speeches.[61] The interpretation of the present as a historical moment in which Christianity was central also figured in the publicly prominent historiography of Arnold Toynbee, Herbert Butterfield and others. In 1948, Toynbee, who we have already met as director of studies for the influential Royal Institute of International Affairs and in regard to the wartime Churches Peace Aims Group, put forward this thesis in *Civilisation on Trial* and on the BBC, and Butterfield's lectures on 'Christianity and History' appeared in print and on the third programme the following year.[62] This was history as a grand narrative of the rise and fall of civilisations, in which that of the West was the highest development; a history where all else served the higher development of religion; in which Providence was the shaper of history and Christians were the leaven in the dough of society. One consequence of all this was that a space existed in public and political discourse in which the voice of the Churches could speak of, and to, the nation. That Sir Oliver Franks, whose father was a Congregationalist minister, and who was holder of the key appointment of ambassador to Washington, should write on 'The Tradition of Western civilization' in the *Congregational Quarterly* during these dangerous years was eloquent of the role of religion in the cultural politics of the early Cold War and the way in which Church and State found common cause.[63]

'Spiritual union' offered a means to link Britain into the Truman administration's representation of the East–West struggle as a moral conflict; a clash between Christianity and atheistic materialism, but was also important to foreign policy in another way.[64] The opening of the Cold War required that Britain's flank be secured against the Soviet threat by continental Europe being rebuilt and militarily reinforced and only America had the resources to achieve this. Both practically, and according to the United States demands, the reconstruction of continental Europe required Britain's full participation but this was seen to conflict with its wider interests. In terms of political power, economic interest, and cultural identity, Britain was still a global and imperial power. A not unfounded fear was that to draw closer to the continent would send out a signal to the Dominions and precipitate a further loss of Britain's global position to the United States. Therefore, foreign policy required some means of drawing Europe together and a conduit for British involvement which did not threaten the political and economic bases of its wider global interests. As Avi Shlaim has suggested, these contending imperatives 'created a very low ceiling of European integration beyond which Bevin was not prepared to advance'.[65]

After Bevin's speech one critic noted that 'his language was, no doubt purposely, more than usually vague'. The seemingly open quality of Western Union created a space into which every sort of vision could be projected – Maurice Edelman pointed out that 'Western Union is no more than a number of widely differing ideas in the mind of the onlookers'.[66] However, while Western Union might be seized on as a basis for a federation or to create a socialist 'third force' between the superpowers, its vagueness served other, alternative purposes. In both its form and implied content, Western Union took as its point of reference the totalitarian Other but also articulated norms of British political culture: A preference for the informal, evolutionary, and gradualistic over the rigid and formulaic, and for inter-governmental structures which preserved national sovereignty over supra-national formations which ceded it.[67]

Thus, in addition to juxtaposing the unities of Western Union and the Soviet bloc, Bevin in his speech also distinguished Western Union from the federalist vision of European integration, damning with faint praise 'ambitious schemes of European unity' and 'neat looking plans on paper', which he contrasted with his slow, gradual and practical approach.[68] That spiritual union was viewed as offering an acceptable form of 'unity', which left political and economic independence untouched, is suggested in Bevin's cabinet paper detailing Western Union:

> ... our treaty relations with the various countries [of Western Union] might differ, but between all there would be an understanding *backed* by power, money and resolution and *bound together* by common ideals. When the idea was ventilated in my speech in the Foreign Affairs debate ... this conception of a "spiritual" union of the west met with a very favourable reception abroad ...[69]

Recruiting the Churches

Bevin's seriousness is also indicated by the creation of a working party in the Foreign Office's Information Policy Department to study the 'spiritual aspects' of Western Union and seek 'factors common to the Western Union countries other than political, strategic and economic, which can contribute to building up the Western Union conception'.[70] Why religion was discussed at the inaugural meeting, but ignored thereafter might be explained by the only significant mention on the subject. Describing religion as 'the most elusive, and perhaps deceptive' of the possible bases for unity, Paul Gore-Booth, head of the European Recovery Department, reflected on the fragmented and fractious nature of European Christianity and suggested that 'the religious approach to the question seems to be quite impossible on any denominational basis' and that the 'only possible approach to matters of the spirit ... is through ideas such as tolerance'. In the end the group failed to get beyond vague references to 'tolerance' and 'freedom' and 'shelved' its search.[71]

However, 'spiritual and cultural', as the third of four 'practical steps' to implement Western Union outlined by Frank Roberts, Bevin's principal private secretary, led to a purposive engagement with the

Churches.[72] Bevin held discussions with Geoffrey Fisher, and then with Bernard Griffin. Both men agreed to do what they could. Similar invitations went to J.M. Richardson, moderator of the FCFC and Dr. Matthew Stewart, moderator of the General Assembly of the Church of Scotland, who met with Stafford Cripps.[73] Cripps, it was agreed, would 'assume primary responsibility' for the campaign.[74] Compared to the foreign secretary – a lapsed Baptist – the chancellor of the exchequer was much better placed to recruit the Churches. A devout Anglican, he was determined that his faith infuse his public role and had close personal contacts among leading churchmen. Obviously this was a duty outside of the usual brief of the chancellor of the exchequer, but, in any case, the intention was that the State would remain in the shadows and that it would *appear* that these were ecclesiastical initiatives.[75]

Following Bevin's approach, anti-Communism combined with calls for the spiritual unity of Europe figured in the utterances of leading churchmen. For Fisher, as we have seen, this was already a familiar territory. Whereas the UEM was distrusted by Labour, it shared Bevin's preference for cultural bases for unity over federalist blueprints so after his meeting with Bevin, Fisher merely continued in the same vein. His Easter address for 1948 contrasted communism with 'the tradition of European civilisation' as described recently by Lord Pakenham, in the House of Lords. Taking a tone similarly apocalyptic to Bevin's memorandum on 'The Threat to Western Civilisation', Fisher declared that: 'The future good of mankind rests ... with those who will not despair of these moral postulates, but will uphold them with a strong and vital faith and hope'.[76] The Archbishop of York, who had marked out for himself a special role in international affairs and worked closely with the Foreign Office, also gave explicit support to European unity.[77] Later, at the Convocation of Canterbury, Fisher highlighted 'Totalitarian Communism's policy of subversion and aggression' and then noted that 'unities in Western Europe, in the Commonwealth, and across the Atlantic in the fields of defense and of economic life' would only succeed if they were founded on a 'growing unity in clear spiritual values'. To overcome communism it was necessary to 'create a new civilisation with the Christian faith at its heart and in all its limbs'.[78]

Through the sub-committee on International Interests of its Committee on Church and Nation, the Church of Scotland also had an established interest in this question. Apart from its general public influence, the Committee circulated its reports to Scottish MPs and maintained contacts with government departments, including the Foreign Office.[79] Although it is unclear whether the Foreign Office's approach to

Dr. Stewart precipitated it, once again there was agreement between Church and State. The report submitted to the General Assembly referred to Bevin's January speech and discussed the government's policy, suggesting that the Church had a 'special concern for Europe as the traditional bastion of our faith' and that it should 'attempt to give a moral and spiritual lead' The assembly moved that the government's 'efforts ... towards closer co-operation with our European neighbours in order to provide a unified Western European Society' be welcomed.[80] Similarly, the International Congregational Council in its public statement of June 1949 endorsed the organisation of 'regional associations within the ambit of the United Nations'.[81] With the exception of a Dutch representative, The Council was exclusively composed of Congregationalists from the English-speaking world and reproduced the ruling Western secular political assumptions of the Cold War without significant modification.

Griffin – speaking to students at the Newman Association's Summer Conference some months after his interview with Bevin – commented on his listeners' future influence on the 'intellectual life of the country' and concluded with the statement that: 'European unity will not come about merely by economics and politics. These are material things. Europe was united through the Faith and the nations of Europe will be re-united through the same Faith'.[82] *The Tablet* welcomed Bevin's Western Union speech as offering the beginnings of a European policy.[83] However, as *The Christian Democrat*, the journal of the Catholic Social Guild, indicated, English Catholics agreed with their federalist cousins on the continent by wishing for economic and political integration far beyond anything suggested by Bevin. This was a future in which Britain would make 'a decisive break with the past' and take the 'plunge' to become a 'European power'.[84]

Amsterdam and The World Council of Churches

Frank Roberts's memorandum outlining the 'spiritual and cultural' measures promoting Western Union also suggested that in order to 'harness spiritual forces behind ... Western Union' that all of the great world religions should be 'brought together ... in opposition to Communism', by means of the linkage of the 'freedom of the individual' to 'religious freedom and the general spiritual values' of these faiths. However, before this could be done, it was deemed 'essential to arrive at some unity among the Christian Churches'. Standing in the way of this was the not inconsiderable obstacle of the historical and continuing fragmentation of Christianity. While great progress had been made towards unity among the Protestant and Orthodox Churches in the ongoing process of the formation of the WCC, the Catholic Church still remained aloof. Nonetheless the Secretary of State demanded 'further effort ... to get all the Christian Churches together on the basis of the defence of religion, peace, liberty and social justice'. The 'objective' was a 'world congress of Christian Churches' to be held later that year, perhaps in Geneva.[85]

The WCC, which had been in the process of formation since 1937 as a forum and common voice for the non-Catholic Churches, had already planned to hold its inaugural assembly in Amsterdam from 22 August to 4 September 1948. This fact was included in a memorandum on the WCC drawn up a few days later for Bevin by Frank Pakenham, Chancellor of the Duchy of Lancaster and minister responsible for the British occupation zones in Germany and Austria.[86] Lord Pakenham was also a convert to Catholicism and maintained close contacts with the hierarchy of that church. The passages that he highlighted for the foreign secretary indicated the strength of the British, United States and German delegations and the fact that the Catholic Church, while remaining aloof had been exploring the sending of unofficial representatives. It was also noted that the Archbishop of Canterbury was named among the presidents of the Council.

During the years from the decision to found the WCC in 1937, it had paid considerable attention to international relations, and during the war years its various national committees had discussed the future of Europe.[87] In 1948 the chairman of the WCC Commission of the Churches in International Affairs (CCIA) was Kenneth Grubb.[88] It would be consistent with his previous career if, as Kirby suggests, the contacts he made in the wartime MOI created a channel for 'secular policy making elites to exert influence on WCC officers'.[89] It is likely that Grubb was contacted in such a way by the FO at this time as, on 9 March he wrote to Visser t'Hooft in Geneva, to suggest that, in view of 'the present crisis in Europe', 'a small conference of responsible Christian politicians from the countries of the rather loosely so-called "Western Union"' be called under the auspices of the CIIA.[90] That Grubb was responding to a request for such an action rather than himself initiating it, may be inferred from his own doubt as to the value and practicality of such a meeting and his disinclination to press the matter.[91] Should such a meeting go ahead, Grubb noted that it might be financed by an application to 'the Rockefeller Grant'. As already mentioned, the EM floated on American money. He also questioned whether such a meeting would be worthwhile without Catholic participation and suggested Pakenham as a possible British Catholic representative. Grubb also suggested the Labour MP Eric Fletcher as another possible name.[92]

In this respect, the approach of the British government parallels that of the Truman administration that was taking place at the same time.[93] However, The WCC, while being opposed to totalitarianism, also strived to avoid becoming the religious auxiliary of a western crusade against communism and fended off approaches from the US administration towards that end. Visser t' Hooft believed that it would not be prudent to call such a conference under WCC auspices as it would add to 'the already too wide spread impression that the World Council is linked up with the Western Powers' and he was in contact with churchmen from behind the Iron Curtain whom he hoped, along with members of the Russian Orthodox Church – would attend the Amsterdam assembly. As an alternative he suggested that 'a small conference of Christian political leaders' be organised by Nils Ehrenstrom of the WCC in June to discuss the attitude of the forthcoming Assembly to the international situation. This could be used 'at the same time for the wider purpose of a very frank facing of the responsibility of Christian leaders in the present situation'. Once again, in order to avoid the identification of the WCC with the West attendance would not be restricted to 'Western Union' (WU) leaders although most taking part would come from that part of the world.[94]

In the event, the Amsterdam assembly, which Eric Fletcher, MP who attended it, described as 'the most notable event in Protestant Christianity since the Reformation', could not avoid being identified with Western political influence by the Russians, who pulled out at the last moment.[95] The Assembly, which took as its general heading 'Man's disorder and God's Design' and as one of its four themes 'The Church and the International Disorder' debated the disharmony between East and West, and included in its official message a general call for Christians to resist 'every system, every programme, every person' which disregarded justice, the sanctity of human life, or fermented war.[96] In the report of the CCIA on 'The Church and the International Disorder' there where no specific references to supra-national structures, other than the United Nations, although there was a pragmatic acceptance of the need for 'immediate practical steps' while 'comprehensive and authoritative world organisation' was not possible.[97] One of its leading participants, John Foster Dulles, whose long involvement in foreign affairs would culminate in his appointment as Eisenhower's Secretary of State, continued to be a strong advocate of unity for Europe.[98] Among the 'intermediate steps' towards 'universal world order' which his paper endorsed were 'steps towards political, economic and monetary unity' in Europe: 'A Europe divided into a score or more of separate unconnected sovereignties can never again be a healthful and peaceful part of the world'.[99] However, perhaps inevitably, European unity played only a small and subsidiary role in discussions preoccupied with the future of the world polity and the UN, the superpowers, and the threat of atomic Armageddon.

Frederick Nolde, the director of the CCIA, later noted that the global focus and limited resources of the WCC precluded significant involvement on European questions.[100] In fact, the preparatory meeting for the Amsterdam gathering, held at Bossey the year before, when it was discussed how the Churches could influence international affairs, agreed that national councils of Churches should deal with questions of regional unity.[101] Hence, in the British case, the International Department of the BCC, also headed by Grubb, took up the issue of European integration. This was the beginning of several years of tentative involvement by the BCC and, in particular by the secretary of its International Department, the Rev. Herbert Waddams. As has already been mentioned, Waddams had served in the MOI. At the end of the war he became secretary to the Church of England Council on Foreign Relations.[102] The next year the International Department appointed delegates to the Ecumenical Commission for European Co-operation, a group of Christian laymen from different countries in Europe, formed in April 1949.[103] Later that year it discussed whether the Churches had 'any special responsibilities towards the movement for European unity'. It was decided that while they should not get involved in 'political questions concerning a united Europe, there were spiritual issues and concerns of the Churches to be considered'. The BCC offered itself as a point of contact between the EM and the Churches with Waddams acting as go-between.[104]

The Congress of Europe

But perhaps Waddam's most significant contribution in this area was as part of the British delegation to the EM's inaugural conference at The Hague in May 1948. The interest of the Churches in the conference was notable. When Sandys of the UEM had requested Catholic support for the Congress of Europe, the Pope had shown a 'keen interest in the European cause' and gave his approval.[105] The Vatican appointed an observer to the Hague conference, the inter-nuncio Mgr. Jobbe.[106] Similarly, archbishop Fisher responded positively to Sandys's request for a message of good will to be read at the Conference.[107] There was also a powerful representation of the Christian interest among the British delegation, which was to play a significant role in proceedings.

As both an expert on foreign affairs and editor of *The Tablet*, Douglas Woodruff was well qualified to estimate the significance of the Conference. He wrote at the time: 'Everybody recognized that perhaps the Congress really is an historic occasion and a new beginning and if so every phrase in every resolution may prove unexpectedly significant later on'.[108] This was particularly the case in the conference's 'cultural' committee, the work of the Conference outside of its central congress being divided into three committees: political, social and cultural. Even before the Conference, there had been some skirmishes in the Christian interest. Denis de Rougemont, joint rapporteur of the cultural sub-committee, was also the primary author of the cultural report to be considered by the Conference. Before publication, he circulated the draft report for comment to colleagues including T.S. Eliot. Eliot, a prominent Anglo-Catholic, was a significant and influential protagonist for the importance of the historical inheritance of Christendom and the necessity for society to be underpinned by Christian ethics and governed by Christian elites as an alternative to totalitarianism.[109] He gave a series of wireless talks to Germany on this theme which were then published the same month as Bevin's Western Union speech.[110] During wartime he had participated in discussions on post-war reconstruction in Joseph Oldham's 'Moot' and in the later 1940s and 1950s contributed to the EM and to the cultural dimension of the Cold War generally.[111] On this occasion, he pointed to the absence of references to the place of Europe's history and, specifically, Christianity in the creation of the continent's essence and identity. There was, Eliot wrote, 'no place for the "militant atheist"'.[112]

Although the report was duly amended, it was necessary to fight the same battle again at the conference over the resolution.[113] Waddams explained afterwards, that '[t]here was a strong British delegation and it quickly became clear that there were two parties at the Conference, one which felt it important to emphasise the values of Christian civilisation and another, a group of nationalists, which did not. The Christian party succeeded in getting the importance of Christian values included in the Conference report'.[114] Besides Waddams and Woodruff, the heavyweight British party included such illustrious names as Group Captain Leonard Cheshire, VC; Sir Adrian Boult; Sir David Maxwell-Fyfe, MP

(Conservative); Bertrand Russell; and the Poet Laureate, John Masefield. Woodruff wrote of the proceedings:

> ... It was obvious that there was no sort of agreement between the Christians and non-Christians about what the history of Europe has in fact been. There is left in my mind a strong impression that I have been listening to men who are among shadows; that the Europe they invoke is an imaginary subjective thing, that they are homeless post-Christians who are not in complete forgetfulness trailing clouds of glory from a home of whose form they have a vague idea. ... They search for words which will unite them because what they, being men, need, is a religion and a communal, institutional religion. But the corner stone is still rejected by the builders.
>
> From the Bishop of Truro's first declaration that the Christian faith had been, carefully or carelessly, put to one side, there was a strong English Protestant representation, affirming transcendental religion against the liberal humanists who are so convinced that their attitude is the only civilized one that they do not realise that they, too, are militant missionaries.[115]

Besides Joseph W. Hunkin, the Bishop of Truro, other Britons making the Christian case were Cheshire, Boult and Canon John Collins.[116] In contrast, those continental Catholics who were there, were either silent or preoccupied with national or other secular political concerns. The published cultural resolution began:

> Believing that European Union is no longer a Utopian idea but has become a necessity, and that it can only be established on a lasting basis if it is founded upon a genuine and living unity;
>
> Believing that this true unity even in the midst of our national, ideological and religious differences, is to be found in the common heritage of Christian and other spiritual and cultural values and our common loyalty to the fundamental rights of man, especially freedom of thought and expression;
>
> Believing that efforts to unite must be sustained and inspired by an awakening of the conscience of Europe ...[117]

Woodruff wrote of how the nuncio Mgr. Jobbe's presence at The Hague 'represented the active sympathy of the Holy See towards a movement for greater European unity. His silence indicated the prudence and reserve of the Church towards a movement whose character and aims could not be assessed'.[118] In the Papal allocation of November 1948 the Vatican expressed its appreciation of the reference to Christianity in the cultural statement and generously blessed the Europe Movement: 'En tout cas, avec la plus vivante sympathie, Nous prions le Père de lumières de vous éclairer, de vous assister dans vos travaux et de bénir vos efforts tendus vers la paix si ardemment convoitée'.[119]

*

In its argument for Christianity to be the 'cement of the new Europe',[120] as it had been of the old, The Hague conference presaged and anticipated many later debates and controversies. The Churches' victory in 1948 was in a single engagement in what would be an ongoing struggle over the cultural definition of the continent, a struggle inextricably tied into the politically potent question of the ownership of the idea of Europe.

5
Christian Action and the Christian Movement for European Unity

As William Temple once said, when people say 'why doesn't the Church do something' what they mean is 'why doesn't the Bishop say something'. In the eyes of policymakers, public statements by church leaders were part of the gradual moving of public opinion to build coalitions of support behind political projects. However, at the beginning of the Cold War, radical times were not amenable to gradualism. With the breakdown of negotiations at the conference of foreign ministers in London at the end of 1947, a *coup d'état* in Czechoslovakia in February 1948, a communist threat in the elections in Italy to come in April, events seemed to be sliding out of control. A decade earlier, the takeover of democratic Czechoslovakia by another totalitarian power was the penultimate step before war; in 1948 war again seemed a real possibility. The urgency of the need to hold the line against communism in Italy and unify Europe against the Soviets demanded more than words from the bishop, but nonetheless Christians could play an important role.

Canon Collins, Christian Action and Western Union

As part of Ernest Bevin's strategy, an immediate public demonstration of Britain's support for Western Union was called for. Lord (Frank) Pakenham, Chancellor of the Duchy of Lancaster and minister responsible to the Foreign Office for the British zones of occupation in Germany and Austria, was delegated to approach – unofficially – his friend Canon L. John Collins to organise a meeting at the Albert Hall.[1] Pakenham's pro-European credentials were impeccable: In addition to his advocacy of reconciliation between Britain and Germany, he had assisted the British People and Freedom Group (PFG) to attend the Christian Democrats' Congress of Luxembourg in January 1948 and sent his own 'messages of good wishes'. He also knew the leading German Christian Democrat and pioneer of the European movement, Konrad Adenauer, whom he enabled to attend the Congress of Europe at the Hague.[2]

Collins was the obvious choice. Dean of Oriel College, Oxford and shortly to become a canon of St. Paul's Cathedral, he had converted to socialism in the 1930s. As a Royal Air Force Chaplain during wartime, he endeavoured to bring Christianity to bear on public issues through the Fellowship of the Transfiguration of Our Lord, and in 1945, participated in talks initiated by Stafford and Isobel Cripps towards the same purpose. In the end, the London Reform Group, which also included Bishop Bell and Sir Richard Acland – after Cripps, perhaps Britain's most visible Christian politician – could not achieve sufficient agreement. However, in December 1946, Collins, having returned to Oriel College, organised a meeting under the slogan: 'A Call to Christian Action in Public Affairs'. It was out of this that Christian Action (CA) emerged, to work to realise the resolutions of the meeting, including: 'To give support by active democratic means to the government of the day in any attempt made to maintain the application of Christian principles in national and international affairs, and to press for a policy more and more in line with these principles'.[3]

Besides Collins's fervent activism and his contacts with the leading Christians in British political life – in addition to Cripps and Pakenham, he also secured the Anglican and Conservative Lord Halifax and the Catholic and liberal Lord Perth as patrons of CA – he also had an established interest in the fortunes of Europe. In addition to the resolution above, the inaugural CA meeting called for Christians to act personally and lobby the government to further the reconstruction of, and reconciliation with, Germany. Victor Gollancz spoke in support of his campaign 'Save Europe Now!', to which the proceeds of the meeting were donated.[4] Collins was a member of the publisher's campaign and, additionally, of the Oxford Famine Relief Committee.[5] In March 1947, the Oxford Committee for Promoting Friendship and Understanding with Europe was set up.[6] The Committee was intended to 'support Christian and Democratic forces in Europe'. Its aims were 'a) To strengthen the spirit of friendship and understanding between Britain and the nations of Europe; b) to help in relieving their intellectual and spiritual isolation; c) to bring a measure of the Christian spirit of reconciliation to bear upon the relations between victors and vanquished'.[7]

Although the suggestion for the Albert Hall meeting came from Pakenham, Collins organised it with Cripps's help, and it was to the chancellor that he sent a detailed memorandum detailing its aims.[8] The extent to which this reflected Collins's rather than Foreign Office's thinking is unclear, although he had taken advice from someone 'in close touch with Cardinal Griffin and the Apostolic delegate'. This was almost certainly Douglas Woodruff, editor of *The Tablet*, to whom Collins was introduced at this time. Edith Ellis, a Quaker who had previously been successful in persuading Cardinal Hinsley to add his signature next to those of Protestant leaders on the 'ten points' letter in *The Times* in 1940, was once more influential here in bringing together leading figures in the different Christian traditions.[9] Unlike Collins, Woodruff was a traditionalist and politically conservative. One observer wrote that he seemed to have 'completely ... lost his progressive instinct' and become 'a sort of political and social Julian the Apostate' inasmuch that, like the Emperor who tried to return Rome to paganism, he seemed 'to dream, probably through fear, of a static world in which the state of affairs of pre-1914 would be crystallised'.[10] However, despite the political gulf between the two men, Woodruff was ideally placed to offer such advice, he also took a considerable interest in foreign affairs, writing on European questions in – apart from *The Tablet* – *Free Europe*, *Soundings* and other journals.[11]

There was no discernible friction between Collins's thinking and the Foreign Office's, and following discussions 'at a high level' his proposal was approved.[12] Collins called for a:

a big-scale meeting as soon as possible ... The aim of the meeting would be to stir up Christians to give full support to the policy of a Union of Western Europe and to demonstrate to Europe that such a policy, in the view of this country, needs behind it a Christian ideology to support it and inform it.

He hoped that the event might be 'an immediate means of helping towards the defeat of political Communism in Italy and France; and ... a step in the direction of getting a United Europe upon sound foundations'. It was hoped that it might assist anti-Communist forces in the Italian election on 18 April and also redress an impression among the Catholic-dominated Christian Democrat parties on the continent that Labour was snubbing them in favour of socialists. One means to this end was to engineer a political balance among the participants by having the meeting chaired by someone 'acceptable to the centre groups on the Continent'. Alongside leading Christian figures in continental and British politics, Collins hoped that the platform would be graced by the leaders of the British churches. Given that Collins would later be accused of being a communist dupe or even a fellow traveller on account of his activities in Campaign for Nuclear Disarmament (CND) and the peace movement, his role here and his close collaboration with the reactionary Woodruff was not without some superficial irony.

With the facilities of the British State at his command, Collins was able to achieve much of this, although, at such short notice, the Albert Hall was only available after the Italian elections.[13] Cripps took time out from his busy schedule to request Cardinal Griffin to attend, to ask British embassies abroad for speakers, and to arrange for the BBC to report the meeting.[14] The Churches also swung their resources behind the event: Griffin worked though the English College in Rome to secure an Italian speaker and encouraged supporters of the Sword of Spirit organisation to attend to 'make the meeting a magnificent demonstration of our belief in the need for a spiritual basis to European unity'.[15] The Church press and Fleet Street also gave the event considerable publicity.[16]

On the day, the platform was packed with church leaders and also boasted Pakenham, and, representing Churchill's UEM, Lord Layton. A conservative, Lord Halifax – also a patron of CA – took the chair and Cripps gave the concluding address. The only major absence was Bevin himself. Collins had agreed with Woodruff that the foreign secretary's participation would have gone a long way to demonstrate the support not only of individual Christians in the Government, but the Government *itself*, and agreed to discuss this with Cripps.[17] The other speakers included a Catholic Christian Democrat (Karl Arnold) and a Protestant Socialist (Dr. Adolf Grimm) from Germany, a Dutch Protestant (Dr. Egbert Emmen) and a Protestant diplomat from Sweden (Baron Carl Hamilton), an Italian Catholic and member of the Italian National Assembly (Igino Giordani), Protestant socialist (André Philip) and Catholic Christian Democrat (Maurice Schuman) members of the French National Assembly, and the Leader of the Christian Democrats in Belgium (Auguste de Schryver). Florence Hancock, the chair of the Trades Union Congress (TUC) and a Congregationalist and Richard O'Sullivan, chair of the Catholic Social Guild also spoke. The eight continental speakers clearly represented the organisers' attempts to construct a political and religious balance. The inclusion of German representatives also represented a step towards reconciliation with former enemies, a process with which Christians particularly identified.[18] Given that the achievement of a *modus vivendi* between France and its hated three times enemy and the eventual incorporation of a domesticated Germany within the Western bloc were also essential moves in the conjoined projects of

European integration and the Cold War, reconciliation was a process in the interests of both Church and State.

Halifax opened the meeting with messages from both Attlee and Churchill: the former, offering a general affirmation of 'the absolute moral values on which our Christian civilisation is based', the latter stressing that the 'new Europe' must be built on 'moral and spiritual foundations'. References to the historical heritage of Christendom and to the necessity of a Christian, 'spiritual' basis, for social and political life, combined with support for European unity, constituted the major themes of the speeches. Maurice Schuman's endorsement of Europe as a 'Third Force between the blocs' and André Philip's anticipation of the creation of 'new economic and social conditions' were rare gestures towards specificity among a positive but general message. Not surprisingly, the spectre of communism haunted the evening's proceedings and there was an unmistakable polarisation in the speeches between the Christian, democratic West and the totalitarian East.[19]

Although there had been no time to co-ordinate the speeches, the meeting effectively signified Britain's linkage to the continent and the need for the West to be united against the threat of the East but without the political dangers of specific proposals. As to its success, it was sold out over a week in advance, two thousand persons were turned away, and it drew a 'young and attentive' audience of eight thousand. The meeting was reported at length on the BBC and widely in the press and on the day six hundred people committed themselves to the aims of CA and most of the twelve hundred letters received afterwards were adjudged to be sincere.[20]

The Christian Movement for European Unity

After the Albert Hall meeting, Bevin's Western Union was progressively eclipsed, becoming even less than a 'military alliance and a *mystique*', as one critic had described it.[21] It is a matter for debate whether Western Union was dropped by the government primarily because the Marshall Plan and the North Atlantic Treaty made it superfluous or because the increasingly federalist turn in the debate on European integration also made it unattractive. However, while the government's agenda moved away from Europe, it had nonetheless set in train a Christian pro-European movement.

Although Collins later came to regard the Albert Hall meeting as 'something of a noisy but empty tin can', at the time he accepted Cripps's urging that he follow it up with more activities. Cripps also persuaded the prime minister to offer Collins a canonry at St. Paul's so that he could relocate from Oxford and be able to help to 'rouse the public to a serious consideration of European Union'.[22] The Oxford Committee for Promoting Friendship and Understanding with Europe continued to arrange Anglo-German exchange visits and a visit of the Berlin Philharmonic Orchestra went forward with help from the Treasury and the Foreign Office. The tour, originally intended to foster reconciliation, was now cast as playing 'an important part in the process of building up a United Europe on Christian lines to become a bastion for world peace'. CA meetings in connection with the pro-integration forces on the continent were also planned.[23] Collins also joined the EM's Cultural Committee. As discussed above, as one of the religious representatives to the seminal Congress of Europe at the Hague in May 1948, he contributed to the British delegation's successful amendment of the cultural resolution of the Congress to acknowledge Europe's Christian tradition.[24]

Collins also forged links to the wider European movement, beginning contacts with, among other bodies, Nouvelles Equipes Internationales (British Section) (NEI-BS) and the UEM.[25] These two were the most significant of the British groups interested in Europe: the UEM, which as already been discussed above, on account of having Churchill's considerable political weight behind it, NEI-BS as the British representative of the umbrella organisation of continental Christian Democracy.[26] At its formation in 1947, NEI had invited the BCC to become affiliates, but the Council was unwilling to link itself to a political body. In consequence, the British Section was only founded in March 1948, as an initiative of the small Christian Democratic People and Freedom Group. NEI-BS brought together representatives from a number of interested groups. Katharine, Duchess of Atholl took the chair. A Conservative and member of the Church of Scotland, she also chaired the BLEF, whose concern was that part of Europe behind the 'Iron Curtain' and which had began fighting the Cold War long before official policy turned in that direction.[27] NEI-BS styled itself as a body of Catholics and Protestants from all parties: Professor George Catlin, a Catholic and Labour party member long interested in international relations, became treasurer; Miss Barclay Carter of People and Freedom, its secretary, and Collins became one of its vice-chairmen.[28]

NEI-BS made an early start to develop a policy on Western Union, in July 1948 approving a paper based on a draft from Catlin on the political aspects of the Union.[29] While rejecting a federalist solution as likely to be dominated by Germany and unpopular with the Dominions the paper did favour a confederation with a united policy for defence and foreign affairs and economic co-operation. The *Equipe* also enlisted the Christian thinker Maurice Reckitt, a friend and collaborator of executive member Patrick McLaughlin – McLaughlin, Vicar of St. Thomas', Regent Street, was also secretary of the Church Union Committee for Church Social Action.[30] Reckitt described the paper that he sent to Atholl, 'The Church and "United Europe"',[31] as 'merely first aid'.[32] Discussing whether Christians should speak for European unity as such, Reckitt commented that while uniting Europe against the Soviet Union might be strategically necessary, strategy was not the business of the Church and this would hazard ecumenical relations with the Orthodox Church. A united Europe could be politically controversial on account of its relations with the United States, colonial territories overseas and the United Nations. And, where, if anywhere, could Christians stand in the argument over federalism? The Churches' own mission might be compromised by controversy. Even the Christian heritage of Europe had to be balanced against the recognition that many of its later formative influences had been 'neutral' or even anti-Christian. Furthermore, 'superficial optimism' about the heritage of Christendom had to be weighed against the acutely divided nature of Christianity in Europe.[33] Despite Reckitt's pessimism and his rigorous criticism of Christian assumptions, NEI-BS became an affiliate of the UK Council of the EM.

However, NEI-BS was dogged by chaotic administration, personality clashes, and conflict over its insufficient representation of Labour opinion. In the end, after changing its name to the British Group of the Union of Christian Democrats, it finally collapsed in 1952.[34] Even without these problems, NEI-BS was poorly adapted to the British political environment, being associated with the Catholic 'right' and an umbrella organisation for Christian Democratic political parties extended over a territory where no such force was ever likely to exist. On the latter point Collins, when asked whether CA might take part in the emerging 'European Christian Democratic Front', was unequivocal in his rejection. To speak of 'Christian Democratic parties' was 'a complete misuse of the term Christian' and 'not the way in which to get the greatest and strongest moral background for political action, national and international'.[35]

In view of these problems, a significant initiative occurred in early 1949 when Douglas Woodruff suggested to Collins the creation of what became the CMEU. This proposal followed on from the inaugural meeting of the United Kingdom Council for United Europe at the House of Commons on 16 February 1949.[36] Hoping to ensure that the 'special interests of the Protestant Church and the Catholic Church ... be safeguarded' by the Churches' being represented on the UKCEM Executive,

Woodruff had primed Collins to ask for the Archbishops of Canterbury and Westminster and the moderator of the Free Church Federal Council to be put 'on a par' with the leaders of the three chief political parties as honorary presidents with the right to appoint representatives. Woodruff's motivations were strongly religio-political: to avoid the body being dominated by 'non-Christians, largely Liberal and Socialist' who would 'intervene on Liberal or Social[ist] sides in European controversies'.[37] In the event, Collins was unsuccessful and Woodruff then suggested that he – in concert with Herbert Waddams of the Council on Foreign Relations (CFR) and BCC – persuade Fisher to get together with the other church leaders to make their acceptance of the position of patrons be conditional on the appointment of such representatives. In addition, Woodruff pressed that they should 'lose no time in founding a Christian Association in the United Kingdom open to all Christians which could then claim the same treatment as the other bodies, which are keeping the executive so far in their hands'.[38] Although Collins had to confess that he did not always 'see eye to eye' with 'gentleman Waddams' he agreed to use what influence he had and to throw CA's resources behind Woodruff's second suggestion, which he liked 'very much'.[39]

At first sight, given that NEI-BS was strongly pro-European and already an associate of the EM, it is puzzling that a Catholic should propose a competitor, which it was feared would starve the existing body of support and funds. The most likely explanation is that Woodruff hoped to create an organisation free of associations with Catholicism and Christian Democracy. This is indicated by his later opposition to proposals that NEI-BS and CMEU work more closely – 'on the grounds that all that is needed from the CMEU is to encourage Christians to join in the work of the EM and have the right to appoint Christian delegates to the various European conferences'. This interpretation is also supported by the fact that while Woodruff was on the committee of the CMEU, which met in the offices of *The Tablet*, the movement was never mentioned in a publication which otherwise promoted European integration at every opportunity. Finally, when discussion was underway to merge NEI-BS with CA, Lord Perth, a Catholic and also a Patron of CA, counselled against the move 'from the point of view of upsetting Labour, having regard to the extent to which the Christians on the Continent are organised on a party basis'.[40]

Given that Catholics tended to seek clerical approval before acting in the overlap between faith and politics, it is likely that Woodruff's initiative originated with, or was at least approved by, the Catholic Church's hierarchy as part of its Cold War strategy. He was certainly in close touch with the hierarchy in the Vatican, for example, visiting Rome in November 1949 at the time CMEU was being established, when he saw leading figures including Dr. Gedda, Chairman of the lay organisation Catholic Action.[41] As we have already seen, the Vatican and Gedda had taken a close interest in the EM from the outset.[42] Pius XII was also aware of CA. Edith Ellis – described as a 'visionary busybody' and as having 'one of the woolliest minds' one critic had come across – had visited Rome in October 1948 as a representative of CA.[43] Ellis met with Giovanni Montini, secretary to the Holy See – Montini would in time become Pope himself – to hand over CA literature and a memorandum seeking Papal advise on how Catholics and Protestants could work together such that 'spiritual harmony can be given us without prejudice to any matter of religious jurisdiction'.[44] During her visit Ellis worked closely with the Rev. H.L. Duggins, the rector of the American Episcopal Church in Rome. Duggins knew the Republican 'cold warrior' John Foster Dulles and also had Myron Taylor in his Congregation.[45] Taylor, President Truman's representative in the Vatican, played a vital role in forging an anti-Communist alliance between America and the Catholic Church, and, earlier that year, had also been involved in the abortive attempt to recruit the WCC to the same purpose.[46]

Following on from the suggestions in the memorandum presented by Ellis, Collins met with Bishop William Godfrey, the Pope's representative in Britain, to make arrangements for Cripps to meet Pius XII. The Apostolic Delegate suggested that 'a useful field for discussion' between the two men would be the circumstances in which 'full Catholic support' might be given to CA. Godfrey provided Cripps with Papal pronouncements stressing the 'common ground among all followers of Christ' which he suggested that the chancellor refer to, in addition to stressing 'the desire of Christians in Great Britain to conform with the Pope's desire for common action'. Godfrey was also asked to find out what the Vatican's mind was on the 'concrete actions' in which Christians could take part.[47]

Whether this last request was fulfilled is unclear, but at the audience in May 1949 the Pope discussed with Cripps what Collins described as ways in which 'the Anglican and Roman Communions could co-operate in the cause of a united Western Europe'.[48] Given the deep divide between Catholic and Protestant, the Pope's concession that members of the two traditions might work in 'parallel' in CA and even share 'some very simple and non-controversial form of worship' marked a genuine breakthrough.[49] Collins then held extensive discussions in

Rome with Dr. Gedda which produced an agreed statement which Collins described as going 'further than even the famous Malines Conversations in providing a possible basis for a *modus vivendi* between Rome and Canterbury'. However, he had vastly exceeded his authority in operating without reference to the Archbishop or the Church of England's CFR, within whose ambit lay inter-church relations. Consequently these negotiations came to an abrupt end when Fisher heard of them.[50] Although Diana Collins later blamed Cripps for what became the first engagement in an increasingly acrimonious relationship between her husband and the archbishop, it was Collins not the chancellor who should have known the correct protocol.[51]

Despite this, as chairman of CA, Collins called a meeting that September, to explore the creation of an 'organisation with the special object of working for the advancement of European unity, in order that we may play our full part, as Christians, in the work of the British section of the European Movement'. Collins explained that he had involved himself in this question because 'apart from NEI' Christians in the EM had not worked in concert or even participated primarily as such.[52] Of the approximately fifty leading British Protestants and Catholics invited, twenty attended and a provisional committee under Collins' was established.[53] In her report to Sandys of the UEM, Lady Juliet Rhys-Williams, who was a member of this new committee and the honorary secretary of UEM, suggested that although 'the preliminary meeting was not very auspicious' there were 'real forces' behind it which would make it into 'something important'. Similar sentiments were expressed by Collins, who suggested that there was 'potentially vast support to be found throughout the country' and Woodruff who stated that their aim was to create a mass-movement.[54]

Most of the finance for the new movement was provided by a 'loan' of £100 from UEM, half of which was used for a quarter's subscription as an affiliate to the UK Council of the EM.[55] Major Edward Beddington-Behrens of the UEM, pledged 'all possible support, including financial, within his power' and was elected onto the council of CMEU. Generously financed by British big business and the political and commercial interests represented by Friends of United Europe in America, Churchill's UEM provided funds for most of the pro-European groups in Britain and on the continent. Inasmuch that the Friends of United Europe was a conduit for CIA money and Beddington-Behrens worked with MI6, the CMEU was, therefore, also a minor – if largely unwitting – player in the clandestine dimension of the cultural Cold War.[56]

At its first formal meeting the new organisation agreed to:

> Actively ... foster the cause of European Unity as long as it is com-
> patible with Christian principles, by all means within its power: to
> gain support, within the various denominations, and among sympa-
> thetic individuals, for the cause of European Unity: to cooperate as
> far as possible with all other movements working wholly or partially
> for European unity in Great Britain; and to assert the observance of
> Christian principles in their activities and declarations, by examin-
> ing and criticizing whatever by omission or contradiction appears to
> be in conflict with those principles.[57]

The implications of this aim were later fleshed out in the movement's
leaflet drawn up between Woodruff and Collins which took the deliberations of the Council of Europe established earlier that year at
Strasbourg as its point of reference.[58] 'Christian influence' would serve
as the 'cement for unity', by providing a common set of principles. In this
way a 'spirit of mutual helpfulness', would be fostered 'so that, within a
strong framework, diversities can flourish and European peoples as they
are and as their histories have made them can unite'. An earlier draft[59]
had spoken of the need for a 'framework in which diversities, national
and economic, can flourish' but even in the less explicit final form, it
was clear that religious principles were being offered as the means of
transcending the apparently irreconcilable ideological differences then
dividing socialists and Christian democrats. In the absence of any
'avowedly Christian political party' on the continental model in Britain,
the CMEU would serve to represent 'specifically Christian interests' in
such areas as arguing for 'parental rights in education' and to 'resist ...
humanist and agnostic opposition to any recognition of the Christian
foundation and character of Europe'. In both areas Christian opinion
had been insufficiently represented at Strasbourg. The CMEU would
'work for the safeguarding of the Christian heritage in Europe and to see
that all Christians ... are free to live the full institutional and personal
life of their religion'. A unity of Europe built on Christian principles
would be 'an essential prelude to any world unity'; it would 'stand up
against all disintegrating forces which threaten and undermine its material, moral, and spiritual stability'.

A continuation committee was selected, with Collins as chairman and
as vice-chairmen Woodruff and Gordon Lang. Other members included
Atholl, Catlin, Richard O' Sullivan, Lady Ravensdale, Lady Rhys-Williams,
the Conservative MP David Eccles, and the Labour backbencher Richard

Stokes. Walter Matthews, the Dean of St. Paul's, and Edward Myers, Bishop of Lamus, represented the Anglican and Catholic denominations respectively. As we have seen Matthews also served alongside the Bishops of London, Peterborough, Lichfield, Truro and Bath & Wells on the General Committee of the UEM. Similarly, Myers was on the UK Council of the EM and had attended the Hague Congress.[60]

As he was soon to be elevated to the cabinet, Stokes was a catch. Like Collins, he had been on the executive of Save Europe Now, and attended CA meetings at the House of Commons.[61] He actively took up the cause and in the lecture tour he undertook in Italy shortly before becoming Minister of Works, spoke on 'Western Union and the Italian place in Europe'.[62] He also knew the Pakenhams well and, like Frank, mixed with leading members of the EM, for example, dining with Signor de Gaspari at the time of the Italian premier's visit to Britain. At another time he was among a party including Pakenham and George Beck, Catholic Bishop of Brentford. Such occasions, and Stokes's close and responsive relationship with Cardinal Griffin, indicate the secret voice Catholic church leaders had not only on issues such as education – over which the Church claimed a special concern – but also on more 'worldly' questions.[63]

Following the first meeting, Woodruff and Collins wrestled with drawing up a denominationally and politically balanced list of persons who were, as Woodruff wrote, 'doctrinal and convinced Christians ... that ... really mean business about United Europe' to sign an appeal letter to be circulated nationally on behalf of CMEU.[64] Collins had earlier rejected approaching church leaders to sign because of the intractable problems of precedence this would create, so instead the signatories would be restricted to lay persons.[65] He had wanted to include Cripps, Pakenham, the First Lord of the Admiralty A.V. Alexander, and the Minister of Education George Tomlinson[66], but after Cripps had refused to sign, serving members of the government were also struck off the list. Nonetheless, even with these subtractions the final list of fifty five names was a virtual Who's Who of eminent Christians in politics, academia, the arts and public life generally, including Harold Macmillan, Quintin Hogg, Lord Vansittart and the Earl of Halifax; A.J. Toynbee and A.D. Lindsay (Lord Lindsay of Birker); J. Arthur Rank, T.S. Eliot and John Betjeman.[67]

However, more negatively, when the CMEU's statement was published as a leaflet and then distributed after a UEM meeting in November, there was no response whatsoever. Collins wondered if 'something more concise and direct' was needed 'to capture the public imagination'.[68] However, after this the CMEU Committee did not meet again after February 1951,[69] although Woodruff and Collins participated in the work of the UK Council of the EM in its name. Woodruff attended the EM's Social Conference in Rome in June 1950 as the representative of CMEU and Collins was active in the deliberations of the Council.[70]

It was not until 1951 that CA/CMEU intervened publicly again. The idea of a meeting to 'test public opinion', held by CMEU in conjunction with the Christian Frontier Council – a group founded in wartime by Joseph Oldham with similar aims to CA – and the Christian socialist 1950 Group was floated in October 1950 and Collins cautiously agreed to organise it.[71] The meeting, at the Central Hall, Westminster was chaired by Lord Jowitt, the Lord Chancellor, and included R.A. Butler and Stokes – now Lord Privy Seal. Although Fisher's relationship with Collins had become increasingly strained, the archbishop continued to be represented on the CA Council and was included among the church leaders attending.[72] At the time of the founding of CMEU Waddams condemned Collins's creation of CMEU without consulting the CFR or the BCC. He attended a number of EM meetings alongside Collins and described the Canon as an 'ignoramus and bungler' in his dealings with the Catholics and accused him of having 'led the European Movement up the garden path as far as explaining Church support is concerned' and suggested that Fisher withdraw Anglican endorsement.[73] For whatever reason, Fisher continued to back Collins. Writing to Halifax, Collins described the event as 'the natural follow-up of the Albert Hall meeting' but stipulated that 'a common purpose [among] the various movements concerned with making Christian influence felt in the affairs of Europe' needed to be generated first.[74] The size and response of the audience suggested that the event was a success, but Collins later felt that it 'lacked cohesion' and was 'neither sufficiently challenging nor sufficiently down to earth'. Accounts of the meeting indicate that its contributors did not venture beyond wholesome but general pronouncements and that, even in comparison to the Albert Hall meeting, references to European integration were meagre.[75]

At another conference, 'Religion and European Unity', held in London in 1951, Collins also spoke of the British Christians working for representation on the various organisations and commissions of the EM and CMEU's presence on the UKCEM.[76] This gathering was organised by the Religious Bodies Consultative Committee (RBCC), of which Collins was also a member. The RBCC was established in 1950 by the BCC as an independent body to encourage consultation and co-operation in the field of international affairs. The Committee not only included

Catholics alongside Protestants, but also included representatives of British Jewry, the Rabbis I. Livingstone and I.I. Mattuck.[77] The Committee was chaired by Arthur Duncan-Jones, Dean of Chichester and also included Lord Layton (of the UEM/EM) and representatives of the Baptist, Methodist, Presbyterian and Quaker denominations. Cardinal Griffin appointed Fr. John Murray, S.J. and the Very Rev. J.L. Dockery to represent the Catholic Church.

The RBCC's 1950 declaration 'The Spiritual Inheritance of Europe' was published in *The Times* and as a leaflet. This argued that the contribution of Europe to the world was in the 'ethical outlook' that had grown up in Europe and the near-east over nearly four millennia, which stressed the rights and duties inherent in the 'sanctity of human personality'.[78] The representatives of the different faiths voiced their acceptance of the spiritual principles behind the 'idea of Europe' in the RBCC statement. Lord Layton pointed to its similarities to the work of the EM to define the common elements uniting European nations and to found the Council of Europe and create a European Convention of Human Rights. He also hoped that the British government would come to accept the authority and jurisdiction of a European Court. The conference ended with a resolution supporting the struggle for human rights and religious freedom 'throughout Europe and to assist in winning these rights and freedoms for those who do not now enjoy them'. It also called for religious leaders to give greater guidance on the 'meaning of European unity', especially in regard to its 'moral and spiritual considerations'. Religious leaders in Britain were urged to bring the situation on the continent before their Congregations and 'strengthen lines of communication between us and them ... and to join a fresh endeavour to practice in the life of our own community the deep convictions which are the spiritual inheritance of Europe'.[79]

Despite Collins promoting the CMEU at this conference it petered out as an active body. CA's interest in Europe continued a little while longer. In November, at a 'lunch-hour forum' Stephen Spender spoke on European unity and the following January Collins wrote to Cardinal Griffin asking for support for the Conference of the Central and Eastern Commission of the European Movement. Linking the conference to the Albert Hall meeting, the Canon described it as being to 'prepare constructive political and economic policies for the countries concerned with the framework of greater European unity', while giving 'a strong emphasis to the moral and spiritual aspects'.[80] The following month André Philip, delegate general of the EM and a speaker at the Albert Hall returned to lecture on 'European Unity: Its Moral and Spiritual Base' at a CA meeting chaired by the pro-European Tory MP Robert Boothby. At the CA conference at High Leigh at the end of that year Monica Wingate, who was also a leading activist in Federal Union, lobbied for CA to include federalism among its interests.[81] Collins's energies, however, became absorbed elsewhere.

Church and State turn away from 'Europe'

Ever since before the war the relationship of the British to the project of European unity was deeply ambiguous, almost schizophrenic in its varying moods of enthusiasm and engagement, disenchantment and retreat. The frequently emphasised preference for 'unity' based on cultural or 'spiritual' forms of community and identity provided the flexibility and space for such double mindedness and what might also be seen as an attempt to enjoy the benefits of unity but without paying the full cost of its attendant commitments. With the proposal of the so-called Schuman and Pléven plans in 1950 this approach met its Waterloo. In May the French foreign minister Robert Schuman announced a scheme to 'pool' French and German coal and steel production under supra-national authority. Later that year the French prime minister, René Pléven proposed the creation of a 'European army'. Out of the former – in fact devised by Jean Monnet – came the European Coal and Steel Community while the latter proposal aimed to create the European Defence Community (EDC). While the EDC came to nothing when the French Assembly rejected it, the ECSC was the political and economic base from which the European Union would grow. The Labour government rejected both the ECSC and the EDC initiatives. There were a good many infelicities and political mistakes on both sides on the road to this outcome, but ultimately the longstanding disinclination to be drawn into any European commitments which might compromise wider British interests and a chronic allergy to federalism blocked the way.

It was at this point in the history of European integration that religion had what was perhaps its most decisive influence. At the time it was widely rumoured that the Schuman Plan had been 'conceived ... in Moral Re-Armament Circles'.[82] Moral Re-Armament (MRA) was inspired and lead by Dr. Frank Buchman, an American and ordained Lutheran minister. It originated with the First Century Christian Fellowship Buchman founded among students at Oxford at the beginning of the 1920s, which later became known as the 'Oxford Group' in the 1930s. Originally the Group had been broadly Trinitarian in its theology but by the late 1940s it had become much more doctrinally vague, still having a definite religious flavour but being much less specifically Christian. As such, it was strongly criticised by the established Protestant and the Catholic Churches, although not formally proscribed. The essence of MRA teaching was that wider social and political transformation was rooted in men and women first becoming 'changed' by dedicating themselves to the four 'absolute standards of honesty, purity, unselfishness and love'. Although this anodyne, intellectually simplistic and indeed commonplace stress on personal change, which formed the heart of what MRA called its 'ideology', was a prerequisite of the movement's influence it was not the primary reason for it. The value of this 'ideology' was that it was compatible with virtually any religion or even none and that it focussed on atomised individuals rather than offering a specific programme which might arouse the opposition of social fractions or political groupings. However, the twin catalysts for its success at the outset of the Cold War were, firstly, that it was also strongly anti-Communist and, secondly, that it had many influential friends, especially in the United States. It has been suggested elsewhere that the Cold War was not a 'decisive influence on Franco-German reciprocal attitudes until *after* the two sides were already on the verge of effecting their reconciliation by means of the Schuman Plan and the ECSC'.[83] This is completely at variance with the history of British and American foreign policy and those nations' involvement in the European movement after 1946, and it also exaggerates the role of MRA as an independent agency.[84]

To encourage European unity and, in particular, to dissolve the 'centuries-old fear and bitterness' between France and Germany became stated MRA aims. The claim that the circulation of MRA literature and the presentation of its sentimental stage revue 'The Good Road' could have caused the 'spirit' of MRA to begin to 'sweep through' France and Germany is unverifiable but intuitively unlikely.[85] Nonetheless, although it was also not correct that the Schuman Plan had been 'conceived' by the Buchmanites, there is good evidence that MRA had a significant role in fostering French and German agreement over the plan. In the later 1940s the MRA centre at Caux in Switzerland invited many German political leaders to join its international gatherings at a time when they were – with the important exception of the European movement[86] – otherwise still otherwise largely ostracised from the international community. Furthermore, Konrad Adenauer, the German chancellor and Robert Schuman, the French foreign minister, were both described as 'friends' of Buchman.[87] It was claimed that, except for a conversation between Buchman and Schuman, the Frenchman would have 'retreated into private life in 1949'.[88] In these respects, MRA may have served as a private forum or network for elite contact away from the more circumscribed environment of formal public talks. Following the signing of the Treaty of Paris in 1951, Adenauer, stated: 'In recent months we have seen the conclusion of important international agreements. Moral Re-Armament has played an unseen but effective part in bridging differences of opinion between the negotiating parties and has kept before them the aim of peaceful agreement in search for the common good'.[89] It is also indicative that Buchman was awarded high honours by both France and Germany shortly afterwards.[90]

It might also be asked, as a topic for further research, whether the MRA circle also functioned to connect the European movement to those elements of American opinion which were strongly in favour of European unity. As Tom Driberg notes of Adenauer: 'his friendship with Dr. Buchman seemed to grow steadily when Western Germany was consolidating its position as ... John Foster Dulles' favourite ally'.[91] Given that Roman Catholics were strongly discouraged from involvement with MRA, except 'under certain conditions and within certain limits', there must have been some very special instrumental reasons for a leading Christian Democrat to publicly endorse them. Recalling the abortive contacts between the Vatican and CA mentioned above, it seems that the Catholic Church was prepared at this time to tolerate some otherwise unpalatable alliances for reasons of political expediency. At the other side of the chain of influence, O'Brien has noted that MRA was 'supervised' by the Psychological Strategy Board, which was responsible for the CIA's psychological warfare programme in the early 1950s and there were also rumours at the time that MRA was in some part financed by the Agency.[92]

MRA, although not exclusively 'British' and becoming increasingly international in its interests and American in power base at this time, did have strong British roots going back to the 1920s. It was thus yet another irony that this movement, with its vaguely disreputable cultish and deviationist reputation, was so influential on European unity at the time when the established Christian Churches in Britain were turning away from the cause. There were exceptions, *The Tablet* did not falter in enthusiastically backing British participation in the ECSC. The paper recognised the Schuman proposals as a 'step of quite peculiar importance ... a step which is quite as much political and military as economic'. It also hoped that this might be a step towards the 'integration of Europe' which would be part of a larger community spanning the Atlantic and Africa.[93] Inevitably, the paper regretted the Attlee government had not been prepared to show 'a little genuine enthusiasm for the great vision of European unity' and Woodruff repeated the pro-unity message at every opportunity.[94] Elsewhere, the Jesuit John Murray described the Labour government's response as 'a party stand, not a national stand, and most certainly not a stand for and with Europe'.[95] The Bishop of Chichester took a similar position in a long speech in the House of Lord's debate on the Schuman Plan.[96] Whereas the Archbishop of Canterbury and other Lords spiritual generally restricted themselves to matters of specifically ecclesiastical interest, Bell gave a speech that any ardent, intelligent and well-informed pro-European might have made.

However, beyond these reliable sources of support, the British Churches remained largely silent at this crucial moment in the history of European integration. The BCC issued a memorandum on the contribution of the Churches to European Unity in February 1950[97] and the next year the subject was the second among its 'seven-point policy for joint action in international affairs'.[98] But the BCC's approach was particularly low key on this topic. In contrast to its significant activism concerning 'race relations' at home and in the Commonwealth, the Churches had 'not yet made any very conscious efforts to carry out the policy' of the BCC on European unity. Rather activities stayed at the level of inter-church contacts and material assistance to Continental churches through the Inter-Church Aid Department.[99] The Council hoped to promote its international policy through the departments of its constituent churches concerned with social and international affairs, to thereby 'reach the grass roots'. Aside from any intrinsic merit to this approach, the resources of the Council were limited and its structure of local Councils of Churches weak, meaning that this was really the only possibility. The fact that member Churches had to refer the BCC's policy to their own assemblies, which generally met only once a year, is also indicative of the considerable inertia build into the structure of the Churches.

In December 1951, *The Frontier*, reflecting on the consequences of the election of a new Conservative government headed by Churchill, noted that this development was being closely watched from the Continent by those hoping for a more 'affirmative line about the integration of Europe'. The use of a pseudonym 'Libra' – 'a student of European affairs, with considerable practical experience in the cultural and in the political field' – suggests that the author was in some form of government service.[100] Whoever it was, they showed an astute grasp of the political prospect: 'Individuals from Britain have done much to advocate this idea, but when it comes to action both national parties begin to lean backwards'. Assessing the national position in the world, Libra noted that the Commonwealth was by no means the passport to world power that the Empire had been and that the 'financial ghost' of British imperialism, the sterling area, was 'increasingly tenuous and precarious'. The nation's industries were in the process of being overtaken by Germany and Japan and its trading position was slipping away. Already British governments could no longer pursue their international policies independently and no matter that a common language might seem to relate Britain to America, the Superpower preferred that 'Britain should count herself in with Europe'. For these and other important reasons, Libra called for a definite commitment: 'We have now paid so much lip service to the ideal of Britain as part of the European political community that any more of it, unless accompanied by some practical commitment, begins to feel like a sin'.

'Libra's' analysis of the Britain's national position was acute and realistic. However, the new government's response to the ECSC and the EDC showed that it is no more willing to turn words into action than its predecessor. Concerning the EDC, Churchill commented 'I meant it for them, not for us'.[101] British policy remained unchanged at the time of the Messina Conference of 1955 and the Treaty of Rome two years later which established the European Economic Community (EEC). It was at this point that the opportunity to take a leading role in European integration was finally discarded by Britain. However, given their frequent references to the cultural tradition of European Christendom, and the claim that Christians' religious identity as members of a universal Church and human 'brotherhood' put them above the parochial claims of national identity, we might have anticipated that the Churches should have been the exception to the general British response. In fact the British Churches followed the same line of retreat.

British Churches and European Christendom

As a preamble to discussing the various reasons behind this it should first be recognised that Christian support for the European movement in the UK was, despite appearances, a shallowly rooted plant. For example, while the bald facts of the Albert Hall meeting seem to indicate a significant pro-European constituency among British Christians, closer examination throws this into question. The meeting's message was, one member of the audience suggested, indistinct, being mainly composed of 'honest platitudes about the strength of the "forces of Materialism," – implicitly Russian Communism – and the approach of the atomic war'.

'European Union' was only 'discreetly hinted at'.[102] Of the considerable correspondence that followed the meeting most focussed on the general conception of CA rather than European unity.[103] Whereas a capacity audience at the Albert Hall *could* be taken to indicate the basis of a popular movement, in all likelihood the pro-European lobby among Christians was a narrow group of activists and leaders and as shallow-rooted as the European movement in British society generally. The London correspondent of the *Manchester Guardian* noted that while the meeting should have been 'impressive' since the 'hall was packed ... and the platform ... was really notable', in fact 'the enthusiasm was tepid. The audience seemed to consist of middle-class churchgoers innocent of politics'.[104]

In reality, European unity was a cause introduced from above rather than something growing from popular concern. Even here, Collins's leadership had something of the 'tepid' quality of the Albert Hall audience. Persuaded to move from a humanitarian concern for the peoples of Europe to participation in the politics of European integration, an air of duty rather than conviction marked his involvement. This was detectable in CA's official explanation of its involvement that: 'whether Christians like it or dislike it, the Union of Western European Nations is a policy to which the government of Great Britain is now committed'.[105] Western Union was a matter for CA inasmuch that it was a question of public concern, and when it ceased to be, it slipped easily from Collins's agenda too. In contrast, when he was awakened to the evils of apartheid at the end of 1949, that became a matter of passionate and lifelong conviction. Writing to Lord Hailsham, Collins commented: '... somehow this South Africa business has got under my skin and I feel quite unable to keep quiet'.[106]

Part of the explanation for the decline of Christian interest in European unity was also that, in Collins's case, he was advocating a notionally 'right-wing' project opposed by many socialists. This indicated a deep flaw in Collins's general conception of CA. It was intended to be a non-party ginger group for Christian influence on public affairs and, thereby, to avoid the pitfalls of mixing faith and politics exemplified by Christian Democracy. However, at the same time Collins aimed to 'get away from generalising' and repudiated the common clerical hesitation to risk what he called 'the scandal of particularity'.[107] Inevitably this emphasis on specifics instead of platitudes made CA a political vehicle for Collins's own ideals and negated its original aim. However, where Christians agreed to eschew specifically political positions (for example, as in the BCC at this time), they were left uttering generalities about the spiritual component of the European tradition because almost all other aspects of the question involved specific technical questions or partisan issues.[108] Similar problems haunted Christian forays outside of the Churches' specific sphere generally.

Collins was equally unsuccessful in courting Christian opinion in the Labour Party.[109] Whereas the Labour government had originally encouraged the Churches to support Western Union, the party was deeply divided over the form integration should take or whether it should occur at all. Following Woodruff's suggestion to found CMEU, Collins had explored with Tina Bruce, Cripps's secretary, possible questions to put to the chancellor concerning its relationship to Labour: Was there any chance that the Party would change its negative attitude to the EM or should Collins go ahead with the creation of CMEU regardless? 'The urgency for this action' Collins argued, was that whereas French, Belgian and Dutch socialists were co-operating directly in what was becoming an increasingly influential movement on the continent, the Labour Party had remained aloof from what it regarded as a rightwing movement, dominated by Churchill and other Conservatives.[110] Bruce suggested that Collins should put his points to Cripps formally in a letter, but this probably did not occur. When the chancellor was asked to endorse CMEU his response was cool, writing that '[i]f we are to butt into Christian politics on the Continent we must consider much more carefully how it is to be done and what we are to say', and he closed the subject by refusing to trespass into the Foreign Secretary's 'domain'.[111]

In the Labour movement as a whole Christian opinion was represented by the Christian Socialist League and at Westminster by the Parliamentary Socialist Christian Group (PSCG). These two co-operated in 1949 to found the 1950 Group. Chaired by Thomas Skeffington Lodge, the PSCG had eighty odd members in both houses, including – besides Cripps – Acland, Stokes, Roy Jenkins and Harold Wilson and the Lords Jowitt, Pakenham and Lindsay. However, while Collins's pro-European moves gained the support of Stokes and Pakenham, other socialist Christians stayed aloof.[112]

If Collins was correct that the group was 'very much influenced by Communists, if not actually controlled by them', then the communist stance on European unity was a significant element barring co-operation.[113] Woodruff had been apprehensive about asking for signatories for the CMEU's appeal letter from the 1950 Group, fearing 'a resignation over the Soviet Union and our lack of co-operation with it'.[114] However, wrecking activities from Labour's crypto-communists were pretty much superfluous given the approach of the party generally.

Fearful of being drawn into discussions about a federal Europe and sus-
picious of the EM as Churchill's creature, the general party line was indicated by its ban on party members attending the Congress of Europe
in 1948. Even for socialists who favoured federalism there were fundamental political and ideological barriers to their involvement.[115]
Christian socialists identified Christian Democracy with 'Right and
Centre parties which do not look forward eagerly and positively to a
new society'.[116] Concerning the EM, Skeffington Lodge was dismissive
of '[v]ague co-operation with anti-Socialists' who opposed the principle
of social ownership, which Christian socialists believed was essential to
Europe's future. Without agreement on fundamentals, they would be
committing themselves to a coalition whose only unity would build
around anti-communism rather than the construction of a positive
alternative to it. Skeffington Lodge and three other PSCG members
appeared among the sixteen signatories of a pamphlet from R.W.G.
Mackay's Socialist Europe Group which warned 'socialists who join with
non-socialists or anti-socialists in a campaign for Western Union' that a
union run by 'anti-socialist movements' would not only be doomed to
failure but increase the risk of war.[117]

Among the exceptions to this stance were Catholics like Stokes and
Pakenham. This raises the linked question of how these Catholics managed to square membership of a socialist party with the teaching of their
Church. Although many Catholics did join Labour, and the attitude of
the Church's hierarchy to the British model of socialism was more
accommodating than to the more straightforwardly Marxian socialism
of the continental parties, there were significant tensions between
Church and Party. In any case, Stokes's socialism was not based on the
ideas of Marx or the Fabians but those of Henry George, and his 'single
tax' beliefs aside, his background and other opinions would have fitted
him well to cross the floor to the Liberals or even the Tories. One close
but critical friend described him as an 'avowed non-socialist' and his
anti-communism led him into some very murky waters.[118] Although
Pakenham saw himself as a socialist, it is significant that *The Tablet* preferred to describe his stance as one of 'personalism', and thus compatible
with Christian Democratic thought.[119] *People and Freedom* had suggested
that figures who bestrode the Labour movement and Christian
Democracy were tokens that Christian principles could be the basis for
a joint political movement. But this was a triumph of hope over what
were deep differences, and as Joan Keating has shown, the paths of
Labour socialism and British Christian Democracy diverged during the
1945–51 Labour governments.[120]

If these ideological and political cultural differences were not enough, an element of lingering Protestant suspicion of the 'Roman' flavour of European integration also existed. During the 1950s Mervyn Stockwood, a Christian socialist and close friend of Cripps and Collins, who later became Bishop of Southwark, spoke disparagingly of the European project on account of the political complexion of Christian Democracy.[121] He also counselled against any contacts with the Catholic Church, on account of the Sword of the Spirit episode having 'left a nasty taste in the mouth all round' as an 'insult' which would not be forgotten for a long time.[122] The roots of anti-Catholicism were many and varied. Collins pointed to a vein of 'extreme anti-Catholicism' among Christian socialists and Halifax also reported the expression of 'old Protestant prejudices' at a CA meeting.[123] Neither was this a tendency which was restricted to Collins's organisation.

Religion was a vital aspect of national identity and anti-Catholicism was central to constructions of British national identity from the Eighteenth century onwards.[124] However, as Hugh McLeod suggests, by the Twentieth century this foundation of Britishness became less important.[125] France was now an ally, and two wars fought against foes, who were not primarily identified in religious terms, provided new means to construct a common identity. Similarly, after 1870, imperialism provided another alternative basis for Britishness, in which the Other, if conceptualised religiously, was 'heathen' rather than Catholic. In any case, 'race' rather than religion increasingly became the primary element for constructions of national unity and difference. Apart from the in-coming tide of secularism, which had much diminished the social role of religion, the growth of Anglo-Catholicism in the Anglican Church during the nineteenth century had also diluted the purity of Protestantism and moderated its position. While Irish Catholics remained distanced from full social acceptance, increasing assimilation and the removal of the 'Irish question' from mainland politics had taken much of the heat out of that source of anti-Catholicism. On the positive side, during 1939–45 Catholics had worked to show themselves to be playing a loyal part in the 'peoples war'. Some leading Anglicans – in particular George Bell – attracted opprobrium for their critical positions. In contrast, Cardinal Hinsley in his public statements on the BBC and elsewhere lent an uncomplicated support to the war effort, while appropriating the symbols of Britishness as a sport-loving Yorkshireman. From 1940 onwards Hinsley's Sword of the Spirit movement and his co-operation with other church leaders had also begun to tentatively bridge the post-Reformation chasm of mutual rejection.[126]

However, whereas *popular* anti-Catholicism was much diminished, this ancient conflict was not negligible among many who were more than *nominally* Protestant. A significant minority of Evangelical Christians remained implacably hostile. From this perspective, Protestants appearing alongside Catholics at the Albert Hall was a 'dreadful apostasy'. *The English Churchman and St. James Chronicle* rejected co-operation to build a front against Communism: '... in the light of Holy Scripture's teaching, ... a working alliance with Romanism under any circumstance would be wrong. What fellowship can light have with darkness?' Catholicism was as much a threat as Communism. A reader's letter commented: 'The choice is not between Communism and Vaticanism, both are from a common source and are characterised by the same spirit and practises'. Furthermore, national identity remained closely linked to anti-Popery. An advert for the National Union of Protestants exhorted: 'If you are of the JOHN BULL breed you will not take these things "lying down". Romanism is trying to knock out, not only Protestantism, but any suspected rival to world domination'. This way of thinking led to a rejection of integration with continental Europe. *The English Churchman* warned its readers 'that "Christian," as a prefix to political party names on the Continent, commonly means "Romanist", and there is very general apprehension among true believers that Rome is endeavouring to create a Rome-sponsored *bloc* of nations'. The linkage of faith, national identity, and the rejection of integration was indicated in the view that the Schuman plan promised 'a union between ourselves, a Protestant nation and others, some—not all—Roman or godless'. 'Legis' continued: 'By all means co-operate, but not amalgamate. For England to surrender her sovereign power to a super-state would be yet another step towards our downfall'.[127]

Opinion among other Evangelicals about integration was frequently more positive.[128] However, alongside was a view of Catholicism which, while expressed more moderately, was not altogether dissimilar.[129] As the Congregationalist Nathaniel Micklem suggested, although the 'bad old rancour' had 'practically disappeared', a wary suspicion of Catholicism remained, and it continued to be seen as a definite threat – 'the Roman menace'. Micklem explained that while there was good in the Catholic church, much of its ecclesiology, doctrine, theology and aesthetics of worship were repellent to Protestants; its reactionary politics, corruption and worldly intriguing made it a 'terrible menace to freedom and even in many places to true religion itself'; in some countries it brought 'a blight upon the political, the intellectual and even the spiritual life'.[130] Tellingly, when Paul Blanchard's investigation of the threat of Catholicism to democracy in America appeared in a new edition with a first chapter 'It is a British problem too', the Free Churches Federal Council's official organ commended it as a corrective for those who believed there was 'no danger of Roman Catholics gaining power in this country'.[131] As long as such thinking existed, it would be a potential influence on evaluations of Christian Democracy and, therefore, of the European movement. A correspondent to the otherwise pro-integration *British Weekly* noted the 'quite remarkable degree of cordiality and unanimity between Catholic and Protestant' at the Albert Hall meeting but questioned the reality of this amity and criticised the presence of Free Church leaders on the same platform as Catholics while Church and State in Italy connived to deny non-Catholics full religious freedom.[132]

If these political and religious barriers to involvement in the European movement were not enough, British Christians were also no less subject to the influence of national identity than other groups. From one perspective they might have been expected to be less susceptible to nationalistic sentiment. While they endorsed the world of nations as part of the richness of God's creation, at the same time they represented the community of Christians as supra-national and declared that the claims of religious identity preceded all others. However, whereas the Churches' supra-nationality might loosen the bonds of nationality, and Christendom as a historical formation was European, universal brotherhood implied a global rather than regional target. A Christian linkage of Christendom to modern Europe was questionable. Whereas the Church, Christendom, Europe and the known world were once virtually one and the same, in the twentieth century, life was global, and Christianity a world religion. The association of a *reborn* Christendom with Europe was not universally accepted. There was nothing preventing specific regional arrangements within a global order, but was there anything specifically Christian about a united Europe, except perhaps as a step to world brotherhood?

Hence, CA involvement was not rooted in a belief that European unity was something good in itself, but only as 'a step towards world peace'.[133] The Society of Friends were not represented at the Albert Hall meeting and refused CA the use of one of its halls because they objected to it being 'only in support of Western Union and not World Union'.[134] This was typical of the wider Christian ambivalence concerning European, as opposed to, world unity. For this reason, any association of a *reborn* Christendom with 'the West' or Europe was fundamentally problematic. CA's response was to stress that its support for Western Union was fundamentally pragmatic, and only as a step towards other things: 'World Union is still as important as ever and must be our constant aim; European Union however is an emergency and is vital to our very existence'.[135] Similarly, Collins reassured Edith Ellis, who was 'anxious lest Christian Action should get caught up with the politics of Western Union and neglect to stand for the principles of world peace', that CA was 'only concerned with Western Union insofar as we can influence it in a Christian direction'.[136] It was stressed that it was not accidental that African, Chinese and Indian Christians were also represented at the Albert Hall meeting.[137]

In addition to their identification with the Church, with human 'brotherhood', and – via Christendom – to Europe, every Christian was also part of a national community. How then did 'Britishness' relate to these other modes of identity? Bell had represented himself as 'a lover of my country ... as a profound believer in the ideals of liberty and justice in defence of which Great Britain went to war', but also as speaking 'with a faith in something more than patriotism', as 'a minister of the Church of Christ, which ... is universal in its range' and which would be 'the principle source of the spiritual recovery of Europe and the world'.[138] This suggested the harmonious interrelationship of the four modes of identity discussed here. However, Christian cosmopolitanism was no less susceptible to being overridden by national sentiment than the internationalism of secular groups. But this reversion was typically not to a *European* consciousness but to formations which were either insular in their Englishness or global in their Britishness.

In terms of the former, the Church of England was not only the national Church, but also a central part of the pastoral, pre-modern mythic core of 'Englishness'.[139] As to the 'Britishness' of the Churches, comments in the journal of the Christian Frontier Council were typical. Surveying 'the British Attitude' to 'Europe', *Frontier* suggested that if Britain lacked:

> ... the same feeling of urgency about Europe, the obvious reason is that her sense of an imperial mission, strengthened through several generations has never been weakened by a major defeat. ... It is naturally harder for Britain than for the continental nations to feel conscious of an organic relation to Europe, or to accept a more intimate part in its affairs with positive conviction ...[140]

Certainly the BCC shared in the allegiances and global focus of British foreign policy. Alongside its commitment to European unity, it stressed that it would also maintain 'the close partnership of the Commonwealth countries and the membership of the Atlantic community, based on Anglo-American friendship'. It was telling that its study of 'the "Future of Europe and the Responsibility of our Churches"' was undertaken by the British members of an 'Anglo-American group'.[141]

A significant cultural difference was also perceived to separate Britons and Continentals. Grubb, replying to Ronald Rees's suggestions for 'increasing the moral and spiritual vigour of Europe' through contacts with sympathetic Continental churchmen and meetings, suggested that the latter 'despised' the 'slow, small but very practical steps' of the British approach. Grubb suggested that the most fruitful approach might be to tour the continent with the message: 'We British Christians are taunted that we stand aside. We don't want to. But we must first discovered just where to make our contribution, and want to learn from you'.[142] In the end, Waddams commented that, in the absence of clear objectives, no action should be taken.[143]

Given that anti-Catholic feeling was particularly strong among Protestants in Scotland,[144] the sustained support of the Church of Scotland for a project generally identified with Rome is perhaps surprising.[145] However, despite its stance on Catholicism, and being an established state church tied closely into the British imperial project, the Church of Scotland was also denominationally joined to continental Calvinism, such that it could stress 'its historic links with European countries'. Among the factors that its Committee on Church and Nation identified as being behind the British rejection of integration, included 'commonwealth responsibilities' and 'insular traditions'.[146]

In this respect, Christian attitudes paralleled those in the wider debate around the question, as posed by Sir Harold Butler: 'Can We Be European Patriots?'[147] Butler's answer – he was also of the ELEC – was 'yes', but all the evidence suggests 'no'. As Hugh Dalton explained when the Labour conference debated the formation of a 'United States of Europe', the difference between the Commonwealth and the continent was that '[i]f you go to those countries you find yourself at home in a way that you do not if you go to a foreign country as distinct from a British community overseas'.[148] Such sentiments may even have been stronger among the Churches than elsewhere. The Church of England was at the head of a worldwide communion which was almost completely extra-European – not until 1980 was a diocese of [continental] Europe created, jurisdiction over that area being previously divided between the Bishops of London and Gibraltar. While the empire was only occasionally at the forefront of the British imagination it was

deeply implicated in the underlying assumptions and emotional economy of Britishness. Through their overseas missions, the Churches had
been at the heart of imperialism from beginning to end and their continuing commitments and denominational links to the 'young' churches
in the Commonwealth meant that the Churches had more reason to
still think in global terms than perhaps any other domestic institution.
As late as 1964, the general secretary of the BCC would state: 'We British
feel we only belong in a very partial way to Europe. It is not only our
island state ... It is that our lines have gone out to Canada and
Nyasaland, to New Zealand and India every bit as much as across the
narrow straits of Dover'.[149]

*

For a brief moment in the late 1940s it seemed that the aims of the
Churches and the British state were aligned to take a leading and positive role in the building of a new Europe with Britain at its head. When,
some years later, Harold Macmillan began what was effectively a forced
turn towards Europe the influence of both parties in the process was no
longer what it was: Britain was now a weakened supplicant and the
social role and influence of the Churches in the life of the nation was
advanced further in its rapid and accelerating decline. But could it have
been any different? Beneath the surface of spiritual union, be it in the
vague secular form envisioned by Churchill or Bevin or as the Churches'
reborn Christendom, lay barely repressed differences of ideology, theology, history, culture and identity, which any move from the rhetorical
to the concrete brought to the surface. In a society which lacked an
emotional identification with Europe, and had no compelling reason
yet to turn away from the fading dream of world power, both spiritual
union and Western Union were seeds sown on stony ground.

6
Christendom, Communism and the Division of Europe

It was one of the many ironies of the integration of Western Europe that the grounds for its rapid progress in the 1940s and 1950s owed so much to Cold War forces and polices which were simultaneously destructive to the unity of Europe as a whole. The forced separation and isolation of the nations of the eastern half of the continent for over forty years was even, in a limited, but real sense, a consequence of unity in the West. That the Churches, which spoke so much of recovering the unity of Christendom and thus of Europe, were active agents in these divisive processes illustrates further the tragic irony of the moment.

But then it is the nature of politics that ideal ends are pursued with impure means, that power, pragmatism and principle are often complexly and problematically muddled together. British relations with the Soviet Union in the 1940s, which were at the intimate heart of this unity making and breaking moment, exemplify this almost without peer. Winston Churchill, who, in wartime, often represented the British as fighting in the cause of 'Christian civilisation', defended the Anglo-Soviet alliance of the time by saying that, had 'Hitler invaded Hell, I would at least make a favourable reference to the Devil in the House of Commons'. In other words, if the liberal 'British way of life' could only survive the onslaught by one totalitarian power with the support of another, so be it. In both war and peace, international relations see a continual negotiation between power and principle. 'Negotiation' implies that while principles might begin pure, they must almost always be compromised to be realised at all.

The problem of international relations in the 1940s

In the 1940s, the general idealistic aim of British diplomacy might be crudely summarised as being to create the conditions for liberal

conceptions of freedom, peace and prosperity to return. The first prerequisite of this was the defeat and removal of fascism in Germany.
Space and light would thereby be created for the liberal ideal to grow
again in Western Europe, but the cost of this was a transfusion of Soviet
blood and totalitarian military might to supplement democratic economic power and wealth. Satan was to be cast out by Satan, or at least
with Devil's help.

Consequently, the Anglo-Soviet treaty (1942) was signed and gestures
of friendship exchanged. Among the British public a genuine and
appreciable respect grew for the Soviet peoples and their fighting forces.
The wartime British national government was party to the series of
meetings between the leaders of the 'Big Three' Allies where the conduct
of the war and its aftermath were agreed, at Teheran in 1943 and Yalta
and Potsdam in 1945. It was also at Yalta, and at conferences at
Dumbarton Oaks (1944) and San Francisco (1945), that the Allies successfully planned and negotiated the creation of the United Nations to
replace the failed League. In 1945 Britain's first viable socialist government was elected with a landslide majority. 'Left understands Left', it
was claimed at the time, and there was a genuine will from the incom-
ing prime minister, Clement Attlee and many other British decision
makers to work out a functional and stable post-war international
order.[1]

On the Soviet side, there were also signs of a readiness to establish a
modus vivendi. The traditional symbol of Soviet world revolutionary
ambition, the Comintern, had been abolished in 1943 and would only
be replaced by Cominform in September 1947. The Communist Party of
Great Britain and the other more important western communist parties
were directed to explicitly disavow the 'revolutionary' path and take the
'parliamentary road to socialism'. Limited, but real, co-operation continued between the wartime 'big three'. Stalin abided by his earlier
agreement with Churchill that Greece should remain in the western
sphere and kept out of the civil war there. In Moscow in 1944 and at
Yalta Churchill had correspondingly agreed with Stalin that the Soviet
Union should be predominant in Poland and the rest of Eastern Europe,
to ensure the security of its western borders. These agreements had
come with the rider that free elections should be permitted. The Soviet
Union did not comply with the spirit of this part of the agreement, but
then the Western powers also fostered coups d'etat and maintained corrupt client governments in their spheres of influence. The withdrawal
of Soviet forces from Iran in 1946 and, later, from Austria in 1955
showed that the Red Army could leave peacefully.

At the same time nothing had changed fundamentally. The Soviet Union remained an object of suspicion in the Foreign Office and among politicians of all parties. Ever since 1917, Marxism–Leninism as theory and praxis had been seen as fundamentally incompatible with a world made safe for bourgeois democracies. Even while fighting together against Germany, Britain's military leaders planned for possible conflict with the Soviet Union. Following the defeat of Germany it was increasingly 'business as usual' in the Foreign Office's approach to Bolshevism, with its return to a defensive politics of power by 1946. Even within the British 'left', the Labour party had consistently stood for democratic socialism and explicitly rejected Soviet totalitarianism and state terrorism. Apart from their knowledge of communism in the Soviet Union, British socialists had experienced the Communist Party of Great Britain as a duplicitous source of endless friction within the Labour movement. Likewise, in Moscow fear mingled with intense, paranoid suspicion. Neither was Soviet paranoia groundless. The country was devastated after the third major offensive from the west in 40 years. Whereas western liberal democracies posited fascism and communism as brothers from the same totalitarian family, seen from the east bourgeois democracy was the bitch that gave birth to fascism. In the 1940s fascism had aimed to destroy socialism in the USSR; after the Great War the Western democracies had pursued the same counter-revolutionary objective. If, from the perspective of historical materialism, fascism was the product of the later stages of the decay of bourgeois society, then it was also clear that the bitch was still fertile. The circumstances were such that relations could only be fundamentally unstable, potentially explosive. In the short term, the best that could be expected was that delicate handling could delay the critical moment as long as possible, perhaps so long that its explosive force might gradually decay.

However, Winston Churchill's 'sinews of peace' speech of March 1946 – delivered in careful co-ordination with the foreign ministries of Britain and the United States – articulated the emerging policy and its rhetorical tone. An 'iron curtain' had divided the continent, and in the West, communism was 'a growing challenge and peril to Christian civilization'. Strength was all, and 'appeasement' in the 1940s would bring the same disaster as appeasement in the 1930s. The great difference was that, whereas 1917 had prompted British military intervention against the Bolsheviks, by 1945 the red spectre of the inter-war period had become a monster of a different order. The Soviet Union was no longer a distant menace contained behind the bulwark of a strong Germany but a military behemoth casting a shadow over western Europe. As already suggested, the support of the United States was vital to British plans. After 1945, British foreign policy returned to a version of the old 'balance of power' model but, as things stood, the scales were heavily weighted towards the East. Germany was out of the picture, France short of everything but pride and America was rapidly returning to its own domestic concerns. Thus the reversal of policy and rhetoric was not simply for domestic consumption or to signal British resolve to the Kremlin but also to help 'educate' America to play its role in the post-war world.

From 1946 onwards, dialogue broke down, such that, by 1948, the relations between East and West had become a trial of strength conducted in a deadly atmosphere of fear and hatred, under a fog of misapprehension and suspicion. With the breakdown of wartime's alliance of convenience even the limited objective of the coexistence of the two incompatible systems was apparently impossible, leaving the West facing a totalitarian, military superpower whose supposed ideological aim was world revolution and which now dominated not only the former Russian empire but also the east of a now divided Europe. But it was also the case that more total war – should it have been palatable to any of the exhausted erstwhile allies – was in any case soon made impossible by nuclear weapons.

As we now know, the 'solution' to this problem went as close to world war as was possible without pressing the doomsday button. Vast wealth and human energy was squandered in decades of arms race. In the West politics – and so propaganda – became war by other means. However, this was merely the rhetorical side of long and bloody conflict which elsewhere in the world was anything but 'cold'. On the so-called periphery – in the Middle East, Africa, South East Asia and Latin America – territorial conflicts, civil wars and the tensions of de-colonisation were massively exaggerated by the global bipolar disorder. In Europe itself, most of the eastern and central area of the continent remained frozen in a coma-like condition under the sterile conditions of totalitarianism. And here too the populations of Poland, Hungary and Czechoslovakia were subject to armed intervention to maintain the status quo. In short, the wartime hopes for a new European unity were exchanged for 45 years of bitter division during which the continent was cut in two.

*

The second half of the 1940s was a moment of wasted opportunities. The hot war against fascism was not followed immediately by cold war against communism. For the first few years after 1945 the classic 'bipolar' ordering that would dominate world affairs until 1991 was absent. America had withdrawn the mass of its military might from Europe and was showing many signs of retreating back to its traditional isolationism. As we have already noted, in this dawning age of the superpowers Britain had the ambitions and responsibilities of a world power but without the material and political resources to support them. However, although weaker than either of the new superpowers at the beginning of the nuclear age, Britain was not entirely without advantages. Unlike wealthy, powerful but historically isolationist America, bankrupt Britain was rich in the experience of wielding world power. Despite her economic weakness and critically overstretched military resources, Britain had a median position and potentially pivotal role between the superpowers at the outbreak of the Cold War. In a few years this position and the possibility for forging a workable global polity would be gone as world affairs assumed the bi-polar form in which everything, including British policy, was subordinated to the logics of the superpower conflict.

Political culture and the power of the Churches

If a *modus vivendi* between East and West had emerged in the 1940s, the character of the meetings of allied foreign ministers before their breakdown in 1947 indicates that any dialogue would have necessarily been deeply problematic. The radical differences between the values, assumptions and histories of the individualistic, liberal capitalist West and the authoritarian, collectivist and state-socialist East meant that any dialogue was always going to be – at best – tentative, fragmentary and painfully slow. Ultimately, hopes for fundamental progress or fraternal friendship where futile between sides so radically divided. However, the continuation of meaningful dialogue, no matter how compromised, would have nonetheless been a basis for a more workable and less costly relationship between opponents.

One important determinant variable in this respect was the political culture of the time, that is the discourses and rhetorical tropes within which questions of policy were framed, and which contributed to the background assumptions informing specific discussions and negotiations and the emotional economy surrounding relations. It was because this political culture *was* important that both sides devoted so much energy and resources to the war of words. This was why during the war years British government departments had worked to encourage a limited but real sympathy for the Soviet Union by conducting all public voices, including those of the Churches. As a leading official in the wartime MOI stated, 'the Russians study the pronouncements of Archbishops and are sensitive to almost everything in daily, weekly and even sectional press of this country'.[2] To seek a dialogue in a political culture such as that of the late 1940s – one which was rhetorically violent and polarised – was to weight that effort towards failure. The importance of the war of words was why the British State then reversed its policy, working to make communist Russia the ogre of world affairs in the eyes of the British public but most importantly of all, in the official mind of the United States.

In contrast, the Churches claimed not only to have a special duty to foster peace and comity between the nations, but also perceived themselves to have a particular historical relationship with – and therefore, duty to – Europe as a 'spiritual' community. As to their capacity as forces in this struggle, the Churches possessed the influence accrued from their long histories, their interconnections to state and/or political power and their unique authority in individual and communal lives. In continental Europe during the 1940s the Christian Democratic parties offered an explicit conduit for Christian influence. While party politics did not take a confessional form in the United Kingdom, the Churches were not without power there either. They were an important former of opinion in the public sphere and common life generally, but were also connected intimately into the State and ruling elite. Furthermore, this traditionally close relationship with the state had been enhanced and extended by the leading role which the Churches played in the war of words against Germany. Political culture was a crucial theatre of operation in the Cold War, in some ways the most important in as it was the basis on which so much action was premised, and it was a sphere in which the Churches were well adapted to operate, where their power lay and the reason that they mattered.

The Churches and Soviet communism

By the 1930s, the Churches had their own theologically founded critique of totalitarianism. Totalitarian systems were rejected as incompatible with Christianity inasmuch that, by claiming that there was no higher authority than the State, they denied the sovereignty of the values and laws which the Church held to be God-given, transcendent and universal. On this the Churches were united, as evinced by the message of the Protestant Churches at the Oxford ecumenical conference of 1937 – from which the WCC came later – and in the Papal encyclical

'Mit Brennender Sorge' of the same year.[3] As we have seen, during the war years there was an almost ideal fit between Christian ideals and an uncompromising opposition to fascism and, while sometimes resisting the description of the war as a 'crusade', almost all church leaders (except for those who took an absolute pacifist position) aligned themselves behind the war effort. Although not without much agonising, the Archbishop of Canterbury, William Temple, defended Britain's bombing campaign against German cities. As one cynical observer noted: 'The Anglican Church ... lost no time in supporting the principle of "Gott mit uns", and in this was backed up by most other well-known and reliably advertised brands of Christianity'.[4] However, if pagan Nazism was damned in the eyes of the Churches' for its totalitarianism and terrorism, so was Britain's wartime ally, atheistic Soviet communism.

The Christian critique of the Soviet system took a number of directions: The abrogation of religious freedom, the persecution of individual Christians and churches in state policy and day-to-day practice in the USSR and its satellites. Alongside these specifically religious concerns and their sympathy for persecuted believers, the Churches also had a powerful systemic critique of Marxism–Leninism. The rise of the secular state and the various economic, political, and intellectual-cultural transformations which together constituted modernity had increasingly eroded but not closed the space for Christianity in European society. In this regard, Soviet communism, while a development from the general historical trends of modernity, was more ambitious. Liberal democracies might have progressively usurped the social functions of the Churches and generally secularised state and society but they nonetheless left open a space for a plurality of beliefs to exist. Soviet communism was a totalitarian system in the purest sense: It not only invaded both the public and private spheres of society but also possessed its own complete and hermetic belief system, worldview and cosmology. Totalitarianism elevated the State to become the supreme source of morality and subordinated individual men and women according to amoral, collectivist materialism to become merely devices for the achievement of the ideological aims of the State. By so doing, Marxism–Leninism had displaced the God's moral order from its position as the transcendent datum of all actions and rejected the Christian concept of the individual human life as sacred. Backed by the intellectual conviction and sense of historical mission of its bearers and the surveillance and disciplinary apparatus of an authoritarian state, this alternative social order and culture would tend, and intended to, expel all other belief systems, spiritual or secular from society. Communism was a materialistic pseudo-religion which not only rejected Christian teaching but sought to fill the role of the Church in society.

Whereas some Christians might see in socialism egalitarian, liberating and empowering aims and so see Soviet communism as a good thing gone bad, it remained the case that for all it was, as George Bell wrote in 1953, 'the most powerful challenge to the Christian religion today'.[5]

Falling in love with Soviet Russia

For the British State in wartime the black and white rhetoric of the struggle against Nazism was obviously impossible in respect of Soviet totalitarianism. Such an alignment of power and principle would be radically inexpedient. Instead the propaganda apparatus of the British wartime state set out to warm political relations by fostering Anglo-Soviet 'friendship'. William Paton wrote in 1942 of how 'Russia is in possession of the hearts of the masses of the people of Britain to-day, and in many other countries it is thought that we have gone too far and too fast in our change of emotional attitude'.[6] How stood the Churches in the face of the messy struggle between power and principle, *realpolitik* and idealism?

At one level, the Churches were unworldly and 'cloistered', speaking for principle and holding up an icon of the ideal. But it was also their appointed duty to go out into 'the world', to work for the good, with all the moral compromises and ambiguity that implied. Furthermore, having watched so closely and spoken so loudly but impotently during the decades of crisis leading to the 1939–45 war, Church leaders were also acutely aware of the relationship between power and ideals in the world. They understood that to pursue the latter without the former was futile. Joseph Oldham wrote: 'This element of power, as this generation is far more fully aware than its predecessors, is not a transient or subsidiary element in human life but an essential and cardinal factor in the historical process. Ideas and ways of life can become effective in history only embodiment in systems of power'. The responsibility of believers was to 'act responsibility in the conflicts of our time on the plane of the struggle for power'.[7]

Thus, despite their misgivings about the persecution of religion in the USSR and their rejection of totalitarianism, the British Churches managed to balance ideals and political expediency and play a full part in the State's propaganda effort. As Dianne Kirby has so effectively shown, the Church of England worked in concert with the Foreign Office and the MOI, notably in the visit of Cyril Garbett, Archbishop of York, to

Moscow in 1943.[8] Garbett's visit was a symbol for consumption at home and abroad, among friend and foe. Churchmen were also prominent in official efforts to warm opinion towards the Soviet Union in neutral countries.[9] A volume dealing with the European Churches' resistance to Nazism, authored by leading members of the Religions Division at the MOI, noted the 'position of Christianity in Russia' was 'complicated', before gratefully putting the topic to one side. Looked at objectively, the extent and severity of the persecution of the Church by the Bolsheviks since 1917 far exceeded that of Nazism in Germany and Western Europe. However, a fig leaf to shade ecclesiastical blushes came in the shape of the moderation of Soviet policy towards the Orthodox Church after 1941. The authors commented that 'present co-operation' between Church and State in the USSR held 'out hopes for a more fruitful partnership in the days to come'.[10] Bishop Bell, who was closely in touch with the thinking of German and other continental Christians, spoke of how it seemed to them that 'Britain had "fallen in love" with Russia'.[11]

Before the fall of the Iron Curtain

At the same time, the Christian approach was not – or at least it aimed not to be – conventional political realism in a dog collar. New testament teaching emphasised hope underwritten by self-sacrifice. In 1947 a 'distinguished Churchman', whose public position was such as to make it 'desirable that he should write anonymously', offered readers of the Student Christian Federation some notes towards understanding relations with the Soviet Union. He emphasised an open-minded approach and warned against too easily accepting predispositions which were 'fatally easy to adopt'. The Christian attitude should be 'permeated with the spirit of love'. He wrote: 'This does not mean that facts are misinterpreted, but it does involve the exclusion of condemnation until all the facts are so well established and overwhelming that it is inevitable'. Such an attitude might result in 'betrayal and loss', but such a danger was 'not incompatible with New Testament teaching'.[12] A similar attitude of mind was advertised by Joseph Oldham, who wrote that 'If the love of God possesses our being, we shall be filled with overflowing goodwill towards the Russian people'. Christians should 'spare no pains to break down all barriers ... in the way of mutual understanding', and exhibit an 'attitude of goodwill'. While defending the liberal, 'free society' of the West, this must be combined with 'open-mindedness towards communist Russia, an infinite readiness to learn and determination to understand'.[13]

After 1941 the imperatives of the politics of power could combine with this open-mindedness to encourage an approach to the Soviet Union combining not only realism but also hope. On the basis of 'two long talks' with Sir Stafford Cripps and the British ambassador to Moscow, Sir Archibald Clark Kerr, William Paton noted that they were 'convinced, rightly or wrongly, that Russia is now overwhelmingly nationalist and not much interested in trying to subvert the economies of other nations from within'.[14] As noted above, in March 1944, after PAG had a final draft for 'The Future of Europe', it began a survey of Soviet domestic and foreign policy through a sub-committee chaired by Kenneth Grubb. This time there was no intention for the group to make a public statement, the situation was too delicate. Instead it was hoped to prepare a 'short, well-reasoned document' for circulation among a 'limited influential circle' and to provide a source of 'discreet guidance' for any 'prominent person' preparing a public statement. Grubb mentioned Peace Aims Group's close relationship to the Commission to Study the Basis of a Just and Durable Peace in America and the 'wide difference' between public opinion on the subject between the two countries. In comparison with Britain, a preoccupation with the war in East Asia, where the Red Army was not engaged and the anti-Russian animus of Polish-American opinion were more likely to foster a negative opinion in the United States. The unspoken implication here was that, once again, Peace Aims Group could act as an oblique lever on American public opinion. A similar aim was envisaged at home – 'Britain's foreign policy, as much as her domestic depends on the endorsement of her people'.[15]

At this point in the war thinking about Anglo-Soviet relations was naturally focussing more and more on the future. The German armies were retreating inexorably before the Red Army in the East and the long-awaited invasion of Western Europe was imminent. The defeat of Germany was now only a matter time and then, Grubb wrote, the West would be 'faced with a non-Christian Russia, flushed with power and victory, able to play, if it wishes, a leading part in the community of Europe'. The 'obvious danger of to-morrow', was 'the division of Europe into two camps. The East led by the USSR, the West led by Britain'.[16] One of the principal aims of the sub-committee was to work to encourage public understanding in those aspects of British and Soviet relations which were 'liable to misunderstanding'.[17]

Grubb decided to begin by looking at the USSR's external relationships and the implications for the 'Christian conscience' of the 'doctrine of political expediency', of issues relating to the possible 'cultural autonomy' of the Baltic nations and conflicts over the future of

Germany. Acutely foreseeing the future challenge, Grubb wrote of how '[i]n the next few years much intelligent understanding, forbearance and firmness will be needed in awkward passes if Anglo-Soviet relations are to be traversed with success'. Among the topics for discussion was the question of how often 'difficulties' in such relations arose from differences of 'tactics or of principles'.[18] As to what the Russians' own approach to the post-war settlement would be, typically that appeared to be enigmatic, even for someone with access to the best sources. As he stated when the group met: '... very little could be prophesied of what the Russians' approach to the peace was likely to be'. Grubb's own interpretation of Russia's aims was cautiously positive, he wrote a few months later that: '[T]he USSR still remains an enigma. My own view is that Russia does not desire too prominent a part in continental affairs, but defined and secure boundaries, peace for internal development and a dominant interest in East European questions'.[19] Beyond that the USSR 'would probably throw her weight wherever possible on the side of collective friendship for peace'. However, he conceded that Soviet appetites might grow as they became more conscious of their strength.[20]

Two years later, tension was growing in East–West relations. Oldham commented how Soviet policy had adopted a stance of 'aggressive independence' coupled with a 'ruthless disregard for human rights and a callous indifference for human suffering'. He noted the conviction of his influential US ecumenical colleague Reinhold Niebuhr that the Soviet aim was to conquer the whole of Europe.[21] But both sides in this mounting struggle had a case:

> The Russians have plenty of grounds for distrust of the Western Powers. America is establishing military bases within striking distance of Russia. It has the atomic bomb and no assurances can efface from Russian memories the fact that America with the concurrence of Great Britain has used it. Behind much of the manoeuvring at meetings of the United Nations lies the rivalry of national interests in oil. To what lengths will the economic drives of American capitalism be pushed? How far will business demand military protection? To what extent is the American Government in effective control of hidden and anonymous forces, which may force it into courses other than it may wish to follow? Great Britain also has started a drive for world trade to re-establish its position.[22]

Oldham wrote this in the context of prevalent talk in America 'about a preventative war before Russia gets the atomic bomb'.[23] The Committee on Church and Nation of the Church of Scotland believed that the 'fear and suspicions' arising from the Western monopoly of nuclear weapons, and its jealous guarding of the vital scientific knowledge to manufacture them were 'poisoning the whole atmosphere of negotiations'.[24]

It is probably significant that, when Grubb and Temple discussed the formation of the USSR sub-committee, one of the reasons given for not inviting the Catholic bishop Matthew was that the difference between Catholic and Protestant approaches to Russia was too 'wide'.[25] If there was an exception, which proved the rule in this respect, it was Barbara Ward. Ward was an authority on economic and foreign affairs, who had been the assistant editor of *The Economist* since 1940, and had also co-operated in wartime with the MOI, on speaking tours in the United States. She was also well known as a broadcaster for the BBC on international affairs and on its long running 'Brains Trusts'.[26] Already an incisive voice on foreign affairs at Chatham House and in Christian circles, at the beginning of the Cold War she gained a much wider general audience. During the period between the end of the war and the beginning of the Cold war, her thinking exemplifies the lost possibilities of this moment.

Writing around late 1946 and early 1947, Ward provided a detailed and critical survey of both Western and Eastern systems. At this time she wrote against the notion of 'taking sides', that the contending superpowers possessed an 'underlying resemblance'.[27] Both systems were materialistic, and ultimately amoral and anti-human. At this point in history she did not see that East and West were 'completely irreconcilable' and even held that their dialectic might be 'fruitful'.[28] At the same time the tendency of the times was worrying:

> At present mutual hostility is accentuating the worst elements of each side. The more the Russian Government fears and distrusts the West, the more it reinforces the system of iron dictatorship, the more rigidly it imposes Communist control and orthodoxy on neighbouring countries ... Equally, fear of Russia is driving the United States into a mood of hysterical nationalism in which all hope of genuine international co-operation is fading, and instead, an aggressive and expansive American foreign policy is taking place of the old isolationism. This policy for Europe has the result of resurrecting and supporting many of the men and groups who formerly supported the Nazis ...[29]

This increasingly explosive situation posed what Ward called a 'test of British statesmanship'. Britain was 'no longer a Titan among the

Powers' but might be hold the 'balance between peace and war'. Ward continued:

> The world is tending to become polarised between the two extremes of Russia and the United States. This division is creeping into every economic and political problem ... Can this tension be resolved? Can the polarisation be broken? Almost certainly the answer lies with Britain, but British statesmanship can meet this challenge only if it pursues its domestic and foreign policies with the utmost fore-thought and at the same time the utmost courage and resolution. ... [S]uccess turns on Britain's ability to maintain a policy independent of both Russia and America and to associate itself with like minded nations of Europe and the Commonwealth. ... These are the stakes for British statesmanship. No nation ever faced so great a task.[30]

Writing around the same time, Oldham had also pointed to a British role in diffusing the immediate danger of war '... a right foreign policy on the part of Great Britain may do something, perhaps much, to miti-gate existent tensions and diminish the risks on an explosion'.[31] By the summer of 1947 the issue was not so much preventing the division of Europe but avoiding war. In anticipation of the Christendom group's summer school, it was noted that such a division was 'must be accept-ed by anyone not wilfully blind as ... now unavoidable ... The only question remaining open is whether this arbitrary dichotomy must sooner or later involve armed conflict'. Even when the group had met to discuss similar questions five years earlier, when Nazi Germany was still at the height of its power, the 'mood was ... incomparably more hopeful and high-hearted' than in 1947.[32]

Ward's approach was in great contrast to what Ronald Preston of the Student Christian Movement described as Rome's 'blank hostility to Communism everywhere' and its tendency to ally itself with 'reactionary groups', in a fashion similar to the American recruitment of former fas-cists, which Ward had noted.[33] Preston was well aware that the International Union of Students (IUS) – which was to be formed in Prague that summer – was yet another Soviet 'front' and that 'Communists may well be short-term allies, under certain curtain circumstances, even though they may be long term enemies'. Nonetheless, dialogue between Christians and communists was 'urgent' and the IUS offered an 'invalu-able place where Eastern and Western Europeans can meet and learn from one another', anything which crossed 'the "iron curtain"' was 'to be encouraged'. Hence, Preston recommended a positive but clear-sighted rather than naïve engagement. In the context of the anticipated ending of the US monopoly of atomic weapons, and the certainty that a nuclear war would see the end of civilisation, these contacts were expedient and urgent to preserve 'the peace of the world'. Preston continued: 'It may be the tackling of short-term problems may so modify circumstances that a head-on collision can be avoided and the world achieve the minimal unity necessary for its preservation'. Around the same time, a similar fusion of realism and flexibility was shown in the *Free Church Chronicle*.[34] Apart from pointing to the importance of prayer to the solution of what was 'in the last analysis' a spiritual problem, this article noted that in the political and economic sphere: 'If Russia has ... a just cause or a sound claim, we must acknowledge it. If there is anything wrong in our policy, too obviously the pursuit of our own secular interest, we must remove it. We must use every means of finding a *modus vivendi* between Russia and the West, so long as it does not involve a compromising of truth and righteousness'.

Part of the problem was that, as Grubb had judged earlier, the Kremlin's thinking was enigmatic; and Church and Nation stated in 1947, Soviet diplomacy was so often 'obscure and incalculable'.[35] The truthful answer to many questions about Soviet intentions was to reply, as the former British Ambassador to Moscow, Lord Inverchapel (formerly Archibald Clark Kerr), had at the Paris Conference, 'I don't know'. However, Oldham saw that ignorance could not be blissful: 'We don't know. And yet incalculable consequences may depend on our guessing rightly and acting in accordance with our guess'.[36]

Taking sides

In early 1948, the Parliamentary Socialist Christian Group (PSCG) conceded that '[r]ecent Russian diplomacy' had been 'irritating' but rejected the fatalistic conclusion that war was inevitable. A *modus vivendi* – to use the term employed in its pamphlet *In This Faith We Live* – was possible. What was required was a 'positive approach ... A determined attempt to understand Russia's hesitations and doubts, to recognise her achievements for good, and then to seek earnestly for every point of agreement'. The PSCG also hoped that the Christian community, because it crossed the East–West barrier would provide 'a foundation on which it may be possible to build a bridge across the chasm which presently divides them'.[37] Despite the communist coup in Czechoslovakia in early 1948, which made up so many other minds against the Soviet bloc, Christian socialists continued to seek positive engagement. Elsewhere they noted 'professing Christians' who had turned to 'indiscriminate denunciation of Communism and uncritical acceptance of all anti-Communist propaganda'. This was 'inexpedient' because it fuelled 'persecution-mania' on the Soviet side and made world war more likely.[38]

However, the predominant response of the British Churches was instead to follow the lead of the State in changing to a squarely oppositional position at what became the opening of the Cold War. Having earlier accommodated himself to the wartime rapprochement between Britain and Russia, in the first half of 1948, the Archbishop of York committed himself to the new line. As in other cases discussed here, Garbett confidently deferred to official advice and information, endorsing it with the Church's authority in his public speeches in the House of Lords and elsewhere, and in his books. The archbishop as Cold War warrior became what Dianne Kirby calls 'an ecclesiastical propagandist for the Foreign Office'.[39] As the Churches' most authoritative and publicly recognisable voice on international affairs, Garbett's contribution was not without weight.

At the Lambeth Conference that year, the first gathering of the worldwide leadership of the Anglican Communion for 18 years, communism was on the agenda. Although the encyclical letter of the conference to the whole Anglican church also alluded to Western economic practices which 'show something of the same ruthlessness' as communism, its representation of Soviet intentions was uncompromising, depicting 'Mankind ... threatened by the new menace of Marxian Communism which exults atheism ... and proclaims its gospel with a militant enthusiasm which expects to conquer the world'.[40] The Report of the Committee on Church and Nation delivered to the General Assembly of the Church of Scotland in May 1948 also marked this shift. The opportunity to 'achieve a mutual understanding and a *modus vivendi*' with the Soviet Union had passed. Europe was divided and such were the conditions of that division the world was divided. In this situation there was a 'a Christian interest in the emergence as a unified political force of those Western European powers which, through their Christian traditions, offer most favourable conditions for reconciling social and economic justice and individual liberty'. The Committee went on in penitent mode to write with a 'tragic sense of relief' that it was now possible to denounce Soviet actions in the east which had 'weighed on our conscience for some years past'.[41]

Part of the Church of Scotland's response to the Cold War was the appointment of a Commission on Communism. In the Commission's report of 1950, communism was cast as a monolithic force which, like some spreading plague, was progressively taking over the world. It was 'Christianity's most serious competitor', the grounds of an 'invisible faith' in its proponents. When not a plague it was an occult power which exerted a 'powerful, distortative effect on those who come under its spell', disintegrating personality and morality and exacting a 'devotion' from those it captured.[42] Elsewhere a Methodist Committee on Communism was established and George Bell, with the approval of the Archbishop of Canterbury, initiated Anglican discussions on the same topic. As an important part of the hardening of positions, Christian attention was increasingly focussed on the Cold War as an ideological clash between 'Communism' on one side and Christianity (and Western liberal democracy) on the other.[43] Rather than ideology being only one important part of a complex problem, which was also political, cultural, economic and historical, ideology increasingly emerged as the predominant point of reference in the discourse. Because the claims of communism as an ideology were all encompassing this focus on ideas tended to polarise the opposing sides and radicalise the terms of their argument. This concealed the reality that communism as a system of ideas was not inevitably pre-eminent in governing the conduct of the USSR but existed alongside competing political imperatives and other historically and culturally grounded assumptions.

The United Europe Movement seen from East and West

As stated above, this shift in 1948 was not so much a fundamental change of attitude as the public voice of policy coming into alignment with assumptions which were already dominant and had been since before the end of the war. Thus, the construction of a Western bloc to stand up against the Soviet Union had been well underway with ecclesiastical assistance for some significant time. As prime minister, Winston Churchill appointed Fisher and, as we have seen, in opposition he recruited the archbishop to support his new UEM.[44] Leo Amery, one of Churchill's collaborators in the project, approached Fisher not long before the landmark 'Sinews of Peace' speech at Westminster College, in Fulton, Missouri that introduced the term 'iron curtain' and its attendant concepts into common usage in the political culture. The UEM, which was an integral part of Churchill's strategy to strengthen Western Europe in the face of the Soviet threat, was formally inaugurated at the beginning of 1947. He explained to Fisher the need for a united Europe to prevent the 'catastrophe of a third World War'.[45] Initially the archbishop was cautious about lending the official support of the Church to a body 'which is in some quarters being criticised as anti-Russian'.[46] However, he indicated that he would talk the issue over with Garbett. Whether because of his contact with York, by the time of the UEM's inaugural meeting Fisher was prepared to bless the movement with his full support.

Writing in March 1948, Gordon Lang hoped to rebut critics who claimed that a united Europe would be either 'an anti-Soviet bloc' or lead to the revival of Germany as a military power. The reconstruction of Germany was vital to the future internal peace of Europe and this could be achieved without a resurgence of either fascism or militarism. Otherwise a degraded and subordinate Germany would become a 'plague spot' spreading infection across the continent. As to the wider world, Rev. Lang spoke optimistically of securing the 'full co-operation' of both of the superpowers.[47]

Lang wrote as if Europe could be treated separately to the rest of the West, as if there were not already countless political, strategic, economic, cultural, ideological and practical ties knitting together that continent and North America which formal unity would further solidify and advance. No matter that the revival of Germany was good for the peace and prosperity of Western Europe, it was also the nation which only two years earlier had been defeated by the USSR after four years of genocidal war. No matter that Churchill might deny that 'the ideal of United Europe is nothing but a manoeuvre in the game of politics, ... A sinister ploy against Soviet Russia',[48] whatever the positive virtues of European unity it was neither realistic nor even possible for Moscow to view such a project with equanimity. In Russian eyes, if Churchill's rhetoric served to polarise the two sides of Europe, then the function of the UEM was to unite Western Europe and then attach it to the Anglo-American alliance to thereby create a Western power bloc. The deep Soviet fear of 'capitalist conspiracy' against them would have aroused a latent paranoia even if these plans for unity were entirely benign but, obviously, the Soviet reading of events was correct. It was, in this context, as *The Congregational Quarterly* wrote, 'simply a closely knit military alliance against Russia'.[49] This model of European unity, both as proposed by Churchill after 1946 and then in the form of the Western Union, developed by Foreign Secretary Ernest Bevin in 1948 sought this end. The alliance of North America, Britain and Western Europe in the North Atlantic Treaty Organisation (NATO) in April 1949 was the fruition of this. For the Kremlin to also see this bloc as defensive rather than a potential threat would have required a miracle of faith and optimism which neither Marxist teleology nor contemporary Russian history made possible.[50]

The Congregational Quarterly suggested that should a 'union' be formed 'everything must be done to bring Russia into it', although it would be 'no easy matter to overcome her suspicion that the Union is a cunning device directed against her'.[51] To believe for such an outcome was 'perfectionist', the journal acknowledged. If this was so, a united Western Europe would also be an anti-Soviet bloc and would therefore itself cause the East–West division to harden and become permanent. Among Christians this second opinion was the rarer, although not completely restricted to the minority of those who – if not actually fellow travellers with communism – were sympathetic to the Soviet point of view. *Religion and the People*, a newsletter edited by the Anglican Rev. Stanley Evans certainly suggested this in its comments on the Archbishop of Canterbury's and moderator of the Free Church General Council's support for the UEM.[52] Similarly the same publication, commenting on George Bell's argument at the Convocation of Canterbury that if the whole of Europe could not be unified on 'a basis of freedom and respect for justice' then it would have to go ahead with those nations which were willing to do so, noted that this meant 'the formal dividing of Europe and not its unity'.[53]

As was remarked at the time, one consequence of this was to erect a barrier to the future integration of Europe at a whole. This was certainly noticed by one of the few Anglican critics of these moves, Ernest Barnes, the Bishop of Birmingham. At the Convocation of Canterbury in October 1947, George Bell, Bishop of Chichester referred to the Conference of Foreign Ministers the next month and proposed a motion welcoming the 'progressive establishment of a United States of Europe with a common foreign, military and economic policy'. In reply, Dr. Barnes argued that Convocation 'should seem to imply nothing which could suggest an alienation of Western Europe from the Slav peoples and in particular from the great Soviet Republic'. The Bishop went on to outline the 'vast' difference in Western and Russian political traditions which were such that 'that although the Russians like themselves, were striving for freedom, yet their efforts were along lines which seemed almost in opposition to British ideals'. Referring to the increasingly violent atmosphere of the times, he concluded with the hope that the words of the House would 'be seen by their Russian friends to be an attempt to dispel the suspicions and distrust which had shown themselves so menacingly alike in Russia and in the United States of America'.[54]

A month later, in the House of Lord's debate on Germany, held on the eve of the Conference of Foreign Ministers, Bell again stressed the linkage of Germany's future to that of Europe as a whole and endorsed

Pakenham's statement of intent to prevent a 'definitive split of Germany and Europe and the world into east and west' (594). Noting that Russian proposals for a political unification of Germany had been countered by British suggestions for economic unity, Bell stressed the former as necessary for the latter and proposed the creation of a 'provisional political regime for a united Germany (595). As part of his specification for such a regime was that it be 'free and democratic' (596). Given that the communists and their allies yet only represented a minority in Germany such a government need not be communist dominated. Such a proposal would be 'a long step forward towards the recovery of Germany and, therefore, of Europe' (597). But would the Russians accept it, Bell asked. It was 'not impossible' he continued but offered no reason why it should be so. Once again, in the case of Russian intransigence he argued that the three Western zones should unify on their own.[55] Replying for the government, Lord Pakenham, reiterated the specific British aim of economic unity, but allowed that 'other political and economic expedients' would be introduced if necessary. Overall, the door would never be shut on a united Germany 'because to shut it would be not only to do Germany an irreparable mischief but to effect a division of Europe which might not be ended in our time'.[56]

It was ironic that George Bell, who had been prepared to make himself so unpopular with influential people – including Churchill – by his brave and principled opposition to the policy of unconditional surrender and the area bombing of German cities, should then be implicitly aligned with them at the outbreak of the Cold War. At this key juncture, for good or ill, the Soviet Union found itself without an advocate who could speak critically, but wisely, on its behalf. If communism and the clergy were coupled together in the British context it was in the figure of the 'Red' Dean of Canterbury, Hewlett Johnson. However, Johnson's support was so staunch and uncritical he would have been dismissed as a paid-propagandist if he had not already been pigeon holed as an Anglican eccentric alongside the vicar of Stiffkey. Barnes's words at Convocation were only reported in the liberal *Manchester Guardian* and the *Daily Worker* (published by the Communist Party of Great Britain). Even Canon John Collins, who would later be accused of being a 'fellow traveller' with communism for his preparedness to enter dialogue with the Soviet 'peace movement', at this time worked with the Foreign Office and the ultra-reactionary Catholic Douglas Woodruff to draw Christian opinion behind Western Union.[57] In this latter case, the only notable Christian critics were the Society of Friends, who refused to participate in the great CA meeting at the

Albert Hall in 1948, in part because they feared that Western Union would divide East and West.

Within the historical meta-narrative of Christendom 'Europe' was posited first and foremost as a unity not based on geographical, linguistic, economic, political or 'racial' criteria but a community unified by a shared system of values rooted in a common spirituality and the authority of the Church.[58] For this reason, in the eyes of the Churches the Iron Curtain represented not merely a boundary geographically separating the east of Europe from its west, but the sundering of half of Europe from Christianity and the Churches which were the core of it as a cultural community. This understanding of the particular threat of Soviet communism to the east of Europe was among the points raised at the 1951 conference on 'Religion and European Unity' organised by the Religious Bodies Consultative Committee. A Catholic commented that: 'The materialism of the West is the exaggerated pursuit of material things while professing religion, while dialectical materialism excludes all spirituality. We need a religious counterblast to the cominform – a "spiritual cominform", to which East Europe could look for moral support. Prayer can penetrate the Iron Curtain'. Taking up the slogan, 'Europe must unite or perish', the Dean of Chichester declared that Europe was confronted by an anti-Christian force which must be met with a 'resistance ... inspired by a glowing faith'. He called for British 'religious communities' to support the work of 'rebuilding European unity on a religious basis'.[59]

Similarly, around the same time following suggestions from Garbett at meeting at Central Hall, Westminster in March 1951 for a response to counter the pro-Soviet British Peace Committee's attempts to secure church support for the declaration of the Stockholm Peace Conference, the BCC issued its 'seven-point policy for joint action in international affairs'.[60] Among these was the pledge to 'emphasise the common spiritual inheritance which binds the people of the British Isles to the other peoples of Europe and to promote a deeper understanding of their problems, so that the Churches may make their distinctive contribution to European unity'.[61]

That European unity and the 'spiritual inheritance of Europe' were important parts of the struggle against communism was clear when the Dean brought a resolution derived from the RBCC declaration before the Anglican Church Assembly. He noted that the statement distinguished:

> ... this spiritual inheritance which he might say was a biblical inheritance of our civilization, quite sharply from the Communist theories

of life and man. That was regarded as dangerous by some at the time, because it was thought better not to draw that distinction too sharply. They were then living in the days when people thought that somehow or other Communism and Christianity could be regarded as much the same thing. Since that time, that illusion has been largely dissipated, though not entirely.[62]

This was a parody of much intelligent and subtle thinking about the relationship between the two belief systems, but Arthur Duncan-Jones's words did indicate that the climatic change in thinking on this issue. With the Berlin Blockade, the explosion of a Soviet atomic bomb and the establishment of a communist state in China in 1949 and, after 1950 war between Western and communist forces in Korea, the Cold War had entered an even more deadly phase. Hence, the statement was drawn up in the context of a 'fight' against communism, in which spiritual resources were to be committed alongside 'economic and political methods'.[63] Mary Hardcastle, who argued against the resolution, said that: 'It would not be right if ... it went out that they were urging the Church of England to take part in an anti-Communist crusade. When she met communists she could not with complete faith believe that absolute justice was on only one side'. She concluded that 'If it went out, a great many people who knew nothing about Communism might take it up as a sort of war cry, and it might in the end make world relationships even worse than they are now'.[64] The Dean's response was uncompromising: '... no communist had the slightest hesitation in saying that he believed that the things which they (as Christians) held as vital were disastrous and destructive to the future of mankind, and why should not Christians be equally strong in saying that the things they held as vital for the future of mankind?'[65] The resolution was carried.

The first cold warriors

The ease with which Garbett and other church leaders took up an anti-communist stance was by no means inexplicable. The archbishop and many of his colleagues were not only part of the British ruling classes, but by their upbringing, education and experience naturally and unconsciously identified themselves with the State and the Nation. Furthermore, York's dealings with the Foreign Office were characterised by the same deference to 'expert' knowledge which a few years earlier William Paton accorded Arnold Toynbee.[66] Given that the Soviet Union's totalitarianism and state atheism already put it high on the Church's poisons list, any other outcome would have been a near miracle. However, while Anglicans could expect to approach this issue with some small degree of detachment and coolness this was not the case among Catholics. In the statement issued by the hierarchy of England and Wales in May 1948 that Church stated 'We are faced with a great challenge. That challenge is whether we are for God or against God. No Catholic can be a Communist, nor Communist a Catholic. We accept the challenge'.[67] However, this unambiguous call to holy war was in reality a restatement of a stance which had already placed Catholics among the earliest 'cold warriors', speaking in terms which would not become dominant in political discourse until later.

Although Vatican-Soviet diplomacy in the interwar years had, on occasion, attempted to go beyond mutual rejection, its general approach remained unswervingly and violently anti-communist.[68] Pius XI and his successor, Pius XII, condemned fascism in Italy and Germany for their totalitarianism and its attendant deification of the State, Nazism for its racism and 'euthanasia' policy, and were alarmed by the implications of its paganism. Despite this, the Catholic Church pursued what might now be called a policy of 'constructive engagement' with the regimes of Mussolini and Hitler, and refused to fully employ the weapons at its disposal. Elsewhere in Europe, Spain and Portugal, Slovakia and Croatia, the attitude of the Church to authoritarian dictatorships of a conservative or para-fascist variety was often supportive. In contrast to the ambivalence and pragmatism of its reaction to radicalism of the so-called right, the Vatican remained vocally and implacably opposed to 'Communism' during the war years, refusing to copy the friendly gestures made by Britain and the United States to their wartime ally, and refusing to be influenced by Stalin's moderation of Soviet persecution of the Churches. The influential Catholic journal *The Month* wrote of the wartime alliance that the 'process was nearly all *Take* on the Russian side, and mighty little *Give*'. Hence it was 'both foolish and unreal to stir up in Britain, as was done between 1941 and 1945, a wave of propaganda enthusiasm for Russia'.[69]

After the defeat of the Germans at Stalingrad, and as the Red army steadily advanced westward, the fears of the Vatican increased. With the occupation or 'liberation' of the countries of Eastern and Central Europe the catastrophe worsened as more and more Catholics fell under Soviet hegemony, and were lost to Rome. The expedient politics of the agreement made by the allies at Yalta were anathema to Pius, and were condemned as a betrayal. The only answer to communism was an unequivocal and uncompromising opposition. The Vatican's stand-firm stance was indicted by its decree in 1949 reiterating that communism and Christianity were incompatible and that henceforth any Catholic who also was seen to 'profess, defend or propagate' communism would be subject to excommunication.[70] This opposition was expressed not only in the Vatican's own denunciations and threats of excommunication, but in its encouragement of the EM and its efforts to draw the United States back into Europe.

Hence, although a minority denomination in Britain, the Catholic Church represented a powerful force in world affairs. In this respect it mirrored the status of the CPGB in British politics and followed the policy laid down by the Vatican with a degree of flexibility similar to its opponents' treatment of the 'party line' from Moscow. The nature of Catholic opinion was expressed clearly in *The Tablet* in October 1947, which spoke of 'a long-established historical fact, the profound and hostile division between the Communists and world they exist to destroy'. The co-existence of the democracies of the West with the Soviet communist system was thus an impossible wish-dream: 'The conflict in Europe is between a spiritual and a material interpretation of life, nothing smaller or less profound, and it does not lend itself indefinitely to compromise at the expense of weaker third parties. It is conflict. There was a war declared in the last century by a movement which has been waging it ever since'.[71]

The voice of the editor of *The Tablet*, Douglas Woodruff, was heard not only through the pages of his paper but also in a number of politically conservative journals. Like Woodruff, Ivor Thomas also had a background in journalism, in his case, on the editorial staff of *The Times* and then at the *News Chronicle*. In wartime, he joined the MOI and firmly believed in the need for 'a religious and revolutionary quality' in British wartime propaganda.[72] In 1942 Thomas became MP for Keighley and from then on provided a parliamentary voice for Catholic foreign policy concerns, in particular those relating to Poland and Italy.[73] Thomas was uncomfortable with socialism, even of the democratic British variety, deeming its ends to be similar to those of Soviet communism, and left Labour even before the end of its first term in government.[74] However, the Catholic who had the widest public audience on this subject was Barbara Ward. Her thinking in the immediate post-war period – as discussed above – had been criticised for reproducing 'some of the usual clichés of pro-Soviet writers'[75] and not been well received by Catholic reviewers.[76] The BLEF campaigned against Ward's pamphlet, writing to both the prime minister, the secretary of state for war, to the Bureau of Current Affairs (BCA) which published it, and the Carnegie UK Trust which financed the BCA.[77] Woodruff recorded his hope that the woman who he described as a 'personal friend' was 'getting this bias out of her system little by little'.[78] By early 1948 her position shifted to a more orthodox, albeit highly intelligent and nuanced position.

In a book hurriedly written at the time of the announcement of the Marshall Plan in 1948 and in a Penguin 'Special' published during the Korean war, Ward provided analyses of the Soviet threat and suggestions to meet it.[79] Following these 'heat of the moment' texts she offered her thinking at greater length in *Faith and Freedom*.[80] Ward's work stood out among the many Christian and secular political voices speaking on this topic by fusing expertise in the latter sphere with belief and insight in the former. Her readers were provided with a calm but clear-sighted analysis of Soviet ideology and world view, intensions and capacities, accompanied by a realistic and balanced estimate of the constructive liberal social and economic policies, and military and political ramparts necessary for the West as a whole to 'contain' what she believed to be communism's ultimate aim of world-domination. In 1951 she wrote that '[a]rrogance and fear, contempt and distrust, scorn and inferiority – these are the strands that have been woven together to make the fabric of Soviet thought'.[81] Ward was torn between her insight into the Soviet mindset and her liberal revulsion at its consequences but still called for a Western response which was 'at once sustained, calm and supremely positive'.[82]

'Military containment' and 'social containment'; NATO and the Marshall plan were the twin indispensable wings of the defence of the West.[83] Integral to Ward's thinking was Western unity, mediated though both shared culture, informal co-operation and practical action but also by means of formally constituted political structures. Already in 1945 she was writing of the fear of 'a growing terror' among Europeans of being 'being divided' as the 'battleground' between the Soviet and American systems.[84] Seeing the problem of containment as necessarily global she focussed on 'the West' as a whole rather than just Europe and stressed structures which were Atlanticist in the first instance and looked towards ultimate world-government. As with other like-minded thinkers, she shared the three circles model of British foreign affairs, which imagined Britain as positioned at the intersection between the United States, the Empire and continental Europe. From this point of view Britain was a world power, which – speaking to the RIIA in 1942 – she anticipated would, alongside the United States, also need to '"go into" Europe'. For 'Europe' itself she advocated a 'super-national' economic and political system.[85] At the beginning of the Cold War she continued to support European unity, supporting the Council of Europe and the Schuman Plan, but going beyond other advocates of the 'three circles' model, by criticising the British government's 'acute economic myopia' and 'misguided determination' in rejecting participation in the latter.[86]

Alongside her acute and informed insights and policy proposals was a stress that their efficacy also drew on the Judeo-Christian and classical cultural heritage of the West and depended on a living and inspirational 'faith'. Ward pointed to 'the resources of Christianity' for creating the loyalty, enthusiasm and 'obligation and fellowship which transcends the limits of a nation state' which a united federal Europe would require.[87] Facing the external threat of communism, she argued that an appropriate policy alone was not sufficient because communism also fed the 'human heart' with its 'appetites and despairs which rational codes alone are unable to control'.[88] 'Where there is no vision, the people perish and with them all the plans and policies and projects ever drawn up in their name'.[89] Hence the importance of Christianity to the containment of communism. Christian faith, philosophy and institutions were the essence of the West. 'Europe' was such because its 'frontiers mark the frontiers of Christendom'.[90] Europe and its 'extension into the New World' were created and sustained by a particular conception of humanity, Christianity had created 'a double order of reality and a division of power out of which the possibility of freedom' had grown.[91] Christianity and democracy had grown up 'so closely intertwined' that the failure of one might mean the 'decadence of the other'.[92] The importance of the Church was that 'of all organized bodies [it] alone can look Caesar in the face and claim a higher loyalty'.[93] The other religions of the wider world confronted the materialism and atheism alongside Christianity. The West would 'reassert its powers of attraction only if its material achievements' could be seen to 'express a vision of spiritual order'.[94]

The British League for European Freedom

Just as their belief in Western unity had brought many Church leaders to support the EM, so their concern for the fate of the nations under Soviet hegemony brought them into involvement with the BLEF. Despite its highly politicised nature and the murky background of some of its supporters, the League had Arthur Duncan-Jones, the Dean of Chichester, as the vice-chairman of its executive committee, which also included Mr. Tracey Phillips, a member of the Church of England Council on Foreign Relations.[95] Woodruff represented the Catholic interest on the executive. He also secured the support of Cardinal

Bernard Griffin, the Archbishop of Westminster, who joined other leading clergy on the BLEF Advisory Council.[96] Other clerical supporters
included the Bishop of Gibraltar[97] and Arthur Headlam, formerly the
Bishop of Gloucester.[98] During the 1930s Headlam had chaired the
Church of England's Council on Foreign Relations, during which time
his fellow bishop, Hensley Henson, described him as 'the pertinacious
apologist of the Nazi Government'.[99]

The BLEF was founded in late 1944 by Elma Dangerfield to lobby the
British government in the interest of refugees from Eastern Europe and
to publicise the nature of the Soviet occupation of their countries. The
League organised public meetings, often providing a platform for exiled
political opponents to publicise conditions in Soviet occupied Europe.
For instance, 'religious persecution in Europe', was the title for a joint
meeting with Sword of the Spirit, held in March 1947.[100] Leaflets and
pamphlets were also published and a weekly press bulletin issued. The
committee also sent out memoranda to important international gatherings and conducted 'indirect work' such as suggesting Commons'
questions to sympathetic MPs. It also continually lobbied the Foreign
Office in the interests of refugees and East European 'volunteer work-
ers'. In one such case, Katharine Atholl believed that Francis Blackett,
secretary of the BLEF helped to avert the deportation of Dr. Wladislaw
Dering.[101]

Dering's wartime career well illustrated the type of alliances that anti-
communism could descend to.[102] While some of the most influential
critics of Stalinism were themselves democratic socialists, the BLEF drew
the bulk of its support from the political right.[103] Although its constitution required that its membership be British citizens, it worked closely
with émigré nationalists, some of whom were tainted with fascism and
collaboration with the Nazis. Consequently it tended towards a doctri-
naire and visceral opposition to 'communism' and 'socialism' generally.
Another consequence of its membership and objectives was, as Stephen
Dorril has shown, that it was almost certainly encouraged, financially
supported and utilised by the British and American secret intelligence
services in the early years of the Cold War.[104] The minutes of the
Executive Committee show some significant donations made by certain
unspecified 'friends' of the League, and also a small donation from
Major Beddington-Behrens.[105] Behrens controlled the flow of money
from America and British big business through Churchill's UEM to suitable recipients. Thus, support by British Catholics and other Christians
for the League was certainly ethically problematic and may even have
had the sulphurous aroma of a Mephisthophelean bargain.

At the beginning of the EM in the UK, the BLEF stood aside from involvement. Before the foundation of the League, Dangerfield had been involved in the Middle Zone Association, which had discussed plans for a central European federation of states. However, when the BLEF's attitude to European unity was discussed it was decided that, while favouring close co-operation between the nations of Europe, it should not be diverted from its purpose of publicising the 'existing situation in Europe'.[106] Following Bevin's call for a Western Union, this changed, with the executive committee agreeing to its published aims: 'The closer integration of the free nations of Europe'.[107] The following year it became an associate of the EM with a seat on its UK Council.[108]

The particular contribution of the BLEF to the European movement was to stress that the Soviet occupied countries should also be included in a future united Europe. For example, in March 1948, the chair of the League wrote to its members noting that while 'all the major parties' recognised the need for 'some form of Western Union, there is a terrible and almost universal tendency to write off as lost the countries ... behind the Iron Curtain'.[109] This reflected a wider concern that Eastern Europe might pass into the Soviet sphere without protest. *The Tablet*, for example, reacted strongly to attempts to justify the emerging status quo which suggested that those nations trapped in the Soviet sphere of influence were not properly part of Europe at all. There was 'no historical justification' for such a move, references to 'Roman or Carolingian frontiers' were not enough to dismiss a 'thousand years of history in communion with the Christian West that have fashioned the Poles and Hungarians'. The paper went on to argue that despite their present situation those nations enjoyed an 'historical advantage' in respect of the project of unity, having already successfully participated in federal systems in the past. From this perspective the division of the continent offered the West an opportunity to catch up, 'to do much preliminary work in the breaking down the narrower tradition of nationalism ... to make the peoples of the west as ready as those of the east for the re-integration of the whole of Europe'.[110] Harking back to the days of the Austro-Hungarian empire as the 'best solution to the linguistic and national problems of the Danube sphere', it was argued that to draw the nations of that former Empire into an Eastern bloc was 'an offence against the organic life of Europe and against her history and culture'; the surrender of the 'very gates of the West'. Catholics were determined to represent these countries as 'an integral part of Western Europe'.[111] The nations of Central Europe were: 'People who know very well what ... Western values are and who want desperately to live in the larger and freer air which we know'.[112]

Hence, BLEF members were among those who encouraged the creation of the CECEM and in 1952 the League was involved in the organisation of a conference of exile groups sponsored by the Commission. G.E. Hildred, of Sword of the Spirit, stressed the need to resist 'any tendency to acquiesce in the Communist domination of Eastern Europe' and commended the CECEM which included exiled leaders from the Soviet satellite countries and sent a deputation to the Strasbourg conference of the EM, and worked to assure the peoples of those nations that the West had not accepted their 'enslavement'. Relating this to European integration, Hildred claimed it as 'not merely an end in itself, but a means to a larger end, to be achieved when the Communist tyranny is broken up or collapses of its own rottenness, and when its noisome debris has been swept away'.[113]

Dialogue versus opposition

Despite the BLEF stressing the ideal of a Europe united across both west and east, its violently anti-communist reflex prevented it from making any real contribution to that end. The prerequisite of any step towards unity was dialogue and the BLEF would not grant the other side any legitimacy. Their position was rhetorically combative and aggressive, and their energies devoted to publicising abuses of human rights and denouncing the Soviet Union in theory and practice. This uncompromising position implicitly stressed the polarity of positions and that strength was the only thing that counted; its logic was one of warfare, of the zero-sum game or rather – in the nuclear age – of a game without winners. It was not that totalitarian persecution of Christians or the heroism of many in the 'underground' Churches was untrue, it was just that it was not the totality of the question. Neither was this approach politically effective. Stephen Neill, Assistant Bishop to the Archbishop of Canterbury, and co-director of the Study Department of the WCC, wrote of how days of prayer for 'persecuted Christians in Russia' were 'not altogether helpful as they have always fallen under the suspicion of being political propaganda'.[114] In retrospect, when Christians indulged in what Donald Mackinnon called the 'pulpit thunders of the anti-Communist crusade'[115] they contributed to the sterile political culture of the Cold War.

At the same time, alongside these 'thunders', were whispers of another possible approach. In the immediate post-war years the ecumenical movement resisted being highjacked by the Western powers as an anti-Soviet tool.[116] Joseph Oldham explained their approach while preparing for the WCC's inaugural assembly, that: 'Every effort is being made to establish friendly relations with the Russian Church, which may be an important factor in promoting understanding and strengthening the bonds between East and West'.[117] Kenneth Grubb, the first chair of WCC's Commission of the Churches in International Affairs, noted that although a debate on the Christian attitude to communism might provide an 'exciting' or 'dramatic' spectacle at the 1948 meeting, it would make it impossible for the Eastern Orthodox Churches to join the Council.[118] This line was maintained even as East–West relations degenerated over the next coming months. Grubb's colleague Stephen Neill recognised that opinion among the world's Christians was so divided that if the Council was to take a clear anti-communist position it would be 'stamped as being the organ only of those Churches which stand on this side of the iron curtain', and would 'regarded as aligned on the anti-communist front' and contact with the Churches beyond the Iron Curtain could be lost for decades.[119]

Grubb chaired the commission appointed in advance of the Amsterdam assembly to study and publish a volume on 'The Church and the International Disorder'. The contributions in this work of John Foster Dulles and, the Czech, Joseph Hromadka dealt in detail with the reconstruction of international relations in the context of the ideological polarisation of world politics and the paralysing effects of the Soviet veto in the United Nations.[120] As has already been noted, Dulles was a highly influential voice on international affairs, who a few years later would serve as secretary of state for foreign affairs under President Eisenhower.[121] He was, as Grubb wrote, 'a man who has been very close to the transaction of considerable affairs'.[122] Joseph Hromadka was professor of Systematic Theology at the University of Prague. Dulles's paper gave an opportunity for typical Cold War anti-communist sentiment to be ventilated but Hromadka's courageous words, empathetic and full of historical insight and political realism presented a model which was regrettably rare at this time. It was, he said, '... the great mission of Christians in all countries to keep the rival fronts in close touch with each other, and not to allow a petrifaction of the international *blocs* which would make further discussion and debate impossible. So long as the two sides speak to one another, so long as they revile each other, the situation is not beyond repair'.[123] One observer wrote how Hromadka 'moved us strangely by the tension with which he spoke of the dilemma on many Christians behind the Iron Curtain'.[124] During the harrowing years from 1938 to 1948, of Nazi hegemony and the beginning of Soviet dominance, the professor had taught at Princeton Theological

Seminary. This may have granted him a little more critical and emotional distance than was available to others among his contemporaries. In 1957 he was the founder of the Christian Peace Conference, established to encourage reconciliation, dialogue and peace. He was widely accused of being an unwitting agent of Soviet propaganda.

Conflict between approaches respectively stressing opposition and dialogue remained a constant feature of Christian approaches to the Cold War. In Britain Michael Bourdeaux and Keston College (later Institute) represented the confrontational and rejectionist approach to the East, whereas dialogue was pursued by John Collins, CA, which was often criticised for its association with anti-nuclear protest and 'peace' movement, and the BCC. The leading figure at the BCC was Paul Oestreicher, the Eastern secretary of its International Department (1964–69), and later (1981–85) head of the International Division, as it was later called. Oestreicher, whose parentage was German, moved from pastoral work as an ordained Anglican minister to the Religious Affairs department of the BCC, and was then recruited to the BBC by Noël Salter. As the next chapter shows, Salter and Oestreicher both sacrificed salary for the sake of ideals: Salter strove for unity in western Europe, Oestricher worked to create lines of contact with the East. He was involved in the Coventry-Dresden project which enabled British Christians to visit and work with their counterparts in the East Germany, with Christian-Marxist dialogues, and had an intimate contact with the shadowy world of Cold War secret diplomacy and intelligence.[125] There was a natural affinity between those interested in European Unity and those working to end East–West division which Salter and Oestreicher personified as the halves of what was ultimately one purpose.

More widely, the WCC and the Council of European Churches (CEC) both committed themselves to dialogue with the official representatives of the Churches in the Eastern bloc. In so doing, they opened themselves to the criticism that they had become the instruments of a bogus Soviet fostered 'peace movement'; that they were sitting down with those who were tainted with cowardice, quietism or even active collaboration with totalitarianism. They were also censured for not raising their voices in support of Christians in the Eastern bloc who bravely opposed the abuse of human rights. For example, in the 1970s the Czech Charter 77 movement was strongly supported by members of the 'underground' Protestant and Catholic Church in Czechoslovakia, but pointedly ignored by the WCC and CEC, neither of which was prepared to endanger their links with the official Church.[126] During the decades of East–West dialogue and contacts the issue of division was a primary issue, even if it was not always explicitly spoken of as such. However, concern for the negative consequences of division is not identical with advocacy of the positive issue of European integration. Ironically, part of the price of CEC's support for East–West dialogue was that, in deference to the eastern churches compliance with the long-standing Soviet line of opposition to European unity, the Council itself stayed silent on the topic.

*

Kenneth Grubb conceded that his approach to communism in 1948 might be seen as 'sacrificing the prophetics of conviction to the ineffectuality of prudence'.[127] Following the unanticipated and largely bloodless collapse of the Soviet bloc it has been easy to portray the advocates of dialogue as vacillating and even morally tainted; that they sold themselves for a process which led nowhere and was then brushed aside by more powerful forces in 1989. History will always be written by the victors. However, there is one question that should be at least posed here, even if it cannot be answered. Did dialogue, even a dubious one, make some contribution to creating the conditions for a largely peaceful revolution? Did ecclesiastical contacts between East and West help to drain the wells of fear, hatred and suspicion which might have provoked a European 'Tiananmen Square' or worse?

Earlier, in the 1940s, the grounds for dialogue were difficult and stony, but we might suggest that they existed even if their potential was not realised. In altered circumstances, the European order that might have emerged would probably have still been expensive for freedom in Central and Eastern Europe. The strategic retention of that territory within the sphere of Soviet influence was probably a necessary price to assuage Russian security fears. But still this might have been preferable to the Cold War as it happened: wasted decades of sterility, death and mortal danger. It is an open question whether the radical division of Europe by the Iron Curtain would have persisted so long in such alternative circumstances. If this is possible, then in times which would permit nothing more than a fragile and compromised *modus vivendi* between West and East, the British Churches helped to close the space in which such a delicate plant might have grown.

7
Christians and the Common Market

At the beginning of the 1950s the British political classes had rejected the opportunity to take a lead in building the new Europe. The Attlee government declined an invitation to join the embryonic community based around the strategic materials of coal and steel, proposed by Robert Schuman in 1950. Winston Churchill was one of the parents of the emerging united Europe, but when he became prime minister the following year, he explained that while Britain might be a 'closely – and specially related friend' to a United Europe, it was not only to remain separate but that Europe came third behind the Commonwealth and the Britain's Atlantic links.[1] At the time, the adjustment of foreign policy required did not seem politically or economically desirable, necessary or expedient. The cultural roots of European patriotism among British ruling elites were too shallow, while the habits of global power were still too ingrained and comfortable. In Britain's absence the 'utopian' project of European unity began to be realised through the Schuman plan, the Messina Conference of 1955 and the Treaty of Rome in 1957. The door of opportunity, opened at such great cost in the 1940s, would never be opened so fully again.

*

The emphasis on the role of 'power elites' or the so-called establishment here, rather than of any collective or popular agency, is intentional. In a representative democracy public opinion was either indirectly – through parliamentary elections – or directly – via a referendum – the ultimate arbiter of a question of such political and 'constitutional' importance. However, with the exception of wars or major international sporting fixtures (war by other means), the consequences of Britain's relationship with the rest of the continent were too remote from the lives of most Britons for the issue of European unity to have an organic life at a popular level. Consequently, the form and magnitude of the question of 'Europe' in the popular imagination at any given time derived significantly and often *primarily* from its treatment by the elite voices which formed opinion and had the means to disseminate it in the public sphere. During the 1950s, elite abstention from European integration begat a corresponding absence of popular interest; then, from the announcement of the Macmillan government's intention to seek membership in 1961 until it received democratic approval in the referendum of 1975, public opinion seesawed back and forth as the persuaders – anti and pro – seduced or stampeded it.

A similar relationship existed between the leadership of the British Churches and the large constituency of opinion who either filled the pews on Sunday mornings or were receptive to Christian opinion. Given the frequent references of clerical and lay elites in the 1940s to the cultural tradition of European Christendom, and to a universal human 'brotherhood' above the parochial claims of national identity, they might have been expected to resist British disengagement from European integration. Instead, as we have seen, they also retreated into silence at the beginning of the 1950s. Notwithstanding the ecumenical movement, denominational conflicts remained. The claims of British national identity continued to be influential on Churches whose relationship to the state and nations in the United Kingdom was intimate and whose involvement in the creation of a global and imperial Britishness close and enduring.[2] In consequence, the Churches also ignored European integration until the beginning of the 1960s. But by that time the cultural changes through which Britain would become an increasingly 'un-churched' and post-Christian society were underway.[3] Nonetheless, the Christian voice still had, and was perceived to have, a definite weight. In July 1967, at the time of second British bid for European Communities (EC) membership, the foreign secretary, George Brown, sent to the 'Vision of Europe' conference at Coventry cathedral the message: 'Our vision of Europe includes Eastern as well as Western Europe: it embraces not just political and economic activity, but all fields of endeavour. And to this vision the Church, with her own message of peace, reconciliation and understanding, has her own special contribution to make'.

The turn back to Europe

Just as the question had been closed in the 1950s, it was reopened from the top rather than in response to any popular movement. In 1961

Conservative prime minister Harold Macmillan announced that Britain would seek membership of the European Communities or what was then misleadingly – but significantly – called the 'common market', and so began what would turn out to be a long and tortuous process. This reversal of policy was the consequence of pragmatic calculations of political expediency. Not only was the sun setting rapidly on the remains of British imperial power but also the ultimately one-sided nature of the Anglo-American 'alliance' had been made plain. Since the 1940s the survival of Britain as a world power rested on American support and during the Suez crisis in 1956 the United States removed this and humiliatingly crushed Britain's ambitions. Over the same period Britain's industrial and commercial performance was entering a steeper decline, while the productivity and standard of living inside the new Europe of 'the six' was rising. So a turn towards the European Community was reluctantly taken. Unity was a political and economic necessity for 'the six' too, but necessity combined with less ambivalence and a greater identification with European unity as an end in itself.

In 1967 the BCC noted the 'almost complete silence of the British Churches during the past twenty years concerning European Unity'.[4] This silence was first disturbed after Macmillan's application to join the EC in the summer of 1961. The names of eminent Christians appeared among the great and good signing the Common Market Campaign's statement in support of British membership. These included J.C. Wand, Canon of St. Paul's and former bishop of London; Lord Longford; and Donald Soper, the former president of the Methodist Conference. Two ecclesiastical statesmen involved in the Churches' earlier dalliance with the European movement, Father Thomas Corbishley and Sir Kenneth Grubb, also signed.[5] Around the same time, the Committee on Church and Nation of the Church of Scotland touched fleetingly, but positively, on the possibilities of western European unity as a 'nucleus of international co-operation'.[6] Catholic circles also noted the role that the late Pius XII had played in encouraging European unity and discussed the pros and cons of British membership.[7] Most significantly, in October 1962 the BCC directed its International Division to set up a working party, which produced an interim report 'Britain and Western Europe'.

Christians and the Common Market

However, the activities of both the BCC and the Common Market Campaign came to a halt after French President Charles de Gaulle vetoed Britain's application in January 1963. It was not until 1967, after

Harold Wilson's Labour Government decided the previous November to seek membership again, that the Churches' silence was definitively broken by the BCC's report *Christians and the Common Market*. This was not only the first detailed and authoritative Christian treatment of the question of Europe since the 1950s, but signalled a resurgence of Christian interest in the topic which would continue up to and beyond the entry of Britain into the EC at the beginning of 1973. Furthermore, this document articulated a paradigm shift at the heart of Christian discourse on the question of European unity.

Noël Salter

Christians and the Common Market was published by the Working Party on the European Communities, established by the Joint International Department of the BCC and the Conference of British Missionary Societies in October 1966. The working party brought together interested churchmen, politicians, academics and experts. However, undoubtedly it was the secretary and *rapporteur* of the group, Noël Salter, who was most influential upon its report. Although Salter's significance has been little recognised, he was the most significant figure in this episode of the British churches' involvement with European integration. His involvement brought about a rare intersection of Christianity with European federalism, idealism with political savvy, influence with historical opportunity.

Salter attended the minor public school of Taunton which was – as he later remarked – near to Crediton, the birthplace of St. Boniface, the Englishman credited with making a historic contribution to the creation of Europe by converting pagan Germany.[8] It was at his school during wartime that he heard John Hoyland preach on the text of Revelation ch.11, v.15: 'Till the sovereignties of this world become the sovereignties of our Lord and our Christ'.[9] Hoyland was a Quaker, author of *Federate or Perish* (1944) and a long-time activist with FU. From this point on to the end of his life, Salter remained intellectually convinced by, and passionately committed to, world federalism. In August 1947, before starting at New College, Oxford, he attended the annual meeting of the Movement for World Federal Government at Montreux. Whereas federalists at the time were often dismissed as head-in-the-clouds idealists, Salter was able to conjoin idealism with a grasp of politics as the 'art of the possible'. He also attended the inaugural meeting of European Union of Federalists held at the same time and found there a realistic first step towards global community.[10]

He was later described as having 'out of religious convictions dedicated his career to European Integration and trans-national understanding'.[11] Besides the ethic of service inculcated by his public school education, a genuine and earnest Christianity inspired Salter. This was initially nurtured by his close relationship with his Baptist mother and he continued to tend and develop his faith in adult life.[12] Alan Bullock, Salter's tutor at Oxford, wrote of his conjoined religious and political faiths that:

Noël ... used every occasion presented by an historical essay ... to preach the federalist faith, the hollowness of national sovereignty, the futility of inter-governmental arrangements, and the blindness of those who believed that Europe could ever be reconstructed except by federation. None of the practical arguments on the other side made any impression on him: the foundations of the political beliefs to which he devoted his life were already laid and were not to be shaken. The same was true of his religious beliefs.[13]

Sheila Kitzinger, who was a world federalist in the 1940s and knew Salter from his school days until the end of his life, remembered him as being on fire with 'puritanism, idealism and a desire to change the world'.[14]

As a first year student in 1947, Salter founded the Oxford University branch of the UEM and soon moved towards the inner circles of influence in the EM. He was invited by Churchill to attend the Hague Congress as the youngest member of the British delegation, and was appointed to the UK Council of the EM. During the first session of the Consultative Assembly of the Council of Europe, in 1949, he served as the personal assistant to the leading British socialist federalist, RWG ('Kim') Mackay, MP.[15] In 1950, immediately after gaining a first in history, Salter became a civil servant to the Secretariat General of the Council of Europe in Strasbourg. Later in 1955–63 he served in one of the pan-European institutions that Britain belonged to while outside the EC, becoming the deputy secretary general of the Assembly of Western European Union (WEU).[16]

Alongside his political career, Salter strengthened his religious faith. In 1957 he spent six months at the famous ecumenical community at Taizé, in France. Founded immediately after the war, 'Taizé' became an important symbol of the breaking down of barriers, not only between Churches but also those dividing European nations. The next year he studied theology at Mansfield College, Oxford.[17] When working for the WEU in Paris, Salter's melding of European patriotism and Christian belief with activism was clear when he was a founder and chairman of a group concerning itself with 'The Christian vocation in international civil service and diplomacy'. Beginning in 1959 this brought together Christians serving in the various European and international agencies based in Paris with theologians and clergy in a series of meetings and retreats.[18] Over the course of these years of work, study and discussion Salter came to articulate a closely argued and theologically founded understanding of his purpose in life. Ultimately a materially bountiful, free and peaceful European community, even as a step on the way to a world community, was insufficient in itself. Such an end could equally be achieved by the 'intelligent secularists and humanists' which had primarily built the new community to date. Such a purpose was only valid inasmuch as it preceded the realisation of 'the vision of a Europe United for Jesus Christ'.[19]

It was indicative of his religious commitment that Salter left Paris for London in 1963, to become the executive secretary of the International Department of the BCC.[20] He understood political attachment as a visceral, emotional thing, as something which demanded sacrifices. Some years later he wrote: 'What matters is what makes people tick – what are they prepared to give, suffer, fight and die for. For me, Europe has been a prosperous thing really ... How much would I *really* sacrifice for the European cause? ... The answer is one can never tell how much one will give, until the challenge is presented'.[21] It must be significant that Salter, despite his taste for the good things in life and a young and growing family, was willing to move from the WEU for a much more modestly rewarded and politically obscure position at the BCC.

This brought the Council a man who, like William Paton, was terrifically hard working and meticulous, and who combined idealism with an intimate familiarity with the workings of the machinery of power. Sometimes carrying the minutes of his next meeting inside a special pocket sewn into the jacket of his tailor-made suit; one colleague described him as 'dining the powerful on behalf of the weak, lobbying in the service of God'.[22] However, a crucial difference was that Salter, unlike Paton, was not first and foremost an insider of the Church but of the secular world of power and politics which it aspired to influence.

Salter had the highest security clearance ('Cosmic') at NATO, and belonged to the elite bodies the Royal Institute for International Affairs and the Institute of Strategic Studies (from 1951 and 1957, respectively). In the same year that he joined the BCC he was also invited onto the Executive Committee of the EM (UK).[23] It is also significant that in 1956 he was invited to join the Christian Study Group for European Unity, which included such influential members of the European movement as the Belgian Dr. Jean Rey (1902–83), a leading federalist who served as president of the European Commission (1967–70) and Max Kohnstamm, another name synonymous with European federalism.[24] Kohnstamm was secretary general of the high authority of the ECSC when Jean Monnet was its president and, after Monnet moved on to run the Action Committee for a United States of Europe, Kohnstamm became its vice-president. Kohnstamm's name is also associated with the private elite fora, the Bilderburg group and Trilateral Commission.[25] In this way Salter was 'linked' – to use the usefully vague but portentous term beloved of conspiracy theorists – to the subterranean network of power and influence which exists beneath legally constituted, publicly visible and – at least in theory – democratically accountable national and international institutions. However, rather than being a cause for naive surprise or synthetic outrage, such 'links' and 'networks' should be understood as an inevitable and necessary part of a functional polity. The democratic element in any political system can only ever operate successfully as a basic check on wayward or corrupt leaders and a crude arbiter of the relative competence of competing elites to govern. What is more interesting is that one of the overlapping networks of the circuitry of power operated in the name of Christ.

Whereas so much of this narrative has recounted wholesome words uttered into an empty room, Salter joined together Christian ideals with power, and did so consciously, in both theory and practice. While at the BCC he wrote:

> United Europe is a power concept, as well as a concept of power. ... As Christians we have no fear of power, because we serve Him to Whom all power has been given in heaven and earth (Matthew 28, v 18). God himself is power, the Creator and Sustainer of all things. Yet the nature of that power ... is love. ... When we exercise power ... we therefore exercise something which should bear the characteristics described in the thirteenth chapter of 1st Corinthians. The heart of this is self-giving rather than self-assertion. ... as Christians we are called not to shun power, but to use it ...[26]

A few months before joining the BCC he stated that the first reason for a Christian to enter the European civil service was because they could there '... have enormous influence. A Christian can bring Christian purpose, standards and, above all, love into shaping the future framework of society'.[27]

While at the WEU in Paris Salter closely followed the negotiations and 'pre-negotiations' of Britain's first attempt to join the EC.[28] When he accepted the invitation to join the BCC in November 1962 these were still in progress – it was only in January 1963, two months after he resigned, that the French veto put a stop to this. It is likely that the BCC, which – before it asked Salter to join it – had set up a working party to consider the question of British membership, was expecting to benefit from his expertise. Is it also possible that, in anticipation of a long campaign at home and abroad to secure membership, Salter believed that he would be better placed to serve European unity at the BCC? Whatever his motivations, the move traded a senior civil service position with its 'princely' salary[29] for a post which would allow him to be openly politically active and at the heart of an unfolding struggle.

'The second try'

As we now know, before Salter could even take up his new post, the French veto would slam the door shut against the first British application. Despite this, his tenure at the BCC was busy and fruitful from the start. He acted as secretary/rapporteur on three working parties which published reports on 'The British Nuclear Deterrent' (1963), 'The Future of South Africa' (1964) and 'World Poverty and British Responsibility' (1966). At the same time Britain's future in relation to the EC was not forgotten, and in 1965 he circulated a long and detailed background paper on the topic.[30]

Then, in October the next year, a month before the new Labour prime minister, Harold Wilson, formally announced his intention to apply again for EC membership, Salter proposed that the BCC organise a working party on that topic.[31] The working party met 11 times between January and July the following year and entered into discussion with government departments, including the Foreign Office, with which Salter was in regular contact throughout this period.[32] He was also simultaneously in touch with grass roots opinion, speaking about Britain's role in international affairs and as a member of the EC with local Councils of Churches across the country. He believed this contact to be '[o]ne of the most instructive aspects' of his time at the BCC.[33]

Kenneth Johnstone, who had an established interest in and sympathy for European integration[34] and was head of the International Department and former deputy director of the British Council, chaired the working party. From the Church of Scotland came Rev. E. George Balls (convenor of the Church and Nation Committee) and the Roman

Catholic interest was represented by the Jesuit Thomas Corbishley, who had first been involved with the European movement in the 1940s as Cardinal Griffin's representative to CA. Rev. Glynmor John, minister of Blackheath Congregational Church, also attended. Theological expertise came from Rev. Canon Professor G.R. Dunstan (professor of Moral and Social Theology at King's College, London) and Rev. Canon Ronald Preston (lecturer in Christian Ethics at the University of Manchester). The group also included two Conservative MPs, Michael Alison and Peter Kirk. Kirk was also a member of the International Department of the BCC, and had a long and active involvement with the European movement.[35] From the Labour side came John Bowyer, a barrister and former Labour parliamentary candidate and J.M. Wood, the parliamentary secretary of the Co-operative Union. As mentioned above, since the 1940s there had been a relationship between the Churches and the influential think tank PEP, and the director of PEP, John Pinder, was particularly active at the meetings. Like Kirk, Pinder was also deeply involved with the EM. Sir Philip de Zulueta, who had served as private secretary for foreign affairs to successive prime ministers (1955–64), also took part. Although not mentioned in the published list of members[36] the sssociate secretary of the International Department, the Rev. Paul Oestreicher, attended many meetings as well.[37]

Christians and the Common Market set out to be an examination of the moral dimension of British membership of the EC and the overall purpose of the Community (7). Notably, the working party did not include anyone who even expressed scepticism about British membership, which was accepted *a priori*. At the opening of the first meeting Salter commented that '[t]he discussion should not centre on whether or not Britain should join the EEC but on what kind of European Community Christians hope may develop'.[38] This assumption was later reiterated by the chair,[39] who returned to the same topic two meetings later, stating that what 'was emerging was the need to have something for the Churches, accepting the political decision as having been taken, and pointing out why this was good, what possible perils were but how overwhelming it was a decision Christians should wholeheartedly endorse'.[40] Salter also commented in his opening introduction – apparently without conscious irony – that '… if the churches entered this debate it was not as an adjunct to some political cause: the Body of Christ must never be demeaned into becoming a political pressure group'.[41]

It is misleading to describe *Christians and the Common Market* as a 'report' of the business of the working party. It *was* the business of the working party. The discussion of each meeting was framed by the draft chapters which Salter provided. Comments, amendments and subsidiary papers from other group members were then taken into consideration. These tended to deal with questions of detail and, in any case, a major rewrite before publication to reduce the text by around 50 per cent gave considerable control to the author over the finished product. Towards the end of the working party's existence it was agreed that any suggestion of disunity be removed: 'phrases like "The majority of the working party" and "your rapporteur" should not ... be used, since they suggested rather more disunity than there was'.[42] Both Salter and others thought of the report as his own.[43] In its foreword it was described as a 'fitting monument to a devoted servant of the Council', which also praised his 'keenness, expert knowledge and warm-hearted Christian concern'.[44]

The report

The report reproduced Salter's vision of a Europe not only united, but in a federal form. It adamantly asserted that the 'nation state is both too small and too big', and suggested that '[o]nly within a united Europe can problems be allocated to an appropriate level' (35). On the next page Salter went so far as to claim a 'congruence of Christian and federalist insights' (36); and elsewhere that the 'earthly goals' of Christians and federalists were 'complementary' (110). Christians could 'welcome ... that the exercise of sovereignty is henceforth a sovereignty shared between the European institutions in Brussels and national institutions of Member States' (37). To those who believed that the Community was an exclusively economic entity – merely a 'common market' – Salter offered no comfort. Economic powers pooled on such a scale were inherently political in the consequences of their execution. An economic community was a first step and an 'overt European Political Community' a second (38). 'Once a member', he wrote, 'our country is on a potential political as well as an economic escalator'. Once again, a congruence of the political and spiritual was seen, for with such aims 'the Christian has no quarrel', it was asserted (38).

The conflict between so-called functionalist and federalist approaches to integration and national 'sovereignty' was divisive at the time and has continued to be so. However, the report's treatment of federalism did not share the tendency of Christian pronouncements on politically sensitive issues towards wholesome vagueness.[45] Neither was there any sign of controversy over the issue among the working party.[46] This was not because there was an inevitable affinity between Christianity and federalism. As Salter wrote, 'the nationalist sin' deriving from the origins of Protestantism was influential.[47] In the 1940s Archbishop Fisher had combined patronage of the UEM with a rejection of federalism with no apparent discomfort.[48] Alternatively, political pragmatism caused even an ardent federalist like William Temple to reject what seemed to him to have become a 'utopian' solution.[49]

To some extent the working party was weighted inasmuch that at least four of its most active participants were convinced federalists. Although pro-European sentiment in the Conservative party was much stronger at this point than later, a federalist pro-European Tory was a rarity, whereas the BCC group contained two: Salter and Peter Kirk.[50] John Bowyer was of a similar conviction[51] and John Pinder was – and remains – one of Britain's most prolific advocates of federalism. However, the report's stance cannot be explained simply as the reflection of the *idée fixe* of a cabal of federalists. Just as Temple's renunciation of federalism was based on a critical examination of the relationship between power and ideals in the historical situation of the time, so too was this espousal of federalism 20 years later.

In the first instance Salter's stance was premised on a Christian argument for the 'sharing' or 'pooling' of authority central to federalism. It entailed, he wrote: *'giving up the claim of ultimately being the judge in one's own cause. It is here that there lies a specifically Christian insight'* original emphasis (OE). Just as an individual's inherent sinfulness required that he or she surrender their own will to the sovereignty of God, so was it necessary that a nation-state no longer be the 'ultimate judge' in its own case.[52] In *Christians and the Common Market*, an appendix prepared by G.R. Dunstan provided the theological grounds for 'transcending local and national sovereignties'.[53]

However, this theological argument, while necessary, was not itself decisive. As we have seen, in the 1940s, Christian realism in seeking the lesser evil had justified support for Britain jealously guarding its sovereignty and remaining aloof from the rest of Europe.[54] But, by the late 1960s, Britain's geopolitical position was weakened due to decolonisation, economic decline and the failure of the 'special relationship' with the United States, while the united Western Europe was increasing in power. In these changed circumstances, for Britain to be able to able to contribute in any way to the realisation of Christian ideals in the world, a geopolitical shift towards Europe was necessary. Salter expressed this succinctly when promoting the report to the annual assembly of the Congregational Church: 'In a nutshell ... There is NO future for Britain as a small off-shore island. ... It is simply a question of doing together what we can no longer do separately'.[55] Kenneth Johnston had come to a similar conclusion: 'the days of liberty of action are gone'. The country could only make a 'useful contribution to the world in a far closer and more permanent association with other nations than she has ever accepted since she became a major power'.[56] In the report it was suggested that while Christians should be wary of Europe emerging as a third "Big Power", they should recognise the opportunities for the 'positive influence' that such power would confer.[57] Obviously this was the basic calculation of many politicians too, albeit often with the hope that it was possible to take strength from an alliance without a corresponding sacrifice of sovereignty. As both Christians and Europeans, Salter and his colleagues rejected that stance. Arguably their understanding of the ineluctable nature of the political logic entailed in creating Europe as a power bloc may have been the more realistic.

As to the purposes envisaged for a united Europe, at the outset of the meetings Salter returned to the three key themes – 'Reconciliation, Stewardship and Service' – which he had sketched out two years earlier.[58] The second of these offered existing arguments for an integrated European economy, infrastructure and so on under a Christian nomenclature. Similarly, the report's comments on integration to avoid further European wars and to foster reconciliation (28–29, 47–48, 81–83) dealt with a topic which had long been of special concern to the Churches. Indicating its federalist inclination in this area, the report noted that the search for peace in the world more widely would benefit if there were 'an effective common European foreign policy' (30).

Themes of federalism, reconciliation and stewardship were nothing new in Christian writing on Europe. Where *Christians and the Common Market* was innovative was in its treatment of the 'Christendom narrative'.[59] As has been shown above, during the early and middle decades of the twentieth century 'Christendom' was integral to Catholic utterances about Europe and – despite its Roman associations – was often a touchstone for the post-Reformation churches too. In one of his earliest published writings Salter argued of the consequences of the Reformation for the unity of Christendom that 'there can be no Christian who does not regret that the split should have occurred'.[60] In contrast, *Christians and the Common Market* brusquely noted that: 'There can still occur a certain sentimentalism about the unity of medieval Christendom, which is tempted to see European unity as a way back, not forward. In fact, the medieval synthesis carried within it the seeds of its own decay'.[61] Any 'dream of recovering lost unity, whether Roman or Carolingian' was dismissed as 'romantic nonsense, since conditions have changed so profoundly'.[62]

A few years later Peter Hebblethwaite, commenting on the discussions of the Roehampton conference, recognised this as a general change, noting that:

> There was a time in Europe when the 'Christian contribution' seemed to mean rhetorical talk about 'our heritage' and other grand themes. There were a few final tributes to this style at the Conference. But in the main Christians have become more modest and more technically competent. And they do not find that their faith enables them to agree on political questions.[63]

That this observation should come from a co-religionist of Christopher Dawson is telling. When the working party discussed what Salter called the 'Vatican Europe bogey', Oestreicher 'said the issue was not between Protestants and Roman Christians but those who thought in terms of a reborn Christendom and those who were modern secular Christians'. Glynmore John 'denied that there was evidence for suggesting that those who sought European Unity did so from a desire to re-establish the medieval relationship between Church and State'.[64] This did not mean that special claims could not be made for the historical relationship of the Church to 'Europe as a spiritual conception',[65] or that a special historical role might not be attributed to the continent. Salter wrote of Europe as 'a uniquely privileged area of the world', which had made a 'unique contribution to the development of man's physical, intellectual and moral resources' (27). Nonetheless – and irrespective of whether an unjustified hubris persisted here or not – such comments were altogether less ambitious in their claims than those previously signified by references to Christendom.

Given the previous salience of the Christendom narrative in the argument and rhetoric of Christian discourse, its banishment was one side of a paradigm shift in the Churches' thinking. The space vacated by Christendom did not remain empty but was occupied by new ethical considerations. In its resolution accepting the report the BCC particularly stressed the service which Britain in Europe 'could render to the advancement of the developing countries'.[66] The new core of Christian discourse on Europe was not about the continent itself, but rather its external relationship to the countries of the so-called third or developing world.

The salience of this point in Salter's thinking was demonstrated in his unpublished paper two years earlier. There, on the first page, after outlining his understanding of the United Europe as a 'concept of power', devoted to 'self-giving rather than self-assertion', he went on to state that '[i]t follows that "A Europe united in order the better to serve" is something that Christians humbly offer up'. The unacceptable alternative was 'a Europe united in order the better to allow ex-colonialists to throw their weight around again', a statement which went on to be a much quoted passage of the published report.[67] Salter also wrote there that a 'wider European unity must pursue justice in terms of the east-west and north-south divisions of mankind, or it will come under the divine judgement' (46). In the first draft of the report Salter conjured up: '... the spectre of a great mass of emaciated faces with hatred in their eyes, the unnumbered army of the international poor and starving, surging through the glass behind which the RWW (Rich White West) gorges its luxury food. ... Here there is a central theme to Christian support for Britain's entry into the Community'.[68]

The utility of a united Europe was that it could do more to address the 'North-South divide' than any individual nation (28). The industry and efficiency of a 'Europe united in order to serve' (72) would benefit its own citizens but would also help to 'alleviate world poverty' (55). 'God expects a great deal of his European children. Our stewardship dare not be selfish, throwing crumbs from our table to the poorer members of the human family'. (26) The report also made a link to Britain's decline as a world power, noting that whereas '[o]utside of the EEC the UK is of diminishing importance to the developing countries. Within the EEC Britain, if she so chose, could be their most persuasive advocate'. This geo-political dimension was crucial in Salter's argument for Britain's membership, in relation to the key role of service. Two years earlier under the heading 'Britain and the world situation in 1980', he predicted that, due to the coming population explosion, '[t]he key North-South problem will have emerged in all its Dives-Lazarus starkness', whereas a politically diminished and economically decayed Britain outside the EC would be 'unlikely' to be able to meet this challenge. He imagined a decadent Britain 'shorn of her power and modern economic base', grubbing for the meagre 'takings of American tourists who visit the island museum'.[69]

Inevitably the paradigm shift articulated in *Christians and the Common Market* was possible because of success in building the common institutions of the new Europe and the rapid reconstruction of the economic infrastructure and general fabric of the continent's life. To anyone with the slightest insight into the material, political, cultural and psychological aftermath left by six years of total war, the results were incredible. Similarly, after decades of being menaced by war or the threat of war, a mere 20 years after 1945 the possibility of another 'civil war' in Western Europe was unthinkable. With these achievements the whole direction of thinking could move from building for survival to discussing the wider purpose of the new construction, even to enquiring whether its moral health might be imperilled if its success made it a 'rich man's club'.[70] In the words of Thomas Corbishley, quoted in the BCC report, it was feared that it would become 'a new sort of Assyrian Empire – powerful, wealthy and dead'.[71]

This change was also a correlate of wider transformations to the basic identifications and assumptions of Christian political theology in the second half of the century. As previously discussed, Temple and his colleagues imagined the British Empire as a leading agency for good in the world. By the 1960s, this liberal imperialism was fading rapidly from the scene. At one level, this reflected political realities: while many of the links forced during the age of empire lived on, decolonisation combined with a general decline of Britain as a world power could not be ignored. Alongside these changes came a transformation of the emotional economy of the culture of imperialism. Whereas up to the 1950s colonialism was still widely accepted as something, which, while it might be criticised in its details, was fundamentally good, after the 1960s it became increasingly seen as predominantly negative, associated with racism and ruthless exploitation, a source of regret and shame, and a cause for penitence, recrimination and restitution. These changes reflected the permeation of what, in comparison to the 'realism' which dominated the 1940s,[72] might be called a 'new idealism'. Whereas political power had been the first concern in the earlier debate, in this later period a greater emphasis was placed on ethics, on universal 'human rights' and international institutions, most especially the United Nations.

While, at the macro level, individuals like Salter were the objects of this wider transformation, they were also its agents, both generally and in the particular way in which these changes were manifested and in their political outcomes. Uwe Kitzinger noted the changing emphases of his friend and colleague's thinking on European unity:

> ... from representing in the forties and fifties the consummation of post-war forgiveness and reconciliation, and the reassertion of one proud continent's historic creativity, it became for him, in the sixties and seventies, a means for atonement of the past, the instrument of bridge building, and the foundation of a new future era in relations between the old continent and the rest of the human race.[73]

As such, Salter's 'chief concern' became 'how we were going to use our European community once it had been achieved. What kind of foreign policy would an enlarged EEC follow?'[74] His particular preoccupation became the relations of the EC to the peoples of the 'third' or 'developing' world: 'I came to see Europe's role and duty in terms of contributing to seek justice for developing countries as the central thrust of her foreign policy'.[75] Salter dated the change in his thinking as occurring between him joining the WEU in 1955 and the first British application for EC membership in 1961. Concerning the origins of this thinking, Salter suggested that Jean Rey, president of the European Commission (1967–70), with whom he had close contact through the Christian Study Group for European Unity, and 'many civil servants' as having 'a vision of a world helped by Europe ... but this was restricted by the Commission'.[76] He also cited a long trip to South Africa[77] and 'special opportunities of seeing Europe through the eyes of fellow Christians in the developing countries' as particularly influential. It was also, he explained, because of this change in his thinking that he did not go back to the WEU from the BCC but moved on to the Commonwealth Secretariat. There relations between the EEC and developing nations in the Commonwealth became his particular concern. During the 1960s Salter and his wife, Elizabeth were also among those who initiated the World Development Movement.[78]

Also significant was an ongoing discussion between the Salters. The two had first met while Elizabeth was working at the WCC in Geneva and she later moved to Paris to also work for the WEU. Having previously been continually reminded of the yawning chasm between rich and poor, developed and 'developing' world, she was shocked at the lavish expenditure of the international civil service in Paris on 'maintaining status'. Such money, if transferred into the lives of the poor would have made a 'real difference'. Salter maintained that it was necessary that Eurocrats lived and entertained in the same rich style as their national counterparts. Although his own tastes were hardly puritan, there was a genuine argument for political expediency and effectiveness here. Despite this, Elizabeth Salter's persistence 'started to lay hold of him'.[79] Salter could not impose restraint on his civil service colleagues but he could change his own perspective and make his own sacrifices, such as his move to the BCC.

Similar things had been said before. Years earlier, the Labour MP and Christian socialist Richard Acland argued that 'European unity for its own sake' or as merely a device to improve the standard of living of Europeans was 'not enough'. Instead unity should be a means to better aid the 'impoverished missions of the world'.[80] Obviously concern about poverty and human rights issues in connection with the third world was also universal across the Churches. The Papal encyclical 'Populorum Progressio' of 1967[81] and the WCC meeting at Uppsala in 1968 marked the growing consciousness of this problem among the European Churches. In Britain, for example, the main Catholic body interested in foreign affairs questions, the Sword of the Spirit (after 1965 Catholic Institute for International Affairs (CIIA)), from its beginnings in wartime and through to the early 1950s had been strongly interested in European questions. This was reawakened in 1961 with the establishment of a sub-committee to organise lectures and conferences on the topic of Europe and Britain's part in the Common Market. Then, the year after, it shifted its focus onto the British responsibility towards developing countries, which became its predominant focus for the next two decades.[82] However, within this general change Salter was responsible for incorporating an emphasis on development and social justice into the core of British Christian treatments of the question of Europe. At the very least, if not an innovator, he played a major role in making this the commonplace that a paradigm shift implies.

It was intended that *Christians and the Common Market* would appear when negotiations for entry into the EC began in the autumn of 1967. Johnstone and Salter had lunch with the Sir Con O'Neill[83] at the Foreign Office to discuss the government's plans and consequently 'stepped up' the schedule of the working party.[84] Salter's intention was that the report would contribute to the direction of the public debate. He expected that British membership would ultimately require a popular mandate but, in 1965, he was confident that, should the government put its resources behind a public information campaign, the majority would be 'six to four in favour'. But – crucially – this support would not be for reasons which Christians could endorse. Hence, the role of the Churches was 'to open the great debate in terms of service, not self interest'.[85] Previously they had failed here, since the time of the French veto in 1962 the Churches had 'reflected not led or stimulated or criticised the national mood'.[86] *Christians and the Common Market* set out to change this, suggesting that citizens had a 'special responsibility' to reflect on the strengths and weaknesses of Britain in Europe (76) and in its resolution accepting the report the BCC welcomed its 'contribution to the public understanding'.[87] The working party hoped that Christians would exert a beneficial influence through 'prayerful reflection, by public utterance; by sustained contact with Government, and the discussion of these issues in fellowship with other Churches' (26).

Measurements of the impact of the report can only be speculative. Unlike other BCC reports its print run was no more than a few thousands. However, given the particular role of elites in rousing and moulding wider public opinion identified here, mass circulation was not a prerequisite of influence. The Christian press had already shown itself favourable to membership[88] and gave prominent and – almost without exception – positive coverage of the report.[89] His stress on the role of the EC vis-à-vis the developing world was central in the reportage. One paper, writing on Salter's speech presenting his work, typically commented that 'The goal, Mr Salter remarked, was not to unite Europe in order to allow ex-colonial powers to throw their weight about. …'[90] Coverage was similar in the secular broadsheets too.[91] *Christians and the Common Market* became essential reading on the topic. It was also translated into German and published by the EM, and was believed to have 'circulated widely in continental Churches'.[92]

However, a subtle but very important observation appeared in the *Church Times*. The reviewer there found that although *Christians and the Common Market* was 'a masterly interpretation of the Common Market, its background and aims, and what would happen if Britain became a member. It does not … present specifically Christian ideals as a yardstick for judgement'.[93]

This pointed to a recurrent question that has haunted Christian treatments of the question of Europe. Was there anything which they brought to the discussion which distinguished them from other commentators, justified them speaking legitimately as Christians, and hence made their religious identity more than incidental?

In reality, this was often in doubt. For example, at the important Roehampton conference, the commentator, after marking the disappearance of the Christendom narrative – 'rhetorical talk about "our heritage" and other grand themes' – admitted that the conference had 'barely alluded to anything specifically Christian'. He concluded that 'Christians have no privileged access to knowledge about what to do in the political sphere and consequently … have no specifically Christian answers to offer'. The best he could offer was that there was 'some relationship, however articulated, between their Christian faith and their political options and attitudes'.[94] Discussing the possibility of a 'Roehampton 2' a few years later, Alan Booth, chairman of Christians For Europe (CFE) opened-up the same question: 'What as Christians do we bring to this debate? Many are, like us, temperamental Europeans. We are at home in Europe and resent the tendencies that confine our national life to insularity. It is possible to express these sentiments in terms which use Christian language, and refer to "Christian" values, but lots of people share our sentiments without feeling the need to relate them in any way to Christian ideologies'. Booth continued: 'We are in danger of putting an inessential holy gloss on a respectable human judgement, and claiming some sort of religious sanction for our personal political predilections'.[95]

Britain joins Europe

In November 1967 Noël Salter moved to the Commonwealth Secretariat. At that stage, at least as far as the BCC was concerned, his work was done. He expected that the likely date for entry to the EC was 1968–69[96] and, in any case, he remained involved in a number of secular and church bodies engaged with the issue. But once again de Gaulle's continued opposition to British membership and the formal French veto delivered in May 1968 dashed his hopes. However, with the General's resignation in April 1969 – following his defeat in a referendum on governmental reforms – the EC announced in November at the Hague conference that negotiations with Britain would reopen. These resumed in June 1970 and the European Council of Ministers announced agreement with Britain a year later. Then, after a long, intense and sometimes bitter campaign in parliament and the country, membership was accepted by a majority of 112 in the House of Commons in October 1971. The Treaty of Accession was signed in the next January and the Conservative government of Edward Heath steered the European Communities Bill through the House of Commons that July. Britain – along with Denmark and Ireland – finally became part of the EC on New Year's Day, 1973. While membership has never become uncontentious, it was settled as a political fact by a referendum in June 1975 which supported continued British membership. During the protracted process of external negotiation and internal debate up to 1975 the Churches and the BCC continued to encourage actively a positive public engagement with the topic.

During the campaign leading up to the pivotal parliamentary vote of October 1971 the International Department of the BCC was directly wired into the pro-EC campaign. This was through the British Council of the European Movement, which had been formed by the merger of the UKCEM and Britain in Europe (BIE).[97] The first of these bodies dated from the late 1940s and it was to UKCEM that the CMEU had been affiliated during its brief life.[98] Although the Council continued to sport an impressive roll call of ecclesiastical names on its stationery, including the Archbishops of Canterbury and Westminster, the Moderators of the Church of Scotland and the Free Church Council and the Chief Rabbi, it was not particularly focussed or active. In contrast, Britain in Europe was – as one of its participants suggests – a 'more active, intellectually more committed and politically tougher body'.[99]

Activists from the pro-federalist BIE dominated the new organisation. They were typically of the generation which had come of age in the 1940s, joined FU, the Crusade for World Government or were associates of the Federal Trust for Education and Research, founded in 1945. Politically they came from all three main parties, and included 'some full time trade unionists, some lawyers, some in public relations, one who worked for the BCC, another for *The Economist*, several at Universities or various research institutions'.[100] While disputing any 'conspiratorial theory' about the influence of this group of 'Eurofanatics', Kitzinger writes of himself and his colleagues that: '... what mattered most was that most of them, while pursuing their own chosen careers in different fields in which they could remain useful to the cause had remained in close touch with several others of the larger interconnected "mafia", that their political thinking had remained along broadly parallel lines, ... there were common reflexes as to aims and strategy ...'[101]

During Edward Heath's successful campaign this 'mafia' worked in close co-operation with the pro-integration sections of both major parties and with the government itself through the secretive co-ordination group established by the state for this purpose.[102] The Information Research Department of the Foreign Office was also covertly involved in the campaign.[103] This shadowy body had been established in 1948 and waged a war of words at home and abroad against anything deemed to be working in the interest of Soviet communism. In this case, it was feared that Britain remaining outside the EC would weaken western Europe.[104] The strategy of the EM was not to target MPs directly, or to attempt to influence the public as a whole but to exert an indirect effect on both, by building and sustaining the support of 'opinion-formers' across society.[105] Given that public opinion was particularly malleable by elites on this question, the role of the EM was especially crucial. As Kitzinger shows, in terms of its strategy, organisation, imagination, personnel and finances it completely outclassed the 'anti' campaign. Working in close co-ordination with the government, it engineered a significant shift in opinion among MPs, with party rank-and-file, and in the country, and presents a textbook example of mass-persuasion in a democracy.

The BCC intervened in August 1971, when the public debate was at its height. A pamphlet by Kenneth Johnstone, who had chaired the International Department's Working Party on the European Communities in 1966–67, was produced summarising the findings of *Christians and the Common Market*.[106] 'An outside grant' allowed this document to be sent out to Anglican parish clergy and the leaders of other local churches affiliated to the BCC, to the secretaries of around 700 local Councils of Churches, and to parish priests of the Catholic Church in England.[107] The most likely source of this generosity was the EM, which also distributed 3000 copies of a Church of England report penned by Noël Salter and John Gummer the year after.[108] Johnstone's pamphlet was the first on the issue to be circulated to 'all clergy in England' and had the small distinction of being quoted by John Hall, MP, on the concluding day of the Europe debate in October 1971.[109] The BCC Assembly, meeting a few days before the parliamentary vote, reaffirmed its approval of the 1967 resolution.

As far the leaderships of the different denominations were concerned, the Free Churches were content to be in concert with the BCC.[110] For the Church of England Michael Ramsey, the Archbishop of Canterbury, spoke of the 'immense new responsibility and opportunity' which a 'yes' vote would bring and wrote of how 'Christian influence' would 'prevent a united Europe from being introverted and selfish'. These words in his diocesan newsletter were then released to the press.[111] On 28 October the archbishop and the other Lords Spiritual voted in favour of membership in the House of Peers. In seeming contrast, in May 1971, the General Assembly of the Church of Scotland had voted in favour of a motion tabled by the Very Rev. Lord Mcleod of Fuinery, a patron of the anti-EC Safeguards Campaign. However, this was an interruption of a long established commitment to European unity and, a week before the crucial parliamentary vote, the Assembly voted strongly in favour of the deliverance deriving from the Church and Nation Committee report, which urged that the Church 'accept whole-heartedly the implications of wider European commitment ...'[112] The Catholic Church maintained its solid support. The Catholic Institute for International Affairs (CIIA) published a pamphlet on the implications of British membership[113] and the Commission for International Justice and Peace of the Catholic Episcopal Conference of England and Wales unanimously adopted a positive statement on British entry to the Community in October 1971.[114] Noël Salter was a member of the Commission from 1968 to 1971.[115]

Although it cannot be quantified, the weight of Christian opinion on this issue in 1971 is likely to have been significant. Taken together, the joint membership of the Churches represented one of the largest and most important targets of the campaign. The sociological profile of churchgoers also meant that they were more likely to combine active political participation with scepticism about membership of the EC than the population as a whole. Given the 'top-down' nature of opinion formation on European questions, the 'yes' campaign was extraordinarily blessed in relation to this important target. Church leaders, in contrast to their congregations, were generally positive about membership and the EM had a direct link to this group of opinion formers.

'Going into Europe'

On New Year's Day, 1973 the Dean of Westminster dedicated the national flags of the EC to mark Britain's formal entry to the community.[116] Following entry, the Churches did not lose interest but continued to work to influence EC policy. In March the same year, a conference in Brussels was held under the patronage of the Bishop of Leicester, also to mark Britain's membership. Out of this came the European Christian Industrial Movement, otherwise known as 'the bridgebuilders', which hosted a number of conferences and received the co-operation of Jack Peel, a veteran British unionist who became director of the Industrial Relations Commission of the EC Directorate General, Employment and Social Affairs.[117] The BCC organised visits to Brussels to enable people to see the 'EEC at first hand'. These excursions included a briefing at the headquarters of the Community and a visit to the Ecumenical Centre to discuss the role of the European Churches in EEC affairs.[118]

The BCC's International Department also published a study pack called 'Going Into Europe', intended to act as the starting point for discussions at parish level and for grassroots groups.[119] The BCC also hoped to project the Christian perspective into the wider community: '[w]hatever is done ... it should not be secretive! Use the local newspapers ... start public debate in the correspondence columns. Get onto the local radio and television editors'. The duplicated pack included information about the EC, on the attitudes of the British Churches to the Community and their involvement 'in Europe' [sic], and a number of articles. Suggestions for readings, prayers and a sermon outline, and suggestions about how to use the kit at a local level were also included. Once again the concern that Britain should not be joining an exploitative 'rich man's club' was strongly present. One piece – originally written by Barney Milligan for *The Church Times* – dealt with this issue and it was also the major burden of the text of the CIIA leaflet included in the pack and the suggested sermon outline. This stated that 'Christians must go on asking the question: "What is there in Europe for the rest of the world?" (There are enough people asking: "What is there in Europe for me?")'. The Europe 1973 programme was also endorsed. This originated with the World Development Movement and was supported by the main UK Churches and charities concerned with the third world. Europe 1973 sought to persuade the EEC to 'foster development and to serve the needs of the entire world'.[120]

The Church of England's Board for Social Responsibility aimed towards a similar end in its first major statement.[121] This was yet another instance of Noël Salter's involvement. After leaving the BCC he became the chairman of the Committee on International Affairs of the Congregational Church in England and Wales (1967–70) and, from 1967 onwards, a member of the Board of Social Responsibility's Committee on International Affairs and Migration. In this capacity he worked with his friend John Gummer, MP, to draft the Anglican statement.[122] Gummer was a leading Anglican lay-person and, like Salter, was on the EM executive in the early 1970s;[123] he went on to become a cabinet minister under Margaret Thatcher and John Major.[124]

Although referring to, and quoting *Christians and the Common Market*, 'Britain in Europe' did not evince the federalism of the earlier document. It did reproduce the fear that a united Europe might become a 'rich man's club', and was much concerned with the future of the Commonwealth. This reflected the strong links between the Church and what had been the Empire – 'As Anglicans we have a special relationship with the Anglican Communion, so largely coterminous with what used to be coloured satisfactorily pink on older maps'.[125] But it also indicated Salter's work in the Commonwealth Secretariat. It certainly synthesised his three allegiances into a common vision:

> The vision of the Commonwealth is non-racial and transnational and it points beyond the European Community to a future world order. Far from being of less significance after Britain has entered the EEC, it becomes of even greater value than in the past. As part of the Anglican Communion the Church of England can help to maintain and develop the Commonwealth relationship during the stresses that Britain's future European base – but not Eurocentricity – will involve.[126]

Relations between the EC and the 'developing world' were also among the central themes of the important conference 'Christians and the European Community'. This was the 'area in which Christians have been most active in prodding European consciences', the official report suggested.[127] Held at Digby Stuart College in the London suburb of Roehampton in April 1974, the event was organised by the Catholic European Study and Information Centre,[128] the Brussels Ecumenical Centre and a specially convened committee chaired by Thomas Corbishley.[129] Around one hundred and fifty persons, drawn from the Catholic and Protestant sides of European Christianity, from across the EC and elsewhere came together. The EEC was also represented, by – among others – Noël Salter, who had returned to his work as a 'Eurocrat' in 1973, and Max Kohnstamm.[130]

Among the background papers offered in advance was one by Roy Jenkins, home secretary in the Labour Government and the leading partisan on the pro-EC side of the argument dividing bitterly the Parliamentary Labour Party and the Labour movement.[131] When the conference convened in April 1974, the EC appeared to be in what Peter Hebblethwaite – editor of the conference report and formerly editor of the Catholic journal *The Month* – described as 'state of considerable disarray'.[132] One cause of this crisis was the question mark just placed over British membership by the referendum prompted by Harold Wilson's attempts to hold the Labour Party together.[133]

The referendum campaign

In March 1974 the Conservative government which had taken Britain into the EC was replaced by a Labour administration lead by Harold Wilson. The Labour election manifesto promised to renegotiate the terms of Britain's entry into the EC and to 'consult' the people about continuing membership. With a party that was divided over European integration and a minute majority in the Commons, the only way that Wilson could hold the party together was to make the question one of popular choice in a referendum. The date set for this was 5 June 1975. In the campaign that followed, there were, as before, Labour and Conservative on both sides of the issue. Membership of the EC was an issue over which Christians could also legitimately differ without bringing the common fundamentals of their religion into dispute. Hence, whereas there were good grounds for the Churches to encourage their members towards an informed and socially concerned participation in the campaign, it was more questionable whether they could legitimately take a position on one side or the other. However, once again, there was a very definite bias in support of the 'yes' campaign among Church elites.

Christians in the EM orchestrated the campaign. The previous year an ecumenical group called Christians for Europe (CFE) had emerged from the committee organising the Roehampton conference and this had become an affiliate of the British Council of the European Movement.[134] The group had the Bishop of Leicester as its figurehead and John Gummer as its secretary. In a private meeting organised by CFE in January 1975, Lord Harlech, chairman of the EM, outlined his desire for a 'Churches Committee for Europe' with the Archbishops of Canterbury and Westminster and moderators of the Free Church and Church of Scotland as its patrons.[135] This committee would then be part of the Britain in Europe campaigning group, which was then being secretly formed as the umbrella group co-ordinating party-political and other groups working for a 'yes' vote. Hugh Wilcox, assistant general secretary of the BCC and divisional secretary of its International Affairs Division, explained that the churches' governing assemblies were not equipped for the rapid action necessary. In any case, the presence of influential opponents of membership such as Lord MacLeod in the Church of Scotland and the Anglican Enoch Powell would make this controversial. Nonetheless, he 'personally would see that the BCC's view was "as European as possible"'.[136]

When Hugh Hanning of the Church of England Board of Social Responsibility asked Harlech whether he hoped that the Churches would persuade, or inform, he replied that 'he hoped that they would persuade, but in any case if this is not possible, he hoped they would inform'.[137] His hopes were realised. Once again the BCC was in the vanguard, the characteristic note of the campaign was struck in the conclusion of its paper, 'Staying in Europe', Yes or No?' This issued the strong political direction that 'a critical but committed yes to Europe is a proper response to the referendum'.[138] The issue of service was prominent in the paper's discussion, and it noted that 'many Christians will wish to emphasise the responsibilities to which our nation is called in service to the Third World and to set the issues concerning European Community predominantly in that context'.[139] At the same time, the BCC was less favourable to '... an ecclesiastical romanticism which rather overemphasizes the glories of the Christian Europe of Charlemagne, and tends to see in the beginnings of Community in Europe a return to old splendours'.[140] Originally it was intended to publish a pamphlet but, in the event, matters moved too quickly. However, a press release ensured that the BCC's support was known and the text of its paper 'Staying in Europe' was sent out to church leaders.[141] This also referred anyone requiring speakers or publicity material to CFE.

The centrepiece of CFE's campaign was a letter signed by the Bishop of Leicester, Dr. Williams, Thomas Corbishley and Alan Booth. This was then sent out to clergy asking for 'a personal commitment and for prayer for the community and for a right decision in the referendum'.[142] Also enclosed were suggested forms of prayer and worship. Over 5000 clergy responded favourably to this campaign and large meetings and services patterned on their suggestions were organised in more than a dozen centres.[143] As was noted at the time, the support of Rev. Alan Booth – 'well known as the director of Christian Aid' – was indicative of the importance of the North-South question in Christian support for the EC. David Edwards noted that although the Churches might have been expected to be instinctive 'antis' on account of their empire heritage, he found a '[s]triking absence of anti-Europeanism in the Churches'. He also noted that '[v]ery few pulpits or discussion groups have displayed any profound interest in the EEC apart from the single question of what the EEC can do for the Third World'.[144]

As already noted, the CIIA almost exclusively devoted its energies to the developing world, but in 1975 it published an edition of *Comment* dealing with the EC.[145] Elsewhere, the Church of England's Board of Social Responsibility worked to raise consciousness on the question, reissuing its 1972 report *Britain in Europe* in a revised edition and issuing briefing notes to bishops in the House of Lords. A suggestion from the Board that the *Church Times* carry a 'pull-out' summary of the pros and cons of membership to enlighten the 'bewildered man in the pew and the street' was rejected because, among other reasons, readers would not expect that paper to carry an excessive amount on 'what is really a secular topic'.[146] In fact, the *Church Times* and the religious press generally devoted considerable space to the referendum, and not only to inform but to persuade.[147]

The Churches' campaign did not pass entirely without protest. Neil Marten, MP, for Banbury criticised a statement put out by clergy in his constituency in favour of a 'yes' vote.[148] Nigel Spearing, Labour MP for Newham South and a career 'Europhobe', complained that the BCC appeared to be unaware that there was 'a sincere case "against" which rests on some of the "moral dimensions" mentioned in the study paper'. Spearing also enclosed a press release entitled 'Churches Adrift over the Market'. Wilcox was unapologetic, writing 'I am quite certain that Christian people in Europe, especially Church Leaders and those Christians who are in the service of the EEC, to say nothing of Churchmen from the Third World, will regard a negative decision by Britain as a betrayal of our commitment to internationalism, and the needs of the less developed countries'.[149] To another critic Wilcox argued that because the question was not 'a matter of party politics', it was 'proper for the BCC, in common with all other institutions in national life, to make some judgment on the issue'. Wilcox continued, 'We have been left in no doubt that Christians in the local churches and Councils of Churches have welcomed what we have done, and indeed many of them have been pressing for a study paper and a statement from the BCC for some time'.[150]

As to the success of this campaign, an insider's view appeared in a book by Uwe Kitzinger and the psephologist David Butler the following year:

A particularly notable effort to appeal through the churches was managed independently by John Selwyn Gummer ... who claimed to have secured the explicit support of over one-quarter of all the clergy of all denominations – including almost every single Anglican bishop. There seems to have been no significant protest against this involvement of religion in politics. Prayers for Europe were said in perhaps half the Anglican churches and favourable items were placed in parish magazines. There was also a pro-Market vote at the General Assembly of the Church of Scotland and official statements by the Methodist Church, the British Council of Churches and the Roman Catholic Institute of International Relations. On the eve of the referendum publicity was achieved with a special commemoration at Crediton of the feast of St Boniface, a native son who converted the Germans 1,300 years earlier. The Church campaign was thought important, partly because it might draw those whose idealism might not be attracted by the usual material arguments, and partly because it could forestall any anti-Rome feeling of the sort that had been important in the Norwegian referendum – in the event only a very few extreme Protestants voiced this attitude.[151]

Although the referendum result is open to interpretation, a 'yes' was what it delivered in the ratio of two-to-one in favour, a relatively high turn-out (64.5 per cent), and, with the exception of only the Shetland and Western Isles, all parts of the country being favourable. The particular contribution of the Churches to this result can only be speculated about – opinion polling did not include religious affiliation among the variables it measured. However, if the discourse of elites and the mass public media which they dominate are at all influential and the 'Yes' campaign was successful at all in maintaining, or at least not alienating positive opinion, then it is likely to have been successful among the

Christians too. For there, in comparison to elsewhere in public sphere, contrary opinion was almost completely absent among the leadership and in its public media.

In 1975 and during the earlier campaigns there were Christian voices raised against membership. For a significant minority, the Treaty of *Rome* symbolised the mounting threat of the Catholic Church to the heritage of the Reformation. The Protestant Alliance circulated its pamphlet *The Queen and the Common Market* around party conferences and elsewhere. As in the 1940s, *The English Churchman* was representative of this section of opinion.[152] Favourite themes remained evergreen: 'the Common Market is a Roman Catholic plot to enslave Britain. What Rome could not accomplish through force by the Kaiser, Hitler or Mussolini she is now succeeding by guile and trade'. 'Edward Heath's revived Holy Roman Empire' presaged the reign of the anti-Christ and the 'second coming': 'What is prophesised of internationalism is the appearance of "that Wicked" who seeks to rule the world, and will only be destroyed "by the brightness of His coming"'.[153] Just as the editorial line was strongly affirmative everywhere else, here it was equally unequivocal: 'The time has come to decide and in the light of the true nature of the EEC there is a clear and overwhelming case for saying NO!'[154]

However, in contrast to the 1940s such sentiments were much less visible and so, presumably, less influential. Vatican II and the progress of the ecumenical movement in the intervening years had done much to ease apprehensions among evangelical Protestants about the role of Christian democrats in the EM or Britain entering into a political relationship with predominantly Catholic nations. The evangelical paper *The British Weekly* suggested that whereas 'fears about Roman Catholic influence will doubtless persist among those who entertain them whatever contrary arguments are presented', it was 'a subject in which it is only possible to answer reassuringly'. There was no evidence from elsewhere in the EC that Catholic domination of Britain's 'religious and cultural life' would follow. This editorial continued: 'Relations between the Roman Catholic and other Churches in Britain have seldom been better and the recognition of differences between them has by no means jeopardised this. We trust that a "Yes" vote next Thursday will promote them still further'.[155] In a letter printed alongside the 'Yes' campaign's symbol, Gordon Landreth, general secretary of the Evangelical Alliance, the body bringing together evangelicals across the denominations, encouraged people to set aside the Sunday before the referendum 'to pray for wisdom in exercising the right to vote, and for God's direction of the outcome'.[156]

The veteran rhetorician of 'Speaker's Corner', the Methodist Donald Soper neutralised hecklers with incredulity that anyone could even entertain a contrary notion to his own. There was perhaps a similar technique in play here too. One Anglican document spoke of 'a fair sprinkling of religious bigots and the "lunatic fringe"' among opponents of membership.[157] In a much-publicised comment the Bishop of Manchester, the Right Rev. Patrick Rodger, found it incomprehensible 'how any sane person could vote for Britain's withdrawal from the EEC'.[158] The reality was that in the Churches, as elsewhere in the country, there was a substantial body of opinion that opposed membership or was at least unconvinced but was neither bigoted nor mad. For example, the Committee of Catholics and Anglicans Against the Common Market, originally founded by Catholics in 1963, was still active in 1975.[159] Just as many in the Labour movement opposed membership, so too did some Christian socialists.[160] For others, the Church leadership's blanket support smacked of the 'establishment' closing ranks. One correspondent noted of the Lords Spiritual that: 'The silence of the bench is deafening on so many issues of the day. It is interesting, therefore, that some of them should speak with such clarity on an issue in which they are supporting the Establishment in the preservation of the economic and social status quo'.[161] Another person, 'a life long Anglican and Communicant', objected to 'blatant propaganda for the continuation of Britain as part of the Common Market and eventually Federal Europe' and needed 'no bishop, nor directives from the Anglican establishment or newspapers to tell me where to vote, or where my prayers should be directed'.[162]

*

Although 'Eurosceptics' have tried to play down the significance of the referendum, it made Britain's future as part of an integrated Europe as much of a sealed fact as democratic politics and historical contingency will permit. By word of government, parliament and people Britain was member of the new Europe. The Churches played a significant part in the campaigns of persuasion preceding the vital parliamentary and popular polls. Any scruples about dabbling in the worldly realm of Caesar were forgotten in an unequivocal and energetically active support for British membership. In the political parties, in the press, at home and in the street, opinion was legitimately divided. In the Churches, or at least in the official pronouncements of their leadership, there was a uniformity of opinion which from other perspectives could have appeared stifling. This stance was partly a refection of affinities between the

European project and contemporary political theology but also very significantly the personal achievement of Noël Salter, one of the unseen and unacknowledged makers of modern Europe. Salter had no opportunity to memorialise his own achievements or even to see the referendum result, he died earlier that year, a few months after being diagnosed with pancreatic cancer.

The preamble of the Treaty of Rome spoke of 'an ever closer union' and so the referendum validated an on-going process in which the Single European Act, the treaties of Maastricht (1992), Amsterdam (1997) and Nice (2001) were stages. Since 1975, British Christians have maintained a sporadic interest in this process of integration. The BCC endorsed British participation in the first European elections of 1979, but it was then not until 1989 that Keith Jenkins (BCC Division of Community Affairs) and Michael Smart, (director of the Council's Division of International Affairs, 1986–90) refocused the Council's attention on Europe, in anticipation of the 1989 European elections and the single European Market.[163] Like Noël Salter, Michael Smart was a former European civil servant.[164] Less positively, in 1990 the BCC was replaced by the Council of Churches for Britain and Ireland,[165] which left international affairs to the care of individual churches. One attempt to fill this vacuum was Christianity and the Future of Europe (CAFE).[166] However, while the beginning of CAFE was quite promising, it has managed to do little more than keep a candle alight. Given the relatively low priority accorded to this issue among the individual churches themselves since the end of the 1980s, this has been a valuable service. Their silence has not been total: for example, the Church of England appointed a part-time representative to the EC in 1986 and synod debated European questions in 1990, 1994 and 2004. Nonetheless, in contrast to the considerable resources devoted by the Catholic Church and other continental Churches to making a Christian voice heard in Brussels and Strasbourg, these are modest measures. As a contemporary has commented, in the British Churches' allocation of resources, 'international affairs comes at the bottom of the list'.[167]

Conclusion

'Let the leaves perish, but let the tree stand, living and bare. For the tree, the living organism of the soul of Europe is good, only the external forms and growths are bad. Let the leaves fall, and many branches. But the quick of the tree must not perish. There are unrevealed buds which can come forward into another epoch of civilisation, if only we can shed this dead form and be strong in the spirit of love and creation'.

D.H. Lawrence, 1 November 1915[1]

In the chapters above is a continual juxtaposition of two orders of history. At one level, this study has referred to some of the great institutions at the heart of late-modern societies, most especially Church and State, the democratic polity and liberal civil society. The great cultural formations to which it has referred are of a similar magnitude, all deeply rooted historically and ever present among the cultural archetypes and intellectual traditions of western societies: religious belief systems and political ideologies; the identities of national, faith and cultural communities. Beyond its interest in the myths, narratives, utopias of Britain at the sunset of its imperial epoch, of Christendom and of Europe, the preceding pages have also touched on a more personal history, of the lives of bishops, historians, ecclesiastical statesmen, politicians and other men and women. The socio-economic, cultural, political and historical circumstances of any moment precedes and overshadows the will of individuals, but as leaders, intellectuals and activists, and collectively through elite networks of discourse, power and influence, they may draw on the cultural and institutional reservoirs of power, and channel the historical potential of the moment.

Although most political history is to some extent concerned with the relationship between elites and the great forces and movements of their time, the relative scope for effective action open to the former varies considerably. For instance, the great outpouring of energy and eloquence from many men and women of passion and conviction has not yet availed against the impersonal tide of modernity washing away the sacred in Europe. In contrast, the building of European unity has been a work in which elites have successfully guided and channelled mass forces which, in other circumstances, might have found different directions. Although the complete history of the role of Christians in the building of the united Europe has yet to be written, they made a major contribution. Similarly, a realistic understanding of the ways in which this project of unity has consciously and unconsciously drawn on the storehouse of the continent's Christian cultural traditions is also urgently needed for Europe's future.

If anything, the relative influence of British Churches on this question may have been less significant than those on the continent, although they too played an important role in their country's troubled relationship with European unity. As narrated above, the Churches in Britain followed the general ebb and flow of wider British elite opinion's engagement with this question. This does not mean that they were merely just another passenger on the bandwagon. In the early war years, at the beginning of the Cold War, and in the campaign for British membership from the 1960s to the referendum in 1975, they were in the vanguard of the campaign in both raising public consciousness about, and encouraging support for, European unity. Similarly, at certain key points, Christians played a significant role in influencing the direction of affairs and the content of public discourse on the question of Europe.

With the benefit of hindsight, it is possible to see the war years as a moment when Britain, already deep in economic decline and at the beginning of the end of empire, might have begun the difficult process of realignment to suit these changed circumstances. If the British Churches could ever have encouraged Britons to think beyond conventional assumptions and join in building a new Europe, it would have been in the war years. Through the Peace Aims Group and other agencies they explicitly aimed to influence the British state on the form of international relations and the future of Europe. However, as Jurjen Zeilstra suggests, the Churches' influence 'on the British political decision-making process concerning the post-war organization of Europe was nil'.[2] But this does not mean that they were not highly significant.

Through its efforts to influence public and elite opinion in the United States, the wartime Churches' Peace Aims Group contributed to securing the English-speaking alliance which became the lynchpin of British wartime survival and post-war foreign policy. The degree to which American opinion was influenced in this way is difficult to estimate. It is highly likely that it made a genuine contribution to securing the vital supply of US war materials in 1940. We should also note Heather Warren's argument that the Commission on a Just and Durable Peace, with which the Peace Aims Group worked so closely, was influential in America not retreating back into isolationism in peacetime but actively supporting the foundation of the United Nations.[3] While the Churches hoped to influence policy, from the point of view of the State they were a channel through which public opinion at home and abroad might be swayed in the British interest. All this might also be taken to indicate that the Christians who set out to pressure the State towards the adoption of their peace aims were instead 'turned', but the truth is more complex.

At the same time as dealing with ideals, Christian thinking dealt with the realities of the politics of power as a necessary evil. In comparison to the record of Christian pacifism in the inter-war period and the pathetic hope it invested in the League of Nations, this was a striking development and one arrived at with an agonising knowledge of the realities of total war. Whereas Christian discourse elevated ecumenical communities and identities, in any alliance with ideals, power assumed the only identity it could do, a national one. The ultimate political context within which Christian peace aims were pursued was the development and execution of state policy to maintain British national interests as a world power. Despite their Christianity and ecumenism, William Paton and his colleagues were also *British* and shared with politicians many of the same political and cultural assumptions inherent in their national identity. To answer the 'problem of power', Christians came to speak in the name of their nation, to build alliances to achieve the strength necessary to create global order. When combined with a tendency to elide British history and policy with the working of Providence this could only be more so. There were undoubtedly other forces at work too. Radicalism became blunted by a too uncritical deference to 'expert' knowledge; idealism was stifled to avoid so-called utopianism and its attendant danger of political impotence. Ultimately, this episode also shows how in the relations between Church and State – as in the relations between nations – there is an ever-present danger that the weaker side will find that the cost of maintaining an alliance outweighs its supposed advantages. In consequence, despite the special place that Europe as Christendom had in their discourse, Christians increasingly came to accept the diagnosis and prescriptions of secular politicians who preferred America over Europe, national sovereignty over federal co-operation, and saw the future as one in which Britain would continue to be an imperial world power. As Reinhold Niebuhr observed, it was difficult even for Christians to 'rise above' their 'national selves'.[4]

Although they may not have influenced policy making itself, figures including Temple, Paton and Bell; Fisher, Collins and Woodruff significantly raised the public profile of federalism and European unity in the 1940s and 1950s. Although now generally forgotten, for a short period at the beginning of the 1940s an unprecedented and unrepeated explosion of interest in European federalism occurred which would not have happened in the same way without the support of the Archbishop of York and other Christians. At the joint beginning of the Cold War and European integration the myths and rhetoric of Christendom, of the spiritual unity of the continent, was at the very heart and centre of the British wing of the European movement. While the British were to veer away from the orbit of the rest of the continent, Churchill and Bevin have rightful claims to be numbered among the grandparents of the European Union. It was the Archbishop of Canterbury who blessed both the UEM and Western Union at their births, and the Churches were among unity's chief standard bearers. Given that the clash between the British preference for 'cultural' or 'spiritual' forms of unity and continental advocacy of federalism was one of the major reasons for the parting of the ways between Britain and the European movement, the Churches' contribution to the native discourse on the question of Europe was more than decorative.

The divide between the domains of God and Caesar has always been contested territory, but in this case the boundary was vestigial, if it existed at all. The Churches' definitive functions were in the realm of ideals and moral absolutes, but they also embraced the duty to go out into 'the world' and the need to obey the rules of political 'realism' to be effective there. The often problematic relationship between ideal ends and expedient means could not be more sharply emphasised than it was during these years. The challenge to religious wisdom presented by the twists and turns of official policy towards the Soviet Union during the Second World War and at the beginning of the Cold War was only matched or surpassed by the agonising problem of formulating a Christian response to allied use of the methods of total war. Torn between dialogue and confrontation, the Churches' response to the cultural conflict through which the Cold War was fought in Europe was almost schizophrenic in its double-mindedness. On one hand, the extent to which they threw their support behind the anti-communist 'crusade' and the building of a western power-bloc may have contributed to the decades' long division of the Europe that they had wished to unite. On the other, the preparedness of the ecumenical movement to enter a deeply compromised and problematic dialogue with the East may have contributed to creating the conditions by which this division could be brought to an unexpectedly peaceful end at the conclusion of a violent century.

Christian supporters of the European movement were numerically a tiny minority drawn from among the political and intellectual leadership of the Churches. As such, they contributed to what was itself a narrow political elite, whose worldview and preoccupations were not shared among wider society. However, the centrepiece of Christian discourse on the Continent – Europe as Christendom, past and future – was of universal reference, it referred to a history, institutions, a system of values, a culture, language: a whole civilization. Europe as Christendom signified a pan-national community and identity. For George Bell or Christopher Dawson this was a clear and influential fact; even for those such as William Paton or Joseph Oldham, for whom the claims of their identification with the British empire were compelling, Christendom was not an insignificant myth. Beyond these prominent individuals we can only guess at what claims the discourse of Europe as Christendom had on the minds and hearts of Britons. To what extent did the rhetoric of Europe as Christendom in the 1940s and 1950s draw out identification with Europe and intellectual and emotional support for the goal of integration? How much resting potential was there for such an identification and in what circumstances did, or could it have, been drawn forth?

These are questions to which no definite 'scientific' answer is possible. The forces involved are shadowy, subtle, existing on the borders of social and political consciousness. Nonetheless they were of great importance at the beginning of European integration and may be so in the future too. Thus it is one more of many ironies in this story that Noël Salter, who was perhaps the most influential native Christian contributor to Britain joining the united Europe, stressed not Europe as Christendom but the ethical dimension of Europe's place in the wider world and, most especially, its relations with the 'developing world'. This has continued to be a common and distinguishing characteristic of most British Christian commentary on European integration ever since.[5] However, given that this critique of international relations is one shared by those of different faiths or no faith at all, Christians cannot legitimately claim that their religion brings anything distinctive to the debate on this or any other social or political issue. Not contributing any vital and distinguishing element to the debate Christian discourse lacks substantive and rhetorical power. In contrast, the Christendom narrative provided both a distinctive utopia and a powerful European identity.

Whereas over the course of his long pontificate John Paul II articulated a vision of Europe as a Christian continent, albeit one tolerant of the religious minorities living within it,[6] the increasingly multi-faith quality of contemporary Europe has made the ideal of Christendom increasingly unpalatable to many liberal Christians. At the turn of the century, Ken Medhurst of Christianity and the Future of Europe prefers to write of 'faith communities' rather than 'churches', and notes that 'the concept of Christendom, and later of Europe, was partly developed in reaction to Islam'. In this respect Catholicism's 'officially proclaimed campaign to rebuild "Christendom" is the source of deep concern to those seeking serious dialogue'. He also suggests that in the 'long run conservative advocates of a revived "Christendom" will lack the capacity lastingly to impose their views'.[7] Among Protestant leaders in the Conference of European Churches and elsewhere there is a similar disinclination to endorse the 're-christianisation of Europe'.[8] At a historical moment when politicians are searching for a 'soul for Europe' it seems that the Churches which once provided it have largely withdrawn from the arena.

Europe with a soul but without the Church?

To return to the speech of José Manuel Barroso, president of the European Commission, mentioned at the outset of this study, the draft Constitutional Treaty of the European Union (EU) speaks of Europe as 'united in its diversity'. Without further definition this phrase would be simply a rhetorical slight of hand, a means of claiming identity but without addressing from whence it comes and how it is sustained. In fact it would be an oxymoron. Barroso traced the quality of unity in diversity to a 'concept of human dignity' which, he argued, 'must reconcile identity and openness, dialogue and respect'. Inevitably, this 'concept' cannot be infinitely elastic. It is based on a complex but concrete measure of the proper political, economic, cultural and personal rights of the individual person in his or her collective, social setting. Everything outside of those rights is excluded, by law and ultimately by the State's monopoly of legal violence. What then is the source of this necessarily divisive concept? As Larry Siedentop shows in his vital book, the liberal values, concepts and institutions whose existence are now taken as natural and inevitable in Western societies in fact have a definite historical origin in the melding of Christianity and classical culture.[9] Barroso pointed to a 'shared heritage' which includes classical Greece and Rome, the Enlightenment and 'medieval Christianity'. However, talk of 'heritage' and a 'shared past' smells of ancient dust. 'Heritage' is only relevant in this context to the extent in which it is also shared in the present as a living, illuminating and guiding presence in people's individual lives and in the collective institutions of their society. If not, the teaching and ethics of 'medieval Christianity' are merely an antiquarian curiosity.

In a certain sense the waning of the Christendom narrative is merely one – albeit highly significant – aspect or symptom of the larger question of the collapse of the Church as a core institution in European societies and Western culture. Britain illustrates this general phenomenon pointedly. A society within which liberal values have long been normal and unproblematic, Britain is also a country – despite the presence of influential *individual* Christians – whose people are now almost completely un-churched.[10] Any projection based on the current membership of the Churches suggests that they will have ever increasing difficulties surviving as viable national institutions in the twenty-first century. Even more crucially, Britain is no longer *culturally* Christian in any meaningful sense.[11] In these circumstances Christianity may continue as a living belief system, but reduced from an established, national, mass institution to the concern of exclusive sects which will be increasingly estranged by their beliefs and practices from mainstream society. Inasmuch that it survives in the mainstream, Britain's Christian tradition may only exist as an adjunct of the 'heritage industry', a resource for Sunday afternoon recreation and aesthetic appreciation for sections of the middle classes.[12]

It might be argued that the values of a liberal and democratic Europe would continue to draw on a common Christian heritage even if the Church itself was largely absent from the future life of Europe.[13] In the wider culture undoubtedly the so-called passive religion, which Grace Davie has described as 'believing without belonging', rather than atheism will continue to predominate.[14] However, while this might be interpreted as evidence of the continued social significance of religion, the proliferating role of myth and superstition in contemporary culture better indicates the integral limitations of Reason and the Enlightenment project rather than the bankruptcy of the secularisation thesis. A question mark also hangs over the significance of such beliefs; as William Temple commented: 'If when a man says "I believe in God" what he really mean is "I suppose there is some sort of God somewhere", it is quite unimportant whether he holds that opinion or its opposite'.[15] In any case, current trends suggest that this commonplace 'religiosity' will include progressively less Judaeo-Christian content and be increasing nourished by individualistic consumption from the mishmash of philosophies, methods, therapies, symbols and rituals customarily lumped together as 'new age'.[16] As John Arnold has pithily put it: '... when people cease believing in God and Utopia they do not believe in nothing; they believe in anything'.[17] No matter whether the new Europe is conceptualised as a secular 'modern' or an endlessly relativistic 'postmodern' society, the disappearance of the power of the Church would leave an institutional vacuum in terms of the reproduction of a common body of values underpinning society.

Although the particular prevalence of the processes 'unchurching' Europe varies from place to place, they can be found across the continent. If these trends continue, the question then arises that if the Church – the first basis for a unified Europe – is no longer to be a fundamental common institution in the new integrated Europe what are to be the consequences? The society which may emerge is one in which the materialism, hedonism and solipsism characteristic of contemporary consumer capitalism may simply saturate to the exclusion of all else. Not an especially heroic or purposeful future but perhaps stable in a drugged and bloated fashion. However, the disappearance of the Church and Christianity would not necessarily leave an unchallenged liberal and secular society. What other futures might emerge in the closing stages of this cultural revolution?

At the same time as the influence of the Church has been attenuated, since 1945 immigration has turned Europe into an increasingly multicultural society with significant and growing Islamic and other non-Christian minorities.[18] Britain has been particularly strongly affected by this continent-wide process of change. There, as elsewhere, unlike the majority 'white' population, the strength of attachment of non-Christian communities to their religion tends to be stronger and more important as an ideology of action and a source of identity and cohesion. Tending to be alienated – as a consequence of racism, among other reasons – from identification with British or other UK regional national identities, the identity of members of these communities, even if they have been born British, is often strongly rooted in the faith and nation of their ancestral origins. Once again, while these developments are particularly developed in the United Kingdom they are general across Europe. As has been noted elsewhere:

> We are left with the paradox, that whereas levels of religious practice and the extent of religion's significance for public life are declining in most of Western Europe and Scandinavia, the continent's bound-aries are becoming more sharply defined in religious terms. Europe is perceived to end at the point where Islam begins ... The demise of Soviet-inspired hostility to organised religion has only served to accentuate the uniqueness of Islam's role as Europe's boundary. ... [T]he salience of the geographical boundary (or, better, frontier) with Islam is heightened by the growing importance of Muslim minorities inside a number of Western European counties.[19]

The presence of these growing minorities whose values may not be com-patible with the Christian heritage of a liberal, democratic Europe[20] leaves an open question as to the future of the cultural status quo and hence social and political order in Britain as it does in Europe more widely. At a moment in history when it is possible that the West may be at the beginning of a long and bitter conflict against forces for whom religious identity is an especially powerful force, this may even raise questions concerning the future internal stability and peace of Europe in a new era of tension between 'East' and 'West'.

Meagre levels of interest among Europeans – Christians and otherwise – in this topic belies its importance to the cultural and hence political integrity of Europe itself. Any genuine and viable supra-national com-munity, just like any national one, lives in the imagination, is a cultural construct composed of myths, histories and utopias. If sufficiently held in common such a cultural construct is the robust and flexible basis for a shared identification, a source of energy and direction and so a basis of political allegiances and praxis. For a Europe which is increasingly post-Christian and where the Churches' cultural significance is continuing to decline, Christendom seems unlikely to return to its previous place in the continent's imagination. Even if this should be possible, from one perspective, in a continent which is becoming increasingly multi-faith and multi-cultural it might be a potential cause of social conflict, disin-tegration and even civil war. Alternatively, it may be that an affirmative, active and unembarrassed identification with Europe's Christian heritage is necessary to provide the foundations for a community strong and sta-ble enough to encompass difference and to set the margins of toleration generously, without demanding assimilation.

As recent declarations indicate, the need for a 'soul for Europe' remains. It is an open question whether this can be found, whether the idea of Europe can be reinvented or recovered to successfully retain its integrity and still accommodate diversity, or whether this continent is in a late stage of irretrievable decay, destined to be replaced by more vital historical forces and become one more artefact in the strata of dead civilisations.

Notes

Introduction

1. Jacques Delors, speech to the Churches, Brussels, 4 February 1992; Romani Prodi, speech to the European Parliament, 1999.
2. José Manuel Barroso, 'Europe and Culture', Berliner Konferenz für europäische Kulturpolitik, 26 November 2004.
3. *Ibid.*
4. Address by the Archbishop of Canterbury, Dr. George Carey to the Academie für Zahnärzliche, Fortbildung, Baden-Württemberg [the Advanced Dental Institute], Karlsruhe, Germany, 27 March 1999 (downloaded on 05 October 2005 from http://www.archbishopofcanterbury.org/ carey/speeches/990327.htm.
5. Forum debate: Is Europe at its end?, Sant' Egidio International Meeting of Prayer for Peace – Palais de Congress, Lyons, 12 September 2005 (downloaded on 06 October 2005 from http://www.archbishopofcanterbury.org/ sermons_ speeches/050912.htm).
6. William Penn, *An Essay Toward the Present and Future Peace of Europe by the Establishment of a an European Dyet, Parliament or Estates* (Hildeheim: Olms-Weidmann, 1983).
7. Donald S. Birn, *The League of Nations Union 1918–1945* (Oxford: Oxford University Press, 1981), pp. 3, 8, 20, 76, 104, 129–37; Richard Mayne and John Pinder (eds.) with John C. de V. Roberts, *Federal Union: The Pioneers* (Basingstoke: Macmillan, 1990), pp. 10–11, 13–14, 19, 26, 28.
8. COPEC, *International Relations: Being the Report presented to the Conference on Christian Poltics, Economics and Citizenship at Birmingham, April 5–2, 1924* (London: Longmans, 1924), p. xiii.
9. 'Summi Pontificatus (On the Unity of Human Society)', 20 October 1939, paras. 37–43 (downloaded from http://www.ewtn.com/library/ENCYC/ P12SUMMI.htm, 16 September 2003).
10. V.A. Demant, 'The Christian Doctrine of Human Solidarity', pp. 37–58 in Kenneth Mackenzie (ed.), *Union of Christendom*, vol. 1 (London: Religious Book Club, 1938), p. 40.
11. A.C.F. Beales, *The Catholic Church and International Order* (Harmondsworth: Penguin Books, 1941), pp. 131, 139.
12. *Ibid.*, p. 159.
13. William Temple, *Christus Veritas: An Essay* (London: Macmillan, 1954, first published 1924), p. 84.
14. J.H. Oldham, 'A Bolder View of National Purpose', *The Christian News-Letter*, no. 157, 28 October 1942, unpaginated.
15. Demant, 'The Christian Doctrine of Human Solidarity', p. 40.
16. 'Summi Pontificatus', paras. 44–45, 49.
17. G.K.A. Bell, 'A War of Ideals', pp. 211–18 in *The Church and Humanity (1939–1946)* (London: Longmans, 1946), p. 213 (first preached as a sermon in Chichester Cathedral, 7 September 1941).

18. John Eppstein, *The Catholic Tradition of the Law of Nations: Prepared under the auspices of the Catholic Council for International Relations* (London: Burns, Oates & Washbourne, 1935), pp. 361–62.
19. Oldham, 'A Bolder View of National Purpose'.
20. Joseph H. Oldham, (ed.), *The Churches Survey their Task: The Report of the Conference at Oxford, July 1937, On Church, Community, and State* (London: George Allen and Unwin, 1937), p. 60.
21. William Paton, *The Church and the New Order* (London: SCM, 1941), p. 144.
22. Oldham, (ed.), *The Churches Survey their Task*, p. 59.
23. *Ibid.*, pp. 178–82.
24. AWCC, IMC 26.11.49/19: William Paton, 'The Household of God', broadcast on BBC Overseas Service, 17 November 1940.
25. Oldham, (ed.), *The Churches Survey their Task*, p. 169.
26. *International Relations*, p. 119.
27. *The Christian News-Letter*, no. 311, 12 May 1948, unpaginated.
28. William Temple, 'The Restoration of Christendom', *Christendom*, vol. 1 (1935–36), pp. 17–29: 17, 18.
29. See, for example, John Arnold, 'Europe: Some Biblical and Historical Reflections', *The Reader*, vol. 100, no. 3 (Autumn 2003), pp. 2–5.
30. Temple, 'The Restoration of Christendom', p. 18.
31. Christopher Dawson, *The Judgement of the Nations* (London: Sheed & Ward, 1943), p. 69.
32. 'John Hadham' [James Parkes], *God and Human Progress* (Harmondsworth: Penguin, 1944). p. 32.
33. Temple, 'The Restoration of Christendom', p. 17.
34. *Ibid.*, p. 21.
35. Beales, *The Catholic Church and International Order*, p. 36.
36. Dawson, *The Judgement of the Nations*, p. 142.
37. Temple, 'The Restoration of Christendom', p. 22.
38. Christopher Dawson, 'The Religious Origins of European Disunity', *Dublin Review*, vol. 207, (October–December 1940), pp. 142–59.
39. Temple, 'The Restoration of Christendom', p. 22.
40. John Eppstein, 'The Catholic Tradition in International Relations', *The Month*, vol. CLXXX (November–December 1944), pp. 377–89: 388.
41. G.K.A. Bell, *Christianity and World Order* (Harmondsworth: Penguin, 1940), pp. 22–24.
42. 'Summi Pontificatus', paras. 52–62.
43. G.K.A. Bell, 'University Sermon: Christian Co-operation', *The Cambridge Review*, vol. LXIII (1 November 1941), pp. 62–64.
44. Christopher Dawson, *Understanding Europe* (London: Sheed & Ward, 1952), p. 19.
45. Dawson, The Judgement of the Nations, pp. 5–6.
46. Oldham, (ed.), *The Churches Survey their Task*, p. 58.
47. Beales, *The Catholic Church and International Order*, p. 36.
48. The Bishop of Chichester [George K.A. Bell], 'Christianity and Reconstruction', *The Fortnightly*, vol. CXLVIII (July–December 1940), pp. 558–64: 539.
49. Alec R. Vidler, *God's Judgement on Europe* (London: Longmans, 1940), pp. 71–73.
50. Paton, *The Church and the New Order*, p. 48.

51. Dawson, *The Judgement of the Nations*, p. 100.
52. Oldham (ed.), *The Churches Survey their Task*, pp. 172–73, 176.
53. See, for example, Alfred Zimmern, 'The Decline of International Standards', *International Affairs*, vol. XVII, no. 1 (January–February 1938), pp. 3–25.
54. Beales, *The Catholic Church and International Order*, p. 179.
55. Bell, 'Christianity and Reconstruction', 561.
56. Temple, 'The Restoration of Christendom', pp. 24–25.
57. 'Summi Pontificatus', para. 82; *The Pope's Five Peace Points: Allocation to the College of Cardinals by his Holiness Pope Pius XII on December 24 1939* (London: Catholic Truth Society, 1939); *The Times*, 21 December 1940.
58. Beales, *The Catholic Church and International Order*, p. 148.
59. Temple, *Christus Veritas*, p. 85.
60. Temple, 'The Restoration of Christendom', pp. 26–27.
61. *Ibid.*, p. 22.
62. Bell, *Christianity and World Order*, pp. 129–38; William Paton, *World Community* (London: SCM, 1938).
63. G.K.A. Bell, 'The Church in Relation to International Affairs', *International Affairs*, vol. 25, no. 3 (July 1949), pp. 405–14: 413.
64. Temple, 'Principles of Reconstruction', p. 93.
65. Paton, *The Churches and the New Order*, p. 170.
66. William Temple, *The Hope of a New World* (London: SCM, 1940), pp. 26–27, 30 (originally part of a series of talks broadcast on the BBC, September–October, 1940.
67. Beales, *The Catholic Church and International Order*, p. 21.
68. Paton, *The Churches and the New Order*, p. 188.
69. Bell, *Christianity and World Order*, p. 38.
70. The history of the concept of 'Europe' is discussed in Anthony Pagden (ed.), *The Idea of Europe: From Antiquity to the European Union* (Cambridge: Cambridge University Press/Woodrow Wilson Centre Press, 2002). In particular, see the introduction and chapters by Pagden ('Europe: Conceptualising a Continent', pp. 33–54) and J.G.A. Pocock ('Some Europes and their History', pp. 55–71). See also Richard Roberts. 'European Cultural Identity and Religion', pp. 17–33 in John Fulton and Peter Gee (eds.), *Religion in Contemporary Europe*, Texts and Studies in Religion, vol. 64 (Lewiston, NY: Edwin Mellin, 1994).
71. Christopher Dawson, 'Europe—A Society of Peoples', *The Month*, vol. CLXXXI (September–October 1945), pp. 309–16: 311.
72. Christopher Dawson, 'Europe and Christendom', *The Dublin Review*, vol. 209 (October 1941), pp. 109–19: 111.
73. For a brief critical discussion of the relationship of medieval Christendom to Europe see William Chester Jordan, '"Europe" in the Middle Ages', pp. 72–90 in Pagden (ed.), *The Idea of Europe*.
74. 'The Unity of Europe', *Westminster Cathedral Chronicle and Diocesan Gazette*, vol. XLII, no. 9 (September 1948), pp. 203–5: 204.
75. Bell, 'The Church in Relation to International Affairs', p. 405; Eppstein, 'The Catholic Tradition in International Relations', p. 389.
76. Dawson, *Understanding Europe*, p. 13.
77. William Temple, 'The Crisis of Western Civilisation', pp. 78–82 in *The Church Looks Forward* (London: Macmillan, 1944), pp. 78–9 (recorded on 12 July

1943, for broadcasting on the BBC Overseas Service); Dawson, *Understanding Europe*, p. 12.

78. G.K.A. Bell, 'Christianity and the European Heritage', pp. 177–82 in *The Church and Humanity*, p. 179 (Christmas Broadcast to Germany, 23 December, 1945).

79. Barroso, 'Europe and Culture'.

1 – Christian Peace Aims and Federal Europe

1. See Paul Addison, *The Road to 1945: British Politics and the Second World War* (London: Cape, 1975).

2. A.D.K. Owen, 'BWP 1: Citizen of Britain – What is at Stake', pp. 13–18 in *The British Way and Purpose: Consolidated Edition of BWP Booklets 1–18 with Appendices of Documents of Post-War Reconstruction* (The Directorate of Army Education, 1944), p. 15; booklet first issued November 1942.

3. Dennis W. Brogan, *The English People: Impressions and Observations* (London: Hamish Hamilton, 1943), p. 120.

4. 'Their Finest Hour', House of Commons, 18 June 1940.

5. J.B. Priestley, *Postscripts* (London: William Heinemann, 1940), p. 73 [Sunday, 15 September 1940].

6. 'Cassandra' [William Connor], *The English at War* (London: Secker and Warburg, 1941), pp. 31–32.

7. John Strachey, *The Banks for the People* (London: Gollancz, 1940), p. 7.

8. Initially as the 'Anglican Council of War'.

9. Keith Clements, *Faith on the Frontier: A Life of J.H. Oldham* (Edinburgh: T and T Clark, 1999).

10. New College Library, University of Edinburgh (NCLUE), Joseph Oldham Papers, 13/1: 'The Moot: Notes on the discussion at fifth meeting, September 23 –24, 1939, at Annandale, North End Road, London, NW11'.

11. Martin Ceadel, *Semi-Detached Idealists: the British Peace Movement and International Relations, 1854–1945* (Oxford: Oxford University Press, 2000), pp. 1–11, 376–427.

12. Maurice L. Rowntree, *Mankind Set Free* (London: Jonathan Cape, 1939).

13. Albert D. Belden, *Pax Christi: The Peace of Christ: A New Policy for Christendom today* (Wallington, Surrey: Carwell Publications, 1944 – second, revised edition; first published 1942), pp. 37–38.

14. For reasons of style and simplicity 'in formation', which was part of the World Council of Churches title before 1948, it has been dropped in references to the Council hereafter.

15. *The Christian Church and World Order: A Statement by the Commission of the Churches for International Friendship and Social Responsibility*, with a Preface by the Archbishop of Canterbury, Chairman of the Commission (London: SCM, June 1942).

16. 'The Proposed British Council of Churches', *The Church in the World*, 8 July 1942, pp. 9–10; 'Inauguration of the British Council of Churches', *The Church in the World*, no. 1 (New Series), (November 1942), pp. 2–5; Ernest A. Payne, *Thirty Years of the British Council of Churches 1942–1972* (London: BCC, 1972).

17. Archives of the Archbishops of Westminster (AAW), Griffin Papers, 2/86: BCC, 'Christian Influence on Peace Settlement', 25 April 1944.
18. Hugh Martin, 'A Tribute to Bill', *the Religious Book Club Bulletin*, no. 37 (November 1943), 1–3.
19. *The Pope's Five Peace Points*.
20. *The Pope's Five Peace Points*, p. 19.
21. Bell, *Christianity and World Order*, pp. 97–101; G.K.A. Bell, 'The Church and the Future of Europe' (The substance of a paper read to the Austrian Democratic Union in London, 20 January 1943), pp. 110–22 in *The Church and Humanity* (London: Longmans, 1946), p. 117.
22. Michael J. Walsh, 'Ecumenism in War-Time Britain. The Sword of the Spirit and Religion and Life, 1940–1945', *The Heythrop Journal*, vol. XXIII (1982), pp. 243–58 and 377–94.
23. See also Introduction above.
24. Paton, *The Church and the New Order*, p. 49; J.H. Oldham, *The Resurrection of Christendom* (London: Sheldon, 1940).
25. Clarence Streit, *Union Now* (London: Jonathan Cape, 1939); William Beveridge, 'Peace by Federation?', *World Order Papers*, no. 3 (London: Royal Institute of International Affairs, 1940). See also, W.B. Curry, *The Case for Federal Union* (Harmondsworth: Penguin Books, 1939); M. Channing-Peace (ed.), *Federal Union: A Symposium* (London: Jonathan Cape, 1940); Lord Davies, *A Federated Europe* (London: Gollancz, 1940); C.B. Fawcett, *The Bases of a World Commonwealth* (London: Watts, 1941); W. Ivor Jennings, *A Federation for Western Europe* (Cambridge: Cambridge University Press, 1940); R.W.G. Mackay, *Federal Europe: Being the Case for European Federation, Together with a Draft Constitution of a United States of Europe* (London: Martin Joseph, 1940); Clarence K. Streit, *Union Now With Britain* (London: Jonathan Cape, 1941); [Sir] George Young, *Federalism and Freedom or Plan the Peace to Win the War* (Oxford: Oxford University Press, 1941); Duncan and Elizabeth Wilson, *Federation and World Order* (London: Nelson/Basis Books, 1940).
26. National Archives (NA), FO800-242 (Halifax Papers): 275 Sir A. Hardinge [King George VI's Private Secretary] to Lord Halifax, 5 August 1940; 279: Halifax to Hardinge, 13 August 1940.
27. *Federal Union News*, no. 17, 16 January 1940, p. 6; Derek Rawnsley 'How Federal Union Began', February–March, 1940, no. 23 (Conference edition), p. 4.
28. *Federal Union News*, no. 29, 6 April 1940, pp. 2–3.
29. Edward H. Carr, *The Twenty Years' Crisis, 1919–1939: An Introduction to the Study of International Relations* (London: Macmillan, 1939).
30. *Federal Union News*, no. 29, 6 April 1940, pp. 2–3.
31. 'X' [A.C. Headlam], 'The War', *Clergy Quarterly Review*, vol. CXXIX (January–March 1940), pp. 314–27: 321–22.
32. *Federal Union News*, no. 13, 16 December 1939, pp. 4–5.
33. *Federal Union News*, no. 70, 2 August 1941, p. 3.
34. See John S. Hoyland, *Federate or Perish* (London: Federal Union, 1944).
35. *Federal Union News*, 'Special Continental Number', April–May 1940, p. 4; *Federal Union News*, no. 68, 5 July 1941, p. 3; 'Spotlight on the Executive', *Federal News*, no. 119 (January 1945), p. 16.
36. University of Sussex Special Collections (USSC), Maurice Reckitt papers, 19/2: 'A memorandum on Federal Union', circulated for the meeting of the

Anglican Wartime Council, 12 December [1939]. Minutes of AWC meetings: 25 January 1940; 19 April 1940; 4 June 1940.

37. USSC, Reckitt papers, 19/4: 'A Memorandum Federal Union', undated (ca. April 1940).

38. USSC, Reckitt papers, 19/2: Minutes of the meeting of the AWC, 19 April 1940. By combining patriotism, social credit, ruralism and guild-socialism the Christendom group was by no means incompatible with the thinking of many British fascists. It also operated on the boundary where social-credit condemnation of 'finance-capitalism' shaded off into anti-Semitic paranoia about the 'money power'. For example, Reckitt spoke on 'Social Integration and the way to World Order' to a series of lectures hosted by the New Europe Group in which Arthur Kitson also spoke on 'The Hidden Meaning of the World Crisis' (25/7: Handbill for 'Lectures and discussions on the present situation in Europe', [no date]). This ideological overlap was well illustrated by the involvement of two former leading members of the British Union of Fascists in the Christendom Group: Arthur K. Chesterton, second cousin to G.K., with whom Reckitt had worked closely (*ibid.*, 12/17: S. Sagar to Maurice Reckitt, 21 July 1946); and Jorian Jenks, formerly the BUF's agricultural expert, who spoke at the Christendom summer school ('British Agriculture and International Trade', *Christendom*, vol. XIII, no. 51(September 1943), pp. 83–86). Conversely, scrutiny of the pages of the British fascist press of the inter-war period shows that the full participation of clergy and lay Christians of all denominations in the activities of the British Union of Fascists (BUF) was by no means rare.

39. Reckitt papers, 19/4 Minutes of the AWC Committee meeting, 4 June 1940.

40. 'Report of the Committee on Church and Nation to the General Assembly of the Church of Scotland: Peace and War', May 1940, pp. 377–86 in *Reports of the General Assembly with the Legislative Acts, 1940*, pp. 383–84.

41. 'Editorial Comments', *The Month*, vol. CLXXV (January 1940), pp. 2–3.

42. AWCC, 24.263: W. Paton to A.J. Toynbee, 12 April 1939.

43. Bodleian Library (Bod L), Arnold Toynbee Papers, 119: Paton to Toynbee, 30 May 1939; Paton to Toynbee, 1 June 1939.

44. AWCC, 24.263/Correpondence II: Paton to Toynbee, 12 April 1939; Bod. L, Toynbee Papers, 119: Paton to Toynbee, 30 May 1939; Paton to Toynbee, 1 June 1939; See Jurgen A. Zeilstra, *European Unity in Ecumenical Thinking, 1937–1948* (Zoetermeer, 1995), pp. 41–51. In the event, the British delegation did not include a representative of FU (its members were Paton, Henry Carter (Methodist), J. Hutchinson Cockburn (Church of Scotland), and W.R. Matthews (Church of England) and the academic Sir Alfred Zimmern (Montague Burton Professor of International Relations, University of Oxford and Royal Institute of International Affairs)).

45. See the letters from Temple and others, including Winston Churchill (President of the UK section of The New Commonwealth) and the Archbishop of Wales in 'Leaders of British Opinion Welcome our New Campaign', *The New Commonwealth*, vol. 7, no. 4 (January 1939), pp. 62–63, 79; see also 'From Press and Platform: Current Public Opinion on our Policy', *The New Commonwealth*, vol. 7, no. 7 (April 1939), p. 138.

46. Vivian Carter (ed.), *Religion and the Organization of Peace: An Agreed Statement by Leaders of Many Denominations* (London: Peace Book Company, [1939]).

47. The Archbishop of York [William Temple], 'The Spirit and Aim of Britain', The Listener, Vol. XXII (5 October 1939), pp. 871–72.

48. William Temple, 'Begin Now', supplement to *The Christian News-Letter*, no. 41, 7 August 1940, unpaginated.
49. William Temple, 'The Future of Germany', *The Fortnightly*, vol. CL (November 1941), pp. 405–13: 410–11.
50. Temple, 'Principles of Reconstruction', pp. 91–104 in *Hope of A New World*, pp. 91, 94–95.
51. *Federal Union News*, no. 21, 10 February 1940, p. 5.
52. Temple, 'Begin Now'.
53. *Federal Union News*, no. 5, 21 October 1939, p. 5; *Federal Union News*, no. 12, 9 December 1939; The Archbishop of York, 'A Christmas Message', *Federal Union News*, no. 14, 23 December 1939, pp. 1–2; Archbishop of York, 'Final Comments on Statements of Policy: Hopes and Difficulties'; *Federal Union News*, no. 56, 4 January 1941.
54. *Federal Union News*, no. 84, 28 February 1942, p. 3.
55. G.K.A. Bell, 'God above the Nation, in *The Church and Humanity*, pp. 202–203; Bell, *The Church and World Order*, pp. 95–97.
56. 'Some Supporters of Federal Union', *Federal Union News*, no. 1 (5 September 1939); *Federal Union News*, no. 20, 3 February 1940, Supplement, p. 1.
57. *Hansard (House of Lords)*, vol. 115, fols. 251–56 (13 December 1939); AWCC, 301.1.02/7: Undated typescript, 'Peace Aims and the Future of Europe'.
58. AWCC, 301.1.02/7: Undated typescript, 'Peace Aims and the Future of Europe'.
59. Bell, *The Church and World Order*, pp. 11, 95–97, 102.
60. *Federal Union News*, no. 5, 21 October 1939, p. 5.
61. 'Of the many unofficial war aims canvassed, Federal Union has registered on the widest number of people though its implications are barely understood' (USSC, Mass-Observation Archive: File Report no. 688, 'Report on the end of the war' (5 May 1941), p. 1).
62. Present were: Paton, H. Carter, A.C. Craig, Canon Thompson Elliott, L.K. Elmhirst and J.S. Whale (Zeilstra, *European Unity in Ecumenical Thinking*, p. 145).
63. AWCC, 301.009/3: Study Department of the Universal Christian Council for Life and Work, 'The Responsibility of the Church for the International Order', undated.
64. *Ibid.*, pp. 4–5.
65. *Ibid.*, p. 2.
66. *Ibid.*, p. 8.
67. *Ibid.*, p. 10.
68. *Ibid.*, p. 2.
69. *Ibid.*, p. 11.
70. AWCC, 301.008/6 'The Churches and the International Crisis', July 1939.
71. AWCC, IMC26.11.47/5: William Paton to W. Temple, 23 November 1939.
72. AWCC, 301.008/6 'The Churches and the International Crisis', July 1939, p. 5.
73. Zeilstra, *European Unity in Ecumenical Thinking*, p. 141.
74. AWCC, 301.008/10: 'Notes on visit to Copenhagen (18–22 October 1939), pp. 8–9.
75. AWCC, IMC26.11.47/5: William Paton to W. Temple, 23 November 1939.
76. IMC26.11.46/8: A.J. Toynbee, 'Notes on "The Responsibility of the Churches for a New International Order"', 31 December 1939; A Zimmern, 'Comments on Draft of World Council', 3 January 1940; Bod. L, Toynbee

Papers, 119: Toynbee to Paton, 13 November 1939, Toynbee to Paton; AWCC, IMC26.11.47/5: J Hope-Simpson to Paton, 15 November 1939.

77. AWCC, IMC26.11.46/8: 'Notes of Conversations between York, Chichester, Carter, Demant, Matthews and self [Paton] and representatives of PEP, Nicholson, Mayer, Elmhirst, Lawrence, Zvegintszov', 14 December 1939.

78. AWCC, IMC26.11.46/8: A.J. Toynbee, 'Notes on "The Responsibility of the Churches for a New International Order"', 31 December 1939.

79. *Federal Union News*, no. 11, 2 December 1939; Derek Rawnsley 'How Federal Union Began', *Federal Union News*, no. 23 Conference edition, February–March 1940, p. 4.

80. Deborah Lavin, *From Empire to International Commonwealth: A Biography of Lionel Curtis* (Oxford: Clarendon Press, 1995), ch. 14.

81. Christopher Brewin, 'Arnold Toynbee, Chatham House, and Research in Global Context, ch. 11 in David Long and Peter Wilson (eds.) *Thinkers of the Twenty Years Crisis: Interwar Idealism Reassessed* (Oxford: Clarendon Press, 1995), p. 278.

82. For an outline analysis of the membership for the RIIA in this period see Inderjeet Parmar, 'Chatham House, the Foreign Policy Process, and the Making of the Anglo-American Alliance', pp. 199–318 in Andrea Bosco and Cornelia Navari (eds.), *Chatham House and British Foreign Policy, 1919–1945: The Royal Institute of International Affairs during the Interwar Period* (London: Lothian Foundation, 1994), *passim*.

83. Robert H. Keyserlingk, 'Arnold Toynbee's Foreign Research and Press Service, 1939-43 and its Post-War Plans for South-East Europe, *Journal of Contemporary History*, vol. 21, no. 4 (October 1986), pp. 539–58.

84. Archives of the Royal Institute of International Affairs (ARIIA), 2/1/7 Annex 1 to Minutes of the Meeting of the FRPS Committee, 14 May 1941: 'Foreign Research and Press Service – Outline of Organisation'.

85. University of Birmingham Special Collections (UBSC), DA51 – WCC/BCC Papers, Box WCC Paton Papers – 'Peace Aims': Minutes of Informal Consultation held at Princeton Inn, March 20–22, 1942.

86. AWCC, IMC26.11.47/5: W. Paton to W. Temple, 23 November 1939; see also AWCC, 301.008/8: W. Paton to W.A. Visser t' Hooft, 23 November 1939.

87. UBSP, DA51 – WCC/BCC Papers, Box WCC Paton Papers – 'Peace Aims': Minutes of Informal Consultation held at Princeton Inn, March 20–22, 1942.

88. *Federal Union News*, no. 80, 3 January 1942, p. 4; *Federal Union News*, no. 81, 17 January 1942, p. 3.

89. Martin, 'A Tribute to Bill', pp. 1–3.

90. Bod. L, Toynbee Papers, 119: W. Paton to A.J. Toynbee, 8 November 1940.

91. Bod. L, Toynbee Papers, 119: Paton to Toynbee, 27 October 1941.

92. ARIIA, 9/18: Toynbee to J.V Wilson [RIIA Assistant Director of Research], 18 October 1941; Wilson to Toynbee, 24 October 1941.

93. Bod. L, Toynbee Papers 119: Paton to Toynbee, 26 April [1941].

94. UBSP, DA51 – WCC/BCC Papers, Box WCC Paton Papers – 'Peace Aims': Minutes of Informal Consultation held at Princeton Inn, March 20–22, 1942.

95. *Ibid.*

96. *Ibid.*

97. PEP, *Building Peace Out of War: Studies in Reconstruction* (London: PEP, 1944); Michael Young, 'The Second World War', pp. 81–96 in John Pinder (ed.) *Fifty*

Years of Political and Economic Planning: Looking Forward, 1931–1981 (London: Heinemann, 1981), *passim.*

98. ARIIA 9/18: Arnold J. Toynbee, 'First Thoughts on a Peace Settlement', 26 June 1939.
99. ARIIA 9/18: A.J. Toynbee to L. Curtis, 21 October 1939.
100. Beales, *The Catholic Church and International Order*, p. 12.
101. Bod. L, Toynbee Papers, 119: W. Paton to members of the sub-committee on ecumenical relationships, 26 June 1940.
102. Lambeth Palace Library (LPL), George Bell Papers, 26/129: W. Paton, 'The Problem of War Aims from the Point of View of the Church', undated typescript.
103. Bod. L, Toynbee Papers, 119: W. Paton to members of the sub-committee on ecumenical relationships, 26 June 1940; 'Notes on Peace Aims', undated.
104. William Paton, 'War and Peace Aims and the Church's task', *Christian News-Letter*, no. 68, 12 February 1941, unpaginated; this was also circulated among the PAG in draft form (Bell Papers: 129–38: William Paton, 'The Problem of War Aims from the Point of View of the Church', undated ca. 1941.)
105. The talks were also published as: William Paton, *The Church Calling: Six Talks on The Church and World Order Broadcast in June and July 1942* (London: Cargate Press, 1942).
106. AWCC, IMC26.11.41/2: 'Notes of meeting of Peace Aims Group', 2 June 1943, p. 12; See also Kenneth M. Wolfe, *The Churches and the British Broadcasting Corporation, 1922–1956: The Politics of Broadcast Religion* (London: SCM, 1984), pp. 147, 283–95.
107. Bod. L, Toynbee Papers, 119: W. Paton to members of the sub-committee on ecumenical relationships, 26 June 1940.
108. Paton, 'War and Peace Aims and the Church's task'.
109. *Ibid.*
110. Bod. L, Toynbee Papers, 119: William Paton to members of the sub-committee on ecumenical relationships, 26 June 1940.
111. Bod. L, Toynbee Papers, 119: W. Paton to A.J. Toynbee, 8 November 1940.
112. Paton, 'War and Peace Aims and the Church's task'.
113. *Ibid.*
114. *Ibid.*
115. *Ibid.*
116. Bod. L, Toynbee Papers, 119: 'Notes on Peace Aims', undated.
117. Mark Mazower, 'Hitler's New Order, 1939–45', *Diplomacy and Statecraft*, vol. 7, no. 1 (March 1996), pp. 29–53.
118. Paton, *The Church and the New Order*, p. 85.
119. *Ibid.*
120. Mayne, Pinder and Roberts, *Federal Union*, p. 26.
121. Paton, *The Church and the New Order*, p. 74, no. 1.
122. Paton, 'War and Peace Aims and the Church's task'.
123. Paton, *The Church and the New Order*, p. 110; see also ch. 2 below.
124. *Ibid.*, p. 74.
125. Paton, 'War and Peace Aims and the Church's task'.
126. Paton, *The Church and the New Order*, p. 84.
127. Paton, 'War and Peace Aims and the Church's task'.

128. Temple, *The Hope of a New World*, p. 42; originally given as part of a radio talk and published in *The Listener*.
129. *Ibid.*, pp. 95–101. This idea was circulated for comment as 'Peace Aims as seen from Great Britain' Life and Work; Department, no. 12E/40, WCC Wartime papers.
130. William Temple, 'The Future of Germany', *The Fortnightly*, vol. CL (November 1941), pp. 405–13; See 'Germany and Europe', and 'The Future of Germany', *Planning*, no. 172 (1 July 1941).
131. See, for example, Robert Vansittart, *Black Record: Germans Past and Present* (London: Hamish Hamilton, 1941).
132. Temple, 'The Future of Germany', pp. 409–12.

2 – Britain, America and Europe

1. A.C.F. Beales, 'Catholics and the Peace Settlement', *The Clergy Review*, vol. XVIIII, no. 3 (March 1940), pp. 189–210: 192. Beales was also wrote the Catholic counterpart of Bishop of Chichester's Penguin Special *Christianity and World Order* (1940): *The Catholic Church and International Order* (1941).
2. Avi Shlaim, 'Prelude to Downfall: The British Offer of Union to France, June 1940', *Journal of Contemporary History*, vol. 9, no. 3 (July 1974), pp. 27–63; Mayne, Pinder and Roberts, *Federal Union: The Pioneers*; Andrea Bosco, 'Lothian, Curtis, Kimber and the Federal Union Movement (1938–40), *Journal of Contemporary History*, vol. 23, no. 3 (July 1988), pp. 465–502; Andrea Bosco, 'Chatham House and Federalism', 321–44 in Andrea Bosco and Cornelia Navari (eds.), *Chatham House and British Foreign Policy, 1919–1945: The Royal Institute of International Affairs During the Interwar Period* (London: Lothian Foundation, 1992).
3. Ritchie Ovendale, *The English-Speaking Alliance: Britain, the United States, the Dominions and the Cold War, 1945–1951* (London: George Allen and Unwin, 1985), pp. 3–21.
4. Inderjeet Parmar, 'Chatham House, the Foreign Policy Process, and the Making of the Anglo-American Alliance', pp. 199–318 in Andrea Bosco and Cornelia Navari (eds.), *Chatham House and British Foreign Policy, 1919–1945: The Royal Institute of International Affairs During the Interwar Period* (London: Lothian Foundation, 1992), *passim*; Inderjeet Parmar, 'Chatham House and the Anglo-American Alliance', *Diplomacy and Statecraft*, vol. 3, no. 1 (1992), pp. 23–47: 36–37 and *passim*.
5. ARIIA, 9/18f: Arnold J Toynbee, 'First Thoughts on a Peace Settlement', 26 July 1939.
6. Carr, *The Twenty Years' Crisis*; Peter Wilson, 'Introduction: The Twenty Years' Crisis and the Category of 'Idealism' in International Relations', pp. 1–24 in David Long and Peter Wilson (eds.), *Thinkers of the Twenty Years' Crisis: Interwar Idealism Reassessed* (Oxford: Clarendon Press, 1995).
7. ARIIA, 9/19C: Committee on Reconstruction, 'Discussion meeting on the "The Future of Germany"', 5 March 1941.
8. Wilson, 'Introduction: The Twenty Years' Crisis and the Category of 'Idealism' in International Relations'.
9. Alfred Zimmern, *Spiritual Values and World Affairs* (Oxford: Clarendon Press, 1939), p. 118.

10. William Paton, 'Britain and America', *The Christian News-Letter*, no. 49, 2 October 1940, unpaginated.
11. Paton, 'War and Peace Aims and the Church's task'.
12. Oldham (ed.), *The Churches Survey their Task*, p. 172.
13. Christopher Dawson, 'Peace Aims and Power Politics', *The Dublin Review*, vol. 214 (April 1944), pp. 97–108: 106.
14. Oldham, (ed.), *The Churches Survey their Task*, p. 172.
15. Oldham, 'Anglo-Saxon Responsibilities', The Christian News-letter, No. 115 (7 January 1942), unpaginated.
16. *The Christian Church and World Order*, p. 13.
17. Vidler, *God's Judgement on Europe*, pp. 26–29, 70–78, 86.
18. William Paton, 'Review of Books: Christianity and World Order', *International Review of Missions*, vol. 29 (1940), pp. 270–4: 271.
19. *Ibid.*, p. 272.
20. Paton, *The Churches and the New Order*, p. 66.
21. AWCC, IMC26.11.47/7: W. Paton to A. Zimmern, 6 February 1940.
22. Paton, 'Review of Books: Christianity and World Order', pp. 270–74: 271, 273.
23. Linda Colley, *Britons: Forging the Nation, 1707–1837* (London: Vintage, 1996); Adrian Hastings, *The Construction of Nationhood: Ethnicity, Religion and Nationalism* (Cambridge: Cambridge University Press, 1997), pp. 35–73; Hugh McLeod, 'Protestantism and British National Identity, 1815–1945', pp. 43–70 in Peter van der Veer and Hartmut Lehmann (eds.), *Nation and Religion: Perspectives on Europe and Asia* (Princeton, NJ: Princeton University Press 1999); Keith Robbins, *History, Religion and Identity in Modern Britain* (London: Hambledon Press, 1993), ch. 7.
24. Benedict Anderson, *Imagined Communities: Reflections on the Origin and Spread of Nationalism* (London: Verso, 1991).
25. Bell, *The Church and Humanity*, pp. v–vi.
26. See, for example, J.N. Ogilvie, *Our Empire's Debt to Missions: The Duff Missionary Lecture, 1923* (London: Hodder & Stoughton, 1924).
27. Beales, *The Catholic Church and International Order*, p. 178.
28. Ortega y Gasset, *The Revolt of the Masses* (London: Unwin, 1961; first published 1932), pp. 131–32.
29. Temple, 'The Sovereignty of God', pp. 119–25 in *The Hope of A New World*, p. 124.
30. Cyril Garbett, *In an Age of Revolution* (London: Hodder & Stoughton, 1952), pp. 36–37.
31. Oldham, 'Anglo-Saxon Responsibilities'.
32. Maurice B. Reckitt and J.V. Langmead Casserley, *The Vocation of England* (London: Longmans, 1941), pp. 7–10.
33. Klaus Larres, 'Making Europe Strong Again: Churchill, the United States, and the Creation of a New European Order, 1940–1943', pp. 19–42 in Antonie de Capet and Aissatou Sy-Wonyu (eds.), *The Special Relationship. la "relation spéciale" entre le Royaume-Uni et les États-Unis* (Rouen: Presses Universitaires de Rouen, 2003); R.B. Manderson-Jones, *The Special Relationship: Anglo-American Relations and Western European Unity, 1946–56* (London: Weidenfeld & Nicolson, 1972), pp. 16–31; Ritchie Ovendale, *Anglo-American Relations in the Twentieth Century* (Basingstoke: Macmillan, 1998), pp. 80–98; David Russell, "'The Jolly Old Empire': Labour, the

Commonwealth and Europe, 1945–51", Alex May (ed.), *Britain, the Commonwealth and Europe: The Commonwealth and Britain's Application to join the European Communities* (Basingstoke: Palgrave, 2001), pp. 9–29.

34. Paton, *The Church and the New Order*, pp. 104, 143–44.
35. Temple, *Christus Veritas*, p. 76.
36. Oldham, 'Anglo-Saxon Responsibilities'.
37. William Paton, 'American Opinion and the War' (etc.), *The Christian News-Letter*, no. 137, 10 June 1942, unpaginated.
38. NA, INF1/414, MOI, Publicity Division, Planning Section, Memo 293, 'Protestant Churches', undated, 31 July 1939, pp. 9–10.
39. NA, INF1/775, Huge Martin, 'The BIS and Religious Organizations in USA', 24 November 1941.
40. NA, FO371/24227: BLI Report no.28, 'The Reaction against the Propaganda Phobia', 22 January 1940.
41. NA, INF1/775, H. Martin to Basil Mathews, 30 July 1940, H. Martin to Lord Davidson, 21 July 1942.
42. Paton, 'American Opinion and the War'.
43. NA, INF1/414, Memo, Martin to Maclennen, undated (ca. 1940).
44. NA, INF1/446 Richard Hope, 'Notes on the Early History of Religions Division', 28 July 1945.
45. *Ibid.*
46. *Ibid.*
47. Dean K. Thompson, 'Henry Pitney van Dusen: Ecumenical Statesman' (unpublished Ph.D. thesis, Union Theological Seminary in Virginia, 1974), pp. 211, 245.
48. NA, INF1.775, 'Report of Discussion between Sir Frederick Whyte and Professor Basil Mathews of American Division; Mclennan, Martin, Williams and Hope of Religions Division, 4 July 1940.
49. NA, INF1/414, Memo, H. Martin to Harold Nicolson, 23 September 1940.
50. NA, INF1/775, H. Martin to Lord Davidson, 21 July 1942.
51. NA, INF1/775, H. Martin, 'The BIS and Religious Organizations in USA', 24 November 1941.
52. NA, INF1/775, 'The Work of the Religions Division in the United States of America', undated.
53. NA, INF1/775, H. Martin, 'The BIS and Religious Organizations in USA', 24 November 1941.
54. NA, INF1/777: Memo, Martin to Darvell, 6 April 1943.
55. NA, INF1/414, MOI, Publicity Division, Planning Section, Memo 293, 'Protestant Churches', undated (ca. 1940), pp. 9–10.
56. NA, INF1/776: H. Martin to Professor John Baillie, 30 October 1940; Martin to Baillie; Memo, Martin to Putnam, 10 January 1941; Martin to J. Balfour (FO), 24 June 1941.
57. NA, INF1/776: Baillie to Martin, 4 March and 26 April 1941.
58. NA, INF1/777: H. Martin to Rev James S. Stewart, 22 December 1942.
59. NA, INF1/776: H Martin to Capt Hamish Hamilton, 29 December 1941.
60. NA, FO371/24227: Lord Lothian to D.J.M.D Scott, 20 February 1940.
61. NA, INF1/776: H. Martin to H. Granville-Barker, undated (ca. 1941).
62. Eleanor M. Jackson, *Red Tape and the Gospel. A study of the significance of the ecumenical missionary struggle of William Paton (1886-1943)* (Birmingham: Phlogiston/Selly Oak Colleges, 1980), p. 267. Williams was formerly

Education Secretary at the CMS and later Bishop of Leicester. He followed Hugh Martin as director of the Religions Section. (Kenneth Grubb, *Crypts of Power: An Autobiography* (London: Hodder & Stoughton, 1971), p. 126).

63. Paton, 'American Opinion and the War'.
64. On the British Library of Information see Nicholas John Cull, *Selling War: The British Propaganda Campaign Against American "Neutrality" in World War II* (Oxford: Oxford University Press, 1995).
65. AWCC, IMC 26.11.47/8: Paton to Curtis, 18 January 1940.
66. AWCC, IMC 26.11.46/8; 'Conversation with PEP – Notes', 5 February 1940. Paton also reported having a 'long talk about the whole American situation' with the 'PEP Crowd' the next year (AWCC, 301.1.01/02: Paton to Raymond Gauntlett, 15 July 1941).
67. AWCC, IMC26.11.46/10: Paton to Leonard K. Elmhirst, 10 June 1940.
68. Edward Mead Earle, 1894–1954, professor at the School of Economics and Politics at the Institute for Advanced Study, Princeton. A military affairs expert, particularly in the area of the history of American diplomacy. Earle served in the US Army, 1917–19 and later fulfilled a series of high-level consultative roles for the US military, including, during wartime, the Office of Strategic Services. As chair of the American Committee for International Studies he planned the ACIS North Atlantic Relations Conference on current and post-war co-operation of 1941, which discussed post-war settlement, including the topics 'Can Britain and U.S. Cooperate', 'Rebuilding Europe,' and 'Post-War Order'. He was also a member of the pro-British Council on Foreign Relations, and some years later was part of its Study Group on Anglo-American Relations (1952). In the post-war period he held posts at the Joint Services Staff College, Imperial Defence College and Royal Naval College in Britain. (*Who Was Who in America*, vol. 3, p. 247).
69. Everett Johnston Coil, 1907–1950 (*Who Was Who in America*, vol. 3, pp. 170–71).
70. Bruce Bliven, 1889–1977 (*Who Was Who in America*, vol. 7, p. 56). The American wife of Leonard Elmhirst, Paton's contact at PEP, was the long-term financial supporter of *The New Republic* and other liberal-progressive titles (Beulah Amidon, 'The Nation and the New Republic', *Survey Graphic* (1 January 1940); Downloaded from http://newdeal.feri.org/survey/40a02.htm, 3 July 2003).
71. Margaret Sinclair, *William Paton: A Biography* (London: SCM, 1949), pp. 240–41.
72. Thompson, 'Henry Pitney van Dusen', p. 223.
73. *Ibid.*, pp. 221–24.
74. Heather A. Warren, *Theologians of A New World Order: Reinhold Niebuhr and the Christian Realists* (New York: Oxford University Press, 1997), pp. 96–97.
75. NA, FO371/24241: 'Memorandum on American Aid for Great Britain', undated (ca. July 1940), p. 1.
76. *Ibid.*, p. 4.
77. Llewellyn Woodward, *British Foreign Policy in the Second World War*, vol. 1 (London: HMSO, 1970), pp. 333–54.
78. *Ibid.*, pp. 337–38.
79. Thompson, 'Henry Pitney van Dusen', pp. 226–27.

80. NA, INF1/775: H. van Dusen to W. Paton, 9 August 1940.
81. *Ibid.*
82. *British Security Coordination: The Secret History of British Intelligence in the Americas, 1940–45*, (London: St. Ermin's Press, 1998), pp. 12–13.
83. *Ibid.*, pp. 9–10.
84. INF1/775: H. van Dusen to W. Paton, 9 August 1940.
85. Sinclair, *William Paton*, p. 241.
86. NA, FO371/24241, Paton to Halifax, 2 August 1940.
87. Bod L., Toynbee Papers 119: Paton to PAG, 26 June 1940.
88. AWCC, IMC26.11.47/14: Paton to Charles Raven, 8 November 1940.
89. *Ibid.*
90. NA, INF1/177: Harley Granville-Barker to Hugh Martin, 23 April 1943. Granville-Barker wrote of Paton's second wartime visit: 'Again a highly successful journey, though, of course, a less spectacular one.'
91. Bod. L, Arnold Toynbee Papers, 119: Notes of the meeting of the Group on 'Peace Aims', Balliol College, Oxford, 2–3 October 1941.
92. Paton, 'War and Peace Aims and the Church's task'.
93. Bod. L, Toynbee Papers, 119: William Paton to Arnold Toynbee, 27 October 1941.
94. Federal Council of the Churches of Christ in America Commission to Study the Bases of a Just and Durable Peace, *A Just and Durable Peace: Data Material and Discussion Questions* (New York: Federal Council of the Churches of Christ in America, 1941); Warren, *Theologians of a New Order*, p. 100.
95. Bod. L, Arnold Toynbee Papers, 119: Notes of the meeting of the Group on 'Peace Aims', Balliol College, Oxford, 2–3 October 1941. In addition to Temple, Bell and Paton, the Churches were represented by Dr. A.C. Craig; Rev. W.T. Elmsie, Rev. J. Pitt-Watson, and the Canadian missionary and literature expert Miss Margaret Wrong (based in London). Also attending were A.D. Lindsay, Master of Balliol College, Oxford, Toynbee and Zimmern and Sir Henry Bunbury stepped in to take the place of A.D.K. Owen of PEP.
96. William Paton, *America and Britain* (London: Edinburgh House Press, 1942), p. 4.
97. Paton, *The Churches and the New Order*, p. 25.
98. AWWC, IMC26.11.41/10: W. Paton to H.P. van Dusen, 22 December 1942.
99. ARIIA, 9/18: A.J. Toynbee to J.V Wilson [Assistant Director of Research], 18 October 1941; Wilson to Toynbee, 24 October 1941.
100. UBSP, DA51 – WCC/BCC Papers, Box WCC Paton Papers – 'Peace Aims': Notes of the meeting of the Group on Peace Aims, 15–6 July 1942.
101. Bod. L, Toynbee Papers, 119: H. Cockburn to H. Martin, 9 December 1942.
102. UBSP, DA51 – WCC/BCC Papers, Box WCC Paton Papers – 'Peace Aims': W. Paton to PAG, 11 January 1943.
103. Donald Gilles, *Radical Diplomat: The Life of Archibald Clark Kerr, Lord Inverchapel, 1882-1951* (London: IB Tauris, 1999), chs 7–8.
104. *Ibid.*
105. Grubb, *Crypts of Power*, pp. 106–107, 117–18, 119–21, 132.
106. AWCC, IMC26.11.41/10: W. Paton to H.P. van Dusen, 22 December 1942.
107. *The Times*, 29 July 1943; *The Manchester Guardian*, 29 July 1943. Signatories: Temple; Garbett; Bell; R.D. Whitehorn, moderator of the Free Church

Federal Council; M.E. Aubrey, general secretary of the Baptist Union of Great Britain and Ireland; S.M. Berry, former Moderator of the Federal Council of the Free Churches of England; A.D. Lindsay, Master of Balliol College, Oxford; R. Livingston, president of New College, Oxford; W.J. Noble, president of the Methodist Conference; William Paton; Sir J. Hope Simpson, Head of the Peace Aims Section at Chatham House; R.H. Tawney, Professor of Economic history in the University of London. Members of PAG in government service could not sign.

108. UBSP, DA51 – WCC/BCC Papers, Box WCC Paton Papers – 'Peace Aims': Study Department of the WCC, 'Comments on the "Six Pillars of Peace" of the Federal Council of the Churches of Christ in America of March 1943 (14 E/43) by a Christian Study Group'.

109. UBSP, DA51 – WCC/BCC Papers, Box WCC Paton Papers – "Peace Aims": Minutes of PAG meeting, 2 Eaton Gate, London, 3 February 1943.

110. UBSP, DA51 – WCC/BCC Papers, Box WCC Paton Papers – 'Peace Aims', 28 December 1940, H.P. van Dusen to W. Paton.

111. John Foster Dulles, *Toward World Order: A Merrick-McDowell Lecture delivered at Ohio Wesleyan University on March 5, 1942, on the occasion of the Conference called by Authority of the Federal Council of Churches to study the Bases for a Just and Durable Peace* (No place, no date).

112. Bod. L, Toynbee Papers, 119: Notes of the meeting of the Group on 'Peace Aims', Balliol College, Oxford, 2–3 October 1941.

113. Bod. L, Toynbee Papers, 119: W. Paton to A.J. Toynbee, 26 September 1941.

114. Henry P. van Dusen, 'Issues of the Peace', *The Church in the World*, 7 March 1942, pp. 3–5.

115. Bod. L, Toynbee Papers, 119: W. Paton to A.J. Toynbee, 22 October 1941; Paton to Toynbee, 27 October 1941; Toynbee to Paton, 10 Nov 1941; Paton to Toynbee, 11 Nov 1941; Paton to Toynbee, 25 November 1941; [illegible] to W. Paton, 24 December 1941. Temple – having secretly been told of his impending elevation to Canterbury – was also unable to go.

116. UBSP, DA51 – WCC/BCC Papers, Box WCC Paton Papers – 'Peace Aims': Minutes of Informal Consultation held at Princeton Inn, March 20–22, 1942, p. 2. The American Party was: Frank Aydelotte (Director of the Institute for Advanced Study, Princeton (1940–47), Dr. Roswell P. Barnes, Dr. Raymond Leslie Buell (former Research Director (1927–33) and then president (1933–39) of the Foreign Policy Association), Professor Robert Calhoun, Dr. Samuel McCrea Calvert, John Foster Dulles, Dr. Angus Dunn, Professor Clyde Eagleton, Professor Theodore M. Greene, Dr. Douglas Horton, Dr. Kenneth S. Latourette, Dr. Henry Smith Leiper, Dr. John A Mackay, Francis P. Miller, Professor Reinhold Niebuhr (professor of Christian ethics in the Union Theological Seminary, New York City (1928–60), Rt. Rev. William Scarlett, Dr. George Schuster, Dr. Henry P. van Dusen, Dr. Walter W. van Kirk.

117. *Ibid.*, p. 20

118. NA, INF1/777: H. Granville-Barker to H. Martin, 23 April 1943.

119. Bod. L, Toynbee Papers, 119: Notes of the meeting of the Group on 'Peace Aims', Balliol College, Oxford, 2–3 October 1941, p. 5.

120. Those attending were: Temple, Bell, Hutchison-Cockburn, Dulles, Rev. Eric Fenn, Grubb, Lindsay, Dr. A.D.K Owen, Paton, Dennis Routh, Sir John Hope

Simpson, Dr George Stewart, Toynbee, Dr. Walter van Kirk, Rev. J. Pitt Watson, Professor R.D. Whitehorn, Margaret Wrong and Zimmern (UBSP, DA51 – WCC/BCC Papers, Box WCC Paton Papers – 'Peace Aims': Notes of the meeting of the Group on Peace Aims, ... 15–6 July 1942).

121. *Ibid.*, p. 10.
122. *Ibid.*, p. 14.
123. *Ibid.*
124. AWCC, IMC 26.11.41/10: H. van Dusen to W. Paton, 7–15, 22 and 23 October 1942.
125. Participants were Frank Aydelotte, Roswell P. Barnes, Raymond Leslie Buell, Robert Calhoun, Samuel McCrea Cavert, J. Hutchison-Cockburn, John Foster Dulles, Angus Dun, Clyde Eagleton, Theodore M. Greene, Douglas Horton, Kenneth S. Latourette, Henry Smith Leiper, John A. Mackay, Francis P. Miller, Reinhold Niebuhr, William Paton, William Scarlett, George N. Shuster, Henry P. van Dusen and Walter W. van Kirk.
126. AWCC, IMC 26.11.41/10: van Dusen to Paton, 7–15 October 1942.
127. Bod. L, Toynbee Papers, 119: Untitled and undated draft memorandum sent by W. Paton to A. J. Toynbee, 30 December 1942.
128. Dulles, *Toward World Order*, pp. 11–12.
129. AWCC, IMC26.11.41/4: G. Bell to Paton, 27 January 1943.
130. Bod. L, Toynbee Papers, 119: D. Routh to Paton, 9 November 1942.
131. AWCC, IMC26.11.41/10: Paton to van Dusen, 2 December 1942.
132. UBSP, DA51 – WCC/BCC Papers, Box WCC Paton Papers – 'Peace Aims': J Hutchinson – Cockburn to Paton, 4 January 1943.
133. UBSP, DA51 – WCC/BCC Papers, Box WCC Paton Papers – 'Peace Aims': Minutes of PAG meeting, 2 Eaton Gate, London, 3 February 1943; see also AWCC, IMC26.41.41/4: N. Mickem to W. Paton, 5 January 1943.
134. AWCC, IMC261.11.41/4: A. Zimmern to Paton, 4 January 1943; see also J. Hope-Simpson to Paton, 28 January 1943.
135. AWCC, IMC26.11.41/10: Paton to van Dusen, 2 December 1942.
136. Bod. L, Toynbee Papers, 119: Routh to Paton, 9 November 1942.
137. Bod. L, Toynbee Papers, 119: Paton to members of PAG, 30 December 1942.
138. 'We doubt the feasibility of establishing a special mechanism for the revision of treaties but we hope that a continuing cooperation in economic tasks and the maintenance of world order may create a readiness to negotiate together as would enable the world structure to be responsive to the need for change.' (*The Times*, 29 July 1943).
139. 'A Just and Durable Peace: Report of a Commission of the Federal Council of Churches in America', supplement to *The Christian News-Letter*, no. 179, 7 April 1943.
140. UBSP, DA51 – WCC/BCC Papers, Box WCC Paton Papers – 'Peace Aims': Minutes of PAG meeting, 2 Eaton Gate, London, 3 February 1943.
141. AWCC, 26.11.41/13: 'A Christian Basis for Reconstruction', typescript annotated by W. Temple enclosed with letter from him to W. Paton, 5 April 1943.
142. AWCC, IMC26.11.41/2: 'Notes on the meeting of the Peace Aims Group', 2 June 1943, afternoon session, p. 1.
143. AWCC, IMC26.11.41/13: 'A Christian Basis for Reconstruction', undated typescript marked 'final draft'.

144. AWCC, IMC26.11.41/10: Memorandum, W. Paton to PAG, 2 June 1943; original emphasis.
145. Henry P. van Dusen, 'British and American Approaches to the Peace', *The Christian News-Letter*, no. 186, 14 July 1943, unpaginated.
146. Llewellyn Woodward, *British Foreign Policy in the Second World War* (London: HMSO, 1962), pp. 435–36.
147. AWCC, IMC26.11.41/4: K. Grubb to D. Routh, 30 January 1943. Grubb wrote of Eden delivering his paper to the cabinet 'shortly'. In fact, the foreign secretary had already presented the paper on 16 January. Given that the business of the war Cabinet was highly secret it is not surprising that Grubb would not have known precise particulars of its business.
148. AWCC, IMC26.11.41/1: Paton to Routh, 27 January 1943; IMC26.11.41/4: D. Routh, 'Draft Statement', 31 January 1943.
149. AWCC, IMC26.11.41/4: Grubb to Routh, 30 January 1943.
150. David Dutton, *Anthony Eden: A Life and Reputation* (London: Arnold, 1997), pp. 281–83.
151. UBSP, DA51 – WCC/BCC Papers, Box WCC Paton Papers – 'Peace Aims': Minutes of PAG meeting, 2 Eaton Gate, London, 3 February 1943.
152. *The Christian News-Letter*, no. 138, 17 June 1942, unpaginated.
153. UBSP, DA51 – WCC/BCC Papers, Box WCC Paton Papers – 'Peace Aims': Minutes of the Meeting of the Peace Aims Group, 2 June 1943.
154. AWCC, IMC26.11.46/9: A. Zimmern, 'Comments on the draft of World Council', 3 January 1940.
155. AWCC, IMC26.11.41/4: E. Fenn to Paton, 4 February 1943; Paton to Fenn, 5 February 1943.
156. LPL, William Temple Papers, 51/68: C. Joad to W. Temple, 14 May 1942; 51/69: Temple to Joad, 19 May 1942.
157. AWCC, IMC26.11.41/5: press cuttings from *Christian Science Monitor*, *New York Herald Tribune* and *New York Times*.
158. AWCC, IMC26.11.41/5: J.F. Dulles to Paton, 30 July 1943.
159. Paton, 'War and Peace Aims and the Church's task'.
160. *The Times*, 29 July 1943.
161. Van Dusen, 'British and American Approaches to the Peace'.
162. AWCC, 301.1.01/3: Paton to Margaret Richards, 27 July 1943.
163. Bod. L, Toynbee Papers, 119: Paton to A. Toynbee, 26 September 1941.

3 – The Future of Europe, 1944–45

1. AWCC, IMC26.11.41/4: G. Bell to W. Paton, 27 January 1943.
2. *Hansard: Parliamentary Debates, House of Lords*, vol. 126, cols. 535–45, 10 March 1943.
3. See Lord [Robert] Vansittart, *The Bones of Contention* (London: Hutchinson, undated, ca. 1945).
4. *Hansard: Parliamentary Debates, House of Lords*, vol. 126, cols. 544–45, 10 March 1943.
5. LPL, William Temple Papers, 57/324: Bell to Paton, 12 March 1943.
6. See above, ch. 2.
7. W.A. Visser t' Hooft, *Memoirs* (London: SCM, 1973), pp. 129–31, 136–49, 173–75, 177–81.

8. AWCC, 301.009/8: 'Some Considerations Concerning the Post-War Settlement', undated (ca. March 1941).

9. LPL, Bell Papers 26/155: 'Notes on "Long Range Peace Objectives" (from a Continental European Standpoint)', December 1941.

10. LPL, Bell Papers 26/155: Paton to PAG members, 30 January 1942.

11. UBSP, DA51 – WCC/BCC Papers, Box WCC Paton Papers – 'Peace Aims': Notes for Christian Principles and Reconstruction group meeting, 5 February 1943.

12. UBSP, DA51 – WCC/BCC Papers, Box WCC Paton Papers – 'Peace Aims': Study Department of the WCC, 'Comments on the "Six Pillars of Peace" of the Federal Council of the Churches of Christ in America of March 1943 (14 E/43) by a Christian Study Group'.

13. See ch. 1 above.

14. AWCC, 301.009/9: 'The Church and the New Order in Europe', August 1941.

15. AWCC, 301.009/9: unsigned [Visser t' Hooft] to H. Martin, 12 September 1941.

16. AWCC, 301.009/11: Document headed (and subsequently crossed out) 'Copy of document handed by Dr. Visser t' Hooft to Dr. William Paton: May, 1942.' See also AWCC, 301.09/11: Adam von Trott to Percy Corbett, 16 June 1941; von Trott to Visser t' Hooft, undated [1941]. Von Trott's letter to Corbett gave detailed comments about the latter's proposed book which would be published as *Post-war Worlds* (1942).

17. AWCC, 301.009/10: G. Bell to A. Eden, 18 June 1942; Eden to Bell, 17 July 1942; Bell to Eden, 25 July 1942; Eden to Bell, 4 August 1942; Bell to Eden, 17 August 1942.

18. UBSP, DA51 – WCC/BCC Papers, Box WCC Paton Papers – 'Peace Aims': Study Department of the Universal Christian Council for Life and Work (under the auspices of the Provisional Committee of the World Council of Churches), 'Peace Aims as seen from Great Britain', May 1940, p. 1.

19. UBSP, DA51 – WCC/BCC Papers, Box WCC Paton Papers – 'Peace Aims': Minutes of Informal Consultation held at Princeton Inn, March 20–22, 1942.

20. Temple, 'The Future of Germany', pp. 411–12.

21. UBSP, DA51 – WCC/BCC Papers, Box WCC Paton Papers – 'Peace Aims': W. Paton to PAG, 3 Aug 1943.

22. LPL, William Temple Papers, 57/359: G. Bell to W. Paton, 5 August 1943; original emphases.

23. LPL, William Temple Papers, 57/361: 'Memorandum on the "National Committee of Free Germany"', 30 July 1943.

24. LPL, William Temple Papers, 57/359: Bell to Paton, 5 Aug 1943; original emphases.

25. AWCC, IMC26.11.47/4: D. Routh to Paton, 5 August 1943.

26. AWCC, IMC26.11.47/4: K. Grubb to Paton, 8 August 1943.

27. AWCC, IMC26.11.41/5: A. Zimmern to Paton, 7 August 1943.

28. LPL, William Temple Papers, 57/ 367: Temple to [Miss] Sigrid Morden, 23 August 1943.

29. J. H. Oldham, 'William Paton', *The Christian News-Letter*, no. 190, 8 September 1943, unpaginated.

30. UBSP, DA51 – WCC/BCC Papers, Box WCC Paton Papers – 'Peace Aims': W. Temple to William T Elmslie [the new secretary of PAG], 9 Nov 1943.

31. UBSP, DA51 – WCC/BCC Papers, Box WCC Paton Papers – 'Peace Aims': 'A note for the members from the Bishop of Chichester for the meeting to be held ... on Friday, December 10th, 1943'.
32. AWCC, IMC26.11.41/3: 'Notes of Morning session of Peace Aims Group, 10 December 1943'.
33. AWCC, IMC26.11.41/3: Peace Aims Group, 'Notes of afternoon session in relation to the proposed document', 10 December 1943.
34. UBSP, DA51 – WCC/BCC Papers, Box WCC Paton Papers – 'Peace Aims': Bell to PAG, 23 December 1943.
35. LPL, William Temple Papers, 57/374: 'Thoughts on the European Situation' (undated; no author given).
36. UBSP, DA51 – WCC/BCC Papers, Box WCC Paton Papers – 'Peace Aims': Oldham to Routh, 28 December 1943.
37. UBSP, DA51 – WCC/BCC Papers, Box WCC Paton Papers – 'Peace Aims': Routh to PAG, 3 January 1944.
38. 'Britain and Europe', *Planning*, (9 December 1941).
39. J.H. Oldham, 'Britain and Europe', *The Christian News-Letter*, no. 115, 7 January 1942, unpaginated.
40. UBSP, DA51 – WCC/BCC Papers, Box WCC Paton Papers – "Peace Aims": Oldham to Routh, 28 December 1943; Jan Christian Smuts, *Thoughts on a New World address ... at a meeting of the Study Committees of the Empire Parliamentary Association, held ... on 25th November, 1943* (London, undated [1943]).
41. Temple to Smuts, 21 April 1944 (F.S. Temple (ed.), *Some Lambeth Letters* (London: Oxford University Press, 1963), pp. 156–57).
42. AWCC, IMC26.11.41/3: 'Notes of Morning session of Peace Aims Group, 10 December 1943'.
43. See ch. 2 above.
44. Oldham, *The Resurrection of Christendom*.
45. Kenneth Grubb, 'Europe—The Christian Outlook', supplement to *The Christian News-Letter*, no. 219, 18 October 1944, pp. 8, 11, 12.
46. The Bishop of Chichester [George K.A. Bell], 'The Churches and European Reconstruction', supplement to *The Christian News-Letter*, no. 225, 10 January 1945 (speech in the debate in the House of Lords, 19 December 1944).
47. UBSP, DA51 – WCC/BCC Papers, Box WCC Paton Papers – "Peace Aims": 3 January 1944, D. Routh to PAG.
48. AWCC, IMC26.11.41/7: 'Rough notes of meeting of Peace Aims Group on January 7th, 1944'.
49. 'The Future of Europe', *The Spiritual Issues of the War*, no. 230, 30 March 1944.
50. AWCC, IMC26.11.41/7: 'Rough notes of meeting of Peace Aims Group on January 7th, 1944'.
51. AWCC, IMC26.11.41/7: 'Rough notes of meeting of Peace Aims Group on January 7th, 1944'.
52. 'The Future of Europe', *The Spiritual Issues of the War*, no. 230, 30 March 1944.
53. AWCC, IMC26.11.41/7: 'Rough notes of meeting of Peace Aims Group on January 7th, 1944'.

54. 'The Future of Europe', *The Spiritual Issues of the War*, no. 230, 30 March 1944.
55. AWCC, IMC26.11.41/7: 'Rough notes of meeting of Peace Aims Group on January 7th 1944'.
56. LPL, William Temple Papers, 57/ 347, Oldham to Temple, 14 January 1944.
57. 'The Future of Europe', *The Spiritual Issues of the War*, no. 230, 30 March 1944.
58. *The Christian News-Letter*, no. 207, 3 May 1944, unpaginated.
59. LPL, William Temple Papers, 57/403–407: K. Grubb to S. Morden, 20 February 1944; W. Hope Simpson to S. Morden, 21 February 1944; Oldham to Temple, 23 February 1944; Oldham to Temple, 25 February 1944.
60. LPL, William Temple Papers, 58/22: Zimmern to Oldham, 22 March 1944.
61. AWCC, IMC 26-11-41: E. Fenn to Morden, 25 February 1944.
62. LPL, William Temple Papers, 58/3: W. Temple to Archbishop of Westminster, 3 March 1944; 58/ 9: Archbishop of Westminster to Temple, 10 March 1944.
63. LPL, William Temple Papers, 58/33: R.E. Burlingham to Temple, 5 May 1944.
64. UBSP, DA51 – WCC/BCC Papers, Box WCC Paton Papers – 'Peace Aims': 'A note for the members from the Bishop of Chichester for the meeting to be held ... on Friday, December 10th, 1943'.
65. LPL, Bell Papers 53/433: Bell to Oldham, 25 February 1944.
66. LPL, William Temple Papers, 57/396: Grubb to Temple; 15 February 1944; 57/f397: Temple to Grubb, 16 February 1944.
67. Dianne Kirby, *Church, State and Propaganda: The Archbishop of York and International Relations, A Political Study of Cyril Foster Garbett, 1942–1955*, (Hull, University of Hull Press, 1999), pp. 50–52, 148–49.
68. Bod. L, Toynbee Papers: Untitled confidential memorandum from Grubb to PAG, 4 March 1944; AWCC, IMC26.11.41/6: Minutes of the PAG USSR Sub-Committee, 4 April 1944; IMC26.11.41/6: Minutes of the PAG USSR Sub-Committee, 4 April 1944.
69. LPL, William Temple Papers, 58/34: G. Bell to William Temple, 7 October 1944; 58/36: H. Thomas (Temple's secretary) to Bell, 13 October 1944; 58/37: D.L. Cowper to Thomas, 16 October 1944.
70. LPL, Bell Papers, 26/232: Bell to PAG, 14 March 1945.
71. Present at the meeting were: Bell, M.E. Aubrey, Dr. Marc Boegner, A.C. Craig, W.T. Elmslie, E. Fenn, Rev. W.D.L. Greer, VTH, Rt. Rev. Bishop Oldham (US), Oldham, Dr. A.L. Warnshuis (US), Rev. J. Pitt Watson and Professor R.D. Whitehorn. (UBSP, DA51 – WCC/BCC Papers, Box WCC Paton Papers – 'Peace Aims': Minutes of the Meeting of the Peace Aims Group, 7 November 1944).
72. Visser t' Hooft, *Memoirs*, pp. 129–31, 136–49, 173–75, 177–81.
73. UBSP, DA51 – WCC/BCC Papers, Box WCC Paton Papers – 'Peace Aims': Minutes of the Meeting of the Peace Aims Group, 7 November 1944.
74. Oldham, 'William Paton'.

4 – The Churches, the European Movement and Western Union

1. See ch. 2 above.
2. F.X. Rabattet, 'The "European Movement" 1945–1953: a study in National and International Non-Governmental Organisations working for European Unity' (unpublished D.Phil thesis, University of Oxford, 1962), pp. 11–13.

3. *Ibid.*, pp. 13–27.
4. LPL, Fisher Papers, 27/347: G. Amery to G. Fisher, 25 January 1946.
5. W. Roger Louis, *In the Name of God, Go!: Leo Amery and the British Empire in the Age of Churchill* (London: WW Norton, 1992).
6. Richard N. Coudenhove-Kalergi, *Europe Must Unite* (Plymouth: Paneuropa Editions, undated [1940]).
7. LPL, Fisher Papers, 27/354: Fisher to Amery, 28 January 1946.
8. See Churchill Archives Centre (CAC), Churchill Papers, CHUR2/18: L. Amery To W. Churchill, 20 September 1946.
9. CAC, Churchill Papers, CHUR2/25A: Lettice Marston (Private Sec to WSC) to L. Amery, 28 December 1946.
10. LPL, Fisher Papers, 27/355: Churchill to Fisher, 28 December 1946.
11. LPL, Fisher Papers, 27/361: Amery to Fisher, 31 December 1946.
12. CAC, Churchill Papers, CHUR2/25A: Amery to Churchill, 10 January 1947.
13. LPL, Fisher Papers, 27/362 Fisher to Amery, 3 January 1947; 365 Fisher to Amery, 17 January 1947.
14. CAC, Churchill Papers, CHUR2/25A: Amery to Churchill, 10 January 1947.
15. CAC, Churchill Papers, CHUR2/20B: 'General Committee' of UE – undated [prob early 1947].
16. LPL, Fisher Papers, 27/366: Fisher to Churchill, 17 January 1947; 27/373 Fisher to Churchill, 11 March 1947.
17. LPL, Fisher Papers, 27/370: Churchill to Fisher, 8 March 1947.
18. CAC, Churchill Papers, CHUR2/18: United Europe: Speakers At the Albert Hall, 14 May 1947 (London, undated [1947]), p. 1.
19. *Ibid.* pp. 1–2.
20. CAC, Churchill Papers, CHUR2/25A: W. Churchill to G Fisher, 25 May 1947.
21. LPL, Fisher Papers: 65/255: Address read by Fisher at EM meeting at Kingsway Hall, 28 November 1949.
22. LPL, Fisher Papers, 27/374: Churchill to Fisher, 22 March 1947.
23. LPL, Fisher Papers, 27/375: D. Duncan Sandys to G. Fisher, 3 April 1947.
24. John W. Young, 'Churchill's "No" to Europe; "The Rejection" of European Union by Churchill's Post-War Government, 1951–52', *The Historical Journal*, vol. 28, no. 4 (1985), pp. 923–37.
25. LPL, Fisher Papers, 27/377–80: Letter and enclosures from J K Killby, Organising Secretary of FU, to Fisher; 381–91 Lionel Curtis to G. Fisher, 29 April 1947.
26. See, for example, LPL, Fisher Papers, 27/393: Charles M. Haywood (British Parliamentary Committee, Crusade for World Government) to Fisher, 20 October 1947; 27/395: Fisher to Haywood, 22 October 1947.
27. 'European and World Peace', pp. 244–62 in *The Chronicle of Convocation: Being the Proceedings of the Convocation of Canterbury*, 15–17 October 1947 (1947): pp. 244, 261, 260.
28. LPL, Fisher Papers, 78/62: L. John Collins to Fisher, 7 February 1950, 78/63, 8 February 1950, 'Statement by the Archbishop of Canterbury'. Fisher's statement appeared alongside those of Attlee, Bevin and Churchill in *The Union of Europe: Declarations of European Statesmen* (New York: American Committee on United Europe in Cooperation with the European Movement, undated [1950]).
29. CAC, Churchill Papers, CHUR2/20/B: Frank H. Ballard (Moderator FCFC) to Churchill, 14 January 1947.

30. CAC, Churchill Papers, CHUR2/20/B: No name (page 2 missing) to Churchill, 21 January 1947; D. Sandys to Churchill, 31 January 1947.
31. CAC, Churchill Papers: CHUR2/20/B: Sandys to Churchill, 31 January 1947.
32. CAC, Churchill Papers: CHUR2/20/B: Churchill to J.M. Richardson, 4 February 1947.
33. CAC, Churchill Papers: CHUR2/18: 'UE Albert Hall Meeting', 24 April 1947; *United Europe: Speakers At the Albert Hall*, pp. 21–22; D. Duncan Sandys, 'Albert Hall Meeting, May 14th', 27 March 1947. In the event, the final word went to Oliver Stanley, who spoke on the task of the UEM and the nature of its campaign.
34. *Free Church Chronicle*, vol. 2, no. 2 (February 1947), p. 2; *ibid.*, vol. 2, no. 6 (June 1947): p. 7; 'Diversity and Unity: Paris Conference 1947', *Federal News*, no. 147 (August 1947), pp. 11–14.
35. Evelyn M. King, 'Spotlight: The Chairman of the Executive', *Federal News*, no. 150 (September 1947), p. 8; 'The Plan for World Government by 1955', *Federal News*, no. 150 (September 1947), p. 14.
36. Michael Hornsby-Smith, *Roman Catholics in England: Studies in Social Structure since the Second World War* (Cambridge: Cambridge University Press, 1987), p. 163.
37. Adrian Hastings, 'Some reflexions on the English Catholicism of the late 1930s', pp. 107–25 in Adrian Hastings (ed.), *Bishops and Writers: Aspects of the Evolution of Modern English Catholicism* (Wheathampstead, Herts.: Anthony Clarke, 1977), p. 107.
38. See, for example, 'The Divided Europeans', *The Tablet*, 25 January 1947, pp. 51–52.
39. See Christopher Dawson, *The Making of Europe: An Introduction to the History of European Unity* (London: Sheed and Ward, 1946; first published 1932); *Religion and the Rise of Western Culture: The Gifford Lectures, 1948–1949* (London: Sheed and Ward, 1950); *Understanding Europe* (London: Sheed and Ward, 1952); Barbara Ward, *The West at Bay* (London: Allen and Unwin, 1948); *Faith and Freedom: A Study of Western Society* (London: Hamish Hamilton, 1954).
40. Douglas Woodruff, 'Focus on Current Affairs: The Holy See and United Europe', *The Sword*, vol. 12, no. 154 (January 1952), pp. 88–92; Michael Burgess, 'Political Catholicism, European Unity and the rise of Christian Democracy', pp. 142–55 in M.L. Smith and Peter M.R. Stirk (eds.), *Making the New Europe: European Unity and the Second World War* (London: Pinter, 1990); Anthony Rhodes, *The Vatican in the Age of the Cold War* (Norwich: Russell, 1992).
41. Richard J Aldrich, 'OSS, CIA and European Unity: The American Committee on United Europe, 1948–1960', *Diplomacy and Statecraft*, vol. 8, no. 1 (March 1997), pp. 184–227: 212; Martin A. Lee, 'Their Will Be Done', *Mother Jones*, July 1983, pp. 21–38: 23.
42. Mary Stansfield, 'Federalists Received by the Pope', *Federal News*, no. 164 (December 1948), p. 10.
43. CAC, Churchill Papers, CHUR2/18: L. Amery to W. Churchill, 31 December 1946; B. Griffin to Churchill, 7 January 1947.
44. CAC, Churchill Papers, CHUR2/22: Churchill to Bishop of Nottingham (Edward Ellis), 2 February 1947; Nottingham to Churchill, 5 February 1947.

45. CAC, Churchill Papers, CHUR2/22: Nottingham to Churchill, 28 January 1947.
46. CAC, Churchill Papers, CHUR2/20B: Kenneth Hare-Scott (Organising Secretary), 'United Europe Movement – The Campaign in Great Britain', [Nov 1948].
47. CAC, Churchill Papers, CHUR2/20B: 'General Committee' [of UEM], undated [ca.1947].
48. CAC, Churchill Papers, CHUR2/20A: UEM, 'minutes of a meeting of the Executive Committee held at the House of Commons on April 22nd, 1947'.
49. Rabattet, 'The "European Movement"', pp. 28–32.
50. 'Western Union', *The World Today: Chatham House Review*, vol. 4, no. 4 (April 1949), pp. 170–83: 171.
51. The EM was originally known as the European Liaison Committee, becoming the Joint International Committee of the Movements for European Unity after 13 December 1947 and, finally, after 25 October 1948, the European Movement. For the sake of clarity it is referred to by its final title throughout.
52. Aldrich, 'OSS, CIA and European Unity', pp. 211–12.
53. *Ibid.*, pp. 190–95,194–95.
54. See, respectively, chs 5 and 6.
55. LPL, Fisher Papers, 57/2: Minutes of the Meeting to Constitute the United Kingdom Council of the European Movement, House of Commons, 16 February 1949.
56. John Baylis, *The Diplomacy of Pragmatism: Britain and the Formation of NATO, 1942–49* (Basingstoke: Macmillan, 1993), ch. 5; Sean Greenwood, 'Ernest Bevin, France and 'Western Union': August 1945–February 1946', *European History Quarterly* 14, (1984), 319–38; Klaus Larres, 'A search for order: Britain and the origins of a Western European Union, 1944–55', pp. 72–87 in Brian Brivati and Harriet Jones (eds.), *From Reconstruction to Integration: Britain and Europe Since 1945* (Leicester: Leicester University Press, 1993); Avi Shlaim, *Britain and the Origins of European Unity* (The Graduate School of Contemporary European Studies, University of Reading, 1978), pp. 86–142; Geoffrey Warner, 'The Labour Governments and the Unity of Western Europe, 1945–51', in Ritchie Ovendale (ed.), *The Foreign Policy of the British Labour Governments, 1945–1951* (Leicester: Leicester University Press, 1984); John W. Young, *Britain, France and the Unity of Europe, 1945–1951* (Leicester: Leicester University Press, 1984), chs 9–14.
57. Dianne Kirby, 'Divinely Sanctioned: The Anglo-American Cold War Alliance and the Defence of Western Civilisation and Christianity, 1945–48', *The Journal of Contemporary History*, vol. 35, no. 3 (2000), pp. 385–412.
58. 'British Memorandum of Conversation', London, undated, pp. 815–22 in *Foreign Relations of the United States 1947: Volume II: Council of Foreign Ministers; Germany and Austria* (Washington: Department of State, 1972), p. 815; Alan Bullock, *Ernest Bevin: Foreign Secretary, 1945–1951* (Oxford: Oxford University Press, 1985), pp. 498–99.
59. *Parliamentary Debates (Hansard): House of Commons*, vol. 446, (London: HMSO, 1948), cols. 407–408.
60. Dianne Kirby, 'The Church of England in the Period of the Cold War, 1945–56' (unpublished Ph.D. thesis, Hull University, 1991), pp. 16–41; Keith Robbins, 'Britain, 1940 and 'Christian Civilization', pp. 195–213 in

History, Religion and Identity in Modern Britain (London: Hambledon, 1993); Siân Nicholas, *The Echo of War: Home Front Propaganda and the Wartime BBC, 1939–45* (Manchester: Manchester University Press, 1996), pp. 155–56.

61. See, for example: 'Their Finest Hour', House of Commons, 18 June 1940; 'The Sinews of Peace', Westminster College, Fulton, Missouri, 5 March 1946.

62. Arnold J. Toynbee, *Civilization on Trial* (London: Oxford University Press, 1948); Arnold Toynbee and Pieter Geyl, 'Is there a Pattern to the Past', *The Listener*, vol. XXXIX (15 January 1948), pp. 93–94; Arnold Toynbee, 'Civilisation on Trial', *The Listener*, vol. XL (15 July 1948), p. 75; Arnold Toynbee, 'A Western Tradition still in the Making', *The Listener*, vol. XL (30 September 1948), p. 489; H. Butterfield, *Christianity and History* (London: G. Bell and Sons, 1949).

63. Oliver Franks, 'The Tradition of Western Civilization', *Congregational Quarterly*, vol. XXVII, no. 4 (October 1949), pp. 296–303.

64. Dianne Kirby, 'Truman's Holy Alliance: The President, The Pope and the Origins of the Cold War', *Borderlines: Studies in American Culture*, vol. 4, no. 1 (1997), pp. 1–17; Kirby, 'Divinely Sanctioned, pp. 385–412; Dianne Kirby, 'Harry S. Truman's International Religious Anti-Communist Front, the Archbishop of Canterbury and the 1948 Inaugural Assembly of the World Council of Churches', *Contemporary British History*, vol. 15, no. 4 (Winter 2001), pp. 35–70.

65. Shlaim, *Britain and the Origins of European Unity*, p. 141.

66. Douglas Pringle, 'Towards a Western European Union', *The Listener*, vol. 39, (29 January 1948), pp. 163–64; Maurice Edelman, 'Correspondence: Western Union', *New Statesman and Nation*, vol. 35 (21 February 1948), p. 155.

67. The Labour Party's principles in relation to European integration were spelled out in: *Feet On The Ground: A Study of Western Union* (London: Labour Party, September 1948), pp. 19–23.

68. *Parliamentary Debates (Hansard): House of Commons*, vol. 446 (London: HMSO, 1948), Col. 395.

69. NA, CAB129/25: CP(48) 72 'The Threat to Western Civilisation – Memorandum by the Secretary of State for Foreign Affairs', 3 March 1948; my emphasis.

70. NA, FO953/144: C. Warner to O. Sargent, 13 February 1948.

71. NA, FO953/144: Memo from C. Warner, 19 February 1948; FO953/144: Notes on the first meeting of the Working Party on "Spiritual Aspects" of Western Union, undated, ca. February 1948; FO953/148: Minutes of the Working party on Spiritual Aspects of Western Union, 16 June 1948.

72. NA, FO800/460: Eur 5/3/48, 'Western Union'.

73. NA, FO800/460: Eur/48/15; LPL, Collins Papers, MSS 3290/14–15: F. Roberts to J. Richardson, 12 March 1948; Roberts to M. Stewart, 12 March 1948.

74. LPL, Collins Papers, MSS 3290/16: R. McAlpine [Foreign Office] to R. Spicer [Private Secretary, The Treasury], 15 March 1948. There are brief references to Cripps's role in: Chris Bryant, *Stafford Cripps: The First Modern Chancellor* (London: Hodder & Stoughton, 1997), pp. 460–61; Simon Burgess, *Stafford Cripps: A Political Life* (London: Gollancz, 1999), p. 260; Peter Clarke, *The Cripps Version: The Life of Sir Stafford Cripps* (London: Allen Lane, 2002); pp. 529–39.

75. NA, FO800/460: Eur 5/3/48, 'Western Union'.

76. *Parliamentary Debates (Hansard): House of Lords*, Series 5, vol. 154 (London: HMSO, 1948), Cols, 325–26; NA, CAB129/25: 'The Threat to Western Civilisation', 3 March 1948; LPL, Fisher Papers, 280/63: 'Easter Message 1948' [pencil annotation 'continent'].
77. Kirby, *Church, State and Propaganda*, pp. 177–78 and *passim*.
78. LPL, Fisher Papers, 280/73 (a similar passage also appeared in 'The Archbishop's Letter', *Canterbury Diocesan Notes*, no. 233 (November 1948), p. 1).
79. National Archives of Scotland (hereafter NAS), CH1/37: p. 284, Minutes of Meeting on 21 January 1948, in 'The Church of Scotland Committee on Church and Nation', 20 April 1932–20 April 1954, p. 284.
80. 'Report of the Committee on Church and Nation to the General Assembly of the Church of Scotland', *Reports of the General Assembly with the Legislative Acts, 1948*, pp. 291, 292, 322.
81. 'The Message to the Churches' *The Congregational Quarterly*, vol. XXVII, no. 4 (October 1949), pp. 349–55: 355.
82. 'The Unity of Europe', *Westminster Cathedral Chronicle and Diocesan Gazette*, vol. XLII, no. 9 (September 1948), pp. 203–205.
83. See, for example, 'The Divided Europeans', *The Tablet*, 25 January 1947, pp. 51–52; 'A More Hopeful Course', *The Tablet*, 31 January 1948, p. 65; 'Mr Bevin and All Europe', *ibid.*, p. 67.
84. William Slattery, 'The Politics of Western Union', *The Christian Democrat*, vol. 28, no. 6 (June 1948), pp. 38–40: 39; see also Paul Crane, 'A Time for Decision', *ibid.*, pp. 33–35 and J.R. Kirwen, 'The Economics of Western Union', *ibid.*, pp. 35–38.
85. NA, FO800/460: Eur 5/3/48, 'Western Union', 5 March 1948.
86. NA, FO800/460: Eur 48/14, 'The World Council of Churches', 9 March 1948.
87. See chs 1–3 above; Darril Hudson, *The Ecumenical Movement in World Affairs* (London: Weidenfeld and Nicolson, 1969); Zeilstra, *European Unity in Ecumenical Thinking*.
88. See chs 2–3 above.
89. Kirby, 'Harry S. Truman's International Religious Anti-Communist Front', p. 45.
90. LPL, Fisher Papers, 40/309: K. Grubb to Visser t' Hooft, 9 March 1948.
91. *Ibid.*; 40/308 Grubb to G. Fisher, 17 March 1948.
92. LPL, Fisher Papers, 40/309: Grubb to Visser t' Hooft, 9 March 1948.
93. Kirby, 'Harry S. Truman's International Religious Anti-Communist Front', *passim*.
94. LPL, Fisher Papers, 40/310: Visser t' Hooft to Grubb, 13 March 1948.
95. Eric G.M. Fletcher, 'The Church and International Affairs', *The London Quarterly and Holborn Review*, January 1949, pp. 43–6: 46.
96. W.A Visser t' Hooft (ed.), *The First Assembly of the World Council of Churches: Held at Amsterdam August 22nd to September 4th, 1948* (London: SCM, 1949), pp. 9–11, 38–39.
97. *Ibid.*, pp. 88–105, 92.
98. See John F. Dulles, *War or Peace?* (London: George G. Harrap, 1950), pp. 155–60, 211–23. See also ch. 2 above.
99. John F. Dulles, 'Christian Responsibility in Our Divided World – (a) The Christian Citizen in a Changing World', pp. 73–114 in Kenneth G. Grubb *et al.*, *The Church and International Disorder: An Ecumenical Study Prepared Under the Auspices of the World Council of Churches* (London: SCM, 1948), p. 110.

100. Frederick Nolde, 'Ecumenical Action in International Affairs' in Harold Edward Fey (ed.), *The Ecumenical Advance: A History of the Ecumenical Movement: Volume 2, 1948–1968* (London: SPCK, 1970), p. 269.
101. Kenneth Grubb, 'The Church and International Affairs', *The Church in the World*, 21 November 1947, pp. 6–9.
102. Kirby, *Church, State and Propaganda*, pp. 50–52, 148–49.
103. Church of England Archives (hereafter CEA), British Council of Churches (hereafter BCC) /5/1/2: 'Report of the Twentieth meeting of the British Council of Churches International Department', undated.
104. CEA, BCC /5/1/2: Minutes of ID Standing Committee 1946-53: Agenda for the meeting of the International Department, 8 December 1949; Minutes of the 35th meeting of the International Department, 8 December 1949.
105. Trinity College Library (hereafter TCL), Lord Layton Papers, Box 131/3: Memorandum concerning visit of Duncan Sandys and Dr. Joseph Retinger to Rome, 29 January 1948.
106. Douglas Woodruff, 'Focus on Current Affairs: The Holy See and United Europe', *The Sword*, vol. 12, no. 154 (January 1952), pp. 88–92: 88.
107. LPL Fisher Papers, 44/284: D. Sandys to G. Fisher, 1 May 1948; 285: Fisher to Sandys, 5 May 1948 ('I had the privilege of presiding at the meeting in the Albert Hall at which Mr. Churchill launched his campaign for the promotion of the cause of European unity. I am a whole-hearted supporter of the cause and am convinced that for its success it needs a revival in power of those spiritual and Christian principles form which abiding values of civilisation derive. I have heard with great interest of the Conference to be held at the Hague and I pray that it may be successful in setting forward at all levels a firmly based unity of culture and co-operation among the nations of Europe.')
108. Douglas Woodruff, 'The Hague Conference', *The Tablet*, 15 May 1948, p. 301.
109. T.S. Eliot, *The Idea of a Christian Society* (London: Faber and Faber, 1939).
110. Clements, *Faith on the Frontier*, ch. 17; William Taylor and Marjorie Reeves, 'Intellectuals in Debate: The Moot', pp 24–48 in Marjorie Reeves (ed.), *Christian Thinking and Social Order: Conviction Politics from the 1930s to the Present Day (London: Cassell, 1999); T.S. Eliot, Notes towards the Definition of Culture* (London, 1948).
111. Frances Stonor Saunders, *Who Paid the Piper? The CIA and the Cultural Cold War* (London: Granta, 1999), pp. 48, 245, 248, 250.
112. T.S. Eliot to Denis de Rougemont, 5 April 1948 cited in Rabattet, 'The "European Movement"', pp. 346–47.
113. *Ibid.*, pp. 348–49.
114. CEA, BCC5/1/2: Minutes of 29th meeting of the International Department, 13 May 1948.
115. Douglas Woodruff, 'The Hague Conference', *The Tablet*, 15 May 1948, p. 301.
116. Other participants were Rev. J. Leycester King (a Jesuit and Professor of Psychology), David Eccles (MP, Conservative), Kenneth Lindsay (MP, Independent), Charles Morgan (novelist), Percy Williams (Hon. Treasurer, Independent Labour Party), Hugh Delargy (MP, Labour), source: *Europe Unites*, pp. 72–87.
117. *Ibid.*, pp. 88–89.
118. Woodruff, 'Focus on Current Affairs: The Holy See and United Europe', p. 88.

119. 'United Europe Movement', *The Clergy Review*, vol. XXXI, no. 3 (March 1949), pp. 198–200.
120. Freda Beales, 'The Hague Conference and the Unity of Europe', *The Sword*, Vol. 8, no. 116 (June 1948), p. 12.

5 – Christian Action and the Christian Movement for European Unity

1. L. John Collins, *Faith Under Fire* (London: Leslie Frewin, 1966), p. 135; Diana Collins, *Christian Action* (London: Gollancz, 1949), pp. 76–77.
2. 'The People and Freedom Group: Annual Report', *People and Freedom*, April 1948, p. 4; Barbara Barclay Carter, 'Christian Democracy in the West', *The Sword*, Vol. 7, no. 110 (December 1947), pp. 8–10; Earl of Longford [Frank Pakenham], *Avowed Intent: An Autobiography of Lord Longford* (London: Little, Brown and Co., 1994), pp. 103–107; Peter Stanford, *Lord Longford: A Life* (London: Heinemann, 1995), pp. 208–25.
3. Collins, *Christian Action*, pp. 22–30, 36; Collins, *Faith Under Fire*, p. 101–102.
4. Collins, *Christian Action*, p. 43.
5. Collins, *Faith Under Fire*, p. 120.
6. LPL, Collins Papers, MSS3290/7: Collins to Halifax, 26 February 1948.
7. LPL, Collins Papers, MSS3290/2: Collins, undated letter without addressee; probably early 1947.
8. LPL, Collins Papers, MSS3290/11: Collins to Cripps, 12 March 1948; MSS3290/ 12-13a: 'Plans for a meeting to get the Christians in support of a Union of Western Europe'.
9. Georgetown University Library (hereafter GUL), Woodruff Papers, 18/12: Collins to D. Woodruff, 30 March 1948.
10. Bod. L, Stokes Papers, 2: G. Hannaford (British Embassy, Rome) to R. Stokes, 6 November 1948.
11. Michael Walsh, *The Tablet, 1840—1990: A Commemorative History* (London: The Tablet Publishing Company, 1990), ch. 4. I am grateful to Sue Chisholm of *The Tablet* for providing me with a photocopy of this chapter.
12. Collins, *Christian Action*, p. 77.
13. Archives of the Archbishops of Westminster (AAW), Bernhard Griffin Papers 1/14e: Letter from Collins (no addressee), March 1948.
14. AAW, Griffin Papers 1/14e: B. Griffin to S. Cripps, 23 April 1948; LPL, Collins Papers, MSS3290/20: Cripps to unnamed, undated; NA, CAB127/124: P. Nichols (British Embassy, the Hague) to Cripps, 25 March 1948; V. Perowne [British Minister to the Holy See] to Cripps, 1 April 1948; LPL, Collins Papers, MSS3290/17: Cripps to Collins, undated.
15. AAW, Griffin Papers 1/14e: Rev. G. Tickle (English College, Rome) to Archbishop of Westminster, 10 April 1948; Tickle to D. Worlock, 19 April 1948 (telegram); Tickle to Worlock, 19 April 1948; Westminster to Italian Ambassador, London, 19 April 1948; Worlock to Tickle, 22 April 1948; Circular to Sword of the Spirit members, undated.
16. See, for example: *Church Times*, 'Summary', 2 April 1948, p. 183; *The Tablet*, 24 April 1948, p. 262; *The Times*, 2 April 1948, p. 7; *The Times*, 15 April

1948, p. 15; *The Times*, 23 April 1948, p. 7; Editorial: 'Crisis of the West', *The Times*, 24 April 1948, p. 5.

17. GUL, Woodruff Papers 18/12: D. Woodruff to J. Collins, 7 April 1948; Collins to Woodruff, 9 April 1948.
18. Bod. L, Stafford Cripps Papers, 30: M. Harris to E. Dunstan, 3 June 1948.
19. Christian Action, *A Call to Action by Christians in the Present Crisis: A Report on the meeting held at the Albert Hall, on Sunday, April 25th, at 7.30 pm* (Oxford: CA, 1948), pp. 2, 12–37.
20. AAW, Griffin Papers, 1/14e: D. Worlock to G. Winham, 20 April 1948; *Church Times*, 'Vital Needs of Europe', 30 April 1948, p. 237; LPL, Collins Papers, MSS3290/54: 'CA, "Follow Up" of the Albert Hall meeting – a second memorandum. A Report presented at the second meeting at the Caxton Hall, on July 21st, 1948'.
21. Maurice Edelman, 'Correspondence: Western Union', *New Statesman and Nation*, vol. 35, (21 February 1948), p. 155.
22. Collins, *Faith Under Fire*, p. 141; Collins, *Christian Action*, pp. 115, 124.
23. LPL, Collins Papers, MSS3290/54: 'CA, "Follow Up" of the Albert Hall meeting – a second memorandum. A Report presented at the second meeting at the Caxton Hall, on July 21st, 1948'; MSS3290/8: Minutes of OCPFUE Committee meeting, 1 March 1948; AAW, Griffin Papers, 2/35:J. Collins to CA supporters, 25 October 1948; Collins, *Christian Action*, p. 106.
24. LPL, Collins Papers, MSS3290/61: Chairman's Report, 29 November 1948; AAW, Griffin Papers, 1/34b: *Europe Unites*, pp. 72–89. See ch. 4 above.
25. LPL, Collins Papers, MSS3290/54: 'CA, "Follow Up" of the Albert Hall meeting – a second memorandum. A Report presented at the second meeting at the Caxton Hall, on July 21st, 1948'.
26. See Michael Gehler and Wolfram Kaiser, 'Transnationalism and Early European Integration: The Nouvelles Equipes Internationales and the Geneva Circle 1947–1957', *The Historical Journal*, vol. 44, no. 3 (2001), pp. 773–98.
27. See ch. 6 below.
28. AAW, Griffin Papers, 2/35: 'Christian Action in Britain 1951'; Katharine, Duchess of Atholl, *Working Partnership: being the lives of John George, 8th Duke of Atholl, and his Wife Katharine Marjory Ramsay* (London: A. Barker, 1958), pp. 240–52; Stephen Dorril, *MI6: Fifty Years of Special Operations* (London: Fourth Estate, 2000), ch. 21; George Catlin, *For God's Sake, Go!: An Autobiography* (Gerrards Cross: Colin Smyth, 1972), ch. 16; *People and Freedom*, February, March, and April 1948.
29. LPL, Collins Papers, MSS3291/158: 'The Political Aspects of Western European Union as approved by the British Interim Committee of NEI, July 23rd 1948' (based on a draft by George Catlin).
30. Reckitt was a veteran Christian activist and editor of the journal of Christian sociology *Christendom*. He had been a leading guild socialist alongside G.D.H. Cole but had drifted away from the mainstream of Labour socialist thinking, becoming part of the circle around the periodical *The New Age* (succeeded by *The New English Weekly*) with its preoccupation with the 'social credit' theory of C.H. Douglas. He also wrote and lectured extensively on foreign affairs, including participating in the series of talks hosted by the New Europe Group of the 'mystic' Dmitri Mitrinovic. However, he also worked in the mainstream, during the 1920s serving on the COPEC

commission on International relations and then, during wartime, being involved in the Anglican Wartime Council's discussion of federal union. At the beginning of the war he was a regular participant at meetings hosted by Sword of the Spirit. (USSC, Reckitt Papers 25/7: New Europe Group handbill for 'Lectures and discussions on the present situation in Europe', no date. Reckitt was to speak on 'Social Integration and the way to World Order'. Other speakers include Arthur Kitson on 'The Hidden Meaning of the World Crisis' and V.A. Demant on 'Solidarity and Conflict'. For the history of the New Britain Movement and New Europe Group see Andrew Rigby, *Initiation and Initiative: An Exploration of the Life and Ideas of Dimitrije Mitrinovic* (Boulder: East European Monographs, 1984).

31. LPL, Collins Papers, MSS3291, 239–40: Maurice B. Reckitt, 'The Church and "United Europe": A Memorandum of Policy for NEI', undated.
32. USSC, Reckitt Papers 28/19 MBR to McLaughlin, 22 Sep 1949.
33. LPL, Collins Papers, MS3291/239–240: Reckitt, 'The Church and "United Europe"'.
34. LPL, Collins Papers, MSS3291: *Passim*.
35. NA, CAB 124/124: Transcript of interview of Collins by Paul Bareau,19 January 1949.
36. See ch. 4 above.
37. GUL, Woodruff Papers, 18/12: Woodruff to un-named, 17 February 1949.
38. GUL, Woodruff Papers, 18/12: Woodruff to Collins, 17 February 1949.
39. GUL, Woodruff Papers, 18/12: Collins to Woodruff, 23 February 1949.
40. LPL, Collins Papers, MSS3291/108: undated, unsigned NEI report; MSS3291/ 106: 'Report on the principal matters that came before the Political and Executive Committees at their meeting held just before Easter', 6 May 1949; MSS3291/124: Collins to Lady Atholl, 15 June 1950; MSS3301/322: Lord Halifax to Collins, 25 June 1951.
41. GUL, Woodruff Papers, 18/12: Collins to Woodruff, 5 November 1949.
42. See ch. 4 above.
43. LPL, Fisher Papers 54/249: Dean of Westminster to H. Waddams, 18 February 1949.
44. Bod. L, Cripps Papers, 32: Edith M. Ellis, 'Memorandum on Christian Action given to Monsignor Montini, Secretary to the Holy See', October 1948.
45. Bod. L, Cripps Papers, 32: 'Rome: Friends of E.M.F.'; Ellis to I. Cripps, 25 April 1949.
46. Dianne Kirby, 'Divinely Sanctioned: The Anglo-American Cold War Alliance and the Defence of Western Civilisation and Christianity, 1945–48', *The Journal of Contemporary History* vol. 35, no. 3 (2000), pp. 385–412; Kirby, 'Truman's Holy Alliance', pp. 1–17; Kirby, 'Harry S. Truman's International Religious Anti-Communist Front, pp. 35–70.
47. LPL, Collins Papers, MSS3299/144: 'Sir Stafford's Visit to Rome, Summary of Results of L John Collins' meeting with the Apostolic Delegate', 13 April 1949; MSS3299/146: 'Notes of L. John Collins on Stafford Cripps' visit to Rome'; Bod. L, Cripps Papers, 32: 'Sir Stafford's Visit to Rome – Summary of the results of L. John Collins' meetings with the Apostolic Delegate'.
48. Collins, *Faith Under Fire*, pp. 175–76.
49. LPL, Collins Papers, MSS3299/144: 'Sir Stafford's Visit to Rome, Summary of Results of L John Collins' meeting with the Apostolic Delegate', 13 April

1949; 147: B. Trend (Cripps' PPS from the British Embassy, Rome) to Collins, 3 May 1949.

50. Collins, *Faith Under Fire*, pp. 175–76.

51. 'John had been ill-advised by Stafford ...' (Diana Collins, *Partners in Protest: Life with Canon Collins* (London: Gollancz, 1992), p. 172).

52. British Library of Political and Economic Science (BLPES), Juliet Rhys-Williams papers, 8/4/1: Collins to J. Rhys Williams, undated [Aug 1949?]; LPL, Collins Papers, MSS3291/245–47: Minutes of NEI-BS Committee meeting, 15 October 1949.

53. BLPES, Juliet Rhys-Williams papers, 8/4/1: 'List of those invited to the Caxton Hall Meeting,' undated.

54. BLPES, Juliet Rhys-Williams papers, 8/4/1: Rhys-Williams (to D. Sandys), 'Interim Report', 6 September 1949; Report of the Meeting convened by the CMEU, Caxton Hall, 17 October 1949.

55. BLPES, Juliet Rhys-Williams papers, 8/4/1: Minutes of the meeting of Continuation Committee of CMEU, 21 December 1949.

56. BLPES, Juliet Rhys-Williams papers, 8/4/1: E. Herriot to Rhys-Williams, 29 November 1949; TCL, Layton Papers, 131/1: Lord Layton to W. Churchill, 22 June 1949; 132/2: 'Lord McGowan's Appeal', 15 July 1949; 132/3: 'United Europe Mission to the United States', July 1948; 'Loans from the United Europe Movement to the International Committee and Other Movements', undated [ca.1948]; UEM, Balance Sheet and Accounts, 31 January 1949; Dorrill, *MI6*, pp. 453–68.

57. BLPES, Juliet Rhys-Williams papers, 8/4/1: Report of the Meeting convened by the CMEU, Caxton Hall, 17 October 1949.

58. BLPES, Juliet Rhys-Williams papers, 8/4/1: *Christian Movement for European Unity* (undated; ca.1949).

59. GUL, Woodruff Papers WP18/12: untitled, undated typescript.

60. BLPES, Juliet Rhys-Williams papers, 8/4/1: Report of the Meeting convened by the CMEU, Caxton Hall, 17 October 1949; 'Continuation Committee', 25 November 1949; 'Spotlight on the Chairman of the Executive', *Federal News*, no. 150 (September 1947), p. 8; 'The Plan for World Government by 1955', in *ibid.*, p. 14; LPL, Fisher Papers, 362: G Fisher to L. Amery, 3 January 1947; 365: Fisher to Amery, 17 January 1947; 375: D. Sandys to Fisher, 3 April 1947. TCL, Layton Papers, 131/2: Minutes of the Meeting of the UKCEM, 17 May 1949; AAW, Griffin papers, 1/34b: D. Worlock to F.L. Josephy, 9 April 1948.

61. Bod. L, Richard Stokes Papers, 18: 'Save Europe Now' folder; Diary for 1949: entries for: 19 October, 23 November, 14 December.

62. Bod. L, Stokes Papers, 25: handwritten notes for speech.

63. For example, see Bod. L, Stokes Papers, Diary for 1949: entry for 9 November; Diary for 1950: entry for 18 October; Diary for 1951: entry for 10 April; Diary for 1951: entries for 14 and 15 March, and 10 April; Box 2: B. Griffin to R. Stokes, 22 December 1949; 3: Stokes to Griffin, 9 February 1950; Griffin to Stokes, 12 February 1950; Stokes to Griffin, 17 February 1950.

64. GUL, Woodruff Papers, 18/12: Woodruff to Collins, 28 September 1949.

65. BLPES, Juliet Rhys-Williams papers, 8/4/1: 'Report of the Meeting convened by the CMEU, Caxton Hall, 17 October 1949.'

66. GUL, Woodruff Papers, 18/12: Collins to Woodruff, 26 September 1949.

67. BLPES, Juliet Rhys-Williams papers, 8/4/1: 'Proposed Names to Sign Circular Letter', undated ca. November 1949.
68. BLPES, Juliet Rhys-Williams papers, 8/4/1: Minutes of the meeting of Continuation Committee of CMEU, 21 December 1949.
69. GUL, Woodruff Papers, 18/2: Minutes of the CMEU Continuing Committee Meeting, 2 February 1951.
70. BLPES, Frances L. Josephy Papers, 5/7: Minutes of the Executive Committee of UKCEM, 25 May 1950; Minutes of the meeting of the Council of UKCEM, 25 May 1950; Minutes of the meeting of the Council of UKCEM, 18 October 1950.
71. AAW, Griffin Papers, 2/35: 'Christian Action in Britain 1951'; Daniel Jenkins and Marjorie Reeves, 'Outside Ecclesiastical Organization: The Christian Frontier Council', pp. 80–100 in Reeves (ed.), *Christian Thinking and Social Order*; LPL, Collins Papers, MSS3291/278–79: Minutes of NEI Committee Meeting, 19 October 1950.
72. LPL, Fisher Papers 54/281: G. Fisher to (Rev.) M. Armstrong, 19 October 1949.
73. LPL, Fisher Papers, 54/277: H. Waddams to Fisher, 10 September 1949.
74. LPL, Collins Papers, MSS3301/307 Collins to Halifax, 2 January 1951.
75. Collins, *Faith Under Fire*, p. 177; *The Times*, 1 May 1951, p. 3.
76. 'A Correspondent', 'The Spiritual Inheritance of Europe', *The Sword*, vol. 11, no. 147 (April 1951), pp. 191–95: 194–95.
77. 'The Spiritual Inheritance of Europe', *The Church in the World*, no. 37/38 (December 1950) pp. 4–5.
78. 'Christians and Europe', *The Sword*, vol. 10, no. 139 (July–August 1950).
79. 'A Correspondent', 'The Spiritual Inheritance of Europe', pp. 191–95.
80. BLPES, Juliet Rhys-Williams papers, 6/7/1: 'An Address delivered by Stephen Spender on European Unity at the Christian Action lunch-hour forum at Caxton Hall on November 20, 1951'; AAW Griffin Papers, 2/35: J. Collins to B. Griffin, 2 December 1951. Griffin was unable to attend (D. Worlock to Collins, 31 December 1951).
81. AAW Griffin Papers, 2/35: *Christian Action News-letter and Review*, no. 5 (January 1952), p. 20; *Christian Action News Sheet* (December 1952), p. 2.
82. 'The Schuman Plan: the British Doubts', *Life and Work*, no. 58 (October 1950), p. 218.
83. Edward Luttwak, 'Franco-German Reconciliation: The Overlooked Role of the Moral Re-Armament Movement', pp. 37–57 in Douglas Johnston and Cynthia Sampson (eds.), *Religion, the Missing Dimension of Statecraft*, (New York: Oxford University Press, 1994), p. 54.
84. *Ibid.*, pp. 38, 54.
85. Peter Howard, *The World Rebuilt: The True Story of Frank Buchman and the Men and Women of Moral Re-Rearmament* (London: Blandford, 1951), pp. 24–34.
86. *Pace* Luttwak, 'Franco-German Reconciliation', p. 38.
87. *Ibid.*, p. 33.
88. Anne Wolridge Gordon, *Peter Howard: Life and Letters* (London, Hodder & Stoughton, 1969), pp. 390–91.
89. Quoted in Ole Björn Kraft, 'MRA: A Unifying Force in Europe', pp. 3–5 in R.C. Mowat (ed.), *Report on Moral Re-Armament* (London: Blandford, 1955), p. 5.
90. Howard, *The World*, p. 25.

91. Tom Driberg, *The Mystery of Moral Re-Armament: A Study of Frank Buchman and His Movement* (London: Secker and Warburg, 1964), p. 182.
92. Saunders, *Who Paid the Piper?*, p. 151; Driberg, *The Mystery of Moral Re-Armament*, p. 149.
93. 'Into Europe', *The Tablet*, 20 May 1950, pp. 395–96.
94. 'The Tepid Welcome', *The Tablet*, 3 June 1950, p. 433; Douglas Woodruff, 'Western Union', *The Sword*, vol. 10, no. 139 (July–August 1950), pp. 260–62.
95. John Murray, 'The Rediscovery of Europe', *The Sword*, vol. 10, no. 139 (July–August 1950), pp. 257–60: 258.
96. *Parliamentary Debates (Hansard), House of Lords*, series 5, vol. 167 (London: HMSO, 1950), cols. 1158–64.
97. CEA BCC/5/1/2: Transcript of letter from Ronald Rees to Kenneth Grubb, 1 January [1951] in 'European Unity and the Churches'. To date, a copy of the February 1950 memorandum has not been found.
98. BCC, *World Affairs* (BCC, undated ca. 1951).
99. R.D. Rees. 'British Churches and World Affairs', *Ecumenical Review*, vol. 4, no. 4 (July 1952), pp. 368–77: 375–76.
100. 'Libra', 'Monthly Letter: The Search for a New European Order', *The Frontier*, vol. II, no. 12 (December 1951), pp. 457–64.
101. Quoted in Alex May, *Britain and Europe since 1945* (London: Longman, 1999), p. 21.
102. Tony Gibson, 'Christian Action', *The Times*, 7 May 1948, p. 7.
103. Collins, *Christian Action*, p. 93.
104. *Manchester Guardian*, 27 April 1948, p. 4.
105. Christian Action, *A Call to Action*, p. 8.
106. Collins, *Faith Under Fire*, pp. 180ff; LPL, Collins Papers, MSS3300/97: Collins to Lord Hailsham, 18 February 1953.
107. Christian Action, *A Call to Action*, p. 8; Collins, *Faith Under Fire*, p. 118; see also Collins, *Christian Action*, p. 48.
108. CEA BCC/5/1/2: 'Report of the Thirtieth meeting of the British Council of Churches International Department', 8 December 1949.
109. LPL Collins Papers, MSS3299/54: '"Follow Up" of the Albert Hall meeting – a second memorandum. A Report presented at the second meeting at the Caxton Hall, on July 21st, 1948'.
110. LPL, Collins Papers, MSS3299/133, 139: Collins to C. Bruce, 30 March 1949. In the note (MSS3299/133) summarising the points to be put to Cripps, Bruce also inquired whether she should mention 'Dr. Retinger'. Joseph Retinger – a former Polish minister of state and a wartime SOE officer with close links to MI6 – was secretary general of the European Movement and a friend of Hugh Gaitskell (Dorril, *MI6*, p. 439; Richard Fletcher, 'How CIA Money Took the Teeth Out of Socialism', downloaded from http://www.wcml.org.uk/wattw.html, 14 October 2002).
111. LPL, Collins Papers, MSS3299/134: C. Bruce to Collins, 25 March 1949; NA, CAB 124/124: Cripps to Collins, 24 November 1949; Cripps to Collins, 6 December 1949.
112. Chris Bryant, *Possible Dreams: A Personal History of the British Christian Socialists* (London: Hodder & Stoughton, 1996), pp. 246–48.
113. LPL, Collins Papers, MSS3299/132: Collins to Bruce, 14 March 1949.
114. GUL, Woodruff Papers, 18/12: Woodruff to Collins, 28 September 1949.

115. For Labour's attitudes to European integration see: Roger Broad, *Labour's European Dilemmas: From Bevin to Blair* (Basingstoke: Palgrave, 2001), pp. 1–17.
116. Richard Acland *et al.*, *Faith Hope and 1950: A Christian Socialist Statement* (London, 1949), p. 9.
117. *Manchester Guardian*, 24 April 1948, p. 4; Sydney Silverman *et al.*, *Stop the Coming War: A Plan for European Unity and Recovery* (no place, no date, [ca. 1948]), p. 5. The other PSCG signatories were John Haire, Leah Manning and Ernest Millington. See also The Socialist Europe Group, *A Socialist Foreign Policy for the Labour Party* (no place, no date [ca. 1948]). On SEG see Stephano Dejack, 'Labour and Europe during the Attlee Governments: the image in the mirror of R.W.G. Mackay's "Europe Group", 1945–50', pp. 47–58 in Brian Brivati and Harriet Jones (eds.), *From Reconstruction to Integration: Britain and the World since 1945* (Leicester: Leicester University Press, 1993).
118. Bod. L, Stokes Papers, 3: Eric [rest of name illegible; on House of Lords stationery] to Stokes, 1 March 1950; Dorril, *MI6*, pp. 430–35.
119. Burgess, 'Political Catholicism, European unity and the rise of Christian Democracy', p. 152 in M.L. Smith and Peter M.R. Strik (eds.), *Making the New Europe: European Unity and the Second World War* (London: Pinter, 1990).
120. 'The Congress of Luxembourg: Christian-Democrats and European Reconciliation', *People and Freedom*, February 1948, p. 1; 'Christianity and Politics', *ibid.*, April 1948, p. 1; 'Christians in the Labour Party', *The Tablet*, 15 May 1948, pp. 299–300; Joan Keating, 'The British Experience: Christian Democrats Without A Party', pp. 168–81 in David Hanley (ed.) *Christian Democracy in Europe: A Comparative Perspective* (London: Pinter, 1994).
121. Private communication to the author.
122. Bod. L, Cripps papers 29: M. Stockwood to I. Cripps, 13 March 1948.
123. LPL, Collins Papers, MSS3299/132: Collins to Bruce, 14 March 1949; LPL, Fisher Papers 40/338: Lord Halifax to G. Fisher, 19 June 1948.
124. Robbins, *History, Religion and Identity in Modern Britain*, ch. 7; Hastings, *The Construction of Nationhood*, pp. 35–73; Colley, *Britons*.
125. McLeod, 'Protestantism and British National Identity'.
126. Andrew Chandler, 'The Church of England and the Obliteration Bombing of Germany in the Second World War', *English Historical Review*, vol.108, (1993), pp. 920–46; Cardinal [Arthur] Hinsley, *The Bond of Peace and other War-time Addresses* (no place, no date [ca.1941]); Thomas Moloney, *Westminster, Whitehall and the Vatican: the Role of Cardinal Hinsley, 1935–43* (Tunbridge Wells: Burns & Oates, 1985), pp. 149–67, 186–204, 241–49; Walsh, 'Ecumenism in War-Time Britain', pp. 243–58, 377–94.
127. *The English Churchman and St. James Chronicle*, 7 May 1948, p. 225; 9 December 1949, p. 592; 30 April 1948, p. 214; 4 June 1948, p. 269; 7 May 1948, p. 222; 30 June 1951, p. 314.
128. See, for example: 'Christian Action Campaign to Support Western Union', *British Weekly*, 29 April 1948, p. 3; David Maxwell Fyfe, 'Guest Commentary', *British Weekly*, 6 May 1948, pp. 1–2; 'Western Christian Union', *Christian World*, 8 April 1948, p. 8; 'A European Christian Union', *Christian World*, 29 April 1948, p. 8; 'Congress of Europe' *Christian World*, 13 May 1948, p. 8; 'Notes of the Week', *Methodist Recorder*, 29 April 1948, p. 6; 'Religion and the Nation' and 'Notes of the Week', *Methodist Recorder*,

6 May 1948, p. 6; 'Notes of the Week', *Methodist Recorder*, 13 May 1948, p. 8; 'Notes and Comments', *The Christian*, 29 April 1948, p. 4.

129. See, for example: 'Ilico', 'Religious Freedom Again', *British Weekly*, 3 June 1948, p. 6; 'Ilico', 'A Meeting of Extremes', *British Weekly*, 10 June 1948, p. 6; 'A European Christian Union', *Christian World*, 29 April 1948, p. 8; 'Notes of the Week', *Methodist Recorder*, 29 April 1948, p. 6; 'Notes and Comments', *The Christian*, 29 April 1948, p. 4.

130. Nathaniel Micklem, 'The Pope's Men', *The Congregational Quarterly*, vol. XXX no. 3 (July 1952), pp. 218–30: 222, 223, 228.

131. Paul Blanshard, *Freedom and Catholic Power* (London: Secker and Warburg, 1951; first published 1949); 'From the Editor's Chair', *Free Church Chronicle* 6, no. 3 (March 1951), p. 8.

132. *British Weekly*, 20 May 1948, p. 10.

133. Christian Action, *A Call to Action*, p. 8.

134. Bod. L, Cripps Papers, 30: M. Harris to E. Dunstan, 3 June 1948.

135. Christian Action, *A Call to Action*, p. 8.

136. LPL, Collins Papers MSS3301/264: Collins to Halifax, 7 June 1948.

137. See, for example: 'Western Union', *The Christian News-Letter*, no. 311, 12 May 1948, p. 3; 'Going West', *The Student Movement*, vol. LI, no. 2 (November–December 1948), pp. 1–4; 'Meeting for Sufferings', *The Friend*, vol. 106, no. 28 (9 July 1948), p. 567.

138. Bell, *The Church and Humanity*, pp. v–vi.

139. Martin J. Wiener, *English Culture and the Decline of the Industrial Spirit, 1850–1980* (London; Penguin Books, 1985), pp. 111–18; Jeremy Paxman, *The English: A Portrait of a People* (London: Penguin Books, 1998), ch. 6.

140. 'Monthly Letter: Tensions in Europe', *The Frontier*, vol. 3, no. 7 (July 1952), pp. 253–58.

141. *World Affairs* (undated ca. 1951); 'What Our Departments Do', *The Church in the World*, no. 58 (December 1954), pp. 13–15.

142. CEA, BCC/5/1/2: Transcript of letter from K. Grubb to R. Rees, 5 January [1951] in 'European Unity and the Churches'.

143. CEA, BCC/5/1/2: Comment by H. Waddams, 9 January [1951] in 'European Unity and the Churches'.

144. On sectarianism and identity see: Callum G. Brown, *Religion and Society in Scotland Since 1707* (Edinburgh: Edinburgh University Press, 1997), pp. 191–96; T.M. Devine (ed.), *Scotland's Shame: Bigotry and Sectarianism in Modern Scotland* (Edinburgh: Mainstream, 2000); Raymond Boyle and Peter Lynch (eds.), *Out of the Ghetto? The Catholic Community in Modern Scotland* (Edinburgh: John Donald, 1998).

145. See *Reports of the General Assembly*, Church of Scotland for 1949, 1950, 1951, and 1952.

146. 'Report of the Committee on Church and Nation to the General Assembly of the Church of Scotland', *Reports of the General Assembly with the Legislative Acts*, Church of Scotland, *1951*, p. 328.

147. Harold Butler, 'Can We Be European Patriots?', *The Listener*, vol. XL (5 August 1948), p. 200.

148. *Report of the Forty-Seventh Annual Conference of the Labour Party*, Labour Party, Scarborough 1948 (London, undated [ca.1948]), p. 178.

149. 'Must we be European?', *The Church in the World*, no. 99 (May 1964), pp. 9–10.

6 – Christendom, Communism and the Division of Europe

1. Raymond Smith and John Zametica, 'The Cold Warrior: Clement Attlee reconsidered, 1945–7', *International Affairs*, vol. 61, no. 2 (1985), pp. 237–52.
2. AWCC, IMC26.11.41/6: Minutes of the PAG USSR Sub-Committee, 4 April 1944.
3. 'A Message to the Christian Churches from the Conference', pp. 57–63 in Oldham, (ed.), *The Churches Survey their Task*, p. 60; 'Mit Brennender Sorge: Encyclical of Pope Pius XI on the Church and The German Reich', 14 March 1937.
4. "Cassandra", *The English At War*, p. 36.
5. Bishop of Chichester [George K.A. Bell], 'Introduction', pp. ix–xii in D.M. Mackinnon, *Christian Faith and Communist Faith: A Series of Studeis by Members of the Anglican Communion* (London: Macmillan, 1953), p. x.
6. Paton, *America and Britain*, p. 3.
7. J.H. Oldham, 'Relations with the USSR', *The Christian News-Letter*, no. 275, 11 December 1946, pp. 1–16: 1, 16.
8. Kirby, *Church, State and Propaganda*.
9. Hanna-Maija Ketola, 'Teaching 'Correct' Attitudes: an Anglican Emissary to Sweden and Finland in 1944', *Journal of Ecclesiastical History*, vol. 55, no. 1 (January 2004), pp. 75–101. I am grateful to Dr. Ketola for bringing her article to my attention.
10. Hugh Martin, Douglas Newton, H.M. Waddams and R.R. Williams, *Christian Counter-Attack: Europe's Churches Against Nazism* (London: SCM, 1943), pp. 12, 112.
11. AWWC, IMC20.11.41/9: Minutes of the meeting of PAG, 7 November 1944, p. 12.
12. 'Russia and the West', pp. 24–25 in J. Davis McCaughey, *Encounter: The World's Student Federation in 1947* (SCM of Great Britain and Ireland, 1947).
13. Oldham, 'Relations with the USSR', pp. 5, 6.
14. AWCC, IMC26.11.41/4: W. Paton to E. Fenn, 5 February 1943.
15. Bod. L, Toynbee Papers, 119: Untitled confidential memorandum from K. Grubb to PAG, 4 March 1944.
16. Grubb, 'Europe – The Christian Outlook', p. 5.
17. AWWC, IMC26.11.41/6: Minutes of the PAG USSR Sub-Committee, 4 April 1944.
18. Bod. L, Toynbee Papers, 119: Untitled confidential memorandum from K. Grubb to PAG, 4 March 1944.
19. Grubb, 'Europe—The Christian Outlook', pp. 8–9.
20. AWCC, IMC26.11.41/6: Minutes of the PAG USSR Sub-Committee, 4 April 1944.
21. Oldham, 'Relations with the USSR, p. 3.
22. *Ibid.*, p. 2.
23. *Ibid.*, p. 12.
24. 'Report of the Committee on Church and Nation', May 1947, p. 303.
25. LPL, William Temple Papers, 57/396: Grubb to W. Temple, 15 February 1944; 57/397: Temple to Grubb, 16 February 1944.
26. For example, three of Ward's broadcasts in 1940 were also published in *The Listener* and in a pamphlet (*The Defence of the West* (London: Sands/Sword of the Spirit, undated; ca. 1940).

27. Barbara Ward, 'The Choice Before Europe', *The Christian News-Letter*, no. 289, 9 July 1947, unpaginated.
28. Barbara Ward, *Democracy East and West*, (London: Bureau of Current Affairs, February 1947). The BCA was created in 1946 to encourage and informed and active citizenry and lasted until 1951.
29. *Ibid.*, pp. 49–50.
30. *Ibid.*, pp. 51–52.
31. Oldham, 'Relations with the USSR', pp. 1–16: 3–4.
32. M.B.R[eckitt], 'Editorial: Whither Europe?', *Christendom*, vol. 15 (September 1947), pp. 75–79: 75, 77.
33. Ronald H. Preston, 'Unity in the Church and World', *The Student Movement*, vol. XLVIX, no. 3 (January–February 1947), pp. 1–4.
34. 'From the Editor's Chair: Are the Churches Helpless in this Crisis?', *Free Church Chronicle*, vol. 3, no. 4 (April 1947), pp. 8–9.
35. 'Report of the Committee on Church and Nation', Church of Scotland, May 1947, p. 303.
36. Oldham, 'Relations with the USSR', pp. 3–4.
37. Parliamentary Socialist Christian Group, *In This Faith We Live* (London: PSCG, 1948), pp. 10–12.
38. Acland, *et al.*, *Faith Hope and 1950*, p. 7.
39. Kirby, *Church, State and Propaganda*, p. 120.
40. *Lambeth Conference, 1948: The Encyclical Letter from the Bishops; together with Resolutions and Reports* (London: SPCK, 1948), p. 19; see also Part I, p. 33, Part II, pp. 20–22.
41. The Church of Scotland, 'Report of the Committee on Church and Nation to the General Assembly of the Church of Scotland' (May 1948), pp. 287–91.
42. The Church of Scotland, 'Report of the Commission on Communism' (May 1950), pp. 601–608: 602–603.
43. See, for example, R.J. Wedderspoon, 'Communism', *The Expository Times*, vol. LCI, no. 9 (June 1950), 264–65; M.C.V. Jeffries, *The Kingdom of this World: The Challenge of Communism* (London; Oxford: Mowbray, 1950); Edward Rogers, *A Commentary on Communism* (London: The Epworth Press, 1951); Cyril Garbett, *In an Age of Revolution* (London: Hodder & Stoughton, 1952); Mackinnon (ed.) *Christian Faith and Communist Faith*.
44. LPL, Fisher Papers, 27/347: L. Amery to G. Fisher, 25 January 1946; /354: Fisher to Amery, 28 January 1946.
45. LPL, Fisher Papers, 27/355 W. Churchill to Fisher, 28 December 1946.
46. CAC, Churchill Papers, CHUR2/25A: Amery to Churchill, 10 January 1947.
47. Gordon Lang, 'The Case for United Europe', *Federal News*, no. 144 (March 1947), p. 6.
48. At the inaugural meeting of the United Europe Movement at the Albert Hall, 14 May 1947 (Randolph S Churchill, *Europe Unite: Speeches 1947 and 1948 by Winston S. Churchill* (London: Cassell, 1950), p. 83).
49. 'Editorial', *The Congregational Quarterly*, vol. XXV, no. 2 (April 1947), pp. 98–99.
50. Vojtech Mastny, 'NATO in the Beholder's Eye: Soviet Perceptions and Policies, 1949–56, Working Paper no. 35 (Woodrow Wilson International Center for Scholars, March 2002).
51. 'Editorial', *The Congregational Quarterly*, vol. XXVI, no. 3 (July 1948), pp. 98–99.
52. 'The Official Church Lines Up', *Religion and the People*, June 1947, pp. 1–2.

53. 'A Divided Europe?', *Religion and the People*, November 1947, pp. 1–2.
54. *The Chronicle of Convocation: Being the Proceedings of the Convocation of Canterbury, October 1947*, Church of England, pp. 244–62.
55. *The Parliamentary Debates (Hansard): House of Lords*, Ser. 5, vol. 152 (London: HMSO, 1947), Cols. 587–97.
56. *Ibid.*, Cols. 621–22.
57. See ch. 5 above.
58. For example, see: Gordon Albion, 'The Church and the Cultural Heritage of Europe', *The Sword*, vol. 11, no. 149 (June–July 1951), pp. 229–36: 229–30.
59. 'A Correspondent', 'The Spiritual Inheritance of Europe', *The Sword*, vol. 11, no. 147 (April 1951), pp. 191–95.
60. Rees. 'British Churches and World Affairs', p. 371.
61. *World Affairs* (BCC, undated ca. 1951). As to the success of the BCC in influencing opinion, 15,000 of *Christians and World Affairs* were sold in the year after publication, a not unsuccessful result for a such a specialised publication and better than other initiatives (Rees, 'British Churches and World Affairs', p. 371).
62. Church Assembly, 'The Spiritual Inheritance of Europe', *Report of Proceedings*, vol. XXXI, no. 2 (Summer Session, 1951), 266–71: 267.
63. *Ibid.*, p. 268.
64. *Ibid.*, p. 269.
65. *Ibid.*, p. 271.
66. See chs 1–2 above.
67. 'Communism', *Westminster Cathederal Chronicle and Diocesan Gazette*, vol. XLII, no. 5 (May 1948), pp. 95–96.
68. Jonathan Luxmoore and Jolanta Babiuch, *The Vatican and the Red Flag: The Struggle for the Soul of Eastern Europe* (London: Geoffrey Chapman, 1999), pp. 1–23.
69. 'Comments', *The Month*, vol. CLXXXIV (November 1947), 194–95.
70. Luxmoore and Babiuch, *The Vatican and the Red Flag*, pp. 52–66.
71. 'Britain and the International Community', *The Tablet*, 25 October 1947, pp. 259–60.
72. Ivor Thomas, *Warfare by Words* (Harmondsworth: Penguin Books, 1942), pp. 17–20.
73. Ivor Thomas, *Great Britain and Poland: An Address delivered at the Conference on Poland for Teachers and Students, held at the Central Library, Sheffield, on October 7–8, 1944* (Birkenhead: Polish Publications Committee, no date). Ivor Thomas, *A Free Italy in a Free Europe* (London: Friends of Free Italy, undated; ca, 1944).
74. Ivor Thomas, *The Socialist Tragedy* (London: Latimer House, 1949).
75. GUL, Woodruff Papers 18/2: Lady Atholl to D. Woodruff, 30 May 1947.
76. *The Sword*, vol. 7, no.104 (April 1947), p. 18.
77. GUL, Woodruff Papers 18/2: BLEF, Annual Report, 16 July 1947.
78. GUL, Woodruff Papers 18/2: Woodruff to Atholl, 16 July 1947.
79. Ward, *The West at Bay*; Barbara Ward, *Policy for the West* (Harmondsworth; Penguin Books, 1951).
80. Ward, *Faith and Freedom*.
81. Ward, *Policy for the West*, p. 11.
82. *Ibid.*, p. 65.
83. *Ibid.*, p. 39.
84. Barbara Ward, 'The Fate of Europe', supplement to *The Christian News-Letter*, no. 240, 8 August 1945, pp. 6–8.

85. Barbara Ward, 'Christian Co-operation and Europe', supplement to *The Christian News-Letter*, no. 144, 29 July 1942, unpaginated.
86. Ward, *Policy for the West*, pp. 201, 217.
87. Ward, 'Christian Co-operation and Europe', unpaginated.
88. Ward, *Faith and Freedom*, p. 240.
89. Ward, *The West at Bay*, p. 222.
90. Ward, *Faith and Freedom*, pp. 238–39.
91. *Ibid.*, p. 240.
92. Ward, *The West at Bay*, p. 229.
93. Ward, *Faith and Freedom*, p. 241.
94. *Ibid.*, p. 269.
95. GUL, Woodruff Papers, 18/2: BLEF, 'Minutes of Meeting of the Executive Committee, 30 April [1947].
96. These included Arthur Headlam, the Bishop of Gloucester and Chair of the CFR; W.R. Matthews, The Dean of St. Pauls; Canon Douglas; Rev. Sydney Berry, DD (secretary of the Congregational Union) and Rev. R.F.V. Scott (representing the Church of Scotland in England) (GUL, Woodruff Papers, 18/2: Atholl to Woodruff, 13 November 1944; AAW, Griffin Papers, 1/40: Woodruff to B. Griffin, 8 December 1944; Atholl to Griffin, 2 January 1945). The Bishop of Gibraltar, Cecil Horsley, also collaborated with the League's activities (GUL, Woodruff Papers, 18/2: BLEF, 'Minutes of Meeting of the Executive Committee, 30 April [1947]).
97. GUL, Woodruff Papers: 18/2: BLEF, Minutes of the Executive Committee, 20 August [1947].
98. GUL, Woodruff Papers: 18/2: BLEF, Annual Report, 16 July 1947.
99. Adrian Hastings, *A History of English Christianity* (London: SCM, 1991), p. 322; see also Owen Chadwick, 'The English Bishops and the Nazis', *Annual Report of the Friends of Lambeth Palace Library* (1973), pp. 9–28.
100. 'Religious Persecution in Europe', *The Tablet*, 8 March 1947, p. 119.
101. GUL, Woodruff Papers: 18/2: Atholl to Woodruff, 22 June 1948.
102. Dering had been imprisoned by the Germans for his involvement in the Polish underground but later became deeply involved in the conduct of so-called medical experiments alongside SS doctors at the Auschwitz extermination centre. He was later released and carried on similar work in Germany before returning to Poland after the war. He fled to Britain in fear of prosecution for his wartime activities (Robert Jay Lifton, *The Nazi Doctors: Medical Killing and the Psychology of Genocide* (London: Macmillan, 1986), pp. 246–89).
103. The BLEF Executive Committee was Chaired by the Duchess of Atholl, a former Conservative MP, and, over its life, included Hon. J.J. Stourton, MP (Conservative); Victor Raikes, MP (Conservative); Major Petherick MP (Conservative); Major Guy Lloyd, MP (Conservative); Sir Ernest Bennet, MP (National Liberal); Captain A.R. Blackburn, MP (Labour), Edward Hulton, proprietor of the *Picture Post*, Lieutenant General Hugh Martin, military correspondent of *The Daily Telegraph*, Douglas Woodruff, and Major Lewis Hastings, of the BBC. The BLEF also constituted an Advisory Council to which it attracted many prominent names, including Professor Gilbert Murray and Lord Kennet. (GUL, Woodruff Papers, 18/2: BLEF, 'Minutes of Meeting of the Executive Committee', 7 April 1948).
104. Dorril, *MI6*, ch. 21.

105. £50.00 (GUL, Woodruff Papers, 18/2: BLEF, 'Minutes of Meeting of the Executive Committee', 7 April 1948).
106. GUL, Woodruff Papers, 18/2; 'Minutes of the Meeting of the Interim Policy Sub-Committee', 23 April [1947].
107. GUL, Woodruff Papers, 18/2: BLEF, Agenda of the Annual General Meeting, 11 July [1948].
108. Layton papers, 131/2: UKCEM, Exec Committee, 4 April 1949.
109. GUL, Woodruff Papers, 18/2: Atholl to Woodruff, 15 March 1948.
110. 'Restoring Europe', *The Tablet*, 24 May 1947, p. 251.
111. 'The Meaning of Vienna – The Unity of the Danubian Basin', *The Tablet*, 23 August 1947, pp. 116–17.
112. 'The European Answer', *The Tablet*, 11 October 1947, pp. 227–28: 228.
113. G.E. Hildred, 'The Battle for the Soul of Europe (VI): Western European Union (II)', *The Sword*, vol. 12, no. 152 (November 1951), pp. 56–63: 62.
114. Stephen C. Neill, 'The Church in a Revolutionary World', *International Review of Missions*, vol. 36 (October 1947), pp. 434–51: 450.
115. D.M. Mackinnon, 'Prayer Worship and Life', pp. 242–56 in Mackinnon (ed.), *Christian Faith and Communist Faith*, p. 255.
116. Kirby, 'Harry S. Truman's International Religious Anti-Communist Front'.
117. Oldham, 'Relations with the USSR', p. 9.
118. Grubb, 'The Church and International Affairs', pp. 6–9. The Eastern Orthodox Churches joined the WCC officially, when permitted by the Soviet Religious Affairs Ministry, in 1961.
119. Stephen Neill, 'The Churches and the Iron Curtain', *The Fortnightly*, vol. CLXIII (1948), 232–238: 237.
120. John Foster Dulles, 'Christian Responsibility in Our Divided World – (a) The Christian Citizen in a Changing World', pp. 73–114 in Grubb *et al.*, *The Church and International Disorder*; Joseph L. Hromadka, 'Christian Responsibility in Our Divided World – (b) Our Responsibility in the Post-war World', pp. 114–142 in *ibid.*
121. See ch. 2 above.
122. Grubb, 'The Church and International Affairs', p. 8.
123. Grubb *et al.*, *The Church and the International Disorder*, p. 121
124. J.M. Richardson, 'Amsterdam', *Free Church Chronicle*, vol. III (October 1948), pp. 2–3: 2.
125. Merrilyn Thomas, *Communing with the Enemy: Covert Operations, Christianity and Cold War Politics in Britain and the GDR* (Bern: Peter Lang, 2005), pp. 124–31.
126. Katharina Kunter, *Die Kirchen in KSZE – Prozess 1968–1978* (Stuttgart: Kohlhammer Verlag, 2000); 'Zurück nach Europa. Die Kirchen als politischer und gesellschaftlicher Faktor im demokratischen Tranformations- prozess Tschechiens', *Kirchliche Zeitgeschichte* vol. 8 (2005), pp. 409–422.
127. Grubb, 'The Church and International Affairs', pp. 6–9.

7 – Christians and the Common Market

1. NA, CAB 129/48, c(51)32: Winston Churchill, Cabinet Memorandum on 'United Europe', 29 November 1951.

2. See ch. 5 above.
3. Callum Brown, *The Death of Christian Britain: Understanding Secularisation, 1800–2000* (London: Routledge, 2001).
4. British Council of Churches and the conference of the British Missionary Societies, *Christians and the Common Market* (London: SCM, 1967), p. 9.
5. European Movement (UK) Archives (EMA), Minute book for the Common Market Campaign, 'Statement', 'List of Signatories' and 'Biographical Notes', May 1961.
6. Church of Scotland, 'Report of the Committee on Church and Nation: International Interests' (May 1963), p. 356.
7. F. Jeffers, 'Russia and the Market'; M.E. Tyson, 'Yes – Join'; Sisley Tanner, 'No-Don't Join'; R.P Walsh, 'Catholics and Europe', *The Christian Democrat*, vol. 13, no. 9 (November 1962), pp. 409–13, 414–19, 420–27, 428–30.
8. Noël Salter papers: Noël Salter, 'Britain's Future Role in the World: A Christian Examination – Background Paper no. 5, Britain's Contribution as part of a United Europe', March 1965, p. 45.
9. Noël Salter, 'Confession of a Eurocrat', *Crucible*, April–June 1975, p. 69.
10. *Ibid.*, p. 69.
11. Salter papers: undated paper (ca. 1979) detailing the Noël Salter Prize offered by INSEAD, the global business school originally founded as the European Institute for Business Administration in 1957.
12. Salter papers: Author's interview with Uwe Kitzinger, 25 March 2005.
13. Salter papers: A[lan] L.C. B[ullock], 'Noël Salter', p. 3 (draft for a introduction for an unrealised collective work in memorial to Noël Salter, planned by Uwe Kitzinger).
14. At author's interview with Uwe Kitzinger, 25 March 2005.
15. Salter papers: Curriculum Vitae of N.H. Salter, 2 August 1972.
16. Salter, 'Confession of a Eurocrat', pp. 68–70.
17. Salter Papers: Curriculum Vitae of N. Salter, undated; ca. 1963.
18. See Salter papers: 'The Christian Vocation in International Civil Service and Diplomacy', Report on the Retreat held at Villemétrie, 1–3 May, 1959; 'The Christian Vocation in International Civil Service and Diplomacy: Applied Christianity', Report on the Retreat held at Bièvres, 27–29 May, 1960; 'The Christian Vocation in International Civil Service and Diplomacy: Jesus Christ, the Light of the World', Report on the Retreat held at Bièvres, 12–14 May, 1961.
19. Salter papers: Noël Salter, 'Christian Service and International Civil Service', unpublished lecture, SCM Bristol Congress, 5 January 1963, pp. 4–5.
20. Salter Papers: Curriculum Vitae of N Salter, undated; ca. 1963.
21. Salter, 'Confession of a Eurocrat', p. 70.
22. Salter papers: Uwe Kitzinger, 'European Ideals and Third World Realities (Extracts from the Federal Lecture, May 6 1976, in honour of Noël Salter', photocopy of article, publication details unknown.
23. Salter papers: Curriculum Vitae of N.H. Salter, 2 August 1972.
24. *Ibid.*
25. Mike Peters, 'The Bilderberg Group and the project of European Integration', *Lobster*, no. 32 (December 1996); downloaded from http://www.bilderberg.org/bildhist.htm on 6 May 2005.
26. Salter papers: Salter, 'Britain's Contribution as part of a United Europe', March 1965, p. 1.

27. Salter papers: Salter, 'Christian Service and International Civil Service', pp. 7, 8.
28. Salter papers: Curriculum Vitae of N.H. Salter, 2 August 1972.
29. Salter, 'Confession of a Eurocrat', p. 70.
30. Salter papers: Noël Salter, 'Britain's Contribution as part of a United Europe'.
31. BCC, *Christians and the Common Market*, p. 8.
32. *Ibid.*; Salter papers: Curriculum Vitae of N.H. Salter, 2 August 1972.
33. Salter papers: Curriculum Vitae of N.H. Salter, 2 August 1972.
34. See Kenneth Johnstone, 'Youth and "The European Movement"', *Christian News-Letter*, vol. 2 (new series), no. 4 (October 1954), 175–79.
35. Peter Kirk (1928–1977) was a former vice-president of Federal Union, a member of the Directing Committee of the Common Market Campaign 1961–63 (Minute book of the CMC). He served on UK delegations to the Council of Europe and Western European Union. In 1973 he became the leader of the Conservative Group in the European Parliament and was deputy chairman of EM, from 1975 to his death in 1977.
36. BCC, *Christians and the Common Market*, pp. 130–32.
37. CEA, BCC/DIA/5/2/1a: Minutes of the European Committees Working Party, *passim*.
38. CEA, BCC/DIA/5/2/1a: Minutes of the first meeting, 27 January 1967.
39. CEA, BCC/DIA/5/2/1a: Minutes of the fourth meeting, 21 April 1967.
40. CEA, BCC/DIA/5/2/1a: Minutes of the sixth meeting, 24 May 1967.
41. CEA, BCC/DIA/5/2/1a: Minutes of the first meeting, 27 January.
42. CEA, BCC/DIA/5/2/1a: Minutes of the eighth meeting, 21 June 1967.
43. Salter papers: N. Salter, 'What form of Political Integration Makes Sense? Speech to the SCM Conference, Manchester, 12 April 1969, p. 10; author's interview with Elizabeth Salter, 12 November 2002.
44. BCC, *Christians and the Common Market*, p. 8.
45. This belief in the sympathy between Christian and federalist thinking was not without its critics. The first owner of the author's copy of *Christians and the Common Market* annotated the prayer offered within to express a preference for a 'better' rather than 'United' Europe and to omit the assertion that the future of the peoples of Britain was 'within a United Europe as a step towards a United World'.
46. CEA, BCC/DIA/5/2/1a: Minutes of the European Committees Working Party, *passim*.
47. Salter papers: Salter, 'Britain's Contribution as part of a United Europe', p. 44.
48. See ch. 4 above.
49. See chs 1–3 above.
50. Salter served as a Borough Councillor in Kingston upon Thames (1968–71) and later considered becoming a Conservative parliamentary candidate (Noël Salter Papers: Anthony Grant, vice-chairman of the Conservative and Unionist Party, to prospective parliamentary candidates, 30 April 1974).
51. John Pinder to the Author, 8 August 2005.
52. Salter papers: Salter, 'Britain's Contribution as part of a United Europe', p. 33.
53. G.R. Dunstan, 'National Sovereignty: A Theological Perspective', pp. 123–29 in BCC, *Christians and the Common Market*, p. 127. This document was prepared for the Wyndham Place Trust's Commission on the Limitation of National Sovereignty and had been accepted by representatives of the

Anglican, Roman Catholic and Free Church and also of the British Jewish Community. The Wyndham Place Trust had some contact with the European Movement, for example, three years later the EM funded the launch of the Trust's publication *Man's Wider Loyalties* (EM Archives: 'Public Relations Report', May–June 1970).

54. See chs 2–3 above.
55. 'The Common Market and Christians', *The British Weekly*, 30 May 1967.
56. Kenneth Johnstone, 'Britain's Place', *Frontier*, (Spring 1966), pp. 34–38: 37.
57. *Christians and the Common Market*, p. 31.
58. CEA, BCC/DIA/5/2/1a: Minutes of the first meeting, 27 January 1967; Salter papers: Salter, 'Britain's Contribution as part of a United Europe', March 1965, Appendix (Background paper 7), 'The Christian and the "Abandonment" of National Sovereignty in a United Europe.'
59. See Introduction above.
60. N.H. Salter, 'The Christian and World Federal Government', *Student Movement*, vol. LI, no. 3 (January–February 1949), pp. 41–42.
61. BCC, *Christians and the Common Market*, p. 15.
62. *Ibid.*, p. 103.
63. Peter Hebblethwaite, 'Europe in the London Suburbs', in Peter Hebblethwaite (ed.) 'Christians and the European Community: Reports and Papers of a Conference' (16–20 April 1974, Roehampton, London), p. 5.
64. CEA, BCC/DIA/5/2/1a: Minutes of the second meeting, 23 February 1967.
65. BCC, *Christians and the Common Market*, pp. 18–19.
66. Resolution adopted at the meeting of the BCC, 25-26 October 1967, in *ibid.*, p. 5.
67. Salter papers: Salter, 'Britain's Contribution as part of a United Europe', pp. 1–2.
68. CEA, BCC/DIA/5/2/1b: Christians and the Common Market, unpublished 1st draft of ch. 4, Section C 'Service' (paper H2).
69. Salter papers: Salter, 'Britain's Contribution as part of a United Europe', March 1965, pp. 2–6.
70. Salter papers: N. Salter, 'What form of Political Integration Makes Sense?' Speech to the SCM Conference, Manchester, 12 April 1969, p. 9.
71. BCC, *Christians and the Common Market*, p. 18.
72. See Chs 2–3 above.
73. Salter papers: Uwe Kitzinger, 'European Ideals and Third World Realities (Extracts from the Federal Lecture, May 6 1976, in honour of Noël Salter'.
74. Salter papers: Salter, 'What form of Political Integration Makes Sense?', p. 9.
75. Salter, 'Confessions of a Eurocrat', p. 69.
76. CEA, BCC/DIA/5/2/1a: Minutes of the fourth meeting, 21 April 1967.
77. Salter, 'Confessions of a Eurocrat', p. 69.
78. Elizabeth Salter to the Author, 25 July 2005; Salter papers: Salter, 'What form of Political Integration Makes Sense?', p. 14; Salter, 'Confessions of a Eurocrat', p. 69.
79. Elizabeth Salter to the Author, 25 July 2005.
80. Richard Acland, *What Sort of World?* (London: 1950 Group, October 1949), p. 13.
81. Encyclical of Pope Paul VI, 'On The Development Of Peoples', March 26, 1967.

82. Michael J. Walsh, *From Sword to Ploughshare: Sword of the Spirit to Catholic Institute for International Relations 1940–1980* (London: Catholic Institute for International Relations, 1980), pp. 19–39.
83. O'Neill was a senior civil servant in the Foreign Office. Previously he had been ambassador to the European Communities in Brussels (1963–65) and was later the leader – at the official level – of the British delegation which successfully negotiated entry in 1972.
84. CEA, BCC/DIA/5/2/1a: Minutes of the third meeting, 22 March 1967.
85. Salter papers: Salter, 'Britain's Contribution as part of a United Europe', p. 14.
86. CEA, BCC/DIA/5/2/1b: Christians and the Common Market, unpublished draft of Ch. 1.
87. Resolution adopted at the meeting of the BCC, 25–26 October 1967, in *Christians and the Common Market*, p. 5.
88. For example, 'United into Europe', *Methodist Recorder*, 18 May 1967, p. 2; J.M. Reid, 'What Kind of Europe', *The British Weekly and Christian World*, 11 May 1967, pp. 1–2. 'European Churches can Act together' and 'Comment on the News', *Church Times*, 12 May 1967, p. 1 and p. 3.
89. 'Christians and the Common Market', *The Tablet*, 28 October 1967; 'Pro-Common Market Motion Approved', *Church Times*, 27 October 1967. p. 1; 'Homework piling up for the Churches in 1968', *Methodist Recorder*, 2 November 1967, p. 6; Common market Reconciliation', *British Weekly and Christian World*, 26 October 1967, pp. 1–2; 'Christians and the Common Market', *English Churchman*, 27 October 1967, p. 3; 'Christians and the Common Market: An English Churchman Comment', *English Churchman*, 3 November 1967, p. 7.
90. 'Pro-Common Market Motion Approved', *Church Times*, 27 October 1967.
91. *The Times*, 24 October 1967, p. 3; 25 October 1967, p. 6; 26 October 1967, p. 2.
92. *Christen und der Gemeinsame Markt* (Koln: Europa Union Verlag, 1968); CEA, BSR/IAC/EUR/2/1 Europe (EEC): Draft Background paper for General Synod Debate, February or July 1972, p. 7.
93. J.D. Boyle, 'Going into Europe', *Church Times*, 1 December 1967, p. 6.
94. Peter Hebblethwaite, 'Europe in the London Suburbs', in Hebblethwaite (ed.) 'Christians and the European Community Reports and Papers of a Conference' (16–20 April 1974, Roehampton, London) p. 5.
95. CEA, BSR/IAC/EUR/MISC, misc papers of Peter Haynes: Alan Booth, 'What Sort of Conference', no date [ca. 1979].
96. Salter papers: Salter, 'Britain's Contribution as part of a United Europe', pp. 37, 43.
97. The British Council of the European Movement later changed its name to the United Kingdom Council of the European Movement. At the time of writing, there was another organisation called Britain in Europe, founded in 1999 to pursue campaigns in favour of the single currency and the European constitution. This body does not support federalism.
98. See ch. 5 above.
99. Uwe Kitzinger, *Diplomacy and Persuasion: How Britain Joined the Common Market* (London: Thames and Hudson, 1973), p. 190.
100. *Ibid.*, pp. 190–91.
101. *Ibid.*, pp. 192, 193.

102. *Ibid.*, pp. 196–97. The 'one who worked for the British Council of Churches' was actually Noël Salter who moved on from the BCC in 1967 (U. Kitzinger to the author, 7 September 2005).

103. Paul Lashmar and James Oliver, *Britain's Secret Propaganda War, 1948–1977* (Stroud: Sutton, 1998), ch. 16.

104. *Ibid.*, pp. 150–51.

105. Kitzinger, *Diplomacy and Persuasion*, p. 207.

106. Kenneth R. Johnstone, *Britain and the Common Market: A Christian View* (London: BCC, 1971).

107. Kitzinger, *Diplomacy and Persuasion*, p. 255.

108. Salter papers: Curriculum Vitae of N.H. Salter, 2 August 1972.

109. CEA, BSR/IAC/EUR/2/1 Europe (EEC): Draft Background paper for General Synod Debate, February or July 1972.

110. Kitzinger, *Diplomacy and Persuasion*, p. 255.

111. Quoted in *ibid.*, p. 253.

112. Quoted in *ibid.*, p. 256.

113. CIIA, *Comment: The Common Market* (London: CIIA, 1971).

114. Kitzinger, *Diplomacy and Persuasion*, p. 252.

115. Salter papers: Curriculum Vitae of N.H. Salter, 2 August 1972.

116. David L. Edwards 'Christians and the Common Market', *Church Times*, 30 May 1975, p. 11.

117. CEA, BSR/IAC/EUR/1, European Christian Industrial Movement: BSR, Industrial Notes no. 69 'The Bridge Builders', Tom Chapman (Cof E Industrial Council), 20 November 1972.

118. New College Library, University of Edinburgh: BCC press release, 'British Churches and Europe', 30 September 1974; BCC press release, 'Second Churches Group visit to Brussels', 3 February 1975.

119. BCC, 'Going Into Europe', 'Suggestions iv: At the local level.', undated; ca. 1972.

120. BCC, 'Going Into Europe', 'Suggestions v: The Europe 73 Programme', unpaginated.

121. Church of England Board for Social Responsibility, 'Britain in Europe: the Social Responsibility of the Church', undated (1972).

122. *Ibid.*, p. 19.

123. EMA: EM, 'List of Full Executive', 21 July 1971.

124. John Selwyn Gummer (1939–) was later minister of state for employment 1983–84, chair of the Conservative party 1983–85, paymaster general 1984–85, minister for agriculture 1985–89, secretary of state for agriculture 1989–93, and secretary of state for the environment 1993–97. In 1994, after its decision to permit the ordination of women, Gummer left the Church of England and became a Roman Catholic. Regrettably, Mr. Gummer did not respond to any of my requests for assistance with this project.

125. Church of England Board for Social Responsibility, 'Britain in Europe: the Social Responsibility of the Church', undated (1972), p. 12.

126. *Ibid.*, p. 17.

127. Hebblethwaite (ed.), 'Christians and the European Community', p. 4.

128. Otherwise known as the Office Catholique d'Information et d'Initiative pour l'Europe (OCIPE).

129. Hebblethwaite (ed.), 'Christians and the European Community', preface.

130. *Ibid.*, pp. 141–45.

131. *Ibid.*, p. 1.
132. R[oy] Jenkins, 'The Community as a New Form of Power', pp. 47–51 in *ibid.*
133. Hebblethwaite (ed.), 'Christians and the European Community', p. 1.
134. CEA, BSR/IAC/EUR/MISC [misc papers of Peter Haynes]: 'A "Ground floor" project for European Christians' (undated ca. 1980).
135. CEA, BSR/IAC/EUR/2/2, Europe Common Market Referendum: Hugh Hanning (BSR) to Giles Ecclestone, 30 January 1975.
136. *Ibid.*
137. *Ibid.*
138. New College Library, University of Edinburgh: BCC Assembly, 'Britain, Europe and the European Community', 23 April 1975; BCC press release, 'British Council of Churches Says "Yes" to Europe', 24 April 1975.
139. CEA, BCC/DIA/5/2/4 'The Referendum and Staying in Europe: Yes or No?': BCC Division of International Affairs, 'Staying in Europe: Yes or No?' A Study paper prepared by the Division of international Affairs BCC-CBMS'.
140. *Ibid.*
141. *Ibid.* Noël Salter was sent a copy too. Wilcox wrote 'I am sorry to hear that you had been ill, but it was plain from our conversation that illness has not dampened your spirits' (H. Wilcox to N Salter, 8 April 1975).
142. 'Churches 'yes' to EEC membership', *British Weekly*, 2 May 1975, p. 4.
143. 'EEC-Pro and Anti Give Voice in the Churches, *British Weekly*, 30 May 1975, p. 3.
144. David L Edwards, 'Christians and the Common Market', *Church Times*, 30 May 1975, p. 11.
145. 'After the Referendum', *The Tablet*, 7 June 1977, p. 523.
146. CEA, BSR/IAC/EUR/2/2, Europe Common Market Referendum: H. Hanning to Editor of *Church Times*, 30 January 1975; B. Palmer to Hanning, 6 February 1975.
147. See, for example: 'The world of Shirley Williams', *The Tablet*, 24 May 1975, p. 475; Barbara Ward, 'Europe preserved – a moral necessity', *The Tablet*, 31 May 1975, p. 498–500; 'Vincent O'Donovan, 'Sharing Sovereignty' *The Tablet*, 31 May 1975, p. 500501; 'Churches "yes" to EEC membership', *British Weekly*, 2 May 1975, p. 4; 'Bishops Speak out on Market Issue' *Church Times*, 27 March 1975, p. 1 and 4; David L Edwards; 'Christians and the Common Market', *Church Times*, 30 May 1975, p. 11; '"Yes" to Europe', *Church Times*, 30 May 1975, p. 1.
148. 'Pro-Market Clergy accused by MP of misleading the public', *Church Times*, 30 May 1975, p. 1 and 20.
149. CEA, BCC/DIA/5/2/4 'The Referendum and Staying in Europe: Yes or No?': N. Spearing (MP for Newham South) to K. Sansbury, 29 April 1975; H. Wilcox to N. Spearing, 6 May 1975.
150. CEA, BCC/DIA/5/2/4 'The Referendum and Staying in Europe: Yes or No?': Wilcox to (Rev.) H. Kelso, 6 May 1975.
151. David Butler and Uwe Kitzinger, *The 1975 Referendum* (London: Macmillan, 1976), pp. 82–83.
152. This school of opinion has been robust, surviving on the margins of the debate ever since. See, for example: *Maastricht, Magna Carta, Monarchy and Morality* (Gerrards Cross: Spirit of '88, 1994) and David Samuel, *Rome's Strategy for England* (London: Protestant Truth Society, undated ca. 1992). Travelling in a Glasgow taxi from the interview for my post working on the

Churches and European Integration project, my driver explained his belief that the European Union was a Roman plot.

153. 'The Referendum', letter from Rev. T.G. Manly, *The English Churchman*, 9 May 1975, p. 2; 'The Referendum', letter from Mrs M.L. Goodey *The English Churchman*, 23 May 1975, p. 3.

154. 'European Ecumenical Community', *The English Churchman*, 23 May 1975, p. 4.

155. *British Weekly*, 30 May 1975, p. 5.

156. 'EEC – Time for Prayer', *British Weekly*, 30 May 1975, p. 4.

157. CEA, BSR/IAC/EUR/2/1 Europe (EEC): Draft Background paper for General Synod Debate, February or July 1972, p. 2.

158. 'Bishops Speak out on Market Issue' *Church Times*, 27 March 1975, p. 1 and 4.

159. 'Pro-Market Clergy accused by MP of misleading the public', *Church Times*, 30 May 1975, p. 1 and 20.

160. 'Christian Arguments against the EEC', letter from Edward Charles, Christian Socialist Movement, *Church Times*, 16 May 1975, p. 3.

161. Barry Lynch, 'EEC referendum: mad to vote 'No'? *Church Times*, 4 April 1975, p. 12.

162. Mrs Kathleen M. Glaze, 'Leave it to the Individual to Decide', *British Weekly*, 30 May 1975, p. 6.

163. This paper 'An Open House' was later published as Keith Jenkins and Michael Smart, *An Open House? The European Community – Looking to 1992* (London: BCC, 1990). Noël Salter's widow, Elizabeth, took the chair of the International Affairs Division during the 1980s (1984–90). Although herself a convinced pro-European, she attributed the silence of the BCC on Europe during her tenure to the overwhelming pressure of more urgent international problems (Elizabeth Salter to the author, 3 October 2002). Two years later, when serving as Executive Secretary International Affairs, Peace and Human Rights at the WCC, she was responsible for one of its rare forays into the topic of European unity: Elizabeth Salter (ed.), *Europe 1992: Promise and Challenge* (Geneva: Commission of the Churches on International Affairs World Council of Churches, 1992).

164. Smart was head of the EC branch in the Department of Employment in the early 1980s, (Michael Smart to the author, 3 September 2002).

165. Later known as Churches Together in Britain and Ireland.

166. Derek W. Ford, 'An analysis of the response by the Christian UK churches to the involvement of Britain in the European institutions, 1967–1997' (unpublished MA dissertation, Anglia Polytechnic University, 1999), pp. 57–58.

167. Hugh Wilcox, 'Churches' Foreign Policy', *Audenshaw Papers*, no. 50 (December 1975).

Conclusion

1. D.H. Lawrence to Cynthia Asquith, 2 November 1915, in Herbert Read (ed.), *The English Vision: An Anthology* (London: Routledge, 1939), p. 363.

2. Zeilstra, *European Unity in Ecumenical Thinking*, p. 206.

3. Warren, *Theologians of a New World Order*.

4. UBSC, DA51: 'Minutes of Informal Consultation held at Princeton Inn', March 20–22, 1942.

5. Surveying the British Churches' responses to European Integration up to 1997, Derek Ford finds a 'general consensus' on humanitarian issues relat-

ed to development and 'about the threat a "Fortress Europe" poses to the
Third World' (Ford, 'An analysis of the response by the Christian UK
churches to the involvement of Britain in the European institutions', p. 71);
see also Kenneth Medhurst, *Faith in Europe* (Oxford: Churches Together in
Britain and Ireland, 2004) p. 50.

6. Michael Sutton, 'John Paul II's Idea of Europe', *Religion, State & Society*, vol.
   27, no. 1 (1997), pp. 17–29: 21–25.
7. *Ibid.*, pp. 35, 36, 47. In July 2005 CAFE merged with its sister body the
   Churches' East–West European Relations Network (CEWERN) to form a new
   body called Faith in Europe. The merger of these two bodies marks the final
   achievement of a long frustrated unity after the end of the Cold War in
   1989 and the beginning of the enlargement of the EU to incorporate the
   countries of Eastern Europe. To an outside observer, the choice of the gener-
   ic term 'Faith' rather than any specific reference to Christianity in the title
   of the new body could be seen to indicate multi-cultural hyper-sensitivity.
   Among the purposes of the new body is 'To advance ... the Christian religion' and also 'To promote relationships and appropriate collaboration
   with other faiths in Europe' ('Draft Constitution', June 2005).
8. Jean-Paul Willaime, 'Protestant Approaches to European Unification', pp.
   93–108 in John Fulton and Peter Gee (eds.), *Religion in Contemporary Europe*,
   Texts and Studies in Religion, vol. 64 (Lewiston, NY: Edwin Mellin, 1994).
9. Larry Siedentop, *Democracy in Europe* (London: Allen Lane, 2000), ch. 11.
10. Steve Bruce, 'Religion in Britain at the Close of the 20th Century: A
    Challenge to the Silver Lining Perspective', *Journal of Contemporary Religion*,
    vol. 11, no. 3 (1996), pp. 261–75.
11. Brown, *The Death of Christian Britain*.
12. Edmund Cusick, 'Religion and heritage', pp. 277–311 in Mike Storry and
    Peter Childs (eds.), *British Cultural Identities* (London: Routledge, 1997).
13. Kenneth N. Medhurst, 'Christianity and the Future of Europe', pp. 169–88
    in Martyn Percy (ed.), *Calling Time: Religion and Change at the Turn of the
    Millennium* (Sheffield: Sheffield Academic Press, 2000).
14. Grace Davie, *Religion in Britain since 1945: Believing Without Belonging*
    (Oxford: Blackwell, 1994).
15. Temple, *The Hope of a New World*, p. 27.
16. Reender Kranenborg, 'New Age: The Religion of the Future?', pp. 125–45 in
    Robert Towler (ed.), *New Religions and the New Europe* (Aarhus: Aarhus
    University press, 1995).
17. Arnold, John R., 'Europe, the Churches and the Conference of European
    Churches', *Kirchliche Zeitgeschicte* 12 (2) (1999), pp. 473–87: 483.
18. Philip Lewis, 'Muslims in Europe: Managing Multiple Identities and
    Learning Shared Citizenship', *Political Theology*, vol. 6, no. 3 (2005), pp.
    343–65.
19. James A. Beckford, 'Final Reflections', pp. 160–68 in John Fulton and Peter Gee
    (eds.), *Religion in Contemporary Europe*, Texts and Studies in Religion, vol. 64
    (Lewiston, NY: Edwin Mellin, 1994); see also Grace Davie, 'Unity in Diversity:
    Religion and Modernity in Western Europe', pp. 52–65 in *Ibid.*, pp. 60–61.
20. See, variously, Siedentop, *Democracy in Europe*, ch. 11 and Ziauddin Sardar,
    'European Muslims and European Identity', pp. 153–62 in John Coleman
    (ed.), *The Conscience of Europe* (Strasbourg: Council of Europe, 1999).

Selected sources

Primary manuscript sources

Archives of the Royal Institute of International Affairs (ARIIA), London.
Archives of the Cabinet Office (CAB), National Archives (NA), London.
Archives of Foreign Office (FO), National Archives (NA), London.
Archives of Ministry of Information (INF), National Archives (NA), London.
Archives of the British Council of Churches (BCC), Church of England Archive (CEA) Centre, London.
Clarence K. Streit, *Union Now: A Proposal for a Federal Union of the Democracies of the North Atlantic* (London: Jonathan Cape, 1939).
Minutes of Meetings of the Church of Scotland Committee on Church and Nation, National Archives of Scotland (NAS), Edinburgh.
European Movement (UK) Archives (EMA), EM, London.
Archives of the World Council of Churches (AWCC), Library of the World Council of Churches, Geneva.
Archives of the International Missionary Council (IMC), Library of the World Council of Churches, Geneva.
Lady Katherine Atholl Papers, Blair Castle, Blair Atholl, Perthshire.
George Bell Papers, Lambeth Palace Library (LPL), London.
Winston Churchill Papers, Churchill Archives Centre (CAC), Churchill College, Cambridge.
John Collins Papers, Lambeth Palace Library (LPL), London.
Stafford Cripps Papers, Bodleian Library (Bod. L), Oxford.
Lionel Curtis Papers, Bodleian Library (Bod. L), Oxford.
Geoffrey Fisher Papers, Lambeth Palace Library (LPL), London.
Bernhard Griffin Papers, Archives of the Archbishops of Westminster (AAW), London.
Lord Halifax papers (FO800-242), National Archives (NA), London.
Frances L. Josephy Papers, British Library of Political and Economic Science (BLPES), London.
Lord Layton Papers, Trinity College Library (TCL), Cambridge.
Joseph Oldham papers, New College Library, University of Edinburgh.
'William Paton papers' (comprising notes, photocopies and documents gathered by Eleanor Jackson whilst writing her biography of Paton), University of Birmingham Special Collections (UBSC).
Maurice Reckitt Papers, University of Sussex Special Collections (USSC), University of Sussex Library.
Juliet Rhys-Williams Papers, British Library of Political and Economic Science (BLPES), London.
Noël Salter Papers (held privately).
Richard Stokes papers, Bodleian Library (Bod. L), Oxford.
Arnold Toynbee papers, Bodleian Library (Bod. L), Oxford.

William Temple papers, Lambeth Palace Library (LPL), London.
Douglas Woodruff Papers, Georgetown University Library (GUL), Washington, DC.
Alfred Zimmern Papers, Bodleian Library (Bod. L), Oxford.

Newspapers and periodicals

Audenshaw Papers
British Weekly
CAFE News
Canterbury Diocesan Notes
The Christian
The Christian Democrat
The Christian News-Letter
Christian World
Christendom
Church Times
The Church in the World
Clergy Quarterly Review
Congregational Quarterly
Crucible
Ecumenical Review
The English Churchman and St. James Chronicle
The Expository Times
Federal News
Federal Union News
The Friend
Free Church Chronicle
The Frontier
Headway
The Listener
Life and Work
The London Quarterly and Holborn Review
Manchester Guardian
Methodist Recorder
The Month
The New Commonwealth
New Statesman and Nation
People and Freedom
Planning
Religion and the People
The Round Table
The Student Movement
The Sword
The Tablet
The Times
Westminster Cathedral Chronicle and Diocesan Gazette
The World Today: Chatham House Review

Primary published sources

'Notes of the Month: Britain in Europe and in the United Nations', *The Frontier*, vol. I, no. 8 (August 1950), pp. 283–94.

United Europe: Speakers At the Albert Hall, 14 May 1947 (London, undated [1947]).

'Limitanus', 'A New Europe', *Christian News-Letter*, vol. 2 (new series), no. 1 (January 1954), pp. 41–44.

Acland, Richard, *et al.*, *Faith Hope and 1950: A Christian Socialist Statement* (London, 1949).

Acland, Richard, *What Sort of World?* (London: 1950 Group, October 1949).

Albion, Gordon, 'The Church and the Cultural Heritage of Europe', *The Sword*, vol. 11, no. 149 (June–July 1951), pp. 229–36.

Arnold, John R., 'Britain and Ireland – reluctant Europeans' pp. 50–53 in Gurney, Robin (ed.), *CEC at 40: Celebrating the 40th Anniversary of the Conference of European Churches (CEC) 1959–1999* (Geneva: CEC, undated; ca.1999).

Arnold, John R., 'Europe, the Churches and the Conference of European Churches', *Kirchliche Zeitgeschicte*, vol. 12, no. 2 (1999), pp. 473–87.

Atholl, Katharine, Duchess of, *Working Partnership: being the lives of John George, 8th Duke of Atholl, and his Wife Katharine Marjory Ramsay* (London: A. Barker, 1958).

Baker, A.E. (ed.), *A Christian Basis for the Post-War World: A Commentary on the Ten Peace Points* (London: SCM, 1942).

BCC, *Christians and World Affairs: A Policy for Joint Action* (London: BCC, 1951).

BCC, *World Affairs* (BCC, undated ca. 1951).

BCC, *Christians and the Common Market* (London: SCM, 1967).

Beales, A.C.F., 'Catholics and the Peace Settlement', *The Clergy Review*, vol. XVII-II, no. 3 (March 1940), pp. 189–210.

Beales, A.C.F., *The Catholic Church and International Order* (Harmondsworth: Penguin, 1941).

Belden, Albert D., *Pax Christi: The Peace of Christ: A New Policy for Christendom Today* (Wallington, Surrey: Carwell Publications, 1944 – second, revised edition; first published 1942).

Bell, George K.A., *Christianity and World Order* (Harmondsworth: Penguin, 1940).

Bell, George K.A., 'University Sermon: Christian Co-operation', *The Cambridge Review*, vol. LXIII (1 November 1941), pp. 62–64.

Bell, George K.A., 'A War of Ideals', pp. 211–18 in *The Church and Humanity (1939–1946)* (London: Longmans, 1946).

Bell, George K.A., 'The Church in Relation to International Affairs', *International Affairs*, vol. 25, no. 3 (July 1949), pp. 405–14.

Bell, George K.A., 'Communism and the Churches', *International Affairs*, vol. XXV, no. 3 (July 1949), pp. 405–14.

Blanshard, Paul, *Freedom and Catholic Power* (London: Secker and Warburg, 1951; first published 1949).

Brogan, Dennis W., *The English People: Impressions and Observations* (London: Hamish Hamilton, 1943).

Butterfield, H., *Christianity and History* (London: Bell and Sons, 1949).

Carr, Edward H., *The Twenty Years' Crisis, 1919–1939: An Introduction to the Study of International Relations* (London: Macmillan, 1939).

Carter, Vivian (ed.), *Religion and the Organization of Peace: An Agreed Statement by Leaders of Many Denominations* (London: Peace Book Company, [1939]).

'Cassandra' [William Connor], *The English at War* (London: Secker and Warburg, 1941).

Catlin, George, *For God's Sake, Go!: An Autobiography* (Gerrards Cross: Colin Smyth, 1972).

CCIFSR, *The Christian Church and World Order: A Statement by the Commission of the Churches for International Friendship and Social Responsibility*, with a Preface by the Archbishop of Canterbury, Chairman of the Commission (London: SCM, June 1942).

Christian Action, *A Call to Action by Christians in the Present Crisis: A Report on the Meeting held at the Albert Hall, on Sunday, April 25th, at 7.30 pm* (Oxford: CA, 1948).

Church Assembly, 'The Spiritual Inheritance of Europe', *Report of Proceedings*, vol. XXXI, no. 2 (Summer Session, 1951), pp. 266–71.

Church of England Board for Social Responsibility, *Britain in Europe: the social responsibility of the Church: a report* (London: Church Information, 1975).

Churchill, Randolph S. (ed.), *Europe Unite: Speeches 1947 and 1948 by Winston S. Churchill* (London: Cassell, 1950).

CIIA, *Comment: The Common Market* (London: CIIA, 1971).

Coleman, John (ed.), *The Conscience of Europe* (Strasbourg: Council of Europe, 1999).

Collins, Diana, *Christian Action* (London: Gollancz, 1949).

Collins, Diana, *Partners in Protest: Life with Canon Collins* (London: Gollancz, 1992).

Collins, L. John, *A Theology of Christian Action* (London: Hodder & Stoughton, 1949).

Collins, L. John, *Faith Under Fire* (London: Leslie Frewin, 1966).

COPEC, *International Relations: Being the Report presented to the Conference on Christian Poltics, Economics and Citizenship at Birmingham, April 5–12, 1924* (London: Longmans, 1924).

Curtis, Lionel, *Civitas Dei: The Commonwealth of God* (London: Macmillan, 1938).

Curtis, Lionel, *Faith and Works* (London: Oxford University Press, 1943).

Curtis, Lionel, *World War: Its Cause and Cure* (London: Oxford University Press, 1945).

Dawson, Christopher, *The Making of Europe: An Introduction to the History of European Unity* (London: Sheed and Ward, 1946; first published 1932).

Dawson, Christopher, *Progress and Religion* (London: Sheed and Ward, 1938).

Dawson, Christopher, *Beyond Politics* (London: Sheed and Ward, 1939).

Dawson, Christopher, 'The Religious Origins of European Disunity', *Dublin Review*, vol. 207 (October–December 1940), pp. 142–59.

Dawson, Christopher, 'Europe and Christendom', *The Dublin Review*, vol. 209 (October 1941), pp. 109–19.

Dawson, Christopher, *The Judgement of the Nations* (London: Sheed & Ward, 1943).

Dawson, Christopher, 'Peace Aims and Power Politics', *The Dublin Review*, vol. 214 (April 1944).

Dawson, Christopher, 'Europe—A Society of Peoples', *The Month*, vol. CLXXXI (September–October 1945), pp. 309–16.

Dawson, Christopher, *Religion and the Rise of Western Culture: The Gifford Lectures, 1948–1949* (London: Sheed and Ward, 1950).

Dawson, Christopher, *Understanding Europe* (London: Sheed & Ward, 1952).

Demant, V.A., 'The Christian Doctrine of Human Solidarity', pp. 37–58 in Kenneth Mackenzie (ed.), *Union of Christendom*, vol. 1 (London: Religious Book Club, 1938).

Dulles, John F., *Toward World Order: A Merrick-McDowell Lecture delivered at Ohio Wesleyan University on March 5, 1942, on the occasion of the Conference called by Authority of the Federal Council of Churches to study the Bases for a Just and Durable Peace* (no place, no date).

Dulles, John F., *War or Peace?* (London: George G. Harrap, 1950).

Dusen, Henry P. van, 'Issues of the Peace', *The Church in the World*, 7 March 1942, pp. 3–5.

Dusen, Henry P. van, 'British and American Approaches to the Peace', *The Christian News-Letter*, no. 186, 14 July 1943, unpaginated.

Eliot, T.S., *The Idea of a Christian Society* (London: Faber and Faber, 1939).

Eliot, T.S., *Notes towards the Definition of Culture* (London, 1948).

Eppstein, John, *The Catholic Tradition of the Law of Nations: Prepared under the auspices of the Catholic Council for International Relations* (London: Burns, Oates & Washbourne, 1935).

Eppstein, John, 'The Catholic Tradition in International Relations', *The Month*, vol. CLXXX (November–December 1944) pp. 377–389.

Federal Council of the Churches of Christ in America Commission to Study the Bases of a Just and Durable Peace, *A Just and Durable Peace: Data Material and Discussion Questions* (New York: Federal Council of the Churches of Christ in America, 1941).

Fletcher, Eric G.M., 'The Church and International Affairs', *The London Quarterly and Holborn Review*, Vol. 20 (January 1949), pp. 43–46.

Foinette, T.J., 'Christianity and Communism: An Assessment of the Issue', *The London Quarterly and Holborn Review*, Vol. 20 (January 1949), pp. 38–42.

Franks, Oliver, 'The Tradition of Western Civilization', *Congregational Quarterly*, vol. XXVII, no. 4 (October 1949), pp. 296–303.

Garbett, Cyril F., *Church and State in England* (London: Hodder & Stoughton, 1950).

Garbett, Cyril F., *In an Age of Revolution* (London: Hodder & Stoughton, 1952).

Garbett, Cyril F., *World Problems of Today* (London: Hodder & Stoughton, 1955).

Gollancz, Victor, *Our Threatened Values* (London: Gollancz, 1946).

Gollancz, Victor, *In Darkest Germany* (London: Gollancz, 1947).

Gordon, Anne Wolridge, *Peter Howard: Life and Letters* (London, Hodder & Stoughton, 1969).

Grubb, Kenneth, 'Europe—The Christian Outlook', supplement to *The Christian News-Letter*, no. 219, 18 October 1944, unpaginated.

Grubb, Kenneth, 'The Church and International Affairs', *The Church in the World*, 21 November 1947, pp. 6–9.

Grubb, Kenneth, *et al.*, *The Church and International Disorder: An Ecumenical Study Prepared Under the Auspices of the World Council of Churches* (London: SCM, 1948).

Grubb, Kenneth, *Crypts of Power: An Autobiography* (London: Hodder & Stoughton, 1971).

'Hadham, John' [James Parkes], *God and Human Progress* (Harmondsworth: Penguin, 1944).

Hildred, G.E., 'The Battle for the Soul of Europe (VI): Western European Union (II)', *The Sword*, vol. 12, no. 152 (November 1951), pp. 56–63.

Hinsley, Cardinal [Arthur], *The Bond of Peace and other War-time Addresses* (no place, no date [ca.1941]).

Howard, Peter, *The World Rebuilt: The True Story of Frank Buchman and the Men and Women of Moral Re-Rearmament* (London: Blandford, 1951).

Hoyland, John S., *Federate or Perish* (London: Federal Union, 1944).

Hudson, Cyril E., *Nations as Neighbours: An Essay in Christian Politics* (London: Gollancz, 1943).

Jaspers, Karl, *The European Spirit* (London: SCM, 1948).

Jenkins, Daniel, *The British: Their Identity and their Religion* (London: SCM, 1975).

Johnstone, Kenneth, 'Youth and "The European Movement"', *Christian News-Letter*, vol. 2 (new series), no. 4 (October 1954), 175–79.

Johnstone, Kenneth, 'Britain's Place', *Frontier*, Vol. 9 (Spring 1966), pp. 34–38.

Johnstone, Kenneth, *Britain and the Common Market: A Christian View* (London: BCC, 1971).

Labour Party, *Feet On The Ground: A Study of Western Union* (London, September 1948).

'Libra', 'Monthly Letter: The Search for a New European Order', *The Frontier*, vol. II, no. 12 (December 1951), pp. 457–64.

Longford, Earl of [Frank Pakenham], *Avowed Intent: An Autobiography of Lord Longford* (London: Little, Brown and Co., 1994).

Lothian, Marquess of, *et al.*, *The Universal Church and the World of Nations* (London: G. Allen & Unwin, 1938).

Mackay, R.W.G., 'Why European Union?', *The Congregational Quarterly*, vol. XXVII, no. 1 (January, 1949), pp. 60–71.

Mackinnon, D.M., *Christian Faith and Communist Faith: A Series of Studeis by Members of the Anglican Communion* (London: Macmillan, 1953).

Malvern, 1941: *The Life of the Church and The Order of Society* (London: Longmans, 1941).

Martin, Hugh, 'A Tribute to Bill', *the Religious Book Club Bulletin*, no. 37 (November 1943), pp. 1–3.

Martin, Hugh, Newton, Douglas, Waddams, H.M. and Williams, R.R., *Christian Counter-Attack: Europe's Churches Against Nazism* (London: SCM, 1943).

Medhurst, Kenneth, *Faith in Europe*, (Oxford: Churches Together in Britain and Ireland, 2004).

Micklem, Nathaniel, 'The Pope's Men', *The Congregational Quarterly* vol. XXX, no. 3 (July 1952), pp. 218–30.

Mowat, R.C. (ed.), *Report on Moral Re-Armament* (London: Blandford, 1955).

Murry, J. Middleton, *Christocracy* (London: Dakers, 1943).

Oldham, J.H. (ed.), *The Churches Survey their Task* (London: George Allen and Unwin, 1937).

Oldham, J.H., *The Resurrection of Christendom* (London: Sheldon Press, 1940)

Oldham, J.H., *et al. The Church Looks Ahead: Broadcast Talks* (London: Faber and Faber, 1941).

Oldham, J.H., 'Britain and Europe', *The Christian News-Letter*, no. 115, 7 January 1942, unpaginated.

Oldham, J.H., 'A Bolder View of National Purpose', *The Christian News-Letter*, no. 157, 28 October 1942, unpaginated.

Oldham, J.H., 'Relations with the USSR', *The Christian News-Letter*, no. 275, 11 December 1946, pp. 1–16.

Parliamentary Socialist Christian Group, *In This Faith We Live* (London: PSCG, 1948).

Paton, William, *World Community* (London: SCM, 1938).

Paton, William, 'Review of Books: Christianity and World Order', *International Review of Missions*, vol. 29 (1940), pp. 270–74.

Paton, William, 'The World-Wide Christian Society', *The Christian News-Letter*, no. 10, 3 January 1940, unpaginated.

Paton, William, 'Christianity and Civilization', *International Review of Missions*, vol. 29 (October 1940), pp. 486–96.

Paton, William, 'Britain and America', *The Christian News-Letter*, no. 49, 2 October 1940, unpaginated.

Paton, William, 'The Church and World Order', *The Student Movement*, vol. XLIII, no. 5 (February 1941), pp. 63–65.

Paton, William, 'War and Peace Aims and the Church's Task', *The Christian News-Letter*, no. 64, 12 February 1941, unpaginated.

Paton, William, *The Church and the New Order* (London: SCM, 1941).

Paton, William, *The Church Calling: Six Talks on The Church and World Order Broadcast in June and July 1942* (London: Cargate Press, 1942).

Paton, William, 'American Opinion and the War' (etc.), *The Christian News-Letter*, no. 137, 10 June 1942, unpaginated.

Paton, William, *America and Britain* (London: Edinburgh House Press, 1942).

Payne, Ernest A., *Thirty Years of the British Council of Churches 1942–1972* (London: BCC, 1972).

Penn, William, *An Essay Toward the Present and Future Peace of Europe by the Establishment of a an European Dyet, Parliament or Estates* (Hildeheim: Olms-Weidmann, 1983).

PEP, *Building Peace Out of War: Studies in Reconstruction* (London: PEP, 1944).

Peters, Mike, 'The Bilderberg Group and the project of European Integration', *Lobster*, no. 32 (December 1996); downloaded from http://www.bilderberg.org/bildhist.htm on 6 May 2005.

Priestley, J.B., *Postscripts* (London: William Heinemann, 1940).

Reckitt, Maurice B. and Langmead Casserley, J.V., *The Vocation of England* (London: Longmans, 1941).

Reckitt, Maurice B., *Prospect for Christendom: Essays in Catholic Social Reconstruction* (London: Faber and Faber, 1945).

Rees, R.D., 'British Churches and World Affairs', *Ecumenical Review*, vol. 4, no. 4 (July 1952), pp. 368–77.

Rowntree, Maurice L., *Mankind Set Free* (London: Jonathan Cape, 1939).

Salter, Elizabeth (ed.), *Europe 1992: Promise and Challenge* (Geneva: Commission of the Churches on International Affairs, World Council of Churches, 1992).

Salter, N[oël] H., 'The Christian and World Federal Government', *Student Movement*, vol. LI, no. 3 (January–February 1949), pp. 41–42.

Salter, Noël, 'Confession of a Eurocrat', *Crucible*, April–June 1975.

Silverman, Sydney *et al.*, *Stop the Coming War: A Plan for European Unity and Recovery* (no place, no date, [ca. 1948]).

Smuts, Jan Christian, *Thoughts on a New World address ... at a meeting of the Study Committees of the Empire Parliamentary Association, held ... on 25th November, 1943* (London, [1943]).

Streit, Clarence K., *Union Now With Britain* (London: Cape, 1941).

Temple, William, *Christus Veritas: An Essay* (London: Macmillan, 1954; first published 1924).

Temple, William, 'The Restoration of Christendom', *Christendom*, vol. 1 (1935–36), pp. 17–29.

Temple, William, *The Hope of a New World* (London: SCM, 1940).

Temple, William, 'Begin Now', supplement to *The Christian News-Letter*, no. 41, 7 August, 1940, unpaginated.

Temple, William, 'The Future of Germany', *The Fortnightly*, vol. CL (November 1941), pp. 405–13.

Temple, William, et al., *The Crisis of the Western World, and Other Broadcast Talks* [etc.] (London: George Allen & Unwin, 1944).

Temple, William, *The Church Looks Forward* (London: Macmillan, 1944).

The Archbishop of York [William Temple], 'A Christmas Message', *Federal Union News*, no. 14 (23 December 1939), pp. 1–2.

The Archbishop of York [William Temple], 'Final Comments on Statements of Policy: Hopes and Difficulties', *Federal Union News*, no. 56 (4 January 1941).

The Bishop of Chichester [George K.A. Bell], 'Christianity and Reconstruction', *The Fortnightly*, vol. CXLVIII (July–December 1940), pp. 558–64.

The Bishop of Chichester [George K.A. Bell], 'The Churches and European Reconstruction', supplement to *The Christian News-Letter*, no. 225, 10 January 1945.

The Pope's Five Peace Points: Allocation to the College of Cardinals by his Holiness Pope Pius XII on December 24 1939 (London: Catholic Truth Society, 1939).

Thompson, Elliott W., *Spiritual issues of the war* (London: SCM, 1939).

Toynbee, Arnold J., *Civilization on Trial* (London: Oxford University Press, 1948).

Vidler, Alec R., *God's Judgement on Europe* (London: Longmans, 1940).

Visser t' Hooft (ed.), W.A., *The First Assembly of the World Council of Churches: Held at Amsterdam August 22nd to September 4th, 1948* (London: SCM, 1949).

Visser t' Hooft, W.A., *Memoirs* (London: SCM, 1973).

Waddams, H.M., 'Communism and the Churches', *International Affairs*, vol. XXV, no. 3 (July 1949), pp. 295–306.

Ward, Barbara, *The Defence of the West* (London: Sands/Sword of the Spirit, undated; ca. 1940).

Ward, Barbara, 'Christian Co-operation and Europe', supplement to *The Christian News-Letter*, no. 144, 29 July 1942, unpaginated.

Ward, Barbara, 'The Fate of Europe', supplement to *The Christian News-Letter*, no. 240, 8 August 1945, pp. 6–8.

Ward, Barbara, *Democracy East and West*, (London: Bureau of Current Affairs, February 1947).

Ward, Barbara, 'The Choice Before Europe', *The Christian News-Letter*, no. 289, 9 July 1947, unpaginated.

Ward, Barbara, *The West at Bay* (London: Allen and Unwin, 1948).

Ward, Barbara, *Policy for the West* (Harmondsworth; Penguin Books, 1951).

Ward, Barbara, *Faith and Freedom: A Study of Western Society* (London: Hamish Hamilton, 1954).

Woodruff, Douglas, 'Western Union', *The Sword*, vol. 10, no. 139 (July–August 1950), pp. 260–62.

Woodruff, Douglas, 'Focus on Current Affairs: The Holy See and United Europe', *The Sword*, vol. 12, no. 154 (January 1952), pp. 88–92.

Zimmern, Alfred, 'The Decline of International Standards', *International Affairs*, vol. XVII, no. 1 (January–February 1938), pp. 3–25.

Zimmern, Alfred, *Spiritual Values and World Affairs* (Oxford: Clarendon Press, 1939).

Zimmern, Alfred, 'Christianity in the Atomic Age', *The Congregational Quarterly*, vol. XXVII, no. 4 (October 1949), pp. 335–48.

Secondary published sources

British Security Coordination: The Secret History of British Intelligence in the Americas, 1940–45 (London: St. Ermin's Press, 1998).

Addison, Paul, *The Road to 1945: British Politics and the Second World War* (London: Cape, 1975).

Aldrich, Richard J., 'OSS, CIA and European Unity: The American Committee on United Europe, 1948–1960', *Diplomacy and Statecraft*, vol. 8, no. 1 (March 1997), pp. 184–227.

Anderson, Benedict, *Imagined Communities: Reflections on the Origin and Spread of Nationalism* (London: Verso, 1991).

Arden, H., *Pursing a Just and Durable Peace. John Foster Dullles and International Organisation* (NewYork: Green wood, 1988).

Baylis, John, *The Diplomacy of Pragmatism: Britain and the Formation of NATO, 1942–49* (Basingstoke: Macmillan, 1993).

Beckford, James A., 'Final Reflections', pp. 160–68 in John Fulton and Peter Gee (eds.), *Religion in Contemporary Europe*, Texts and Studies in Religion, vol. 64 (Lewiston, NY: Edwin Mellin, 1994).

Birn, Donald S., *The League of Nations Union 1918–1945* (Oxford: Oxford University Press, 1981).

Bosco, Andrea, 'Lothian, Curtis, Kimber and the Federal Union Movement (1938–40), *Journal of Contemporary History*, vol. 23, no. 3 (July 1988), pp. 465–502.

Bosco, Andrea and Navari, Cornelia (eds.), *Chatham House and British Foreign Policy, 1919–1945: The Royal Institute of International Affairs During the Interwar Period* (London: Lothian Foundation, 1994).

Boyle, Raymond and Lynch, Peter (eds.), *Out of the Ghetto? The Catholic Community in Modern Scotland* (Edinburgh: John Donald, 1998).

Broad, Roger, *Labour's European Dilemmas: From Bevin to Blair* (Basingstoke: Palgrave, 2001).

Brown, Callum G., *Religion and Society in Scotland Since 1707* (Edinburgh: Edinburg University Press, 1997).

Brown, Callum G., *The Death of Christian Britain: Understanding Secularisation, 1800–2000* (London: Routledge, 2001).

Bryant, Chris, *Possible Dreams: A Personal History of the British Christian Socialists* (London: Hodder & Stoughton, 1996).

Bryant, Chris, *Stafford Cripps: The First Modern Chancellor* (London: Hodder & Stoughton, 1997).

Bullock, Alan, *Ernest Bevin: Foreign Secretary, 1945–1951* (Oxford: Oxford University Press, 1985).

Burgess, Simon, *Stafford Cripps: A Political Life* (London: Gollancz, 1999).

Butler, David and Kitzinger, Uwe, *The 1975 Referendum* (London: Macmillan, 1976).

Ceadel, Martin, *Semi-Detached Idealists: the British Peace Movement and International Relations, 1854–1945* (Oxford: Oxford University Press, 2000).

Chadwick, Owen, 'The English Bishops and the Nazis', *Annual Report of the Friends of Lambeth Palace Library* (1973), pp. 9–28.

Chadwick, Owen, *The Christian Church in the Cold war* (Harmondsworth: Allen Lane The Penguin Press, 1992).

Chandler, Andrew, 'The Church of England and the Obliteration Bombing of Germany in the Second World War', *English Historical Review*, vol. 108 (1993), pp. 920–46.

Clarke, Peter, *The Cripps Version: The Life of Sir Stafford Cripps* (London: Allen Lane, 2002).

Claydon, Tony and McBride, Ian, *Chosen people?: Protestantism and National Identity in Britain and Ireland c.1650–c.1850* (Cambridge: Cambridge University Press, 1998).

Cleary, J.M., *Catholic Social Action in Britain, 1909–1959: A History of the Catholic Social Guild* (Oxford: CSG, 1960).

Clements, Keith, *Faith on the Frontier: A Life of J.H. Oldham* (Edinburgh: T and T Clark, 1999).

Colley, Linda, *Britons: Forging the Nation, 1707–1837* (London: Vintage, 1996).

Colls, Robert and Dodd, Philip (eds.) *Englishness: Politics and Culture, 1880–1920* (London: Croom Helm, 1986).

Cull, Nicholas John, *Selling War: The British Propaganda Campaign Against American "Neutrality" in World War II* (Oxford: Oxford University Press, 1995).

Cusick, Edmund, 'Religion and heritage', pp. 277–311 in Mike Storry and Peter Childs (eds.) *British Cultural Identities* (London: Routledge, 1997).

Davie, Grace, *Religion in Britain since 1945: Believing Without Belonging* (Oxford: Blackwell, 1994).

Davie, Grace, 'Unity in Diversity: Religion and Modernity in Western Europe', pp. 52–65 in *Texts and Studies in Religion*, vol. 64 (Lewiston, NY: Edwin Mellin, 1994).

Dejack, Stephano, 'Labour and Europe during the Attlee Governments: the image in the mirror of R.W.G. Mackay's "Europe Group", 1945–50', pp. 47–58 in Brian Brivati and Harriet Jones (eds.), *From Reconstruction to Integration: Britain and the World since 1945* (Leicester: Leicester University Press, 1993).

Devine, T.M. (ed.), *Scotland's Shame: Bigotry and Sectarianism in Modern Scotland* (Edinburgh: Mainstream, 2000).

Dorril, Stephen, *MI6: Fifty Years of Special Operations* (London: Fourth Estate, 2000).

Driberg, Tom, *The Mystery of Moral Re-Armament: A Study of Frank Buchman and His Movement* (London: Secker and Warburg, 1964).

Dutton, David, *Anthony Eden: A Life and Reputation* (London: Arnold, 1997).

Edwards, David L., *Christians in a New Europe* (Jondon: Collins, 1990).

Edwards, Ruth Dudley, *Victor Gollancz: A Biography* (London: Victor Gollancz, 1987).

Fey, Harold Edward (ed.), *The Ecumenical Advance: A History of the Ecumenical Movement: Volume 2, 1948–1968* (London: SPCK, 1970).

Fogarty, Michael, *Christian Democracy in Western Europe* (London: Routledge and Kegan Paul, 1957).

Gasset, Ortega y, *The Revolt of the Masses* (London: Unwin, 1961; first published 1932).

Gehler, Michael and Kaiser, Wolfram, 'Transnationalism and Early European Integration: The Nouvelles Equipes Internationales and the Geneva Circle 1947–1957', *The Historical Journal*, vol. 44, no. 3 (2001), pp. 773–98.

Gilles, Donald, *Radical Diplomat: The Life of Archibald Clark Kerr, Lord Inverchapel, 1882–1951* (London: IB Tauris, 1999).

Greenwood, Sean, 'Ernest Bevin, France and 'Western Union': August 1945–February 1946', *European History Quarterly* vol. 14, (1984), pp. 319–38.

Hanson, Eric O., *The Catholic Church in World Politics* (Princeton: Princeton University Press, 1987).

Hastings, Adrian, 'Some reflections on the English Catholicism of the late 1930s', pp. 107–25 in Adrian Hastings (ed)., *Bishops and Writers: Aspects of the Evolution of Modern English Catholicism* (Wheathampstead, Herts.: Anthony Clarke, 1977).

Hastings, Adrian, *A History of English Christianity* (London: SCM, 1991).

Hastings, Adrian, *The Construction of Nationhood: Ethnicity, Religion and Nationalism* (Cambridge: Cambridge University Press, 1997).

Hebly, J. A., *Eastbound ecumenism: a collection of essays on the World Council of Churches and Eastern Europe* (Lanham, MD: University Press of America, 1986).

Hempton, David, *Religion and Political Culture in Britain and Ireland: From the Glorious Revolution to the decline of empire* (Cambridge, Cambridge University Press, 1996).

Henderson, Ian, *Man of christian action: Canon John Collins: the man and his work* (Guildford: Lutterworth Press London, 1976).

Hope, Nicholas, 'The Iron Curtain and its Repercussions for the Churches in Europe', *Kirchliche Zeitgeschicte*, vol. 12, no. 2 (1999), pp. 426–440.

Hornsby-Smith, Michael, *Roman Catholics in England: Studies in Social Structure since the Second World War* (Cambridge: Cambridge University Press, 1987).

Hudson, Darril, *The Ecumenical Movement in World Affairs* (London: Weidenfeld and Nicolson, 1969).

Irving, R.E.M., *The Christian Democratic Parties of Western Europe* (London: Allen and Unwin, 1979).

Jackson, Eleanor M., *Red Tape and the Gospel. A study of the significance of the ecumenical missionary struggle of William Paton (1886–1943)* (Birmingham: Phlogiston/Selly Oak Colleges, 1980).

Jasper, Ronald C.D., *Arthur Cayley Headlam: The Life and Letters of a Bishop* (London: Faith Press, 1960).

Keating, Joan, 'The British Experience: Christian Democrats Without A Party', pp. 168–81 in David Hanley (ed.), *Christian Democracy in Europe: A Comparative Perspective* (London: Pinter, 1994).

Keating, Joan, 'Looking to Europe: Roman Catholics and Christian Democracy in 1930s Britain', *European History Quarterly*, vol. 26, no. 1 (1996), pp. 57–79.

Kent, John, *William Temple: Church, State and Society in Britain, 1880–1950* (Cambridge: Cambridge University Press, 1992).

Kent, John, 'William Temple, the Church of England and British National Identity', pp. 19–35 in R. Weight, R. and Beach, A. (eds.) *The Right to Belong: Citizenship and National Identity in Britain, 1930–1960* (London: Tauris, 1998).

Ketola, Hanna-Maija, 'Teaching 'Correct' Attitudes: an Anglican Emissary to Sweden and Finland in 1944', *Journal of Ecclesiastical History*, vol. 55, no. 1 (January 2004), pp. 75–101.

Keyserlingk, Robert H., 'Arnold Toynbee's Foreign Research and Press Service, 1939–43 and its Post-War Plans for South-East Europe', *Journal of Contemporary History*, vol. 21, no. 4 (October 1986), pp. 539–58.

Kirby, Dianne, *Church, State and Propaganda: The Archbishop of York and International Relations, A Political Study of Cyril Foster Garbett, 1942–1955* (Hull, University of Hull Press, 1999).

Kirby, Dianne, 'The Church of England and the Cold War Nuclear Debate', *Twentieth Century British History*, vol.4, no. 3 (1993).

Kirby, Dianne, 'Responses Within the Anglican Church to Nuclear Weapons, 1945–1961', *Journal of Church and State*, vol. 37 (1995), pp. 599–622.

Kirby, Dianne, 'Truman's Holy Alliance: The President, the Pope and the Origins of the Cold War', *Borderlines: Studies in American Culture*, vol. 4, no. 1 (1997), pp. 1–17.

Kirby, Dianne, 'The Archbishop of York and Anglo-American relations during the Second World War and early Cold War, 1942–55', *The Journal of Religious History*, vol. 23, no. 3 (1999), pp. 327–45.

Kirby, Dianne, 'Divinely Sanctioned: The Anglo-American Cold War Alliance and the Defence of Western Civilisation and Christianity, 1945–48', *The Journal of Contemporary History*, vol. 35, no. 3 (2000), pp. 385–412.

Kirby, Dianne, 'Christian Faith, Communist Faith: Some aspects of the Relationship between the Foreign Office Information Research Department and the Church of England Council on Foreign Relations, 1950–1953', *Kirchliche Zeitgeschichte*, vol. 13, no. 1 (2000), pp. 217–41.

Kirby, Dianne, Christian co-operation and the ecumenical ideal in the 1930s and 1940s', *European History Review*, vol. 8, no. 1 (2001), pp. 37–60.

Kirby, Dianne, 'Anglican-Orthodox Relations and the Religious Rehabilitation of the Soviet Regime During the Second World War', *Revue d'Histoire Ecclesiastique*, vol. 96, nos. 1–2 (2001), pp. 101–23.

Kirby, Dianne, 'Harry S. Truman's International Religious Anti-Communist Front, the Archbishop of Canterbury and the 1948 Inaugural Assembly of the World Council of Churches', *Contemporary British History*, vol. 15, no. 4 (2001), pp. 35–70.

Kitzinger, Uwe, *Diplomacy and Persuasion: How Britain Joined the Common Market* (London: Thames and Hudson, 1973).

Kranenborg, Reender, 'New Age: The Religion of the Future?', pp. 125–45 in Robert Towler (ed.), *New Religions and the New Europe* (Aarhus: Aarhus University Press, 1995).

Larres, Klaus, 'A search for order: Britain and the origins of a Western European Union, 1944–55', pp. 72–87 in Brian Brivati and Harriet Jones (eds.), *From Reconstruction to Integration: Britain and Europe Since 1945* (Leicester: Leicester University Press, 1993).

Larres, Klaus, 'Making Europe Strong Again: Churchill, the United States, and the Creation of a New European Order, 1940–1943', pp. 19–42 in Antonie de Capet and Aissatou Sy-Wonyu (eds.), *The Special Relationship. La Relation Speciale Entre le Royaume-uni et les Etats-unis* (Rouen: Presses Universitaires de Rouen, 2003).

Lashmar, Paul and Oliver, James, *Britain's Secret Propaganda War, 1948–1977* (Stroud: Sutton, 1998).

Lavin, Deborah, *From Empire to International Commonwealth: A Biography of Lionel Curtis* (Oxford: Clarendon Press, 1995).

Lee, Martin A., 'Their Will Be Done', *Mother Jones*, July 1983, pp. 21–38.

Lewis, Philip, 'Muslims in Europe: Managing Multiple Identities and Learning Shared Citizenship', *Political Theology*, vol. 6, no. 3 (2005), pp. 343–65.

Long, David and Wilson, Peter (eds.), *Thinkers of the Twenty Years Crisis: Interwar Idealism Reassessed* (Oxford: Clarendon Press, 1995).

Louis, W. Roger, *In the Name of God, Go!: Leo Amery and the British Empire in the Age of Churchill* (London: W.W. Norton, 1992).

Luttwak, Edward, 'Franco-German Reconciliation: The Overlooked Role of the Moral Re-Armament Movement', pp. 37–57 in Douglas Johnston and Cynthia Sampson (eds.), *Religion, the Missing Dimension of Statecraft*, (New York: Oxford University Press, 1994).

Luxmoore, Jonathan and Babiuch, Jolanta, *The Vatican and the Red Flag: The Struggle for the Soul of Eastern Europe* (London: Geoffrey Chapman, 1999).

Manderson-Jones, R.B., *The Special Relationship: Anglo-American Relations and Western European Unity, 1946–56* (London: Weidenfeld & Nicolson, 1972).

Marjorie, Reeves (ed.), *Christian Thinking and Social Order: Conviction Politics from the 1930s to the Present Day* (London: Cassell, 1999).

Mastny, Vojtech, 'NATO in the Beholder's Eye: Soviet Perceptions and Policies, 1949–56', Working Paper no. 35 (Woodrow Wilson International Center for Scholars, March 2002).

May, Alex, *Britain and Europe since 1945* (London: Longmans, 1999).

Mayne, Richard and Pinder, John (eds.) with Roberts, John C. de V., *Federal Union: The Pioneers* (Basingstoke: Macmillan, 1990).

Mazower, Mark, 'Hitler's New Order, 1939–45', *Diplomacy and Statecraft*, vol. 7, no. 1 (March 1996), pp. 29–53.

McLeod, Hugh, 'Protestantism and British National Identity, 1815–1945', pp. 43–70 in Peter van der Veer and Hartmut Lehmann (eds.), *Nation and Religion: Perspectives on Europe and Asia* (Princeton, NJ: Princeton University Press, 1999).

Medhurst, Kenneth, N., 'Christianity and the Future of Europe', pp. 169–88 in Martyn Percy (ed.), *Calling Time: Religion and Change at the Turn of the Millennium* (Sheffield: Sheffield Academic Press, 2000).

Mews, Stuart (ed.), *Religion and National Identity: Papers Read at the Nineteenth Summer Meeting and the Twentieth Winter Meeting of the Ecclesiastical History Society* (Oxford: Blackwell, 1982).

Mews, Stuart, 'The Sword of the Spirit: A Catholic Cultural Crusade of 1940', *Studies in Church History* vol. XX (1985), pp. 409–30.

Moloney, Thomas, *Westminster, Whitehall and the Vatican: the Role of Cardinal Hinsley, 1935–43* (Tunbridge Wells: Burns & Oates, 1985).

Moyser, George, *Church and politics today: essays on the role of the Church of England in contemporary politics* (Edinburgh: T. & T. Clark, 1985).

Nielsen, J. S., Muslims in Europe: History Revisited or a Way Forward?, *Islam & Christian-Muslim Relations*, vol. 8, no. 2 (1997), pp. 135–43.

Ovendale, Ritchie, *The English-Speaking Alliance: Britain, the United States, the Dominions and the Cold War, 1945–1951* (London: George Allen and Unwin,1985).

Ovendale, Ritchie, *Anglo-American Relations in the Twentieth Century* (Basingstoke: Macmillan, 1998).

Pagden, Anthony (ed.), *The Idea of Europe: From Antiquity to the European Union* (Cambridge: Cambridge University Press/Woodrow Wilson Centre Press, 2002).

Parmar, Inderjeet, 'Chatham House and the Anglo-American Alliance', *Diplomacy and Statecraft*, vol. 3, no. 1 (1992), pp. 23–47.

Paxman, Jeremy, *The English: A Portrait of a People* (London: Penguin Books, 1998).

Peart-Binns, J.S., *Maurice B. Reckitt: A Life* (Basingstoke: Bowerdean Press, 1988).

Pinder, John (ed.), *Fifty Years of Political and Economic Planning: Looking Forward, 1931–1981* (London: Heinemann, 1981).

Rhodes, Anthony, *The Vatican in the Age of the Cold War* (Norwich: Russell, 1992).

Robbins, Keith, *Nineteenth-century Britain: integration and diversity: The Ford Lectures* (Oxford: Clarendon, 1988).

Robbins, Keith, *History, Religion and Identity in Modern Britain* (London: Hambledon Press, 1993).

Roberts, Richard, 'European Cultural Identity and Religion', pp. 17–33 in John Fulton and Peter Gee (eds.), *Religion in Contemporary Europe*, Texts and Studies in Religion, vol. 64 (Lewiston, NY: Edwin Mellin, 1994).

Russell, David, '"The Jolly Old Empire": Labour, the Commonwealth and Europe, 1945–51', in Alex May, (ed.), *Britain, the Commonwealth and Europe: The Commonwealth and Britain's Application to join the European Communities* (Basingstoke: Palgrave, 2001).

Saunders, Frances Stonor, *Who Paid the Piper? The CIA and the Cultural Cold War* (London: Granta, 1999).

Shlaim, Avi, 'Prelude to Downfall: The British Offer of Union to France, June 1940', *Journal of Contemporary History*, vol. 9, no. 3 (1974), pp. 27–63.

Shlaim, Avi, *Britain and the Origins of European Unity* (The Graduate School of Contemporary European Studies, University of Reading, 1978).

Sinclair, Margaret, *William Paton: A Biography* (London: SCM, 1949).

Smith, M.L. and Stirk, Peter M.R. (eds.), *Making the New Europe: European Unity and the Second World War* (London: Pinter, 1990).

Smith, Raymond and Zametica, John, 'The Cold Warrior: Clement Attlee reconsidered, 1945–7', *International Affairs*, vol. 61, no. 2 (1985), pp. 237–52.

Stanford, Peter, *Lord Longford: A Life* (London: Heinemann, 1995).

Stanley, B., *The Bible and the Flag: Protestant Missions and British Imperialism in the Nineteenth and Twentieth Centuries* (Leicester: Appolos, 1990).

Stehle, Hansjakob, *Eastern Politics of the Vatican, 1917–1979* (Athens, Ohio: Ohio University Press, 1981).

Sutton, Michael, 'John Paul II's Idea of Europe', *Religion, State & Society*, vol. 27, no. 1 (1997), pp. 17–29.

Thomas, Merrilyn, *Communing with the Enemy: Covert Operations, Christianity and Cold War Politics in Britain and the GDR* (Bern: Peter Lang, 2005).

Walsh, Michael J., *From Sword to Ploughshare: Sword of the Spirit to Catholic Institute for International Relations 1940–1980* (London: Catholic Institute for International Relations, 1980).

Walsh, Michael J., 'Ecumenism in War-Time Britain. The Sword of the Spirit and Religion and Life, 1940–1945', *The Heythrop Journal*, vol. XXIII (1982), pp. 243–58 and 377–94.

Walsh, Michael J., *The Tablet, 1840–1990: A Commemorative History* (London: The Tablet Publishing Company, 1990).

Ward, W.R., 'The Way of the World: The Rise and Decline of Protestant Social Christianity in Britain', *Kirchliche Zeitgeschicte*, vol. I, no. 2 (1988), pp. 293–305.

Warner, Geoffrey, 'The Labour Governments and the Unity of Western Europe, 1945–51', in Ritchie Ovendale (ed.), *The Foreign Policy of the British Labour Governments, 1945–1951* (Leicester: Leicester University Press, 1984).

Warren, Heather A., *Theologians of A New World Order: Reinhold Niebuhr and the Christian Realists* (New York: Oxford University Press, 1997).

Whyte, J.H., *Catholics in Western Democracies: a study in political behaviour* (Dublin: Gill and MacMillan, 1981).

Wiener, Martin J., *English Culture and the Decline of the Industrial Spirit, 1850–1980* (London; Penguin Books, 1985).

Willaime, Jean-Paul, 'Protestant Approaches in European Unification', pp. 93–108 in John Fulton and Peter Gee (eds.), *Religion in Contemporary Europe*, Texts and Studies in Religion, vol. 64 (Lewiston, NY: Edwin Mellin, 1994).

Williamson, Geoffrey, *Inside Buchmanism: An Independent Inquiry into the Oxford Group Movement and Moral Rearmament* (London: Watts, 1954).

Winetrout, K. *Arnold Toynbee; The Ecumenical Vision* (Boston: Twayne, 1975).

Wolfe, Kenneth M., *The Churches and the British Broadcasting Corporation, 1922–1956: The Politics of Broadcast Religion* (London: SCM, 1984).

Wolffe, John, *God and Greater Britain: Religion and National Life in Britain and Ireland 1843–1945* (London: Routledge, 1994).

Woodward, Llewellyn, *British Foreign Policy in the Second World War* (London: HMSO, 1962).

Woodward, Llewellyn, *British Foreign Policy in the Second World War*, vol. 1 (London: HMSO, 1970).

Young, John W., *Britain, France and the Unity of Europe, 1945–1951* (Leicester: Leicester University Press, 1984).

Young, John W., 'Churchill's "no" to Europe; "The Rejection" of European Union by Churchill's Post-War Government, 1951-2', *The Historical Journal*, vol. 28, no. 4 (1985), pp. 923–37.

Zeilstra, Jurgen A., *European Unity in Ecumenical Thinking, 1937–1948* (Zoetermeer: Boekencentrum, 1995).

Unpublished secondary sources

Ford, Derek W., 'An analysis of the response by the Christian UK churches to the involvement of Britain in the European institutions, 1967–1997' (unpublished MA dissertation, Anglia Polytechnic University, 1999).

Kirby, Dianne, 'The Church of England in the Period of the Cold War, 1945–56' (unpublished Ph.D. thesis, Hull University, 1991), pp. 16–41.

Rabattet, F.X., 'The "European Movement" 1945–1953: A Study in National and International Non-Governmental Organisations working for European Unity' (unpublished D.Phil thesis, University of Oxford, 1962).

Thompson, Dean K., 'Henry Pitney Van Dusen: Ecumenical Statesman' (unpublished Ph.D. thesis, Union Theological Seminary in Virginia, 1974).

Glossary

ACUE	American Committee on United Europe
AAW	Archives of the Archbishops of Westminster
AWC	Anglican Wartime Council
BIS	British Information Service
BCC	British Council of Churches
BLEF	British League for European Freedom
BLPES	British Library of Political and Economic Science
CECEM	Central and Eastern European Commission of the European Movement
CA	Christian Action
CAC	Churchill Archives Centre
CEA	Church of England Archives
CMEU	Christian Movement for European Unity
CFE	Christians For Europe
CAFE	Christianity and the Future of Europe
CCIFSR	Commission of the Churches for International Friendship and Social Responsibility
CCIA	Commission of the Churches in International Affairs
CFR	Council on Foreign Relations
CIIA	Catholic Institute for International Affairs
ELEC	Economic League for European Co-operation
EDC	European Defence Community
ECSC	European Coal and Steel Community
EC	European Community
EEC	European Economic Community
EM	European Movement
EMA	European Movement Archives
EU	European Union
FCFC	Free Church Federal Council
FRPS	Foreign Research and Press Service
FU	Federal Union
GUL	Georgetown University Library
LNU	League of Nations Union
MOI	Ministry of Information
MRA	Moral Re-Armament
NAS	National Archives of Scotland
NATO	North Atlantic Treaty Organisation
NCLUE	New College Library, University of Edinburgh
NEI	Les Nouvelles Equipes Internationales
PAG	Peace Aims Group
PFG	People and Freedom Group
PEP	Political and Economic Planning
RIIA	Royal Institute of International Affairs

SOE	Special Operations Executive
TCL	Trinity College Library
UKCEM	UK Council of the European Movement
UEM	United Europe Movement
WCC	World Council of Churches

Index

LaVergne, TN USA
22 February 2010
173820LV00001B/30/P